The Devil's Fingernail and Heather Aron Gross

The Devil's Fingernail and
Heather Aron Gross

The Devil's Fingernail and Heather Aron Gross

Alyce Gross

The Devil's Fingernail and
Heather Aron Gross

Alice Gross

The Devil's Fingernail and Heather Aron Gross

© Alyce Gross 2013

All rights reserved. Without limiting the rights under copyright reserved above, no part of this publication may be reproduced, stored in a retrieval system, or transmitted, in any form or by any means (electronic, mechanical, photocopying, recording or otherwise), without the prior written permission of the copyright owner of this book.

Published by
Lighthouse Christian Publishing
SAN 257-4330
5531 Dufferin Drive
Savage, Minnesota, 55378
United States of America

www.lighthousechristianpublishing.com

Acknowledgments

The Psalms gave me divine permission to grieve.

My husband, Denny Gross, my first reader, encouraged me.

Marcia Hornok, my editor, convinced me to change the order of Part One, to help grab the reader's attention from the beginning. In Part Two there was no conflict to be resolved. I was making Heather sound perfect, because I left out the dark side. Marcia advised me to share the larger more complete yet painful truth about Heather, which made this a much more meaningful book.

Finding a publisher was a year long arduous process. I'm impressed by and thankful to LIGHTHOUSE PUBLISHING, because they were willing to take on a first time author with no agent. I respect that they think globally, are ecumenical, and money is not their top priority.

Part One: The Devil's Fingernail

By a mother, Alyce Gross, who grieves for her firstborn, Heather Aron Gross

Author's Preface

Why am I writing this book?

On December 14, 2008, a ski resort avalanche slammed me into a new reality. Although the uncaring, impersonal crush of snow grabbed and killed only my Heather, its icy power threatened to crush my soul.

In a struggle to survive—I write. Writing is cathartic: *purging, the purifying or relieving of the emotions by art; the alleviation of fears, problems, by bringing them to consciousness and giving them expression* (Webster New World Dictionary). I don't intend to insult your intelligence by defining the word; but this definition was my motivation to use art (for me—writing) to express myself.

Writing part one was an important aspect of healing—a way of facing my grief head on, and a process to work through my faith and my doubt. I was compelled to write the first volume, because it felt like God wanted me to. Part two, I wrote, because I felt that Heather would want me to. In the hope that my daughter, who died unexpectedly and suddenly will never be forgotten, and in striving for something meaningful to leave for my living daughter and her progeny—I wrote with the knowledge that Heather would want to continue to spread her God-given love and light. Although her life was short, my hope is that her example will last long, spread far, and continue to motivate others to live life abundantly, as God intended.

Just before Heather's death, I was adjusting to being newly retired after thirty-three gratifying and never boring years of teaching in elementary schools. In that profession one never really finishes. True, the unpaid holidays and summers were rejuvenating, but there were always more classes to take, books to read, and new methods to implement.

With retirement, I had the gift of unhurried time to fill in new ways, and I was still deciding where and how to use it, beyond travel in off-season and skiing on weekdays. I'm happiest when I accomplish something meaningful, so I was looking for ways to donate my time in an altruistic pursuit. Never would I have predicted one of my accomplishments would be writing from the depths of my grief. For me, it has been worthwhile, and my hope and prayer is that this book will be meaningful to you as well.

May those who sow in tears reap with shouts of joy (Psalm 126:5).

I wrote about the beginnings of my grief journey in a small journal I found among Heather's possessions. She had never used it, but I decided to. I've used parts of what I wrote in that journal throughout this book. In the first entry, that covered the time spent in the hospital waiting room, I still had my emotions in control. However, most of my journal entries show raw feelings. I often used writing as a way to spew my anger, pain, or sorrow. Of course, the writing changed through grief stages.

When I decided to write a book I switched from the journal to the computer; but I've used many edited quotes from my travel journals, book journals, and primarily the grief journal that Heather unknowing left for me. The latter reveals my rollercoaster ride of emotions. Sometimes I was progressing to a more positive attitude and then would plunge back to deep sorrow or anger. The entries used are not in chronological order because they fit the headings of the outline. The journal examples should show that a grief journey has mountains and deep ravines; it isn't a consistent upward climb, and it isn't a journey I would choose. You may decide not to come with me.

Part one is not a lighthearted read. It will best be understood by people who are grieving for the loss of their child. After growing in my understanding of grief, I encourage others to do the same; because if you're not grieving, you probably will be some day. Almost everyone has or will face the loss of a loved-one, and surely someone you know will or has experienced loss. This book may help you in your own grief, and/or help you to be a more compassionate, supportive friend to someone who is mourning.

If you knew Heather and want to reminisce (and don't want to get bogged down in my grief journey), or if you just want to read about a unique agape-filled person, much in her own words, skip to part two.

Because Facebook comments, emails, letters, and journaling were and are an important part of my mourning process, I used them in this book to help express my feelings as well as the feelings of others. They help share a little of who Heather was and some of her impact on people who knew her.

My current thoughts will be written in Times New Roman
Facebook, Emails, Letters, and Book Reviews in Verdana or scanned as they are
My Journal Entries in Bookman Old Style Italics
The Scripture quotations are from the New Revised Standard Version or the New International Version, but I recognize that there are many other excellent translations of the Bible.

Outline

Part One: The Devil's Fingernail

Sifted as Wheat
Heather's Death
My Mother's Death
The Devil in the Dark
Doubt, Questioning and Cancer

Things That Helped Most in My Grief
The Knowledge That Heather Lived an Abundant Life
Prayers and Thoughts from Others When I Couldn't Pray for Myself
Family, Congregation, and Friends
Sharing Heather's Possessions
Shared Grief
My Childhood Friends
Emily and Ryan's Wedding
Commitment During Crisis
My Own Prayers, Doubt and Faith
Bible Study
Books
Service
Exercise and Newness
Hope and Peace

Sifted As Wheat

The LORD said to Satan, "Where have you come from?" Satan answered the LORD, "From roaming through the earth and going back and forth in it." (Job 1:7).
Does Satan have free choice?

Like a roaring lion your adversary the devil prowls around, looking for someone to devour (1 Peter 5:8b).
Who does the devil want to devour?

Simon, Simon, Satan has asked to sift you as wheat. But I have prayed for you, Simon, that your faith may not fail. And when you have turned back, strengthen your brothers (Luke 22:31).
Did the Triune God give Satan permission to sift Simon as wheat? Why?

      I don't pretend to be nearly as important as Simon Peter. All one has to do is think about St. Peter's Square in Rome to get a feeling for how important people thought he was in the beginnings of the Christian church. A part of his "sifting" was that he denied Jesus three times. Yet Jesus trusted him and the rest of the disciples to carry on God's work and keep the Christian church alive and growing. His earthly sifting ended when, as legend tells it, he was crucified up-side-down. All of this makes my sifting seem like nothing, and I'm almost embarrassed to share it; but I believe all people are sifted by Satan at times in their life and it may be helpful to hear the lesson I learned the hard way.
      In a sermon by my pastor, Steve Klemz, I learned that one can make Satan happy by thinking about him too much, and one can make Satan really happy by never thinking about him at all.
      Many people don't believe in the devil/Satan. It doesn't seem very intellectual to talk about the devil, but Jesus was tempted by the devil in the wilderness and ministered to by angels, so it is hard to believe in Jesus without understanding that

these good and evil celestial powers exist. I think the devil/Satan exists and evil is the evidence. I've felt it working in my mind when I was so angry at God that I pushed God away and stopped praying. I was actually stupid enough to let the devil into my mind and fight it on my own. No, I didn't see or hear Satan, but I felt the presence of evil and I suffered the consequences. It took well over a month after the avalanche, for those darkest times to corrupt my physical well-being, but their cause started long before. My mother's death introduced me to the Devil, and Heather's death caused my battle.

Heather's Death

. . . and a sword will pierce your very soul (Luke 2:35).

  I was alone. I had attended a long meeting after church, so my husband had gone home. During that early afternoon discussion, I was unaware of the life-flight helicopter that was carrying my child and landing a little over a mile away.
  My awareness and reality changed at about 2:30 PM, in my car on Sunday, December 14, 2008: Turning out of the church parking lot, I called Heather as I so often did. I loved hearing her lilting "Hi Mamacita." [She spoke Spanish and several other languages.] I'll never hear her voice again, and it breaks my heart. Instead, a man answered and asked who I was.
  I said, "I'm Alyce Gross. Why are you answering Heather's phone?"
  "You need to come to the University Hospital Emergency room."
  I asked, "Was it a car accident or a ski accident?"
  He said, "It was an avalanche."
  I persisted, "How serious?"
  "I need you to come."
  I knew from his tone there was little hope.
Hope that is seen is not hope. For who hopes for what is seen? But if we hope for what we do not see, we wait for it with patience. Likewise the Spirit helps us in our weakness; for we do not know how to pray as we ought, but that very Spirit intercedes with sighs too deep for words. And God, who searches the heart, knows what is the mind of the Spirit, because the Spirit intercedes for the saints according to the will of God (Romans 8:24b-27).

  I called my husband, Denny, and left a message on our home phone and his cell phone as I made a U turn, on Foothill Boulevard, Salt Lake City, Utah: "Denny, Heather has been in an avalanche. I don't know yet how she is. Come to the University Hospital Emergency Room."

As I made my way to the hospital, I couldn't pray, except for a silent a cry for help. I felt a "protection" around me—guiding me. I believe it was the Holy Spirit, or Heather's spirit, or both. Because of Bible Study, I knew I could depend on the Spirit to *intercede with sighs too deep for words.* At the same time I felt a deep dread, and was almost certain Heather was dead, although the stranger's voice hadn't told me. From the time Heather was a baby, I had a consistent prayer life; but it ended the day Heather died.

I took care to remember where I parked my car, and rushed to a cold reception of three or four serious men (police officers or officials of some sort) who wanted to get their difficult job done. One of them said, "Write your daughter's full name and birth date on this paper."

Instead I asked, "How long was she under the snow?"

When he told me fifty minutes or more, I couldn't write anything. A shaking crying voice from somewhere behind the reception area said her date of birth. The men assumed I must be who I said I was and handed me a small bag of Heather's personal effects—driver's license, keys, money, and cell phone. They also passed off two large heavy bags of her shockingly cold, wet, cut-up ski clothes. The deep pink of her jacket stood out. My entire being was weighed down with a frigid, damp, heavy sensation. My arms were full. Where was Denny? I thought he may be at his office, where I almost never call. With my cumbersome load, I fumbled for his work number among the cards in my purse, while being escorted by the men.

At the waiting room, there were three skiers, who had been with Heather: Sam—male nurse, Lindsay—nurse/ski patroller, and Mike—camera man for Fox News. Alex came in next. It was his voice who had said her birth date. He had just started dating Heather and had also been skiing with her. He was below her on the mountain and called 911 immediately after she disappeared in the white cloud. Alex wasn't caught by the avalanche, nor was anyone else but Heather. He was sobbing and couldn't look at me. I wasn't crying.

There was a hospital counselor among the men. He advised me to call friends. I just wanted Denny. My cell phone battery was extremely low, so I chose not to make other calls. He asked if I wanted a hospital chaplain. I said ok, but that I wanted my own pastor, Steve Klemz. The other men eventually got to leave. Their job was done. The chaplain asked if we who were still there would mind if she led us in prayer. I can't remember her words, but I do remember her compassion.

Denny finally called, his voice shaken as he asked about Heather. He called again and in a crying voice explained, "Randy is coming to get me. I can't drive." He had been taking a nap during my first calls and didn't hear our home phone or his cell phone. Randy Emery, a close friend, brought him to the hospital. Together we made the hardest call to our other daughter, in Fort Collins.

"Emily, sit down, I have to tell you something. Heather has been in an avalanche and they are trying to revive her now."

Although Emily was twenty-five at the time, she sounded like my baby girl when she asked, "Can I come home?"

"Oh Emmy, of course you can." Her future husband, Ryan, was already arranging their flight.

Pastor Steve, Heather's roommate, Jana, and her mom, and Corrine Emery all came. I remember putting my arm around Jana, who was shaking and sobbing. I think I said something like this: "Heather loved being your roommate. You were really a supportive friend to her." I was trying to comfort her and others.

I remember Corrine telling me, "It's ok to cry."

Sam had been answering Heather's phone and notifying people. Three other close friends of Heather's later told me they had come after we had left the hospital. They didn't get to meet us that night, and they weren't allowed to see Heather. Their memories will always be of the living vibrant person Heather was.

Nurses and doctors took turns coming out to explain that they were trying to warm Heather and get her heart beating. Her core temperature was 27° C (80.6° F). I kept asking to see her.

One East Indian doctor came to let us know that it was hopeless: "We gave her five units of blood to try to help warm her. There was so much bleeding, from her lungs. We couldn't stop the bleeding."

The head surgeon, also East Indian, finally came. He said, "I'm sorry to inform you, I declared the time of death as 4:47 PM. We got one side of the heart to flutter, but we couldn't get a heartbeat. I'm so very sorry."

We thanked him and the others for their efforts.

I believe the efforts were futile. She most likely died about twenty minutes after the 12:24 avalanche.

We again called Emily. "Emmy, our Heather has died."

Through her sobbing she was barely able to tell us the flight information.

It took them a while to prepare Heather's body before we could see her. Pastor Steve went with Denny and me to see our cold, sheet-covered, daughter. Intubation had caused her neck to be enlarged, and she had a black and blue/green swollen right eye. Her lifeless, peaceful face was hard to recognize. I said, "That's not my baby girl."

Denny hugged her and cried, "Did we love you enough, Heather? Did we love you enough?" I bent over his body and said, "Yes, we did. Yes, we did." Denny and I each took off the earrings she was wearing—I the right ear, Denny the left. I cut a lock of her hair. The nurses gave me a plastic bag for the earrings and hair. I still have them in my bed stand. I looked at her right foot and felt it—so cold. I was afraid, with the nurses all watching, to look too much at her body. I recognized her hands and feet and tried to memorize them. She had been washed thoroughly, but when I kissed her forehead I noticed thick blood slowly beginning to come out of her nose. I thought, "How can that be? She is so cold. Her life is over, yet she can still bleed."

The kind nurses said the medical examiner was coming, so it seemed like we needed to leave. Pastor Steve prayed with us. Again, I don't remember the words. He anointed her forehead with oil in the sign of the cross. That is the last time we saw Heather on this Earth.

She was cremated on December 17, 2008. "I'm sorry I don't know the time, Heather." She loved numbers and always remembered her birth was at 11:42 AM. She was given the number: #U4717. It's engraved on a small burnt piece of metal attached to the plastic bag that holds her ashes.

We left the hospital with enough time to go home and call family members and close friends in private, before going to the airport to pick up Emily and Ryan.

The Celebration of Life was held on Saturday, December 20, 2008. I'll write more about that spirit-filled memorial service in both part one and two of this book.

Christmas was spent with my younger daughter, Emily, her fiancé Ryan White, and Heather's former boyfriend, Scott Merkle. I was touched and comforted that Scott wanted to be with us. As was our family tradition, we went skiing. On that stormy Christmas morning, few lifts were open because of high winds, but we met with compassionate ski patrollers at Snowbird and skied a few runs at the very resort where our Heather died just eleven days before. Mt. Baldy, the killing mountain, was not visible.

As I already mentioned, I wrote most of the above in a beautiful small blank, silver-blue, ornately patterned journal that I found among Heather's possessions. In it I made my most life shattering event sound like it was written by an objective bystander with no feelings. The truth is: I felt like a bystander on the day of my daughter's death. I was very aware of all that was happening, but my emotions were tucked safely away. It felt unreal and impossible at the time, so I moved through it and tried to comfort others. Initially I wrote that I floated through it, but it was more like moving through very thick dense air.

Unlike Heather's sudden, unexpected, unwelcomed death; my Mother's came gradually. It took its torturous time, so the arrival was expected, in some ways welcomed, and finally a cause for relief.

My Mother's Death

I write and think about my mother's death from my selfish perspective as though it happened to me. It was her illness, and her suffering, but it took my mother when I needed her.

In my fourth grade year, my mother found she had breast cancer. She made a mastectomy sound like no big deal. She acted like it was not a problem to put false breasts in her bra and go back to work as an elementary school teacher. The example I followed in both career and in facing problems was my mother. Because she wasn't worried, I wasn't worried. All seemed to go fine until she developed keloids (painful growing scar tissue). The treatment with radiation and I'm not sure what all, may have contributed to her getting cancer again. The summer before my sophomore year, the blood she found in her stool led to a diagnosis of colon cancer. Again she put on a brave face, and underwent a colostomy—a surgical procedure removing part of her lower colon, thus the end of the large intestine is brought out through the abdominal wall. A bag is attached to the abdomen so stools can drain into it. As a teenager I thought it was horrific, but my mother made light of the situation. Even with the knowledge that they didn't get all the cancer this time she bravely went back to work, and she hung on to hope for a cure. I recall her strong faith. She often said, "With God anything is possible," and again endured chemotherapy and radiation.

After I got my driver's license I often raced, with her lying in the back seat, to doctors' appointments. She encouraged me to speed because of her pain. A nurse who lived near us was scheduled to come with shots to give some relief. I remember my mother begging me, "Please call the nurse and ask her to come."

In search of a cure, my mother left home for several months to go to USLA Hospital (a five-hour drive from us) for more specialized treatments. She fought to live and suffered extreme pain for three long years. Her last months were spent in the hospital fairly close to home where friends visited bringing her candy and gifts. She loved that because she would give everything away. "The nurses work so hard to care for me and others. Will you make a cake so I can give it to them?"

I recall driving with a group of friends to San Luis Obispo to take our SAT tests for college entrance. After the tests, we all went to visit my mother. It was thoughtless of me and must have been overwhelmingly difficult for her, but she sat up with a bright smile, and did her best to take an interest in each of us.

She lost the physical battle and died at age fifty-four. In her last months, my dad and I faithfully drove thirty miles each evening after work to the alarming sight of her emaciated body. To the end she attempted to give us encouragement.

When she died, her sister, on furlough from missionary service in Taiwan, was praying at her side. At that moment, I was at work cooking hamburgers at an A&W Root Beer Stand. While cleaning and scraping the hot grill and using some force, the big metal spatula flipped, and I scraped the tops of my fingers on the hot surface. The skin peeled back. I now wonder if the devil was laughing. I attended my mother's funeral with big bandages on one hand, but I know Satan's laughing was stifled, because the church was filled with so much love.

Although my mother requested memorial gifts be given to the Lutheran Mission in Taiwan, where my Aunt Alyce served, there were gifts of flowers filling the entire front of the church. Overflowing love was shown with bouquets placed in every window, yet there was enough money donated to build a small chapel. About seven years later, when I worked for the Department of Defense and taught Air Force kids in the Philippines, I went to Taiwan to visit my namesake and saw that little white chapel with its steeple and cross. No, I don't think the Devil laughed about that.

During our time of mourning for our mother, my family didn't talk about our grief. Family friends, relatives, and even my close friends didn't ask about my feelings. I don't blame them. They knew I was too sad to talk. To the few people that asked, "How are you?" I had my answer rehearsed and ready.

"I'm relieved that my mother isn't suffering anymore, but it's still very hard." My sorrow stifled my sarcastic-self, who would have silently said, "How do you think I feel?"

Throughout my high school years, I put on a brave face (like my mother had taught me), but underneath I was dealing with the fear and dread of losing the most important person in my life. Watching her suffer was torture and I wanted it to end, but I selfishly didn't want her to die. My father was a solid, dependable provider, but my mother was the heart and soul of our home. Before she was so sick, the friends of my two older brothers and my friends all loved coming to our house, because my mother made them feel so important and welcome.

Several years after her death, I attended a high school reunion that included five or more grades younger than ours. That was possible because in our whole high school there were only about one hundred and twenty-five students. Before I went to the reunion, I was thinking, "Everyone will remember me; I was a cheerleader."

People did remember me and talked to me, but with no mention of cheerleading. Everyone talked about my mother and how much they loved and admired her. Many had had her as a teacher. They came to me and said things like:

"Your mother was such a good teacher; she taught me how to spell."

One young man from a poor family said, "I loved your mother. She cared about all the students. I remember a field trip by train, though the tunnels to San Luis [Obispo]. That's the only time I've ever been on a train. She made school fun." He and all her students knew she wanted what was best for each of them. I tried to remember that lesson in my own teaching career.

She made her friends feel important too. In August, 2010, while I was visiting my home town, Templeton, California, getting ready for a Gang trip, to Yosemite (You'll meet "The Gang" under the heading "Childhood Friends"), I made a concerted effort to visit Elizabeth Larsen, an old friend of my mother's. Irene and Judy (from The Gang) also went. While we walked to her home, I remember saying, "I don't know if I remember what Elizabeth looks like, and I doubt that she'll remember me." I hadn't seen her in several decades. The minute we walked into her living room, where her hospital bed was set up, I was taken back in time, recognizing everything—the smell, the interior of her home, her lovely face, her voice—especially her voice; and I felt the essence of her goodness and love for me and for my mother. Yes, she remembered me. Shortly after that trip, I received this email from Linda Hamers, one of The Gang who lives in Templeton.

> August 26, 2010
> Hi Alyce,
> I went to Elizabeth Larsen's funeral today. It was very nice. She was loved and appreciated by many people. The new minister's service was intimate, humorous, and positive. During part of the service people were given an opportunity to speak. A woman told a story about being new to the church and how kind the ladies were to her, and she mentioned your mom. I don't know who she was, but she was very fond of your mother.
> Today was the first day of school for 5 of my little ones (grandchildren). Emma came home from K and said it was the best day of her life! And her teacher was the best ever. Nate came home from 8th and said it was boring, but he was up and dressed this morning when I got up at 6:00.
> I miss you. Love, Linda

Emma's Kindergarten teacher had made the children feel important and excited to learn. My mother did the same for her students. She was and is remembered. Her friends remembered her too, although almost all of them have died, her God-given goodness hasn't. It continues to live on. I believe it lived on in her granddaughters Heather and Emily, although they never met her on this Earth.

The Devil's Fingernail

In school, I always enjoyed math and science and did that homework by myself; but with writing, I asked my mother for help. When the time came for writing to colleges, I was on my own. Ironically here I am writing without her, or is she with me?

I had to fill out my college forms and applications for scholarships without her help. She didn't get to come to my high school graduation. Every girl in my class cried at graduation, except me. I was afraid if I cried, I would never stop. My mother died five days before I turned eighteen and one month before I left to go to California Lutheran College, which was a four-hour drive from home. I went with sorrow, insecurity, and dread. Some mornings the black feeling in my chest was so overwhelming I could barely get out of bed. Just writing this is making my throat close.

At college, we were housed in dorms with suites for five girls. I remember some of my roommates crying because they were homesick. I thought, "I wish I could be homesick, but what was my home, isn't there. The foundation has dropped from under me. They are so lucky to be homesick." The one thing that saved me was that my friend, Linda Atkins (now Hamers), was there with me for the first year. It was a secure feeling to have one person from home, who had known my mother and my background. Linda was the perfect person, because she is kind, sweet, and understanding. Just ask her eleven grandchildren.

Prayer was a constant for me through my mother's illness. I prayed for her healing. In praying the Lord's Prayer, although I knew it was wrong, I sometimes left out "Thy will be done." I wanted my will to be done. I needed my mom and didn't trust God's will. Through her sickness and after her death I kept asking God, "Why?" I never quit praying and I never quit asking, "Why did my mother have to suffer so intensely and die? Was it something she did or I did? Was it God's will? Do we get what we deserve?"

Of course I knew we were far from perfect, but that wasn't it. I couldn't believe it was God who caused that suffering. With the help of a college class, (something to do with the Old Testament), I decided it was caused by the devil. I didn't and still don't think of the devil is an individual character. I don't really know what it is, but I do know there is evil in the world and it can mess with people in many ways, through mind and body, to cause suffering. I begin to realize with the suffering of my mother, and I now know that evil and suffering can and does strike anyone—good or bad.

The Adam and Eve story shows how we humans chose and continue to choose the "knowledge of good and evil," and with that knowledge and freedom to choose comes ugly consequences. I believe God knew we would make that choice, and wanted us to have choice and freedom. Without evil and consequences there really wouldn't be choice. Life is burdened with struggle between good and evil.

With Heather's death I learned that being Christian does not protect one from external or internal battles; in fact I believe "religious" people struggle more than most. Douglas H. Gresham, the stepson of C. S. Lewis, wrote in the Introduction of A Grief Observed, by C. S. Lewis (p.xxvi): *"This book is a man emotionally naked in his own Gethsemane. It tells of the agony and the emptiness of a grief such as few of us have to bear, for the greater the love the greater the grief, and the stronger the faith the more savagely will Satin storm its fortress."*

Those were some of the most powerful words for me. I related to them deep in my soul, my mind, and my body. "The greater the love the greater the grief" has been quoted by many because it is true, also it is almost impossible to explain, but writing this book is my attempt. Before I share how Satin "stormed my fortress" I must tell more about my father.

My Father

When I think back I ask, "How did my father deal with his pain and darkness?" I remember how hard it was for me when each of my own daughters went away to college. It was a necessary loss but difficult. I bring this up because my father lost so much in such a short period of time. About a year after my mother's death, my oldest brother graduated from California Lutheran College, got married and went away to Air Force Officers' training. The middle brother was drafted into the Army and went to Korea.

In a discussion with my new sister-in-law about our concern for my father, Bev said, "Every time Al or I call him we wake him up."

I concurred, "He just works and sleeps."

I stayed at California Lutheran College for one year and two quarters and then transferred to Cal Poly, San Luis Obispo, the town where my father worked, to be closer to him and my childhood friends. Four of us from The Gang lived together during that third quarter and through my junior year of college. My father stopped by often to visit. Then he began seeing me less and Dorothy more. Eventually he married Dorothy, whom my mother had consoled years before when Dorothy's husband was suddenly killed in a car accident. Now it was my mother's dear friend, Dorothy, who consoled and was a companion for my father as he was for her.

I felt pleased that they were no longer alone. I am deeply thankful to God that I had wonderful loving parents, including sweet Dorothy.

When my father died after I was married and had young children, my grief felt less intense than that for my mother. It seemed it was his time and he was ready. I wasn't dependent on my father, but Dorothy was, so it was very hard for her. When she died, she too was ready. I remember her saying, "I don't know why I'm still here." They both had long lives and their deaths seemed to fit the natural order.

Ironically grief returned twice stirred-up with the most intense joys in my life—the birth of my daughters—because I missed my mother. I wanted to share my joy with her. Thankfully I had no idea that the intensity of that joy and love would be matched with my deepest grief. The loss of Heather's bright future, and the thought of Denny's and my life without Heather took me to the darkest depths.

Alyce Gross

The Devil in the Dark and the Attack on My Immune System

It is not unusual for a grieving person to become physically ill. Several of the helpful books I read warned that one's immune system may be weakened at this vulnerable time. As a school teacher of thirty-three years, I almost never got sick. I had developed a strong immune system, but within six months of Heather's death, a series of events taught me I wasn't so strong after all. I learned the hard way to never go into battle without armor.

Heather died in the middle of December, and it took me until the end of January before the rage really set in. On January 27, 2009, while I was in a very dark emotional place, Denny drove with me to the Medical Examiner's Office. There I was finally able, through persistence, to collect a copy of the examiner's report, from a heartless, officious, little b---- who worked in the office. The written report was about the condition of my daughter's body. Denny couldn't understand why I was so compelled to read it, but he read it too. Doom set in with the reading of that clinical report about the extent of Heather's injuries. My spirit was being crushed as I so graphically imagined the violent death of my beautiful daughter. My anger grew deeper. I had my session alone with the devil the following day while Denny was at work.

Grieving books had taught me to not avoid the sad and the dark places, so in the basement, with Heather's cut-up pink ski jacket around my shoulders, I sat with the devil in the dark. I believe the insidious attack started that day. Within the week I had a bad cold and sinus infection that made all my teeth on the top right side ache. My right canine tooth (a primary tooth) became very loose, and an ugly abscess formed on the gum above the tooth. It was pulled before it fell out. With my dentist and a periodontal specialist, I went through a year-long process before I got my new tooth, an implant. That length of time for an implant was not unusual then. What was unusual is what the periodontist said when he saw the dead bone and big hole where the root of the tooth should have been. He has worked on hundreds of jaw bones, yet he said, "I don't know what that was! I never saw anything like it! I pulled out soft dead brown bone."

As he said it, I thought to myself, "I know exactly what that was. It's where the devil's fingernail touched me."

Refrain from anger and turn from wrath . . . It leads only to evil (Psalm 37:8).

Journal Entry March 25, 2009 Mom's Thoughts on Heather's Death
(I almost edited this out, because it sounds so crazy, but it shows how distraught I was, so here it is.)

Was it God allowing the devil to mess with my mind? Was I being "sifted like wheat?" The Bible, in 1 Corinthians 10:13, teaches that, "No testing has overtaken you that is not common to everyone. God is faithful, and he will not let you be tested (NIV translation uses tempted) beyond your strength, but with the testing he will also provide the way out so that you may be able to endure it." *Denny and I were and still are being tested/tempted. About a month and a half after Heather's death, I felt like I was sitting with the devil in my basement alone in the dark. The devil loves the dark, and hate, and anger. It was having fun with me and my anger at God. I could feel the evil getting into my head and coming out in my ugly words. I tried to push God away, but God didn't leave me. God is in my every cell, and with that knowledge, I could "kick the devil in the face." An old friend told me that that is what her mother always said to do. It stuck with me, but I got kicked back. The devil doesn't scare me, because* "If God is for us, who is against us?"*(Romans 8:31). God will win.*

Where is my way out, so that I will be able to endure it? God is my way out, but I can't answer for Heather. I need to know she is in "the light." Please, God, help me to know.

Heather, I will never forget you. I will never quit asking questions, because God made me a thinking human being. Even with all this pain and grief, I am so glad I got to be your mother. I'll always be proud to say I am the mother of Heather Aron Gross. Heather, please go to the light. Go with God the Father, Son, and Holy Spirit.

A month later, the end of April, is when I had shingles, which is caused by a chicken pox virus attacking the nerves. The shingles episode made the skin on my left arm and on part of my upper left torso feel very sensitive. It hurt to have clothes touch it. An outbreak of eight sores on my upper left back was arranged in a neat rectangle. I also had a few sores on my chest. Relative to some stories I've heard, it wasn't a bad case, but it was the second immune system attack. The third was far more serious and most probably—deadly.

The following month I discovered a hard lymph node, the size of a small egg, in my right groin. The abnormal cell growth probably started four months earlier, on January 28th, as the third and most frightening reminder of my battle with evil.

Lymph nodes have everything to do with the immune system. The hard rubber egg was removed and biopsied. I found out I had non-Hodgkin's lymphoma the day after what would have been Heather's 28th birthday, six months after her death.

Skeptics could easily say my illnesses were psychosomatic or coincidence, and being a skeptic myself, I know that could be true; but I believe that evil can do some of its most insidious work through one's psyche.

I don't recommend ever asking the devil for battle. In my attempt to kick the devil in the face, I lost a tooth, got shingles, and cancer. You can see how well I did while pushing God away. I believe everyone will have to fight evil, but don't do it on your own, be prepared with the armor of God. The Bible puts it like this:

> *Put on the full armor of God so that you can take your stand against the devil's schemes . . . so that when the day of evil comes, you may be able to stand your ground, and after you have done everything, to stand. Stand firm then,*

> *with the belt of truth buckled around your waist, with the breastplate of righteousness in place, and with your feet fitted with the readiness that comes from the gospel of peace. In addition to all this, take up the shield of faith, with which you can extinguish all the flaming arrows of the evil one. Take the helmet of salvation and the sword of the Spirit, which is the word of God. And pray in the Spirit on all occasions with all kinds of prayers and requests. With this in mind, be alert and always keep on praying for all the saints* (Ephesians 6:10 & 13-18).

I am not saying that "with God" I won't die of cancer, or suffer more illness or heartache, but I do know God will be with me through everything. I know that I need to let God in. I need to pray so I have "armor." God is there waiting to be let in. *I am! I stand at the door and knock* (Revelation 3:20). "I am" is God.

Prayer is one way to open the door to God.

> *Ask, and it will be given you; search, and you will find; knock, and the door will be opened for you. . . . If then, you who are evil, know how to give good gifts to your children, how much more, will the heavenly Father give the Holy Spirit to those who ask him!* (Luke 11:9&13).

When I found out I had non-curable cancer, on top of having lost Heather, my feelings could best be described in the following Psalm:

> *O LORD, the God who saves me, day and night I cry out before you. May my prayer come before you; turn your ear to my cry. For my soul is full of trouble and my life draws near the grave. I am counted among those who go down to the pit; I am like a man without strength. I am set apart with the dead, like the slain who lie in the grave, whom you remember no more, who are cut off from your care. You have put me in the lowest pit, in the darkest depths. Your wrath lies heavily upon me; you have overwhelmed me with all your waves* (Psalm 88:1-7).

Heather's death still sometimes has me in a desolate pit, but God is with me. God is deep in the marrow of my bones and gives me spiritual and physical healing.

He drew me up from the desolate pit (Psalm 40:2).

Do not, O LORD, withhold your mercy from me; let your steadfast love and your faithfulness keep me safe forever. For evils have encompassed me without number; my iniquities have overtaken me, until I cannot see; they are more than the hairs of my head, and my heart fails me. Be pleased, O LORD, to deliver me; O LORD, make haste to help me (Psalm 40:11-13).

He heals the brokenhearted, and binds up their wounds (Psalm 147:3).
For me being brokenhearted is much worse than cancer.

On the day I called, you answered me. You increased my strength of soul (Psalm 138:3).
I don't increase my strength of soul, God does.

I still have angry days and bouts with evil. I know there will be more to come, but I know I'm not alone. After I was diagnosed with lymphoma, my church put me on their prayer chain. As you'll see in the next topic, I also put out emails explaining my condition to friends and family, and asked for their prayers. Thus far it appears their prayers were answered. Oh yes, the eighteen radiation treatments may have helped as well.

Doubt, Questioning and Cancer

Journal Entry February 4, 2009
   From a devotional in the book Hope *by Nancy Guthrie, p.7, "Brokenhearted":*
"Have you determined to trust God with your future? How is that evident in your life?"
I don't know, but I am doing a lot of Bible study and not a lot of prayer. I don't trust that there is a point to my prayers.

   Early in February, just after this negative journal entry of February 4th, I received a beautiful letter from a former coworker of Heather's. I will include the first part of the letter in Part Two of this book, but am including the last paragraphs here, because it motivated my next journal entry.

Bonnie Fletcher
   From my own experiences with death, I have come to realize that surrendering to what is, is the beginning of healing from the suffering, that part of my suffering seemed to come from my resistance to accepting what is. But this is such a very, very difficult thing to do.
But I can say this: Heather would not want her family to remain sad! She would want Denny-Alyce-Emily—all of you—to Choose Life! That is certainly what she did!
   I pray that you are all comforted in the knowledge that Heather touched so many more people than you can know and she will always be loved and remembered by those of us at Tandem [a science lab] who knew her.
And most importantly, I pray to God and wish for all of you:
Strength, love, peace, and healing,
Bonnie

Journal Entry Friday the 13th of February, 2009, in the wee hours of the morning
   I choose life and I choose to live it abundantly. I skied on Heather's fat skis [extra wide and good for deep powder] *today and chose to ski in her honor. They were the last gift Heather gave me, but she didn't know she was*

buying the skis for me. She never skied on them, but I consider them a little part of her. She was so excited about them that she put them in her Facebook photos. Perhaps if she had skied on them on December 14, 2008, instead of her old skis, she would still be alive.

The lifties [kids that work at the ski lift] *coveted my fat skis today and that was fun. It was our last Alta Ski Resort, Ladies Day class. I never told the other skiers that my daughter had just died, but my friend, Corrine Emery told our instructor, Laurie. Corrine is an excellent listener, and the perfect person with which to ride up and down the canyon each week. It was difficult but good to face the mountains and snow every Thursday for the last six weeks. Most ski days were met with dread and foreboding, because Alta is just on the other side of Mt. Baldy where Heather died. But today was a better day. Maybe because it was the last time I have to face that mountain for a while.*

This was a very temporary high. The questioning and turmoil returned. I still haven't accepted Heather's killing through an act of nature. Yes, it was a killing by natural forces, and it is almost impossible to accept.

Journal Entry   March 26, 2009   Talking to God
          ". . . the Lord whose name is Jealous, is a jealous God." (Exodus 34:14b). *Was Heather putting other gods before you? Did you take her to keep her for yourself? Is she with you? I need to know. Please help me know.*
God you are Holy. You are good and faithful. *Were you good and faithful to Heather, to me?*
You are just. *Was it justice to take a beautiful human like Heather from our lives?*
You are gracious. *Is Heather receiving your grace?*
You are immutable (unchangeable). *Didn't you change your mind about destroying some of your people? Why are some saved and some killed?*

You are patient. *Were you patient with Heather? Will you be patient with me and my constant questions?*

You are merciful. *Was any mercy given to my daughter as she was smashed off her feet, surrounded by crushing snow, slammed and plummeted over jagged rocks and around trees which broke her rib and bruised her organs? Was the suffocation with densely compacted ice crystals an act of mercy? What was my daughter thinking as she was being killed? Did she think of me? Did she think of how her family would suffer and never be the same again? Were you with her? Was there an angel to comfort her? Was the devil laughing? I hate that bastard! It took my future son-in law and [potential] grandchildren and my Heather's whole interesting future. Oh God, how I hate that bastard.*

You are omnipotent (unlimited power). *Why didn't you move Heather to safety?*

You are omniscient (knowing all things). *Please let me know she is with Jesus.*

You are wise. *Let me know the wisdom behind her death.*

You are perfect.

You are Holy, Holy, Holy.

Journal Entry   March 27, 2009   Bitter
Exodus 15: 23 & 25

"The water is bitter. . . . The Lord showed Moses a piece of wood to make the water clean."

Where is my piece of wood? I know it is the cross, but did Heather know it? Is Heather with you? Please let me know. I have faith, but did she? I need to know.

Journal Entry   April 10, 2009   Good Friday Baby

Heather, Stone Thomas Emery [Randy and Corrine's grandson] was born today at 2:30 AM. You never got to have a baby. You never got to have a husband. Why was your life cut short? Where are you? Please let me know—Heather, God, Jesus, an angel. Please come and let me know that my firstborn child that I love with my whole heart is in a good place. Please help me know and trust. I'll always love you, Heather.

Journal Entry   April 13, 2009   Yesterday, Easter without Heather

I didn't have the heart to prepare a meal and invite guests for Easter dinner, so Denny and I took quiche to the church brunch followed by the 11:00 AM worship. I felt sad the whole time. There was no Easter joy. Denny and I went home, changed into comfortable clothes, drove to Deer Valley, and found that our passes are still good for credit for next ski season. We then parked near Main Street Park City, and walked, looking at restaurants trying to decide where to eat. We made the mistake of going to the Mexican Restaurant where we took Heather and Koshin on Christmas 2007. It was painful to remember how much fun they made dinner then and would have made Easter dinner. Denny and I worked on a puzzle at home that evening. I was forlorn and lonely. I miss her so much I can hardly breathe. I wish I could die. I know I can't leave Denny and Emily. When will I find any happiness? Please God, help me to know she is with the resurrected Jesus. Help me.

Journal Entry   Thursday, June 18, 2009   Before Surgery

My Heather has been dead for 6 months. She was my pride and joy. My pride and joy have been dead for 6 months. I would rather stand on a beach in Thailand and face a killing tsunami than go through the last 6 months again. My only reason to keep living is my husband and my Emily, who wants me in her life. I do look forward to Emily and Ryan's future. I do need to figure out my future and purpose beyond my daughter. I do need to find my purpose. God help me.

Why do I pray to God who answered my daily prayer, "Like a mother hen protects her baby chicks, please protect my Heather, my Emmy, my Denny and Me," with a crushing avalanche, that slammed my child over rugged terrain, bruising her organs and suffocating her? Why?

I wonder if I have cancer like my Mom. I'll get through the wedding and die. I look forward to death, but I don't want to leave Denny alone. I'll go, stripped of pride and joy. I'll go toward the light and look for Heather and my mother and father and others. It's supposed to feel good. I look forward to feeling good.

Since Heather died, I've had a sinus infection that led to an abscess on the gum above my eye tooth. I lost the tooth. I've had shingles. Now I have a swollen lymph node or a hernia. Is this surgeon any good if he can't tell the difference? I Hope he can figure it out when he cuts me open.

E-mail:
Wednesday, July 1, 2009
Hi Kristi,

Thanks again for coming to the 5K. [More is to follow on this event that Heather's friends planned on what would have been her birthday.] It is so helpful for Denny and me to be around people who loved and remember our Heather. You're a wonderful supportive friend. All is fine with me, but I'm having some more tests today and will save talking about them until after the wedding. Good and peaceful thoughts and prayers are always appreciated.
Alyce

Journal Entry   July 26, 2009

A bone marrow biopsy is a different sort of pain. It's deep and far reaching, but not too intense. I just kept a mantra going: "Dear God please help me, Dear God please. . . ." And I got through without a whimper. Then I went back to Vacation Bible School to do music activities with Susan Swidnicki and the kids. The very next evening, July 9th, Doctor Liz called me with the news that my bone marrow was clear of cancer. She also scheduled a second CT scan for Monday, so I could have a better reading this time, with the iodine contrast, and without charge, as they misread my creatinine levels in my blood test.

I sent the following letter to most of the people on my email list that day:
Sunday, July 26, 2009
Dear Friends,

    Denny and I made a pact not to tell anyone this news until after Emily's wedding. We didn't want to put a dark cloud over the preparations or the wedding.

    The day after Heather's 5K event I was diagnosed with non-Hodgkin's lymphoma. The good news is: after two CT scans and a bone marrow biopsy, I'm only in stage 1 or 2; so it is not only treatable but curable. Because I'm in the expert hands of Dr. Liz Prystas, who attends Zion Lutheran, the tests were started quickly. I have my initial appointment for radiation therapy this Tuesday, 7/28. I'm not sure yet, but I believe I'll have radiation therapy through most of August. One of the side effects is fatigue. Compared to Heather's death, this really isn't a big deal. Denny and I are doing fine with this news, because after a rollercoaster ride of emotions for the first two weeks of July, we are thankful for the words "stage 1 and curable." About 85% of the people with this kind of cancer (low grade, B cell, follicular lymphoma) don't find it until it is stage 3-5. Then it is not curable.

    We're also thankful for a beautiful and joyful three days of wedding celebrations.
I appreciate friends and prayers. Love, Alyce

Many people answered with good wishes. Here are a few:

Alyce,
    Thanks so much for having us at the wedding. It was a beautiful ceremony and reception. Emily was the perfect bride, and it was an honor to be there.

    Thank you for letting us know about your situation. As always, we will keep you in our daily prayers.
"I am strong and of good courage, I do not fear nor am I afraid, for the Lord my God, He is the one who goes with me. He will not leave me nor forsake me" (Deuteronomy 31:6).
Catina Aronson (My niece from Canada)

The Devil's Fingernail

    I am so saddened by this news. I wish more than anything I could be there at this very second to give you a hug. Sorry that I didn't email back straight away. I guess I needed a day to let it sink in. You truly are one of the most wonderful women I have ever known. I think of you as a second mom and a good friend. The more I think about why things happen the less I understand any of it. I have come to the realization that horrible things happen to amazing, kind and generous people. You and Dennis are so strong and have an unbreakable faith that I envy. In my heart I know that you will both get through these trying times and come out of it all that more brilliant. Know that you are always in my thoughts and prayers...there are so many people that love and care about you in this world, I hope the positive energy can be felt in Salt Lake.
    Emmy's wedding was wonderful. . . . She looked so beautiful and happy. It was great to see you as always, and I look forward to seeing you in Sept. Until that day I will pray for you and keep you close to my heart.
Love,
Katie Gracia Dyson (Heather's friend since 7th grade)

July Journal Entries
July 26 and 27, 2009: My legs and body ache like crazy. Is the devil messing with me again?
July 27, 2009: I felt swollen lymph nodes in my left groin and neck.
July 28, 2009: I went to a radiation consultation. The radiation doctor let me know I'm probably not in stage 1 after all. Instead of starting the radiation treatments, he set me up for a PET scan—bad sad news in my mind.
July 29, 2009: I am in such a bad place. I hate life and want to die. God please help me. I feel so alone. Where are you?
July 31, 2009: I waited all day yesterday to hear about my PET scan. Today I called the Radiation Oncologist. He let me know the scan showed increased up-take in the right underarm, and the left and right groin. The neck didn't light up and there was nothing showing in the organs. His

opinion on treatment is "less is better." I'm still waiting to speak to Liz.
1:00 PM: Liz called. She made it sound even better. The groin areas didn't show much up-take (only 2; 10 would be bad), and a 1 cm node in my right armpit (up-take 3.4) so I'm a moderately suspicious stage III.

At some point I finally got on my knees and asked God to help me, and to take the evil turmoil away from me. I felt the ugliness lift and peace set in.

This is what I sent out to people to let them know what was going on with my cancer:

Dear Friends,
    I wrote too soon. The radiation consultation, on 7/28, ended with the conclusion that radiation is not the best treatment at this time. Instead I had a PET (positron emission tomography) scan on 7/29/09. It's an imaging test that uses a radioactive substance (called a tracer) to look for disease in the body. The result showed no cancer in the organs, but lymph nodes in the left and right groin and the right underarm are showing very low amounts of possible cancer activity. That means I'm not stage I (cancer in only one area), but a moderately suspicious, stage III. And remember it is very slow growing. In fact sometimes there is almost no activity for years with this kind of cancer. I've been researching and learning as much as I can about my specific cancer. I'm listening to two excellent oncologists. Their advice, at this point in my treatment, is "watch and wait, less is better." Neither chemo nor radiation are called for now. I feel fine, and with the prospect of no treatment, I plan to go help Emily set-up her new classroom in the middle of August.
    Thank you for your loving responses. Your positive thoughts and prayers feel much better than chemo and radiation. Don't worry, if treatment is called for down the road I'll say, "Bring it on."
Love, Alyce

August Journal Entries
August 11, 2009

Dr. Liz called today to tell me the needle biopsy taken on Friday, of a 1 cm node in my right armpit, showed no cancer, yet suspicious cells. She thinks I should have radiation on my right groin and is going to discuss it with the Radiologist. I'll learn about their conclusion when I return from Fort Collins.

August 12, 2009   Part of a Journal Entry
Today is our 31st wedding anniversary. I'm thankful that I have Denny as a husband. We grieve together. That is not supposed to be the reason I'm writing today. I was going to write about the wedding, but grief is my topic instead. I know I'm a different person. I know I'm not in control. I know God is in control and is more powerful than anything. I know I need God, or the devil takes over my mind and my body. I know when I pray for help, the devil is pushed away. It (the devil) is so powerful, yet completely powerless when God is with me. With the evil gone, is my cancer gone? The tests seem to be showing that.

The Radiation Oncologist later, on August 24th, in my second radiation consultation, said something like this, "With the evidence of several swollen lymph nodes, when I examined you on July 28th, I was sure you were in stage III, but I was wrong." I respect him and his honesty. I don't blame him for misdiagnosis, because I too felt all those lymph nodes and thought I was well past stage one.

I do pray that Dr. Liz and the radiologist come to the best conclusion for me. I do want to live and be Denny's wife and Emily's mother.

Emily just called and talked to me during her whole lunch break, before having to report to back to school trainings. I'm so glad she needs me and looks forward to me helping her in her new classroom. She is such a wonderful daughter and an absolute blessing to Denny and me. We're fortunate to have a condo to go to, and to be able to spend quality time with our Emily and our new son, Ryan.

Last night I attended Compassionate Friends. It was our first meeting at Zion Lutheran Church, where there is no charge. Wilbert, our leader used to collect donations and had been paying $50 a month for a meeting place at Sugarhouse Park. Denny, who was church council president, got permission to move the meetings to our church with no charge. I feel good about saving Wilbert the trouble.

Through reading many books on grieving, and during the meetings, I've learned that I'm not alone in my grief. Many people in this world are hurting, and I feel more compassion and connection to them. I feel my grief puts me at a new level of understanding God and the gift of the suffering of Jesus. Not that I pretend to understand God. I know I can't understand God, and that puts me a little closer to understanding. It doesn't make sense, but if we could make sense of everything it wouldn't be other worldly or godly. It would be too human, and too contained, and too small, and too simple, to be God. I don't understand, and I don't get to control, but I do know a little better that God is all powerful and I am not.

"For my thoughts are not your thoughts, nor are your ways my ways, says the LORD. For as the heavens are higher than the earth, so are my ways higher than your ways and my thoughts than your thoughts" (Isaiah 55:8-9).

Sent: Monday, August 24, 2009 5:16 PM
Subject: treatment change
Dear Friends,

The results of a needle biopsy of the lymph node in my right armpit indicated no cancer. That means I'm probably stage 1 after all. Therefore I start radiation Wednesday, 8/26, and continue through 9/22. I had my second radiation consultation today and got 5 little tattoos and another CT scan. There is now a 30% chance of a cure.

That's better than no chance. Again, I appreciate your positive thoughts and prayers. Alyce

Response from my childhood friend:
September 12, 2009
    Hi girl, glad to hear treatment is going well. I am so thankful that we all have each other. I know that all of you are just like having sisters, probably better!!!!
    The trip sounds great. There is something to be said for having a mission to focus on when you have lost a child, the pain will never go away. It does seem to lessen as time passes. However, for you that is a long way down a heartbreaking and difficult road. For me the year of "firsts" was the worst. As the first anniversary draws near it gets almost unbearable.
    Just remember that I love you and so does your family. Sometimes you just have to keep moving forward because you need to do it for the rest of the family. Remember they are suffering that tremendous loss too. I know you know all of this in your head, but it is really hard to feel it in your heart. Hopefully we can get together before or after your trip to Italy. Leave it to the Italians to have a good and interesting time.
Much love, hugs, and prayers. Barb Condon   Love to Den too!!

Only someone who has suffered through the death of a child can share like this. Sadly, Barb has been there.

Journal Entry   Tuesday, September 22, 2009
First Day of Fall and Last Day of Radiation
    Today is my last day of 18 radiation sessions. I'm taking rice crispy treats to the technicians who so carefully cared for me. I'm writing them this note:

Dear Radiating Women,
    Thank you for being kind, cheerful, and efficient. More importantly, thanks for being precise and careful in your life saving work.
Fondly, Alyce Gross

(I also gave them some of my garden fresh tomatoes. Again, I followed my mother's example.)

These journal entries seem repetitive, because they are. The grief and anger keeps coming back.

Journal Entry: Thursday, October 22, 2009
(It has been a month since I've written.)

I used to be in a happy place on my faith journey with God, until I was slammed into a new reality. I've been stripped of my pride and joy. I now know nothing. I understand nothing. I'm no longer more important or more loved than anyone. My children and I are subject to forces of nature and are not physically protected. Heather was my pride and joy. I prayed almost every day of her life for her protection. My answer came on December 14, 2008, when she was slammed, pushed, dragged, broken, bruised, and suffocated by what journalists call an act of God, or an act of nature. More than two hundred skiers had skied Mt. Baldly that morning. Yet Heather, who had been studying for finals and was cramming in a few runs, was the only skier in the shoot, just after noon, when an avalanche grabbed her and carried her over three hundred yards down the rugged steep terrain on The Fields of Glory. She was buried under three feet of crushing snow for over fifty minutes.

I've made some new discoveries. I'm on this journey alone. I can't expect others to be on my journey. The one person that would be with me, who was brilliant and the most interesting person I knew, who could really listen with empathy, who was open minded, nonjudgmental, understanding, and who deeply loved me, is dead. I miss you so much, Heather.

Grief for a child doesn't ever leave. I climb a little and feel better, but I slide back into dark valleys. I just need to remember not to climb and slide alone. "God, please help me and forgive me. Help me to do your will." It is so simple yet so hard.

Paul in writing to the Romans: . . . *but we also boast in our sufferings, knowing that suffering produces endurance, and endurance produces character, and character produces hope, and hope does not disappoint us, because God's love has been given to us* (Romans 5:3-5).

Email:
Date: Thursday, December 10, 2009, 11:23 AM
Dear Friends,
    I had my first post radiation CT scan, yesterday. My Oncologist just called with good news: They could see no enlarged lymph nodes. 😊 YEA! I'll have a repeat scan in about 6 months or more.
Cheers, Alyce Gross

    My next CT scan was nine months later, September 23, 2010. It showed no changes nor did my latest scan on November 4, 2011. My Oncologist used these words: "It's a miracle."
    Odds have it that this cancer may eventually kill me, but we all must die. For now it is helping me appreciate life.

*O L*ORD *my God, I cried to you for help. And you have healed me. O L*ORD*, you brought up my soul from Sheol, restored me to life from among those gone down to the Pit* (Psalm 30:2&3).

Alyce Gross

Things That Helped Most in My Grief

The Knowledge That Heather Lived an Abundant Life

Denny, Emily, and I agree that the way Heather lived is one of the greatest comforts to us. She breathed in God's gift of life with pleasure and joy. She shared her gifts with love and humor. For those who never met Heather, let me introduce her:

Who Was Heather?
From Heather's memorialized Facebook page:

Este Pizzeria
Every time someone touches your life, even for the briefest of moments, it is important, effective, and affective. Hold your memories, take life's lessons, and be better for having these people in your life.
December 16, 2008 at 2:11pm

March 6, 2010

Our Heather lived life to the fullest, and her pleasure wasn't selfish. Loving humankind was a part of her passion. Anyone who knew her knows this is true. She was too much for some people, but they remember her. When she would walk into a gathering or party (usually late, because she had been making the perfect earrings, or choosing the perfect shoes from the large and interesting assortment she collected) everyone would say in a happy raised voice, "Heather's here." Now the fun could really begin. As her mother, I don't know, nor do I want to know everything that went on in her celebratory life. She did share a lot with me, especially her concerns and love for her friends. I do know that her friends loved being with her, because of the wonderful and funny things they said and wrote about her.

People knew they were "safe" in her company. She had many varied and unusual friends because of this. Her purpose was never to tear down, but to build up. She would ask probing questions to get to the heart and soul of a person. One felt important around Heather, because although she was talking all the time and sometimes in different languages and made up words, she also was listening and remembering and caring about the people she trusted. I will miss talking with Heather for the rest of my life.

If I had a complaint about something or someone, she had the ability to listen in a nonjudgmental manner and not add to the anger or tension. She would help release it, often with humor. When I had something positive to share, she would add to the joy, because she was happy along with me. Heather couldn't resist giving loving advice to me and to her friends: "Mom, this is the nineties—get rid of those clothes." To friends: "You shouldn't slump. Hold your shoulders and chin up." This is a quote from an email she sent inviting friends to a party. "Wear cute attire—jeans and hotness." Her purpose was to help everyone look their best and be their "best self." Her intent was for good and for fun.

When Jesus said, *Love one another*, it wasn't a romantic or friendship kind of love. In Greek there are different words for love. Jesus spoke of *agapao*: the highest form of love. I once heard it explained as "Willing that person the best they can achieve for themselves." That was the kind of love Heather had for people. She certainly experienced romantic and friendship types of love as well, but Heather's love often reached the highest level: *agapao*.

Facebook comments that show her *agapao:*

Jeanne Sims
Heather!
Thank you for the nice comment! :) How have you been!?
December 12, 2008 at 12:05pm

The day after her death:

Xinling Chen
Heather, It hurts so much to click on your page.
I feel like you are still around me everywhere, at my place, in your car, in Union, fixing my English, giving me hugs, telling me to be confident and talking to me in a mixed language of Chinese and English...
My life will be quite different without you. I cannot imagine how it will be.
You are wonderfully weird. I will keep you in my heart for good.
Thank you for being my friend! Peace! Word! Yarrrr! (This is an example of one of Heather's made-up words. Her friends called it G-speak.)
December 15, 2008 at 11:53am

Justin Crowther
For those of you who never met Heather, it's a shame. I met Heather last year as we struggled through intro Syntax, intro Phonology and Sociolinguistics. In all the years of school that I've attended, I never even heard of any particular department being so interactive with one another. Heather was great and kind of like the glue to the group with her infectious personality. We had great times and I will miss the talks we had after class about her crazy adventurous weekends. She was really influential to me and what class I would take. Mainly I wanted to be around her because when you were with her you just felt good.
     Yesterday I found out that Heather died in an avalanche. She was going back to get her ski when the avalanche came down. I know that she is greatly missed not only by me but by many others. I don't really know what else to write but I just wanted to put something up on here in memory of her. The linguist community has felt a great loss in her passing.
Heather I love you and will miss you. It will never be the same without you. Posted by Crowther at 4:08 PM

Dominique Pantophlet Lieve
Heather, Thanks so much for those great last memories. I will always remember you like that; queen of the couch, bed, or anything else comfortable enough to pass out on, but never before dancing your crazy dance and sometimes succeeding in convincing me to join you... I am so glad I got to see you on Friday and say goodbye to you in a somewhat decent manner. All of us are just spending our days sitting together and staring, crying and then laughing at all of the silly memories we have of you. You were the one who told me at 3 a.m. in the morning that really, my theta's were fine, but it is the 'eth's I suck at. I keep feeling that you are just about to come around the corner and join us and that you are just stuck in traffic or something, and in our minds you are still here. Thanks for being my weird dancing buddy and for all the times that you have made me smile. I miss you. ♥
December 15, 2008 at 5:47pm

Alexandra Scott
I don't want this to be the last time I send you an obscene message... but it is. Everyone loves you for different reasons. You loved all of us just the same. I have a secret you should know....you know all my secrets. I will make you cupcakes anytime...just let me know.
December 15, 2008 at 7:11pm
(I think I know Lexy's secret, and I will reveal it in Book Two.)

Ryan Smith
You really knew how to live life and how to treat people, a friend to everyone you met. You were always kind, welcoming, and outgoing, I'm fortunate I had the chance to know you. I'll miss you.
December 16, 2008 at 4:27pm

Bree DeGraw
Your laugh, your silly poses, the way you said things, and like others have said - your crazy dancing skills! You led an amazing life, always to its fullest, and you did it with a smile and a desire to spread the love. I love and miss you so, so much!
December 16, 2008 at 11:52am

Xinling Chen
Me again!!! I hope I am not bugging you. I just need to write something here to release my feelings. Help me, Heather! Help me help me help me! I am desperately missing you!!! I want to grab something and hold it tightly to my heart. That something is you! I cannot think of anything else! How can I go on living like this? You really broke my heart!!!
Give me strength, please!
January 24, 2009 at 12:02am

Jackie Van Buren
I always feel like I see you on campus. Especially when we're all together and I imagine you walking toward us like you used to and we'd all go "Heather!" and wave you over and be so happy to see you, because you always made everything better just by being there. Seriously, whose face wouldn't you put an instant smile...on? I feel like you're there when we're all together, because you're a part of us, such an important part of who we are, what makes us us. Damn Heather, come back.
February 6, 2009 at 3:57pm

We received this kind note in the mail in February, 2009:

Dear Mr. and Mrs. Gross,
    You have my deepest sympathy. Heather and my daughter Emily were on the ASU rowing team together. The rowing team was a turning point for Em at ASU. Heather was a primary reason. She was a good friend to Em when Em needed a good friend. Em didn't stay on the team long after Heather left ASU. I had the good fortune to converse with Heather on several occasions. I loved how she referred to everyone as "dude." She was such a charming young woman. I am so very sorry.

Sincerely, Paul Stevenson

On Facebook a year later:

Bree DeGraw
The poem in yoga class tonight was filled with your energy. May I be generous and helpful. May I be pure and virtuous. May I be patient and able to bear and forbear the wrongs of others. May I be strenuous, energetic and persevering. May I practice meditation and attain concentration and oneness to serve all beings. May I gain wisdom and be able to give the benefit of my wisdom to others. Oh and this song, is you.
December 14, 2009 at 8:31pm
Heather's Mom again: I was privileged to be Bree's fifth grade teacher. Heather first met her in Girl Scouts.

  After working for several years as a scientist, Heather knew she didn't want it as her life's work: instead she felt compelled to continue the study of languages. I think it was the thrill of travel and the love of humankind that motivated her.

Some quotes Heather put on her own Facebook page shortly before she died:
"Language, after all, is the ligature that binds person to person, individual to culture, human to the world of humanity." -Charles Schuster
  Maybe now Heather communicates in a timeless universal language. Through her interest in people, culture and humanity she was bound to so many in her short life.

"Boundless indeed is the science of language,
but life is short and obstacles are numerous.
Hence take what is good and leave what is worthless, as geese take milk from the midst of water." -Pāṇini
  I believe she loved the science of language because it is boundless, and yes her life was short and her obstacles were numerous. It took us until two years before her death, before we really understood how great those obstacles were for her. The devil's fingernail may have even touched my firstborn's DNA.
  While she was pursuing a master's degree in linguistics, she had a part time job as an assistant reviews editor in that field.

The following are her own few words written in the summer of 2008 describing herself for the Linguist List job. I found this by searching Heather Aron Gross on the internet.

Heather Aron Gross
Assistant Reviews Editor
Heather@linguistlist.org

I graduated from Arizona State University with Bachelors degrees in Chemistry and Spanish, and a minor in Italian. I spent my junior year studying abroad in Granada, Spain, where I dared to take Italian and Inorganic Chemistry. Perhaps I should stick to tricky science in my native language.

The fluffy fresh of the Wasatch Mountains called me back to Salt Lake City, where I have worked as a scientist in bioanalytical chemistry for three years. I am now studying Chinese and pursuing a graduate degree in theoretical linguistics at the

University of Utah. I love to alpine ski, dance, run, and travel.

I have had the opportunity to visit many of Europe's countries, as well as Argentina, Mexico, New Zealand, and Australia. (That's Byron Bay behind me.) Many more travel adventures lie ahead. I was at Torino 2006, so Beijing 2008, here I come!

Even with the restriction of a few short paragraphs, Heather was able to convey her love of the mountains and skiing. She also included dancing, running, and travel. Dancing was a way Heather showed and shared her free spirit and love of life, and she could perform in the highest heels with the most creative movements, and not miss a beat. She ran cross country in high school, and continued running for enjoyment and exercise. As you'll see in Part Two, travel was a part of who she was.

Certainly, travel is more than the seeing of sights; it is a change that goes on, deep and permanent, in the ideas of living. Miriam Beard

If you wish to travel far and fast, travel light. Take off all your envies, jealousies, unforgiveness, selfishness, and fears. Glenn Clark

Heather traveled with a respect for humanity and with an open minded willingness to learn from different cultures. Much more is coming about Heather's life, in her own words, through emails that show the kind of traveler she was.

But friends, fun, and travel isn't all that Heather was. When she was working or studying she did it with the same energy and focused effort that she put into everything she did. Following are just a few of the letters which indicate the kind of work ethic she had.

It is with a heavy heart that I express my condolences and also those of everyone in New Jersey on the untimely passing of

Alyce Gross

Heather Gross. I had the opportunity to work with her during my time in Salt Lake. She was a unique woman who was intelligent, a hard worker and also just an overall wonderful person who was not afraid to go after what she wanted. I was fortunate to know her and I am proud to call her a friend. I'm not sure if everyone remembers this, but she used to have a little sign in her workspace in the lab that read "Well behaved women rarely make history." I think she lived her life that way and that's how I will remember her.
Luca C. Matassa, Ph.D.
General Manager, Bioanalytical Division

From: lailiang zhai
Sent: Thursday, December 18, 2008 12:19 AM
To: Scott Reuschel
Subject: Condolences to Heather's family
Hello Scott,
 I was shocked when I heard from Sherry the tragedy that happened to Heather Gross. I had the opportunity to work with her in the lab for two years. She is such an intelligent person who always has optimism attitude and perfect aptitude at the work she had been doing. She is also a warm hearted person who likes to helping others, and I still remember clearly how she taught me to use the many functions in analyst. I would imagine that it is just because of these characteristics she had that you and Jim chose her as the lab trainer, and she did her job really well! I am proud to call her friend and honor the friendship with her. I am sure that many people will miss her... Our condolences go out to her family and we all wish her family well.
 I would appreciate if you could pass the message to her family.
Thank you. Sincerely, Lailiang
 (Some of the foreign nationals that Heather worked with were brilliant scientists, but their English was not always perfect.)

I'm now shifting from her work as a scientist to her part time computer job she did while working on a Master's Degree. In early January, about three weeks after Heather died, Evelyn

The Devil's Fingernail

Richter knocked on my door, with a homemade cake in her hand, and tears in her eyes. She was one of Heather's colleagues at Linguist List. Heather had stayed with her for a few days in September, 2008, when Heather flew to the University of Michigan for training in her work as Assistant Reviews Editor with Linguest List. Evelyn came to express sympathy on behalf of her colleagues and professors in Michigan, and to give me a copy of an excerpt from an email sent to her by Professor Helen Aristar-Dry, written on December 20, 2008, the day of Heather's Memorial Service. Following is a copy of that email:

> What I will remember best about Heather is her great generosity and professionalism during a misunderstanding last summer. We sent Utah what we thought was payment for a half-time GA for 12 months, but in order to give Heather a full tuition waiver, they paid it out in 8 months. So in April Heather's funding ran out—to her surprise, and ours—just as she was about to travel to China. She was very dismayed, as you can imagine. And so were we, since we had thought that her work on reviews would continue all year. In the end, we did find some additional funding for her, but before that, when we thought that she simply wasn't going to get paid in the summer, she wrote me and volunteered to continue her reviews work from China, whether she was paid or not. She said that she felt an obligation to the users that she had been corresponding with, and she also didn't want to leave Randy in the lurch. This generosity impressed me a great deal, since what she was offering was literally hours of unpaid work under quite difficult conditions.
>
> If you get a chance, please tell her parents about this incident. Heather was a lovely, lively young woman, but she also took her responsibilities very seriously. I know they were very proud of her, and they certainly have reason to be.
> Professor Helen Aristar-Dry

In the summer and fall of 2007, Heather gave her unpaid time to help a Dual Immersion Academy (English and Spanish) get started in Salt Lake City. She enlisted help from her friend Michael Peterson to create a computer program for a lottery for admissions. This is copied from a handwritten note of condolence, which the Board President wrote to Denny and me.

12/18/08
Dear Mr. and Mrs. Gross,
We were all shocked and saddened to learn of Heather's tragic death. Your daughter helped us found our school. She was instrumental in the creation of our lottery for admissions and even went door to door with us spreading the word about DIA. We will always remember her contributions!

Fondly,
Barbara Fink
Board President, DIA

PS. The children of DIA are collecting food for the Utah Food Bank.

They were collecting in Heather's memory, because in her obituary, my husband and I requested donations to the Utah Food Bank in lieu of flowers.

Heather accomplished and experienced so much in her short life and her purpose was for good. In the writing and remembering, I'm helped in my grief. Another help was the knowledge that others prayed for us.

Prayers and Thoughts from Others When I Couldn't Pray for Myself

I felt the prayers and thoughts of friends and family at the beginning of my grief journey. I knew my church had included my family in a prayer chain, and many people called sharing that they would pray for us. We received hundreds of cards with kind words of encouragement. I looked forward to those cards with their compassionate messages. They kept coming for months and months. I truly felt strength and comfort from all the prayers and sympathetic thoughts.

My sister-in-law, Bev Aronson, made me a little cross with plastic and yarn, while she and my brother, Allan, were at our home, right after Heather's death. Her church organization made a prayer shawl and a cross for my daughter, Emily; and through networking, a church group from Hawaii sent a beautiful prayer shawl to me, with the same type of little cross. It came with a note saying, "This prayer shawl has been hand crafted for you. The cross, for your pocket, is to remind you that God and our prayers are with you always." There were many nights I woke up and couldn't get back to sleep. I would slip out of bed, take my prayer shawl, and sit in the rocker in our living room with it wrapped around my shoulders. The prayer shawl felt warm and comforting as I sat and rocked and cried for my child. I used to nurse Heather and later Emily in that same rocker.

Family, Congregation, and Friends

My younger daughter, Emily and her fiancé, Ryan White, flew to Salt Lake City from Fort Collins, Colorado, on the evening of Heather's death. Emily stayed home with us until the end of December, but Ryan stayed a few days, then flew back to Colorado to work the rest of the week. On Friday night he and a friend drove ten hours through a snow storm to get to Heather's funeral. His support of Emily during that time cemented my husband Denny's and my respect for him.

Karen Joseph, Denny's sister came within a few days with gifts, good cooking, and much love and helpfulness. She came again for a week in February, 2009. Both of my brothers live in Kalispell, Montana. We've always had a good relationship, but they were extra attentive about calling for more than a year after Heather's death.

The overwhelming love and support that Denny, Emily, and I felt at the memorial service (or Celebration of Life) was truly a gift from God. (I wrote more about it in Book Two.) God's love was poured out through our church congregation, our friends, family, and Heather's many friends from all over the country and world. That Spirit-filled celebration was a beautiful tribute to our daughter.

Our church family all seemed to be there and showed support with wonderful music, singing, prayers, and food. Even the program cover was a work of art, featuring Heather with her arms outstretched and her shadow forming a cross. The artist, Kristi Grussendorf, later gave us a framed copy of the original. It hangs at the end of our hall as constant reminder of our daughter. After the service the pastor invited all to a meal downstairs at the church. Tables were decorated, and the kitchen full of workers from my book club and Bible study groups all demonstrated edification in action. Our church family fed hundreds of people delicious chicken casseroles, vegetables, and desserts. There was even a Champaign toast in Heather's honor. Emily and Heather's former church youth group director organized meals to be delivered to our home every other day, so we didn't have to cook for a month or more.

I wrote countless personal thank-you notes. Following is a generic sample.

Thank You Letter   December, 2008
Dear Church Family,
    When Denny and I were planning Heather's service with Pr. Steve, we wanted it to be a celebration of her life, as well as out-reach to non-members. Your loving presence, beautiful singing, delicious casseroles, veggies, cakes, champagne and all the friendly assistants, were enough to make anyone, including Zion members, see how important it is to have a church family. We truly felt and tasted your love and support. Thank you.
    Our grief comes in waves that threaten to drown us, but we keep swimming. We appreciate your prayers, because we're not able to face this alone.
Love, Denny, Alyce, and Emily Gross

We received many beautiful plants and flowers, and thousands of dollars were given to The Utah Food Bank and other food banks and good causes around the country, in our daughter's memory. It was helpful to know that something positive came from Heather's death that winter.

Letter   January 12, 2009
Dear Director Jim Pugh and Utah Food Bank Workers,
    Thank you so much for the framed letter, which we were able to display at the service for our daughter, Heather Aron Gross.
    Enclosed are donation checks which were received at or after her service on December 20, 2008. If more are received, we will forward them to you.
    Thank you for your vital service in Utah.
Sincerely,
Dennis and Alyce Gross
Parents of Heather Aron Gross

Alyce Gross

Thank You Note   January, 2009
Dear Friends,
   We recently received notification that you made a contribution to the Utah Food Bank in the name our daughter, Heather Aron Gross. Thank you for helping us to pay tribute to her.
   Your gift not only serves needy people, but it helps us in our grief.
Sincerely,
Dennis and Alyce Gross

   At first friends were very intentional about spending time with me. Many people took me to lunch. It was helpful and appreciated, because it required me to get ready and gave me something to look forward to. I sometimes looked forward with dread, but I forced myself to go to be among people. Friends made a point to try to be good listeners and to be attentive and kind. I did learn it was up to me to initiate talking about my feelings or about Heather. Most people weren't and still aren't sure what to say. I don't blame them, because I don't know what to say either. They don't want to force me to talk about things I'm not comfortable with, so people make small talk unless I bring up the deeper subjects of my grieving. Although it is difficult, I've learned it is up to me. Often I hesitate to share my feelings, because some people want to give "helpful" advice. Staying busy seems to be many people's solution to grief.

My Commentary

   In the United States the word "busy" is some kind of badge of honor for women. I think being busy for busyness sake is a silly. I've learned to appreciate the unhurried time I now have for reading, Bible study, and writing. That has done more to help me in my grief journey than any amount of "busy" pursuits. Also in the U.S. we always want to fix pain. We're taught, through advertisements, that there is a pill or cure for all pain, so we shouldn't have to experience it. One who is grieving does experience deep emotional pain; and pills, drugs, alcohol, distractions, busyness, all can dull it or postpone it, but the pain patiently waits and must be experienced. I find it insulting that some people think they can fix my grief.

Everyone can master a grief but he that has it. William Shakespeare

Compassionate Friends
For more information go to: www.compassionatefriends.org

Now that it is over a year since Heather died, I sense even more that people want to offer advice if I don't say, "I'm fine." The one place I feel safe to talk of my sadness is at Compassionate Friends. It is a group of people who come together once a month to share. All who are there have had a child die, so they are empathetic and know better than any professional how we feel. For some who come, the pain is new and raw, but many lost a child years ago. They still come because they have no one else to talk to. I plan to continue attending for a long time, because maybe I can be helpful to others, as they have been and are to me.

Sometimes I feel that people are so full of themselves that if I tried to share my grief with them, it would come bouncing back at me with intensified force. Of course, I'm not giving most people enough credit, but I hesitate to take the chance. Not so with Compassionate Friends. Most of the people who attend Compassionate Friends are not full, they are empty. When one shares with them nothing bounces back. It is more like pouring one's grief into a calm pool of water where it is shared with the grief of others.

All of us are at various stages in our grief, we all deal with it differently, yet all seem to agree it is something we'll never get over. Although we're very different, we have another thing in common: we appear to have been broken and emptied, and it seems to be a part of who we now are. Broken and empty sounds weak, but we're not weak. We know we have suffered one of the worst losses possible, and we're surviving. We're reaching out for help and we're attempting to help each other. In our brokenness we're actually stronger; because we know if we can live with this, we can get through almost anything. I believe that brokenness also makes us more sensitive to human suffering. It makes us able to serve with a compassionate heart. Because of our emptiness and because we're less full of our own egos, we're able and ready to be filled with new truth. We now know a little better what is really important.

It doesn't mean that some don't become bitter and angry. It doesn't mean that we're not still struggling for answers, but we're not so full of our own importance that there is no room to learn. We're still futilely asking "Why?" but we're also asking "What?—What can we do in response to this soul crushing loss?" We know we don't have to do earth-shaking things. We've learned that sometimes small things mean the most—empathetic listening, kind words, or sharing a hug. Some are going on with their jobs and their lives, and are an inspiration because of their quiet strength. Some, who have lost children to drugs or alcohol, are compelled to write and/or speak publically to warn against those dangers. Some, whose children have taken their own lives, have learned that death isn't always the worst option. They have hope that their loved one is at peace, away from the earthly demons that tormented them. Even if we still have living children to consider, we want to honor our deceased children, and we know they would want us to find joy again. They would want us to live life abundantly. We are all survivors.

Sharing Heather's Possessions

Heather shared a cute brick house in an area called Sugarhouse, in Salt Lake City, with a roommate whose mother owned the home and was renting to Heather. Some of her college friends from Arizona State stayed at her house and in her bedroom when they came for her funeral. I believe that it was a meaningful experience for them to reminisce about Heather while staying in her former residence and being around some of her familiar possessions.

Although Heather had paid her rent for December, we knew we should start getting her personal items cleared out. On December 17th, Katie Gracia Dyson (one of Heather's long-time friends), Bev Aronson (my sister-in-law), Emily (my younger daughter), and I went to Heather's house and started talking about what to do with some of her things. We gave Katie a few sentimental items. Emily, of course, wanted most of her sister's personal affects, and I respected that. Bev made sure that I got Heather's bathrobe. It warms and comforts me while I fix my coffee, do my morning reading, and watch the sun rise over the Wasatch Mountains.

About a week later, after our out-of-town guests had left, Emily and I went through Heather's household items more thoroughly. It was an excruciating process for me. Everything reminded me of times and events in Heather's life. It seemed so wrong to be sorting and disturbing items in her sacred personal space. I probably wouldn't have accomplished anything without Emily there. It is still painful to think that that personal space doesn't exist anymore.

We boxed clothes and other items, dividing what Emily would take and what she left for me or for Heather's friends. Heather had numerous books—some I wanted and Emily took a few. We saved most of them for linguistics friends. Heather was working on a Master's Degree in linguistics and had a part time job as an Assistant Reviews Editor. As a result she had many new books through her Linguist List computer job. We boxed those books to save for her study partners.

Alyce Gross

On the afternoon of December 29th Denny, Emily, and I went to Heather's home again, this time pulling a U-Haul trailer. Denny and Emily accomplished more than I. They efficiently stowed Heather's furniture, bicycle, clothing, and other items into the trailer. Emily needed to go back to her home and job in Fort Collins, Colorado; so early the next morning we took Emily home, driving eight hours, pulling the U-Haul filled with my dead child's possessions. The whole experience was heart wrenching for me, but it was necessary. It is also a comfort knowing that the sister that Heather had loved, from the day she was born, now had things she could use and things that would give her a feeling of being close to Heather.

Before Heather died, I decided I needed an all-wheel drive car for getting up the canyons to ski. Heather's deep red Honda CRV was the solution. I drive it still, with its specialized plates—SCIARE (meaning *skiing* in Italian). Many little reminders of Heather are still inside including—some earrings in a little cubby, some colorful hair bands around the gear shift. On the practical side there is a car kit (a gift from her sister) and some warm black gloves which I have used several times. A friend said, "You must feel Heather's spirit while driving her car." I only wish that was true.

On January 4, 2009, shortly after returning home from Emily's, we invited about fifteen friends of Heather's (linguist students and scientists she had worked with) to our home for a buffet dinner and to share Heather's belongings. The students all appreciated the books. Heather had hung some of her clothes on puffy cute coat hangers. Almost everyone got a coat hanger. I asked, "Who didn't get one?" Two boys raised their hands. I quickly went to my own closet where I had the remaining four fancy hangers, and grabbed two for those boys. Everybody wanted one. I had some of Heather's clothes spread all over a bed. The clothes only fit some of the girls, and they were careful about taking what they wanted and leaving something for others. The shoes only fit Lisa and Xinling, and they each seemed delighted in receiving them and being able to walk or dance in Heather's shoes.

It felt good to get some of Heather's friends together and to share some of her belongings with them. We also fed them, and many students happily took food home and to take with them skiing the next day. It felt right.

Facebook:
Xinling Chen
Hey girl, I went skiing yesterday. I fell all the way down the hill. The skis and the shoes were so heavy that I could not stand up by myself (alright, I admit that I really need to work out). People (I mean Justin, Koshin, Tyler, Brian, and Matt) had to pull me up every time. They were soooo nice! I had a lot of fun.... Now I see why you loved skiing!
I will go to SF for LSA tomorrow morning. I will tell you what I see there when I am back. Word. (another example of G-speak)
January 6, 2009 at 6:11pm

Jackie Van Buren
I love you Heather. I think about you every day. I wonder if you realize how many people you brought together, all these people who cherished you. I hope you know how special you are.
And I really hope it was you coming to say goodbye to me in that dream. I'll hold it dear to me forever—hold your memory dear to me. And just so you know, every time I eat edamame I think of you.
January 5, 2009 at 6:21pm
Xinling Chen
I am wearing your coool shoes with maps on the soles!
January 15, 2009 at 11:17pm

Xinling Chen
The lunar New Year is coming. I can't help thinking of the party you threw last year. I was really homesick and sad about not being able to celebrate the Chinese New Year with my family. You have no idea how grateful I was for you hosting that party which made me feel so much better!!! Thank you once again! mua~mua~~~ber~
January 20, 2009 at 9:36pm

Heather had worked with scientists and was studying with linguists. These same young adult friends of hers were having another Chinese New Year's party. I'm sure that meant a lot to Xinling. They invited Denny and me, but we couldn't go because of a trip to visit Emily in Colorado.

E-mail: Lisa (scientist)
Subject: Chinese New Year
Friday, January 30, 2009

Oh, I'm so glad you are going to see Emily! The more I talk to you both the more I admire you and can see where so many of Heather's amazing qualities came from. I've wanted to send you a thank you email for a while, but somehow haven't been able to articulate it very well. I hope that you don't mind it now. I really wanted to thank you both for sharing Heather's clothes and books and shoes and fancy hangers with me and everyone else. It means so much to all of us to have them and be able to keep her memory close. I particularly love having the clothes, because Heather did mentor me in matters of style and fashion. I'm definitely more fashionable now!

These are a few more pictures I took of Heather that you may not have seen. I love all of them. She looks so vibrant and happy in the first three. The last I love because it is from the protest on proposition 8 that we went to. She spent a fair amount of time trying to take a good picture of a rainbow flag with her phone. I love it, because it reminds me of the things that I really loved about her. She accepted everyone, and wanted the world and society to accept them too. What I will treasure about Heather are those very sincere compliments she used to give, to all of us. The compliments that she gave me are among the most cherished I have ever received. They were so meaningful because they were absolutely genuine, and were about my character, my way of thinking, the qualities that she thought made me unique and someone whose friendship she valued. When she respected something about a person, she let them know. And what is amazing is that she found something to admire in everyone.

So thank you for everything you have done, and for the positive impact that Heather had on my life and the world in general. I will treasure her friendship for a lifetime. And I will

send you pictures if we take any, because Heather is the reason we will all be together, and even if she isn't in the pictures she is in our hearts.
All my love, Lisa Rohde

Alyce Gross

Shared Grief

My Uncle Don Anderson (my Godfather) taught me this saying: "Shared joy increases the happiness and shared sorrow decreases the pain." Grieving people need someone who loves them and cries and hurts with them. One of my favorite pieces, in the meditation book, <u>Healing after Loss</u>, was about a little girl who came home late. When her mother asked where she had been, she explained that her friend's doll fell and broke. Her mother said, "Oh, did you stay and help fix it?" The little girl answered, "No, I stayed and helped her cry."

Another book, <u>The Grieving Garden</u> helped me cry and helped me share grief with Heather's friends. The excerpt I used will be found in the chapter entitled "Books." This is an email from Heather's best Junior High and High School friend in response to the quote I sent:

May 11, 2009   Happy Mother's Day, Alyce

Emily is lucky to have you as a mom and Heather was lucky and appreciated you every day. I know this, she told me so :) She was forever grateful for your support through her ever changing goals and dreams...successes and failures.

I will be there on late Wed evening, Mon the 20th and would love to come over for a party with everyone. I am very much looking forward to seeing you and Denny and everyone else.

I have yet to read any books on grieving but that excerpt is comforting in more ways than one. I never thought of it that way...that Heather does not have to lose you or Denny or Emily or me. Many memories of Heather that I haven't thought of in years have come into my daily life during random times. When we were in high school—sometime around 10th grade, Heather had a dream that I died and she was crying in the dream and was heart-broken. The exact details are fuzzy, but it really affected her. I think of that time and realize how incredibly random and unpredictable life can be. I know that her dying has changed me forever and will shape who I am to come, but I find comfort in knowing that the friendship we had made me who I am today. Without her my life would be very different. So I agree. I would not change being her best friend even if I had known she would leave my life so suddenly.

    I am so happy about you buying a condo in Ft. Collins...will be great to be so close to Emmy whenever you want.
See you soon.
Love, Katie

Journal Entry   July 2, 2009   Sharing Joy and Sorrow

    Our big day was Sunday, June 28th—Our Heather's Golden Birthday. She would have turned 28 on the 28th and was born on a Sunday. My mother gave me a gold watch on my 17th birthday, because I was born on August 17th. She called it my golden birthday. By my next birthday, my mother was dead. I didn't get to give Heather a gold watch, but on her birthday, I woke up early and looked carefully through her baby book; something I haven't done thoroughly since I filled it out. I was reminded that in 1981, many people showed their love for Heather, Denny and me, by sending us cards and gifts. I read through lists of people and things they sent us. We didn't have help when she was born, but we had love and support. We also had love and support this 2009.

    On June 28, 2009, we were still at church at 11:42 am, Heather's birth moment (that she never let us forget). We went home and I made three batches of brownies to take to Sugarhouse Park. Denny and I arrived at 3:50 PM to help tape down table cloths and to decorate with streamers and with pictures of Heather. Lexy Scott (who had been doing a bike race for the cure for MS in Ogden), Scott Merkle (Heather's former boyfriend), Lisa Rohde, and Emily Markovitz were there with silly party stuff from the dollar store. These organizers had worked with Heather in a science research laboratory. Lexy went home to get the cake she made in Heather's honor. It was all very Heatherish—cute and fun.

    The event was the 5K for HG. There were about 70 people who took part in some or all of the events. Some people came just to walk/run the 5K at 6:30 PM at Sugarhouse Park. Denny started the motley crew in their race by shooting two dollar-store guns. One went off. The race ended with receiving handmade medals by Emily M. who flew from Michigan for the event. Some came and didn't walk or run, but were there for the bar-b-q. I didn't walk, because of my surgery.

Some dressed in funny costumes, bright clothes, and wigs for the festive and wonderful tribute to Heather. She would have loved it. A friend said she saw Heather there in the form of a dove. There were psychics and psychos. There were scientists, linguists, high school friends, and church friends. It was great for Denny and me to look forward to and experience. We visited with all types of Heather's friends. We both get much comfort from them. It was far better than being home alone grieving. Our Emily and Ryan were in Fort Collins doing hard labor, putting on a shingle roof on the only weekend they had open for that task, before their wedding.

Following are Facebook comments from Heather's memorialized page to tell her Happy Birthday:

Alexandra Scott
G-face, Just wanted you to know that there is an awesome 5K in your honor on the day of your birth. I still think of you every day. Love you more every minute.
June 7, 2009 at 1:23pm

Zebulon Pischnotte
Heather! I'm sorry I couldn't run with the others on your b-day... fieldwork has me elsewhere. But I did run a 10k in Germany today, in your honor of course!
Wish you could have been here, it was great. I'll never stop saying this, but not a day goes by where I don't think of you!
June 14, 2009 at 3:09pm

Andrea Klemz Bagioli
I just heard about the 5K race on your birthday—I'm flying into SLC on the 2nd and wish I would have known earlier, so I could have planned my trip home a few days earlier... I'll run on the 28th here in Phx thinking of you though. Miss you.
June 25, 2009 at 12:06am

Xinling Chen
Hey, Happy Birthday! I miss you every second!
June 28, 2009 at 12:01am

Brian Cragun
祝你生日快乐～ 祝你生日快乐～ 祝你生日快乐～ 祝你生日快乐！生日快乐G! 我们今天为你跑步又做寿 · 想念你但是不能忘记你 ·
June 28, 2009 at 10:46am

Zebulon Pischnotte
祝你生日快乐! I don't care if I sound like a broken record, I'll say it again... I miss you much!
June 28, 2009 at 10:48am

Brittney V
Happy birthday to my beautiful Mercury. 28 on the 28th! I can't give you presents, but I am sending love and energy to you. My heart hurts and I miss you and I wish I could hear your voice other than in my own head.
June 28, 2009 at 10:26pm

Jeff Hortin
miss you, heather. happy bday. i would only run a 5k for you.
June 28, 2009 at 10:28pm

Emily Gross
Happy Birthday sister! I miss you. I was thinking about you all day. 11:42 yo. I love you.
June 28, 2009 at 10:48pm

Jewel Kling

Alyce Gross

Belated Golden Bday Heather GGGGGG. So cool about the 5 K on your special day. I miss you more than words. love you ttmab. jitro
June 29, 2009 at 11:59am

Megan Ream
Happy late bday, chica! I'm headed towards a 2000 mile road trip for the weekend and I'll be traveling through the northeastern corner of UT tomorrow. I'll be thinking of you.
July 2, 2009 at 1:47pm

On Mon, Jun 29, 2009 at 1:45 PM
Dear Lexy,
    You are amazing. Yesterday would have been so difficult without the fun festivities to entertain Denny and me and to help us know that Heather is not forgotten. I'm sure it was helpful to many others as well. The idea was perfect with something for everyone. Some people were able to show support by just running, and some just choosing the bar-b-q part, and many doing both.
    It was so well organized. I'm impressed by your energy level and Heather would be too. Most people would think the MS biking event would be enough for one weekend, but you pulled off both; and made a delicious, perfect-looking cake to top it off.
    I'm so glad Heather brought you into our lives. Now I'll play surrogate mom. Take good care of yourself. You deserve it. I hope you're getting some well-deserved rest and not pushing too hard.
    Thank you so much!! Love, Alyce

Re: 5K
Alyce,
    The fact that you and Denny were able to enjoy Heather's birthday means the world to me. I know that the others found that it was supportive and fun too. The turnout, awesome food, helping hands and running legs are all obvious indicators of how much Heather is loved and remembered. You two are lucky to have such wonderful people around you.
    Thank you for the accolades, but it wasn't all me. Everyone helped, sweated, stressed (a little), and smiled. To

me, it's a nice refresher in the ways of humanity to see parties like that happen. All you need is a little elbow grease and a lot of heart. There was a lot of heart there yesterday.

I feel lucky to call you a surrogate mom. I also feel lucky to have such wonderful friends in my life.

"Yesterday is history. Tomorrow is a mystery. What do we have? We have today. That's why they call it the present."

Much love,
Lexy

Jun 29, 2009 2:47pm
Dear Lisa,

You are so much fun to be around. We loved your wig and sunglasses. Heather would have been proud of how you pulled the outfit together—way cute. Thank you for being a decorating, festivities, support person. Denny and I always enjoy your company. You made our day.

Love, Alyce

6/30/09

Aw, thanks Alyce! I'm so glad we all got to celebrate together. I enjoy your company as well, you two mean a lot to everyone. Take care! And I hope you plan a nice trip to an exotic location, after Emily's wedding, that you can look forward to!

Love, Lisa Rohde

Journal Entry   May 3, 2010   Almost a year later

I haven't written in my journal in a long time, but today I feel so empty and alone. I don't respect people who feel sorry for themselves, so I don't respect myself today. We had an old friend visit us last night, and I had expectations of sharing my grief. I also wanted to tell him that I'm writing a book, but I couldn't break through to share much of anything.

I don't hear from Heather's friends anymore, and I hesitate to intrude into their lives. My friends all seem distant. People seem to think I'm doing well, but I'm not. I don't tell anyone, because it isn't what anyone wants to hear. Also I'm afraid of hearing unwanted and unappreciated advice. I don't even feel I can talk about this with Emily. There is really no one alive I can talk to. Heather was my best listener, and I need her.

Today there is a dramatic change in the weather; finally it's not snowing or raining. It looks like spring again. Maybe there is hope for a dramatic change in me. I'm going for a walk and talk with God. I'll even try to listen.

I'm back from my walk. I didn't hear a voice, but I saw the fresh colors of the spring flowers with the ever-present dominance of the Wasatch Mountains in the background. Today they are snow dusted, yet I'm still warm from the sun. I've lived in Salt Lake City almost thirty-two years, and I've never taken the changing beauty of the mountains for granted. They were always a reminder to me of the fun of snow skiing so close and convenient. Now they are a reminder of Heather's death, but also a symbol of God's power. He can move and fold the Earth to create mountains that look so permanent, yet nothing on Earth is permanent. Heather wasn't permanent. None of us are. The mountains aren't even permanent. Everything will change and be new again.

I didn't hear God's voice as I walked, but I did come to the realization that it is up to me to reach out. I'm going to invite some of Heather's friends to dinner this week. Mother's Day is this Sunday, and I want to hear some good "Heather stories" and let those stories help me through my second Mother's day without her.

Today is Irene Morrison's birthday. I'll call her later. She is my friend from childhood. She has had much heartache, and she lives alone. I'll share with her and I'll listen.

My Childhood Friends

In the chapter on my mother's death, I made my high school years sound terrible, but the fear and dread that I wrote about didn't get really bad until my senior year of high school. Until then, I managed to suppress my sadness through hope. My childhood was wonderful mainly because of a loving family, but also because of adventure and good times with long lasting friends.

A boy, who was in the grade ahead of my friends and me, dubbed us: "The Gang." He later married Irene Saueressig Morrison, and happily announced, "I finally got one of 'The Gang.'" I met these friends in first grade, and we've been friends ever since. For years, after I was married, I prayed for each of them in my Friday prayers. Some of us went on a cruise together when we turned fifty. In August of 1998, when Barbara Condon (one of The Gang) called me to say her son had taken his own life, I drove seven and a half hours from Salt Lake City to Denver to be with her and attend and speak at Carl's funeral. When she called about a year later to say her husband had left her and she needed us, three of The Gang went and spent a week with her. After Irene's husband died in a fiery car crash on their ranch, I went from Salt Lake City to my childhood town, Templeton, California, to spend time with Irene. Four of us went to the Templeton cemetery to put flowers on the graves of Gary Morrison (Irene's husband), Carl Condon (Barbara's son), and my parents. We make it a point to get together once or twice a year.

(I'm adding to this on August 15, 2010.) I just returned from a "Gang" trip to Templeton, for Linda's son's wedding. We helped with the rehearsal dinner and food preparation for the wedding. Of course, we fit in a cemetery event with wind, wine, and flowers. Often at dusk the ocean breezes cool that area quickly. That didn't stop us from enjoying shivery toasts and leaving flowers at the same graves and sadly including some new ones—Barbara's Dad and Mom and Linda's Dad. Five of us then went to Yosemite for four fun-filled days of time together with lifelong friends.

The year before, in July, 2009, these same friends: Barbara Condon, Linda Hamers, Irene Morrison, and Judy Yomans came through in a huge way. They bought, cooked, and served all the food for my Emily and Ryan's rehearsal dinner, as a gift to my kids and to Denny and me.

We didn't think it was right to ask Ryan's parents to do it, because we wanted to invite our out- of-town relatives and friends. Emily and Ryan had had it with wedding planning and working hard preparing their yard, so I realized the rehearsal dinner planning was up to me. My friend Barbara often came from Denver to visit me when I made trips to Fort Collins, so while she was there I shared my concern about the dinner. That night she called The Gang. They stepped up and said they would take care of it. It took place in Fort Collins, in Emily and Ryan's beautiful back yard; with seventy people. A few days before the wedding, my childhood friends stayed at Barbara's in Denver where they had some "Are we crazy? We don't know what we're doing!" moments, but mostly had great fun preparing a Mexican food menu.

The day of the rehearsal, there was some rain and wind as we were putting up tables and tents. We didn't know if the tents were for the rain or the sun. Barb had gathered colorful decorations and flowers so the backyard looked perfect for the Mexican Fiesta. Some of Ryan's groomsmen were there to help, and Emily's Maid of Honor, Sydney Holbrook, and her sister Angie lent support. My "old" friends loved Emily and Ryan's young friends. We all had fun working and stressing together.

I can't express enough how much the effort from The Gang meant to me. It felt like my past was there to support me. Our relatives, our Salt Lake City friends, our new in-laws: Marlee and Rick White and their relatives, the six groom's men and three bride's maids were all impressed by the festive Mexican dinner party. One would have thought my friends were experienced caterers. They graciously served, and talked to all the guests. Judy said, "I haven't had this much fun in forty years."

The week before the wedding, it had been raining on and off, day and night, in Fort Collins, but for the backyard rehearsal dinner, the sun came out just in time and the evening was beautiful. After the last guest left, as Denny and I were going to our car, the clouds opened with a torrential downpour that was only a foreshadowing of the next rainstorm.

He binds up the waters in his thick clouds, and the cloud is not torn open by them (Job 26:8).

Facebook:

Emily Gross
Heather, Parents bought a condo in CO. They will be able to come and see me for longer periods of time. It was a year ago that we ran our marathon. I am so glad that we were able to do that together. Parents were out here last weekend. Besides buying a condo, we finalized wedding stuff. Mom's friends are going to help a bunch with things. That will be nice to have helpers. Also, it will be nice for rents [In Heather and Emily's creative language, "rents" means parents.] to have a home base that is not a hotel. I wish you were there to dance with me. I have a very pretty frame that I am going to use to put the angelic photo of you from April's wedding. That is my favorite picture of you. I love you more than all of the weddings that have ever happened. I miss my sister!
April 25, 2009 at 3:26pm

Alyce Gross

Emily and Ryan's Wedding

For everything there is a season, and a time for every matter under heaven . . . a time to break down, and a time to build up; a time to weep, and a time to laugh; a time to mourn, and a time to dance . . . (Ecclesiastes 3:1,3b-4).

Yes, each should have its own season, but Emily and Ryan's wedding crammed all of those "times" into one event for me. Heather's absence wasn't spoken about during the wedding, but it was there like a loving presence causing the occasion to be charged with spiritual power. Adding to my own raw emotions, I was carrying a deadly personal secret—my cancer.

One month before the wedding, two of my dear friends, put on an elegant shower in honor of my younger daughter, twenty-five-year old, Emily. Her future mother-in-law and sister-in-law flew to Salt Lake City from Denver to share in the happy occasion. It seemed that all who were invited came. The cool rainy spring weather forced us out of Jane's beautiful backyard, but did not dampen the loving spirit shown by so many friends.

I usually think shower games are silly, but Jan, with the help of her daughters, Kate and Kirsten, thought up some creative and fun activities. The first, a good mixer and conversation starter, was about guessing what Bible character's name was taped on your back, by asking others strategic questions. Another had to do with teams working together to "dress" one of its members to compete for which team created the most beautiful toilet paper wedding dress.

In spite of our ever present heart ache that Heather wasn't there to share this, Emily and I had fun. I saw it as an opportunity for friends, who couldn't come to the wedding, to extend their love and support to Emily. It felt wonderful.

That same feeling was a part of the strong and mixed emotions I had about Emily and Ryan's wedding that took place on July 20, 2009, seven months after her sister's death. The day after the wedding, I finally revealed my cancer secret to Emily. As a part of our heartfelt emotional sharing, she revealed how (although she and Ryan thoroughly enjoyed the wedding day) the preparations had been hard. Ryan felt that Emily had no time for him, and he was right. To say Emily was doing too much at the time is a gross understatement. First and foremost, she was grieving for her sister. It was her first year of teaching, and only teachers can understand how much work that first experience is. She had a third/fourth grade combination class at Red Feather Elementary School, a small mountain school, which required an hour commute one way. She was working on a Master's Degree in education, while she was taking care of wedding details.

From my perspective, the wedding was a time I looked forward to as an oasis in my desert of grief. It was another opportunity for family and friends to come together. My brother, Marty Aronson, wanted to come to Heather's funeral, but I told him I would rather he and his wife, Sue, come to the wedding. I also suggested I would love it if his son, Andy, and family could come. As it turned out, my nephew, his wife Catina, and their cute little son, drove from Calgary, Alberta, Canada; and Marty and Sue drove from Kalispell, Montana. The day after Heather died my brother, Allan Aronson and his wife, Beverly, flew from Kalispell to be with us; but their two married daughters, had other family obligations, it being so close to Christmas. They felt torn about not being able to attend Heather's funeral. Like Marty, they opted for the wedding. My nieces turned the wedding into a family vacation, with seven people flying from Washington State. Emily got to see cousins and cousins' children that she hadn't seen in years.

Denny's sister, Karen, flew from Pittsburgh, Pennsylvania, to be with us shortly after Heather died; but her husband, Victor Joseph, does not feel comfortable flying. He too felt a desire to come to the wedding. He and Karen made a road trip all the way across the country to witness the blessed event. Our extended families incurred great expense, effort, and planning to share in the celebration, in Fort Collins, Colorado. It meant everything to Denny and me.

We were able to invite some of our many wonderful Salt Lake City friends. They drove seven hours or flew into Denver and rented cars. Our pastor, Steve Klemz and his wife Norma came and stayed two nights at our condominium while Denny and I moved to the hotel where most of our guests were staying.

In the invitation, Emily thoughtfully tucked in entertainment information for Fort Collins, including no less than four breweries with beer-tasting trays, one featuring the Budweiser Clydesdales and a tour. She listed theatres, parks, golf courses, museums, and Fort Fun for the kids. The day before the rehearsal, Denny and I hosted a lunch buffet at our condo clubhouse and pool and that evening, in Old Town Square, we had a causal dinner at Lucky Joe's Bar complete with peanuts shells on the floor. Our guests all took advantage of some of the pre-wedding activities, especially the Clydesdales, and fell in love with Fort Collins.

On the day of the wedding, after getting my hair done, Denny, with the wedding dress filling our backseat, and food and drinks for the bridal party in the trunk, picked me up for our drive several miles through pastoral scenery to the wedding venue— The Tapestry House, which used to be a very fancy farm house. As we drove, to calm my spirit, I silently prayed over and over, "God, please help me and guide me." Denny did interrupt my meditation to ask, "So, did you order a wedding cake?" I cracked up laughing. Every detail had been covered at a "wedding walk-through" which Marlee, Emily, and I attended over three months before. I still have the organized three ringed binder they gave me.

In plenty of time before the wedding was to begin, a groomsman, Jim Doney, and I put a picture of Heather in the reception room, on a small table, by the table where Karen, Victor, my four childhood friends, and Denny and I sat. With thoughtfulness and consideration, Syd Holbrook, Emily's Maid of Honor (of course that was to have been Heather's position) had an extra bouquet made. It was held together with a little cylinder vase wrapped in thin ribbons arranged in rainbow order.

Sydney held it, along with her own bouquet, in Heather's honor, during the wedding ceremony. Later it was placed at the table with Heather's picture. Many people came by and took a picture of Heather's framed photograph and bouquet.

The setting was country perfect. One would never know the clouds had been pouring buckets the night before. At our 2:00 PM arrival the air still had that fresh, clean smell that only a summer rain can create. The sunshine made the colorful gardens' well-watered flowers look happy. White chairs neatly faced the gazebo backed by tall, stately trees. The gazebo also white and entwined with netting, yellow, orange, and deep red gerbera daisies, and delicate white lights caught every ones' attention, but the dominant feature was the Tapestry House—a beautiful two-story Victorian home. It had been rebuilt in a fashion true to its 1890 beginnings, with beautiful hardwood floors, old-style woodwork, including raised panel wainscot, and an elegant stairway all of quarter-sawn white oak. Ornate Victorian furnishings complimented the interior. Many bedrooms made more than ample space for the entire bridal party to get ready. The grand old house added to the elegance of the event. The lovely railed back-porch happened to be the perfect length for six groomsmen and three bridesmaids to stand in their finery, while waiting for all the guests to be seated. Marlee and I waited by the steps of the porch, while listening to beautiful flute music. It brought memories of my Heather playing the flute and I thought to myself—Emily chose that music because, before Heather died, I had suggested that she play at the wedding.

Right on queue, Ryan came and seated first his mother, then me. I remember giving him a hug before I sat. Next the bridesmaids gracefully descended the stairs from the back porch with a groomsman on each arm. When they were all arranged in front of the gazebo—the young men in their black shirts, silver-gray vests, and black flip-flops (a gift from the groom) and the girls in black heels and flattering black summer dresses (a gift from the bride) which offset their bright bouquets; we waited for the bride. The anticipation became a bit mysterious, because we could barely see through the greenery, but we heard the clip-clop of hoofs. Next we could see glimpses of a white horse and carriage on the ranch road behind the majestic century-old trees.

The carriage driver wore a cowboy hat and vest, but all eyes were on Emily and her father. We watched Denny, beaming with pride, help his beloved daughter out of the carriage. She was stunning, with her highlighted blond hair up in swirls, topped with a small sparkling tiara matching the sparkles in the bodice of her perfectly fitted dress. The diagonal ruching in front and the corset lace-up back with flowing train, created the perfect picture in that country setting.

Although the six groomsmen were capable of party-animal behavior, they stood with a dignity that displayed their respect for Ryan and Emily, and they listened to the pastor's message with rapt attention. The wedding planner's lecture, the day before, and the drill sergeant photographer may have had something to do with their exemplary behavior.

Pr. Steve made the outdoor ceremony a very personal and sacred occasion. At one point he had Ryan and Emily as well as himself, kick off their shoes (made easier by the grooms decision to wear flip-flops). The pastor told them they were standing on Holy Ground. Keeping the message all about Emily and Ryan, he managed to include Heather and Ryan's recently deceased Grandpa Larry, by quoting from Hebrews 12:1: *Therefore, since we are surrounded by so great a cloud of witnesses . . . .*

Denny read passages about love, in his strong confident voice, from the Gospel of John. Marlee and I nervously lit two separate candles, and the bride and groom used them to jointly light one.

The newlyweds exited to snappy guitar music and Josh Turner's deep voice singing, "Would You Go with Me?" The horse and carriage made a few rounds with husband and wife, while the wedding guests, now able to ooh, awe, and chat; moved to the front lawn of the gabled country manor. While wedding planners gently herded us, the photographer relocated to an upper balcony. After waiting a bit we could hear whoops of happiness from an upper room as all the appropriate people signed the wedding certificate. Emily and Ryan appeared on the balcony. They were in the forefront, and all the bridal party made their way to the lawn below, with the guests fanned out behind. The well-planned photographer then took several joy-filled pictures of everyone together. Next the guests moved to the outdoor bar and patio for appetizers and drinks, while the family walked back toward the inviting shade trees for a few more pictures. The efficient photographer took most of the wedding photos there before any guests arrived, because we didn't want to keep people waiting too long for the reception to begin.

The pavilion was white, big, versatile, and perfect. Had there been rain, the ceremony could have been held in the covered patio with walls dropped for protection; but the warm temperatures allowed the patio to remain open. The attached pavilion held a perfect dance floor. Salads and wine were already on the beautifully set round tables. Textured clear glass made lovely place-settings complete with wine glasses and champagne flutes. Candles and the same colored gerbera daisies that filled bridesmaids' bouquets brightened each table. The 140 guests were favored with a cute beer koozy inscribed with Emily and Ryan's names, the date, and two entwined hearts encircled with the words "TO HAVE AND TO HOLD AND TO KEEP YOUR BEER COLD!" Some were used that night, because a few kegs of beer were hidden behind the bar. The delicious smell coming from an inviting buffet, including a tiered fountain flowing with chocolate, tempted appetites. Above, tiny welcoming lights wrapped the white exposed rafters.

I clearly recall telling Irene, who sat on my right, during dinner, "It is such an honor and so fitting that you are sitting by me at my daughter's wedding reception. We have been friends since first grade and will add this to our lifetime of memories." I had more emotional moments to share with her and the rest of the gang, but was saving the foreboding news of my cancer for the following day.

To thank people for coming, Emily, Ryan, Denny, and I circulated separately and enjoyed hearing similar comments: "What a beautiful bride." "The setting is perfect." "I loved the horse and carriage." "Where did you find that wonderful dress?" "The food was delicious." "I've attended a lot of weddings, and I have never listened so carefully to the pastor." We welcomed our guests, but mostly we danced.

Many of the guests knew Heather and how much she loved to dance. She would have so enjoyed capturing some of the attention while showing her moves and sharing in the celebration. Maybe her precious spirit did exactly that. Her dad certainly did.

Denny had smugly kept his own secret—his selection for the dance with his only living daughter—"I Loved Her First," by Hartland. There wasn't a dry eye among the quiet observers. He held Emily tightly as they floated around the dance floor. A little later they were joined by Ryan dancing with his mother. Denny then let Emily go to dance and spend the rest of her life with Ryan.

The expert disk-jockey started with great oldies and progressed to more contemporary tunes. Almost everyone danced, and the few that didn't, enjoyed watching and were swept-up in the celebration. In true Denny style, he once again caught everyone's attention by spontaneously leading a great rendition of Michael Jackson's "Thriller." It got comments for months after. Sydney wrote a thank you note that included: "The wedding was such a great day, but I am still upset that Dennis does a better Michael Jackson than I can."

Many shared, "I never had so much fun at a wedding." including the disk-jockey! Throughout the entire event, we felt like loving arms were enveloping us. The wedding was sacred, celebratory, and downright fun! We laughed, we cried, we danced.

The Devil's Fingernail

You have turned my mourning into dancing (Psalm 30:11).

The organization of the Tapestry House was beyond impressive. Every detail was subtly orchestrated by their expert staff, even the timely way they ushered people out at the 10:00 PM conclusion. All remaining guests (still full of party spirit) were invited out to watch the newlyweds place a brick, with their names on it, in the walkway. Just then it began to sprinkle.

Like the night before, the hands of God, maybe with a little help from Heather's and Grandpa Larry's spirits and the rest of *the great cloud of witnesses*, kept the rain back until all the guests had left. Denny and I collected some last minute items and were rushing to the car when the heavens let loose. I was drenched to my underwear. On the drive to the hotel, the rain slashed across our headlights in beautiful silver flashes. The awe inspiring lightning lit the sky, and the thunder crashed and rumbled across the valley late into the night. The next day it continued raining, and the storm caused flooding and destruction around the valley. My brother Marty's car was flooded in his hotel parking lot.

I wonder why the otherwise tumultuous weather was perfect for the pool party, rehearsal dinner, and wedding amid storms of news-worthy magnitude. I like to believe it was a gift from God. Did God hold back the rain? If so, why didn't he hold back the avalanche?

But the thunder of his power who can understand? (Job 26:14b).

Commitment During Crisis

There is so much I don't understand, but I do know the wedding celebration was charged with love, yet a marriage is so much more. In thinking about the newlyweds I pray they will grow in their commitment to each other. Crisis can sometimes end a marriage, but for Denny and me it was a beginning of a new kind of appreciation for each other.

Journal Entry   August 12, 2009

Today is our 31st wedding anniversary. I'm thankful that I have Denny as a husband. We grieve together. We grieve in very different ways, but it is somehow comforting to me to know someone else misses our Heather as much as I do.

Denny has shorter "fits of crying" as he calls it, and then he moves on; whereas, I get extra sad and it lasts for days. Some of the books I had been reading warned that the death of a child can tear a family apart. With the decision to respect each other's differences we are determined to not let our sorrow destroy our marriage. We're committed to each other. Commitment is the key to any marriage, but now more than ever I feel its importance. I never wanted to be dependent, but at this stage we both appreciate the strong support we offer one another. My husband has been my rock through all of this. We're often able to remind each other of positive moments and share happy memories from both of our daughters. Shared happiness does increase our joy, and shared grief does decrease the pain. Heather would be pleased.

My hope for Emily and Ryan is that they will support each other through difficult times. I also hope they depend on prayer and faith to help them. Denny and I have. I won't speak for my husband, but Heather's death has shaken and changed my faith and my prayers hopefully for the better.

My Own Prayers, Doubt and Faith

Why pray? God wants us to: *My house will be called a house of prayer for all nations* (Isaiah 56:7 & Matthew 21:13a).

Part of a Journal Entry   Wednesday, March 4, 2009
Denny and I agree that our grieving is getting harder. I woke up this morning with my heart aching, because I again realized—I'll never see Heather on this Earth.
I don't know if the anger or the sadness is worse. I'm a little less angry and sadder now. The anger is because for all of Heather's life I've prayed for her protection. I felt that guardian angels really watched over us, because Denny has had so many close calls and has come out "protected."
Why couldn't you protect my Heather? I'm filled with doubt. My faith isn't strong enough even to feel that Heather is with You. I hope she is, but I'm not sure.

I write things important to me in a small calendar which I keep in my purse. I've saved all my calendars from way back, so for some events, I have the exact date recorded. On March 9, 2009, about three months after Heather's death, the Accident Report was available at the Sheriff's Department. Just like the Medical Examiners Report, I was compelled to read it carefully.

Part of a Journal Entry   March 10, 2009   Three Months after Heather's Death
I prayed yesterday as I went to the sheriff's office to pick up Heather's accident report. I had been told, after checking several times, that the report was completed, and I could have a copy. I drove all the way across town to find out that the report had yet to be copied, so I couldn't take it after all. They said they will call me in a few days when it's ready. Normally I would be angered by the wasted trip, but it wasn't wasted time. I used it to finally communicate with God. I don't remember what I prayed, but I talked to God almost all the way. Again that night just before bedtime, I

asked for a good dream about Heather. The prayer was answered! I woke up from my first and only dream about Heather since her death. I felt happy! In my dream, she seemed very natural and not at all surprised to see me. I was able to hug her just before I woke up. I usually forget my dreams, but I made a point to remember this one because of the comfort it brought me. I relished the feeling and told Denny all about it. As we drove to Park City with Randy, he and Denny visited while I quietly basked in my first shred of real happiness in three months. At the parking lot we met-up with Bill and Joanne Baker, good friends who had kindly obtained ski tickets for us. I actually had fun for the first time since Heather's death. It was an answer to a specific prayer, but God gave me more than I asked. We skied on fresh snow, and the sun came out.

Thank you, God.

Journal Entry   March 18, 2009   More on Answered Prayer

Dear God, when Heather died, I quit praying in my regular way. When Heather was an infant, I often prayed while nursing her, that she would grow up to be the best she could be. I believe she worked at that throughout all of her short life. Judging from what her friends said and wrote about her, she really was her "best self." She saw the best in others with an open-minded compassion; and did her best to edify others with love and acceptance.

Through a group called Bible Study Fellowship, which I joined when Heather was just over three years old, I learned, in the study of Matthew, more about the power of prayer. I loved the verses Matthew 23:37 and Luke 13:34 where Jesus said, "How often have I desired to gather your children together as a hen gathers her brood under her wings." I used that and changed it to my own prayer for my children: "Like a mother hen protects her baby chicks please protect my Heathie, my Emmy, my Denny and me. I prayed that almost every morning.

Shortly after Heather died, on December 14, 2008, I pictured that brood hen and its feathers smeared down the

Fields of Glory on Mt. Baldy along with my Heather—like some sick joke. Where was her protection? I knew that the verses were about a spiritual protection, but I wanted a physical protection as well. I wondered, "If I only had prayed differently would she still be alive?"

In my heart, I know spiritual protection is more important than physical protection, but God knew how much it would hurt me to lose my Heather, and he let her, or caused her to die anyway. That hurts so deeply. In some cases being "religious" makes grief much worse.

At the emergency room when I was surrounded with Holy strength, I concluded that God took or allowed Heather to be taken, to protect her from future depression, or just to protect her beautiful spirit while she was at her best or prime. It gave me comfort then, but later I was less sure. My faith was shaken. I'm better now. I still don't know "Why?" and I will keep asking, because God made me a thinking, analytical person. I always ask questions, and I'm proud of it, because it is a part of who I am. It makes studying and learning more interesting. Doubt is a part of faith. I believe with a thinking, studying, yearning, faith. The words, "blind faith," irritate me. Jesus wouldn't have taught using parables if he didn't want us to think.

I've started some of my old prayer life again, but through a shaken, questioning, faith. After my first post-death prayer, on 3/9/9, and my first dream about Heather, my prayer was answered. It was a little miracle.

I'm greedy. I want another one. I'm not worried about my salvation. I should be, but I'm not. I'm a mother who wants assurance about her dead child's salvation. Heather was open minded and searching. Her Facebook says of her religion: "I hear in my mind all this music, and it breaks my heart." I know she believed in and loved God, but I need to know she is with God. I need to know she is ok—more than ok—thriving in her everlasting life, fulfilled and continuing to explore and learn, growing toward her heavenly best self. I want to know her abundant life is continuing in a spiritual abundance. I want to know she is not dead ashes; that she has gone to the light, that she is feeling true joy. I'm asking for a miracle so that I know my baby is living on and I'll see her again. I'm going to pray now.

More than a year later, June 11, 2010, as I proofread this, I still don't know and I probably never will on this Earth. Some might say I just need faith, but my faith isn't Heather's faith. I'm glad for that, because I don't feel I have much faith today. Some days are better, but not today.

Part of a Journal Entry   June 24, 2009   After Surgery to Remove a Swollen Lymph Node
Now Emily [my living daughter] and Nickie, her friend, are driving back to Fort Collins, and I don't even pray for their safety, because I don't know how to pray anymore. I lack faith and trust. I feel empty and unimportant. Maybe it's the anesthetic from yesterday. Maybe I'll quit feeling sorry for myself tomorrow.
My next thing to look forward to is the 5K in honor of Heather on her 28th birthday. God help me.

The day after Heather's Golden Birthday and 5K bar-b-q, I received a call from a nurse who assumed the surgeon had already notified me of the results from the biopsy on my lymph node. The conversation went something like this: "We need to make an appointment for you with one of our oncologists. The first available date is July 16th."

Incredulous I asked, "Why do I need an oncologist? Do I have cancer?"

Embarrassed she answered, "Oh, I am so sorry, the surgeon hasn't called you. He never should have asked me to make the appointment without notifying you first. I'll be having a talk with him about this.

Even in my shock about learning I have cancer, I thought, "She's a little toughie who isn't afraid to let a doctor know what she thinks. Good for her."

"What kind of cancer do I have?"

"He should be telling you this, but—non-Hodgkin's lymphoma."

"Is it treatable?"

"I'll have him call you, but we should make an appointment."

"July 16th is too late. I'll be in Colorado in the midst of wedding preparations for my daughter."

"Oh, I'm so sorry, but that is the first available date."

I answered, "I'll have to think about this and get back to you." I thanked her and hung up thinking "Oh sh--, is God answering my wish to die, or shaking me out of my grief into an appreciation for the time I have left? Maybe the devil is just messing with me, or maybe stuff just happens."

Of course, next I called Denny at work. He and I agreed we really didn't want to wait until after Emily's wedding to start taking action. Denny, who is the personification of action, immediately called Dr. Liz Prystas, an oncologist and church friend.

Meanwhile, I got on-line and learned that 85% of NHL is not curable, because by the time it's found it is usually in stage 3 to 5 and spread all through the lymph system.

A little later I received a call from the surgeon (I'll call him Dr. Smith) saying sorry that he wasn't able to call sooner. He explained that the detailed biopsy indicated that I have a very low grade, slow growing, follicular, B cell lymphoma. He repeated that I should make an appointment with an oncologist and I assured him that I had found an excellent one. He kindly wished me the best.

Dr. Liz immediately accessed my medical records and called me shortly after Dr. Smith. She gave the same information he had, but her assistant was able to schedule a CT scan in two days—July 1st.

During the scan prep I was mistakenly told that my creatinine level was too high to receive the iodine contrast. The technician told me it could cause kidney failure, and it was an indication my kidneys weren't functioning correctly. So she administered the CT scan without the iodine contrast. My next on-line research confirmed that high creatinine levels could be an indication of serious kidney problems, so I thought I had kidney cancer. That dismal night, my GP called to check on me. I told her about the creatinine levels, so she looked at my health records while we were on the phone and let me know they were not out of the normal range and my kidneys are normal. She has never called me at home before, but that call was certainly timely. I only thought I was dying of kidney disease for half a day. The technician had read my blood test incorrectly.

Journal Entry   July 2, 2009
Today Dr. Liz called me with the good news: my cancer is treatable because it is probably only in stage 1 or 2, according to the CT scan. She has me scheduled for a bone marrow biopsy on Wednesday, July 8th. She doesn't mess around. I'm so fortunate to have her as my doctor. Thank you, God. I do want to live and maybe see my grandchildren. This is a turning point for me. This is good. Yes, a bone marrow biopsy—can't wait.

As you can see by the following journal entry, I may have had good intentions about my prayer life, but it still isn't back to "normal" and probably never will be. But what is normal? Nothing will ever be normal again for me.

Journal Entry   Oct 22, 2009
I'm on a new journey now. I've been angry with God and tried to push God out of my life, but God won't leave. My prayer life has changed. I used to have a list of things to cover; too many for one day, so I had different days of the week for different prayer concerns. Monday was for world concerns (not the whole world which was too general for me, but for places where I had a connection). Tuesday—for my brothers and their families. On Wednesday I prayed for my church—the leaders and my church family. Thursday, I covered in-laws. Friday was friends, and Saturday—

thanksgiving. On Sunday I focused on praying with my church family and asking for forgiveness before receiving Holy Communion. My husband, daughters, and myself I prayed for every day, starting with asking for protection and that we develop to our optimum potential: physically, socially, emotionally, morally, academically, and spiritually; also that we use our talents to God's glory. Every day I ended my prayers with, "Please fill me with your Holy Spirit, and the gifts of the spirit: love, joy, peace, patience, kindness, goodness, gentleness, faithfulness, self-control (Galatians 5:22-23 NIV). [Gentleness and faithfulness are actually switched, but this is how I memorized it.] It was often what I was saying, in my head, as I entered school to start my teaching day.

Now I just pray, "Help me and forgive me." I guess I am not alone on this journey. God won't leave me alone.

In the following month, November, 2009, Denny and I felt very much alone after spreading Heather's ashes in Monterosso, Chinque Terre, a town in northern Italy. We were tormented. On November 16, Denny had a night of crying and coughing. I hurt for him.

The following entry is the part that relates to prayer. I'll include entries that relate to spreading of ashes in Part Two.

Journal Entry November 19, 2009 Coach to Carrara, Tuscany

After spending time in a lime-dust-filled studio, watching craftsman chisel copies in white marble, we visited a mountain quarry. This site is where Michelangelo selected the marble he used for his famous sculptures. That evening we had our last dinner at the hotel with our small tour group. Maybe because we were leaving the next morning, leaving a little part of Heather, I had my most anguished night. I couldn't sleep. In my mind I kept questioning the idea of spreading Heather's ashes all around the world. I felt torn and uncertain. Finally I resorted to the most simple but powerful thing. I got down on my knees, on the cold white marble floor, did the sign of the cross and asked for help. "God please forgive me, guide me, and help me." That's all. I got back in bed and felt calmness settle over me. I had my second dream about Heather. Her warm, friendly, happy spirit was with me in a car. Then she was gone. It felt good. Thank you, God. I felt more peaceful. The alarm went off at 3:15 AM for a 4:00 AM coach to Pizza and a 7:00 AM flight to Rome. Then home.

Again skeptics will think that my calmness after prayer was psychological. I understand that, because I'm a skeptic about many things. But I do believe that both good and evil work through the psyche.

Do not fret—it leads only to evil (Psalm 37:8b).

Delight yourself in the LORD and he will give you the desires of your heart. Commit your way to the LORD; trust in him and he will do this: He will make your righteousness shine like the dawn, the justice of your cause like the noonday sun. Be still before the LORD and wait patiently for him (Psalm 37:4-7).

March 11, 2011

I've come to realize through this awful journey—this journey filled with awe—that my prayers throughout my whole life have mostly been about what I want or what I hope for others. Shouldn't prayer help us do and be what God wants?

Faith

Some people think that the loss of a loved one is easier to deal with if one has faith in God. Some will share this, thinking it is comforting. It's not. I used to think it myself, because my faith was comforting and helpful to me when my parents died; but I'm here to tell you that faith and a relationship with God doesn't save one from the deepest grief and sorrow during the loss of a child. It makes it more complex. Anger at God seeps in, and with it a sense of fear, guilt, and inadequacy when you begin to question God and your own faith. Maybe not everyone who loses a child questions God like I did and still do, but I think most parents do. Yes, God is with you in your deepest pain; but, no, being Christian or having a relationship with God doesn't lessen the pain. It expands it to a more universal level.

Losing a child does come with a gift; at least it did for me. It strengthened my relationship with God even though I resisted and fought. With my ego and pride shattered it was more possible to begin to share in a universal pain, to feel a connection to the pain and suffering of others. It helped me to feel a little touch of God's pain. He gave his Son for us. I still can't get my mind completely around that, but having lost a child gets me a little closer to understanding. I don't pretend to understand God, but I do feel the smallest touch of God's suffering. A part of faith in God means sharing in the suffering. There is nothing easy about it, but the anguish intensifies the need for hope in God's promises. Grief and suffering helps strip away all that is unimportant and sharpens one's sense of what is good. If we let that sharpened sense help us, we can become a little wiser and more compassionate.

Friends have shared with Denny and me that we appear to be strong in our faith, but I don't feel strong in any way. I used to think I was a relatively strong and fearless person. My childhood friends could verify this. I've never been filled with worry, and I've always loved adventure; but now I'm shaken. Death is too real, and it's not my death I fear. Denny or Emily and Ryan could die at any time. I fear being left alone with more grief. I know I need to remember that I'll never be alone, that God is always with me.

Without faith it is impossible to please him. For whoever would draw near to God must believe that he exists and that he rewards those who seek him (Hebrews 11:6).

I can't make myself have faith, because faith is a gift from God. But I can seek God. The Bible is one of the best tools for that.

. . . Faith comes through hearing the message, and the message is heard through the word of Christ (Romans 10:17).

Bible Study

When Heather died, eleven days before Christmas, My husband and I were immediately surrounded by friends and family, but with their own responsibilities, they of course, moved on; so in January, I often found myself alone with time on my hands and grief in my heart. I turned to books and especially to the Bible for help. The Psalms were the first place I went. They were primarily written by King David and deal partially with his joy and suffering. I read through all of them in a few sittings, looking for answers and comfort. This was not my first experience with Psalms. I heard different Psalms almost every Sunday in church during my childhood, and again when I returned to regular church attendance during my thirty-plus years of marriage; so I knew I would find comfort in some of them. These are the Psalms that spoke to me most in my initial time of grief—a period of anguish. This doesn't mean that there aren't many more meaningful Psalms for grieving people, but these were mine:

My soul melts away for sorrow; strengthen me according to your word (Psalm 119:28).

My soul clings to the dust; revive me according to your word (Psalm 119:25).

If your law had not been my delight, I would have perished in my misery (Psalm 119:92).

If God's word could help David, maybe it could help me.

The LORD answers you in the day of trouble! (Psalm 20:1)
I am still and probably always will be looking for answers.

My God, my God, why have you forsaken me? Why are you so far from helping me, from the words of my groaning? (Psalm 22:1)

This Psalm is a foreshadowing of Jesus' suffering for us. The first line foretells some of Jesus' final words on the cross, which are recorded in Matthew 27:46b and Mark 15:34b. I found and continue to find them comforting. I'm not alone—Jesus felt forsaken too.

Because of Heather's death, I think not only of Jesus' pain, but also of the pain God went through in allowing Jesus to suffer and die. That pain was for all of us for the forgiveness of sin. But why all the pain? I've asked that question often. I explained my simple conclusion in the chapter on my mother's death. It is the price we pay for choice and freedom. I know there is much more to it, but who can understand?

O my God, I cry by day, but you do not answer, and by night, but find no rest (Psalm 22:2).

I was never suicidal, but I often thought I wanted to die. I still do sometimes. The truth is, I look forward to death in hopes of being reunited with Heather.

For all who are led by the Spirit of God are children of God. For you did not receive a spirit of slavery to fall back into fear, but you have received a spirit of adoption. When we cry, "Abba! Father! it is the very Spirit bearing witness with our spirit that we are children of God, and if children, then heirs, heirs of God and joint heirs with Christ—If, in fact, we suffer with him so that we may also be glorified with him (Romans 8:14-17).

In my mind, this does not mean that we suffer with him to earn glory; but we suffer because God and Jesus suffer. Out of compassion and love we suffer with him.

The earth is the LORD'S and all that is in it, the world, and those who live in it (Psalm 24:1).

I'm coming to understand there is a shared pain of all humanity that Jesus took with him to the cross. I do know I'm not alone in my pain and I'm growing in compassion for others.

Turn to me and be gracious to me, for I am lonely and afflicted. Relieve the troubles of my heart, and bring me out of my distress. Consider my affliction and my trouble, and forgive all my sins (Psalm 25:16-18).

When I don't have words to pray, the Bible has them for me.

Background

I've been interested in Bible study for as long as I can remember. I was raised by Christian (Lutheran) church-going parents. I'm still Lutheran, not because I think it is the one true religion, but because the Evangelical Lutheran Churches recognize the validity of other denominations and welcome all to Holy Communion. I could never belong to a church that was so narrow that it declared itself the only way to salvation. I also appreciate my local congregation, Zion Evangelical Lutheran Church in Salt Lake City, Utah, because we encourage asking questions and don't claim to have all the answers. Denny and I were married there in 1978 and started attending regularly. Both of our daughters were baptized at Zion and attended Sunday School and later Youth Group activities. Early on, I joined in adult Bible studies that were run by the pastor at that time, Harold Nilsson. His thorough preparation was evident; yet he never dominated the discussions, doing his best to encourage all to participate. I respected that and try to model him in the Bible studies I now lead.

As a child, I thought of the Bible as a book of stories which I learned about in Sunday School. I thought of it as important, but it was not something I would turn to for comfort. I didn't learn to do that until I attended Bible Study Fellowship from 1984 to 1990. The program has gone though some changes since that time, but I'm sure it is still a well-organized, excellent Bible study. Some of the teachings at Bible Study Fellowship, in my view, were too literal, which is not how I approach Bible study; however I do feel that the best place to start is with reading what the Bible actually says, not what someone else writes about what the Bible means. I learned a lot in those six years, and I am eternally grateful.

My Own Commentary

Like any group run by people, including all the many denominations of churches, there are flaws and problems involved with religious organizations. One must be careful not to think too highly of oneself, one's organization, or of one's religion, and forget about the underlying message of God's love. Any kind of religion can get way off message when beliefs are used as an excuse to hate and/or attack others. The Bible is not to be read or studied to find ammunition to use against someone else. I believe we are to read it and search our own heart. It's always important to ask, "What is the message for me?" Not, "What can I find to point out the wrong in others?" To me, some people who call themselves Christians are off track, if pushing personal belief has become more important to them than spreading God's love. Often people "cheat" and take Bible verses out of context and use them incorrectly to promote their own agenda. The Bible should never be used as a weapon, but as a way to come closer to God.

Usually it is not meant to be read fast. Some verses are so pregnant with meaning, one must stop and let the words take shape in one's soul. Think or don't think, just let the idea be with you. Later discuss it. Learn from others' impressions as well. Sometimes in rereading familiar passages, new meaning will be revealed, because of different life circumstances at the time.

Science and the Bible should not be in opposition. Science requires evidence. Religion requires faith. I love learning about both. The more I learn about science the closer I feel to God. Our dynamic planet, with its evolving life forms and constant change, is a reminder of the Creator's omnipotent power. Nature's beauty, abundance, healing and renewal are all reminders of God's very personal, ever-present, loving attention to the smallest details. Genesis reveals the powerful and personal aspects of God. In chapter 1, God works through awe-inspiring voice commands beyond human imagination, to create the universe and all that is in it. In chapter 2, God is very personal: walking and talking with man and woman, in the garden. Studying the Bible and studying science are both ways to come closer to our Creator and to try to gain some understanding of our personal place and importance as a part of it all.

One should never be finished with learning. One should always be open minded enough to learn new truths. Through my church, I involve myself in various Bible studies and continue the on-going process. I consider the supportive friends involved in these groups, as sources for learning, even though and especially because, we don't always agree on everything. Also, we never have all the answers.

For who has known the mind of the Lord? Or who has been his counselor? (Romans 11:34).

Comfort

I have often felt comfort while I prepare for the adult Bible study that my husband and I facilitate on Sunday mornings at my church. We study and discuss the lectionary (Bible lessons that are part of the worship on a given Sunday). The lesson for March 1, 2009 was especially meaningful to me. Following are a few excerpts from the passages studied:

God's first covenant with "every living creature (descendants and animals) that is with you (Noah) for all future generations: I have set my bow[rainbow] in the clouds, and it shall be a sign of the covenant between me and the earth . . . I will remember my covenant . . . " (Genesis 9:12,13,15).

Alyce Gross

My daughter Heather's dear friend, Katie Gracia Dyson, gave her a little cardboard rainbow which Heather hung from the front mirror in her car. On it was written, "I'm not gay, I just love rainbows." Heather added to the back, "But it's ok if you're gay." When Heather was a toddler, she started loving rainbows—the science behind them, their beauty, color, order (as she got older, she even put her clothes in rainbow order), and hopefully she loved them for God's promise. So anytime I see a rainbow it reminds me of Heather. Her friends were aware of her love for rainbows as well. They still write to her on her "memorialized" Facebook account. Here are a few about rainbows:

Kristen Schaub Lindahl
Heather, I skied with my dad today at Park City. We saw the most gorgeous sun dog—tons of snow crystals in the sky and a perfect rainbow circle. I couldn't help but think of you.

Thank you for all of the contributions you made to our department, to all of the friends and family who so obviously love you dearly, and to the planet as a whole. You are missed.
December 18, 2008 at 7:59pm

Alexandra Scott
G. there was this really cool rainbow in SLC today. Besos!!
March 9, 2009 at 7:02pm

Ryan Adler
I saw it too and then got home and saw my 5k for HG medal on the wall! Amazing.
March 10, 2009 at 12:11am

Xinling Chen
Hey girl! I saw the brightest and most beautiful rainbow this Tuesday in Cottonwood Heights. That was you smiling at me, right?
Everything about rainbow reminds me of you. You know I miss you every
day and that will last forever! I have so much to tell you. Come to my
dream tonight! Love and Hugs!! March 13, 2009 at 1:13pm

 Another lesson on that Sunday was: *For Christ also suffered for sins once for all, the righteous for the unrighteous, in order to bring you to God . . . He went and made a proclamation to the spirits in prison, who in former times did not obey, when God waited patiently in the days of Noah . . . Baptism, which this prefigured, now saves you* (1 Peter 3; 18-21).
 Christ even reached out to the lost ones of that ancient time. Has Christ reached out to Heather? Is she with him esperiencing the fullness of joy?

 Jesus then said to the Jews who had believed in him, "If you continue in my word, you are truly my disciples, and you will know the truth, and the truth will make you free" (John 8:31-32).

I'm not finished with Bible study. I'll always have it as a part of my life, because it offers a *continued* unfolding of *truth*.

We do not receive wisdom, we must discover it for ourselves. Marcel Proust

The Bible is my most available "friend." It is there whenever I choose to open it. I love books, and my favorite by far is The Holy Bible. Studying it helps me to be less self-involved and broadens my concerns to a more universal level. I don't consider the physical book to be sacred; but its message, when read with the power of the Holy Spirit, is. It is full of the "Living Word," but it must be opened and studied to be living. It is the richest; most relevant, most interconnected, most layered, most complex, most confusing, most simple, book I've ever read.

It is relevant for all people of every culture and time in the history of the Earth. The Old Testament is the foundation for the New. The Old continually points to the necessity of the grace shared in the New. The Bible has layers of meaning and can reveal "truths" to people in their darkest as well as their most joyful moments. It's full of meaningful intriguing symbolism, beautiful poetry, and fascinating action-packed history. Different people can find different meaning in the same passage and both may be right; not to say we can't get it wrong. There is always an underlying "truth" that can be missed if we impose our own agenda to our study, rather than letting the Holy Spirit guide our understanding. There is something for everyone. Open it, read it, discuss it.

I waited patiently for the LORD; *he inclined to me and heard my cry. He drew me up from the desolate pit, out of the miry bog, and set my feet upon a rock, making my steps secure. He put a new song in my mouth, a song of praise to our God. Many will see and fear, and put their trust in the* LORD (Psalm 40:1-2).

Books

Caring friends and family gifted me with many books. I'm certainly not a professional critic, but I will share how some of the books helped me. These are not presented in the order that I read them. I lumped some together because of their similar themes.

<u>The Shack</u>, by W. M. Paul Young, is feel-good fiction about heaven and the Trinity but also involves the tragedy of a child's death.

I read it shortly before Heather died, because my friend, Linda Hamers (from The Gang), was reading it for comfort when her father died. She wanted to discuss it with me. I bought copies for my two daughters' Christmas stockings. Heather never got her copy. I wonder what she would have said about this fictional depiction of the Trinity. I wish I could discuss it with her spirit now. Will I ever?

<u>Experiencing Grief</u>, by H. Norman Wright, is short and covers a lot.

I read it first, just after Heather died, and I think it was helpful at the time; but I can't remember a thing—not to fault the book. A friend shared that she had loved reading fiction, but after her son died, she couldn't focus on a fiction book for two years. This book isn't fiction, but I was numb and couldn't focus. I'll reread it someday. You see, I'm still in this grieving process, and will be for the rest of my life.

<u>Life after Life,</u> by Raymond Moody, MD; and <u>Closer to the Light,</u> by Melvin Morse, MD: Dr. Morse interviewed many different children. He chose children because they're less likely to have preconceived notions and more likely to be honest and open. Both are books about near-death experiences, all of which are different, but have a common thread. The patients were out of their body and, from above, observed doctors and medical people working on them. Most traveled through a tunnel toward a light. Some had a companion (i.e. an angel or dead relative). All said it was not

possible to really describe the experience in words, but the light was wonderful, and full of love and acceptance. Many felt the light was Jesus. They were told in some gentle way that they must return. Most didn't want to. All had revelations they couldn't explain, but they discovered how important love and learning are. They came back unafraid to die, and went on to live "good" lives.

These books were comforting, and offer hope for afterlife. The fact that the "dead" came back from their vision of heaven with a desire for learning, helped motivate my passion for Bible study. Something tells me that some of the most important learning is the "truth" taught in the Bible.

On Life after Death, By Elizabeth Kubler-Ross: She jumps right into the subject through four essays about people of many ages and religions who "died" and came back. They too, were met by someone who deeply loved them.

I found it comforting that people were met by loved ones and aren't alone in death. I don't know who that would be for Heather, but I trust that God does. I want to trust.

90 Minutes in Heaven, by Don Piper with Cecil Murphey: The author was "killed" in a car accident and was in heaven for 90 minutes. He shared this with no one for two years, because it was too personal, unbelievable, and indescribable; but a friend got him to tell all about it and convinced Don to share it through this book. Don's short wonderful stay in heaven is described in the second chapter, and the rest of the book is about the torture he went through wearing the Ilozarov bone growth device. He spent a year of bone-stretching excruciating pain so he could walk again, because he had lost 4-6 inches of bone in the crushing car wreck.

My husband, Denny, kept telling me to read this book that a friend had lent him. It does make dying seem wonderful; because heaven, with its pearly gates, is full of love, light, and beautiful music.

My Glimpse of Eternity, by Betty Malz: Her "glimpse" was very much like 90 Minutes in Heaven. An angel accompanied her to smooth gates of pearl. There was light and love and no concept of time. She saw that God loved all Christian churches, not just hers. The sharing of her glimpse of heaven helped her husband in his death, and helped her to accept his dying.

The last two authors were both very religious people before their "time in heaven." They both saw the pearly gates and certain precious gems described in *Revelation.* It makes me wonder if people see what they expect to see. Maybe our minds take us to a "good" place in a near-death experience. Their minds couldn't have been really dead, because they lived to tell about it.

Good Grief, by Granger E. Westberg is very short and is written to cover all kinds of grief, so it lacks the depth one needs if they have lost a child. You can't tell if Westberg experienced his own grief, so it isn't written with the emotion of a grieving person, but from the perspective of a counselor. It tells about stages though which most grieving people go: shock, emotional expression, depression/loneliness, physical symptoms of distress, panic, guilt, anger and resentment, resistance, hope, and finally struggle to affirm reality. It doesn't suggest a definite order, or that one will experience all of these stages.

The stages that were and are most poignant to me are quite different from what he described. First, I had a sense of being "held together" by the Holy Spirit. Some people might call that shock, but I don't think I was ever in shock. Next I faced deep sorrow knowing I will be living the rest of my life without my firstborn child who gave me untold joy. I never felt much guilt, but I did feel panicky on a few occasions. The anger stage has come and gone and will probably come again, but maybe not with such intensity and danger. For me, physical symptoms came, I believe, as a result of the anger. By writing this book, I'm working on affirming reality, and I'm feeling just a tiny glimmer of hope.

Psalms of Lament, by Ann Weems are similar to the Bible Psalms but are written by a grieving Mother who lost her twenty-one-year old son. As she explains at the beginning, this book is not for everyone. Only a grieving person could relate to the intense pain which her psalms express. They are a poetic, heart-wrenching expression of grief. The author is searching for God.

I should be searching for God. I was mostly searching for Heather, but now I'm searching for both.

How to Survive the Loss of a Love, by Harold H. Bloomfield, M.D., Melba Colgrove, Ph.D., and Peter McWilliams is more for one who lost a spouse or boyfriend. It doesn't touch the loss of a child.

When Will I Stop Hurting? by June Cerza Kolf, who has worked with grieving people and hospice. She lost her husband after retirement. It is a clearly written, short book, which lacks depth.

If God Is So Good, Why Do I Hurt So Bad, by David Biebel: He lost a young son to genetic disease. It is heavy with relying on Jesus.

The Other Side and Back, by Sylvia Brown: She has worked as a psychic for over fifty years. In her book, she comes across as a loving person with very good intentions. She gives some excellent common sense advice. I especially liked her "Affirmations" at the end of the book. She believes in reincarnation and says she has been on Earth about fifty-seven times. She says the "other side" is with us but with different vibrations so we can't see them—like fast moving fan blades. She gives no explanation of how she knows this. She says there is no Satan or hell, but there are dark entities (bad people) and white entities (good people). She is a white entity. She believes parts of the Bible and discounts parts. She does seem to believe in the Trinity.

Sylvia would be an interesting person to meet, and I think she is sincere, but I don't believe much of what she believes, especially reincarnation. I have no desire to live another life on Earth, so I don't want to believe in reincarnation.

Hope, by Nancy Guthrie: The author lost two babies to a genetic illness. It's written as a daily devotion and Bible study.

I don't like or agree with everything she writes, but during my first year of grief, I was drawn to her book every morning. I love that it is totally Bible-based. It is written to last a year. I'm slowly working through it a second time.

Healing after Loss, by Martha Whitmore Hickman is another one-year daily devotion.

At first I felt it lacked depth, because it is written for people experiencing all kinds of grief, but I now feel a bond with all in grief and have found wonderful comfort and "ah ha" moments in reading it. I'm reading it a second time as well. I've given copies of it to grieving friends.

The Grieving Garden, compiled by Suzanne Redfern and Susan K. Gilbert, includes the stories of twenty-two parents with children who died. It is written in such a way that I had to keep flipping back to see how old the children were and how they lost their life.

It is so scary, because this book revealed that it takes years and years for people to feel better. I finished the book five months after Heather's death, just before Mothers' Day, 2009. Pages 256 & 257, by Kathleen Weed, saved me from despair. I'll share it through this email:

May 10, 2009   Mother's Day
My email to Heather's best college friend (I also shared the following quote with Katie Gracia):
Dear Jewel,

I'm so sorry that you lost another close friend on Monday. I wish I could make it better for you. I believe that one who loves deeply runs a great risk of hurting deeply, but it's worth it. I've just been reading one of my many grieving books where a mother wrote: (I'll substitute with Heather's name and I feel the same about Emily.)

"Although I haven't discovered a truth about life or death or grief that can somehow shift the Universe back into place, I do know

that if I could have selected from every child in all the world, just one to be my daughter, I would have picked Heather. Even though she died before me, even though I suffer every day for the loss of her—no matter, I would choose her. . . .

Despite my broken heart, I believe, I know, it was good fortune that allowed me to love and be loved by this child. She died before me. So living without her is the price. So be it. I grieve for her every day. Some days are harder than others. Still, I would pay any price to have had Heather as my daughter. Remembering this helps me to feel less of a victim. It helps me to balance light and dark.

And when I acknowledge that I haven't been singled out for pain, I am more willing to embrace the world, just as it is. My grief mingles with the countless afflictions humans endure, and have endured before me. My loss is personal and irrevocable, but choosing to view it in a wider reality heartens me. And though I sometimes tremble before this staggering vision of the world, I am grateful for its more generous, less bounded perspective. This inclusive view presses me toward a willingness to become less a sympathetic observer and more a compassionate comrade. Authorities on grief often rank death of a child as the greatest loss. But it seems true that pain is a condition of human existence and loss shapes us all. We are all initiated, one way or another, if we live long enough."
(<u>The Grieving Garden</u> p. 256, by Kathleen Weed).

I just read this last night, and it was a comfort to me on Mother's Day.

Another comfort that I thought of myself is that our Heather will never have to live life having lost Denny and me, or her sister, or you, or the many people that she loved

so deeply. Like you, Jewel, she had such a capacity for love, but I'm not sure how she could have dealt with the pain of loss.
    I know you are thankful that you have a wonderful husband and family to give you support through this sad time.
    With love and compassion, Alyce

    I considered the writing of Kathleen Weed a beautiful Mother's Day gift for 2009.
    Also p. 236, by Stathi Afendoulis, from <u>The Grieving Garden</u>, helped me to look to the future. We cannot live our life for our deceased children, "but we can live our lives in honor of them."

<u>The Case for Christ</u> by Lee Strobel, an investigative reporter with a law degree. The book answers many questions an atheist may have about the Bible being legitimate.
    I chose to read this and discuss it with my Book Club, to help me with my doubt. I learned that I can't expect others to be interested in doubt just because I am. I think only one other Book Club member read the whole book. Most skimmed parts of it and decided it wasn't entertaining or well written. I liked it, because I wanted to learn from it. I found the case for the resurrection helpful to me in dealing with Heather's death.

<u>Prayer</u> by Ole Hallesby: The original copyright was in 1931. The author, who was imprisoned for his resistance to the Nazi regime, is able to reach out from Oslo, Norway, before the start of World War Two, and help countless people strengthen their prayer life.
    (Contemplating that reach is a motivator for me to get my book published.) I used to quote to my students, "The pen is mightier than the sword." coined by English author Edward Bulwer-Lytton in 1839. The quote could be the subject for a long essay, but I'll do my quick interpretation. Hallesby's mighty pen has reached across years and miles to stab me with the realization that prayer is not meant as a time to tell God what to do or what I need—It's an opportunity to invite the Triune God into my heart,

mind, and soul to grow in faith that God will give me more good things than I can imagine.

In a Women's Small Group I lead twice a month, we're working through and discussing this thought-provoking book. It is surprisingly small to have so many big ideas. Some are challenging and even a bit insulting. It shakes-up one's complacency with prayer, and starts out with promoting helplessness in approaching God. That didn't sit well with some of the women. Being a product of our culture I would have agreed with them before Heather died; but it did ring true to me, because after her death, I've often felt helpless. Sometimes the only prayerful words I could muster were, "Help me."

Through many Bible Study and Book Club discussions, I've discovered the meaning of approaching a topic as an empty vessel. When one approaches a study or a book, and is full of one's own ego and opinions; there is little room to learn new truths.

Breakfast with Buddha, by Roland Merullo, is a fiction book about a road trip with a holy man. The main character ends up learning from this unconventional, good-natured, thoughtful man.

The lessons of moderation, of not letting the ego get in the way of who you are at the deepest level, and the lesson of taking time to just be, reminded me of Eckhart Tolle's teachings. Although I don't agree with the authors on reincarnation, I did feel a sense of peace from both books. I loved that staying "busy" was not their solution for everything. In fact it is quite the opposite.

Stillness Speaks by Eckhart Tolle: His books should not be read quickly. One should be still and take time for grace, surrender and acceptance to be felt and allowed to take you to peace.

Because of the struggle I've been in since Heather's death, for me the following are meaningful quotes from Eckhart Tolle's book:

Acceptance of the unacceptable is the greatest source of grace in this world (p.71). Sometimes surrender means giving up trying to understand and becoming comfortable with not knowing (p.72). Whatever you accept completely will take you to peace, including the acceptance that you cannot accept, that you are in resistance (p.73).

I still have a long way to go on this journey of hills and valleys. To "accept the unacceptable, to give up trying to understand, and accept completely" I believe is much easier if you haven't had a child die, but if you have, maybe it is more necessary. I can accept that I am in resistance.

If you had not suffered as you have, there would be no depth to you as a human being, no humility, no compassion. You would not be reading this now. Suffering cracks open the shell of ego, and then comes a point when it has served its purpose. Suffering is necessary until you realize it is unnecessary (p.118).

I'm not so sure about the necessity of suffering, but I do realize that Eckhart Tolle, whether he knows it or not, is reinforcing a quote from the Apostle Paul:

Therefore, to keep me from being too elated, a thorn was given me in the flesh, a messenger of Satan to torment me, to keep me from being too elated. Three times I appealed to the lord about this, that it would leave me, but he said to me, 'My grace is sufficient for you, for power is made perfect in weakness.' So, I will boast all the more gladly of my weaknesses, so that the power of Christ may dwell in me. Therefore I am content with weaknesses, insults, hardships, persecutions, and calamities for the sake of Christ; for whenever I am weak, then I am strong (2 Corinthians 12:7b-10).

I'm working on making my focus become doing God's will in this world. After Heather died, I tried to push God away, but I couldn't. In my sorrow, I am closer to God.

Loss is a part of who I am. Life has lost some of its luster and death seems a greater gift (p.152).

Heather brought luster to my life, and now it's gone. Or is it?

<u>Tuesdays with Morrie</u>, by Mitch Albom, who visits his old professor. In this non-fiction book Mitch shares many words of wisdom from Morrie, who is dying with a peaceful acceptance that is inspirational.

It was a great comfort to me for many reasons. The one I'll share was how Morrie would live his last day, if he could be well again. On his last day he would get up and exercise. He would go for a walk and appreciate the beauty of nature. Next he would enjoy delicious food while spending quality time with a few close friends. And finally he would dance the night away.

He also stressed that the most important thing is love. Morrie did not consider himself religious, but near his death he was talking to God.

Heather was similar to Morrie in what was most important in her life. She actually lived most of her life like "his last day" without knowing of her impending sudden death. Or did she somehow understand her life would be short?

<u>Have a Little Faith</u>, also by Mitch Albom, was a similar book. Mitch again was sharing inspired messages, this time from men of faith: his rabbi, who wanted Mitch to write his eulogy, and a preacher who had turned away from a life of crime and drug addiction. Both taught that we don't get to question God, but it is ok to ask God questions.

I'm learning there is a difference between questioning God, and asking God questions. I wish I could reach a place of acceptance—like Morrie, but I haven't yet, and I don't feel like I ever will. I haven't quit asking "Why?" even though I know it is answered with silence.

<u>A Grief Observed</u>, by C. S. Lewis is a beautiful book (a journal) about C. S. Lewis' grief after the death of his wife. It bothered him that his stepsons never seemed to want to talk about their mother after she died. In the Introduction one of

The Devil's Fingernail

the sons, Douglas H. Gresham, explains that they didn't talk because they didn't want to break down crying.

It reminded me of and explained the silence in my childhood family, after my mother died.

At the end of this journal, he writes about an experience of his dead wife's mind facing his mind. It was an intellectual exchange, not an emotional one. He didn't experience joy or sorrow, "yet there was an extreme and cheerful intimacy. An intimacy that had not passed through the senses or the emotions at all" (p.73). He said, *'If you can—if it is allowed—come to me when I too am on my death bed.' 'Allowed!'* she said (p.75).

This gave me some hope. Heather is always in my heart and memory. I think of her constantly, and sometimes talk to her in my mind, but I don't get answers. I have experienced "cheerful intimacy" with Heather in four dreams, but no communication. I'm still hoping.

<u>A Grace Disguised</u>, by Jerry Sittser is the best of the grief books I read. It was written by a theologian who lost his wife, mother, and a child in a horrific car accident. It was first published in 1996, and written a few years after the accident. (He updated it in 2004.) He shares some of his real grief and writes his reflections on loss and on his response to that loss. I reread it, but from my first reading I learned to not live in denial (although one's self-preservation system puts one there for several months or years). He teaches that we should not repress grief, but should write about it, deal with it, talk about it, and choose friends who will listen.

The most important thing I learned was to allow myself to go to the "dark" places. The title of my book came from that dark place. I explained it in the "Devil in the Dark" chapter. It was the hardest lesson of my life, but I'm so thankful I learned it. It may kill me, but I'm still thankful.

In my second reading, I realized that his reflections make his book deal with the "universal" experience of loss. My book may have some "universal" aspects, but it is written about my personal grief and my own particular experience. For him the writing of the book was meaningful, but not cathartic. His journals were cathartic, but he doesn't share his journals.

He teaches that the soul is elastic and can enlarge through tragedy and suffering. When we experience loss it is natural and legitimate to experience despair, anguish, depression, and even anger which can increase the capacity for joy, strength, peace, and love.

I wish I could believe that is true. At this time, I don't feel that my soul has expanded. In contrast, I feel it has been irreparably wounded, but I know it all depends on one's response to one's grief. I have to not allow myself to become bitter and closed, but I must open myself to how I can grow through this life-changing grief.

The depth of sorrow is the sign of a healthy soul, not a sick soul . . . . 'Blessed are those who mourn' (Matthew 5:4a). *. . . Sorrow is good for the soul. . . . It is wonderfully clarifying* (pp. 73 & 74).

Because of my sorrow, I do feel more clarity and focus about what is important. Some things that seem to be extremely bothersome and worrisome to others and used to be to me, I now know are just not that important.

In the preface to the first edition, Jerry Sittser, explains that he thinks it's probably not possible to describe the *utterly devastating nature of one's suffering. Some experiences are so terrible that they defy description* (p. 19).

Yet, C. S. Lewis in <u>A Grief Observed</u>, does boldly describe his grief. He explained, in the first chapter of this book that sometimes grief felt like the sensation of fear, with the fluttering in the stomach and restlessness. Some of his other key words were self-pity, agony, and laziness—yes, even laziness. With grief, sometimes one doesn't want to make the effort to read, write, or even get cleaned up.

I understood what he meant. I felt so bewildered and fragile in the beginning. Although the grief is not so raw now; sometimes still, my sorrow causes a mental agitation that makes it almost impossible to concentrate. That is why I've had to read some of these books more than once. I often have to force myself to "get cleaned up" and go do productive things, even simple things like grocery shopping. Productivity, thinking outside of myself, and making commitments to do service has been good for my spirit.

Service

Experts suggest that service to others will help one focus less on self, and thus lighten grief. In true altruism, the focus is unselfish. I picked two service projects to help others, young and old, but also with the hope that it would help me. In the 2009-2010 school year, I began volunteering in an "I Can Read" program at the school from which I retired. I work one-on-one with students who are below grade level in reading. My other choice, started in May, 2010, is a church visitation team. Our aim is to visit elderly shut-ins. I feel both endeavors are, and will continue to be, mutually beneficial.

With the young, reading is the area I chose because of its importance: one must learn to read before one can read to learn. After teaching in classrooms of 23 to 35 students, it is such a pleasure to be able to really focus on one student and not be constantly thinking, checking, anticipating what creative, destructive, and sometimes actually productive antics the others are up to. In our small reading center, there are always other students with their tutors, but all are so engaged we don't disturb one another. While my student is reading a book that is at her instructional level, I'm able to take note of words that we need to review later. The student doesn't have to be embarrassed in front of peers, so feels safe to make mistakes. Also I'm able to ask open-ended questions to teach and check on comprehension—all without ever being interrupted.

As I was walking one reading student back to the classroom to pick-up the next, I was praising her. "You have excellent comprehension of the material you read. That is so important. Sometimes people can read really fast, but they don't know what they've read."

She proudly answered, "When I read to anyone else they never ask me questions. I understand it because you ask me really good questions."

On the older end of my volunteer spectrum it really isn't volunteering, it's visiting with widows who I consider to be my friends. My specialty is getting friends together who have a true understanding of what it means to lose a spouse and a way of life. Dorothy, a ninety-plus year-old widow with a positive attitude and a sharp mind, has come with me to visit people several times. Mildred, now deceased, didn't know me from one visit to the next, but the most gratifying visit we had was when I brought Dorothy (an old friend of hers she hadn't seen in years). Mildred's eyes lit up with pleasure and a spark of recognition. Her son happened to stop in while Dorothy and I were there and was so pleased. He said, "Hi mom, it's good to see you visiting with your lady friends."

On a few occasions I was privileged to take Dorothy to visit a couple with whom she and her husband had been friends and traveling companions. Bob was bed-ridden. His wife, Millie, requested that I come and do Bible study with them. I was happy to, and it was more fun because Dorothy was there. Along with the Bible study we enjoyed talking about their travels. In spite of vision and hearing problems Millie also is very "with it" and likes to attend Bible study and church. I sometimes drive her there. Once when I dropped her off at home she said, "I enjoyed it. I found the discussion stimulating."

Other outings with Dorothy included visiting, Ray, also recently widowed. She is a sympathetic listener and gives much encouragement. She encouraged her friend Millie to move into the assisted living facility where she is, and Ray may be considering it as well. Dorothy knows not to tell anyone what to do, but she shares how secure she feels being in her own apartment, but with the knowledge that meals and help are there when needed or wanted. Because Dorothy has been through it, she understands the loneliness that comes with the loss of a spouse, and the difficult decision to leave one's home. I think she too feels the visits are mutually beneficial.

Volunteering is uplifting for me because I see young and old dealing with difficulties but growing through them. It feels good to help a bit and to realize I'm not the only one with challenges. Truly, I cannot think of one instance when time in service, whether with young people or old, has not given me a sense of gratification. Being less self-absorbed is a key that helps unlock the trap of grief. The grief is still with me, but it no longer has me trapped. Another way out of the trap is to open the door, put the key in my pocket, and step into nature's beauty for exercise.

Exercise and Newness

Because I had a history and habit of exercise, it was easy for me to continue it, even at times of deepest despair. As a child I got plenty of exercise, because I lived in a small sunny California town. It was a time and place for outdoor, carefree freedom. With friends, I played at the park, explored at the Salinas River, climbed trees, rode bikes, and swam almost every day of the summer. When I was a young adult I began doing different types of intentional exercise which changed and evolved though time. When Heather died, I was determined to continue. I knew it would make me feel better, and it almost always does.

In the winter I ski two or three times a week. Although skiing is a reminder of Heather's death; there is nothing to compare to the exhilaration and challenge of trying to do it well, while enjoying an ever changing winter display. Here in Salt Lake valley, surrounded by mountains, we sometimes have to deal with inversion (dirty smog that can settle in for weeks). Skiing takes one out of that, up spectacular canyons, into the thin clean mountain air. Heather would never want me to give up skiing or stop climbing up out of the smog.

When the ski season is over I get exercise and pleasure working in my yard and gardens. I love the feeling of hope and promise that comes with seeing new plants peeking up in the spring. There is a satisfaction even in raking and weeding—pulling out that which is harmful or unwanted and making room for new growth. One can grow spiritually in a garden.

Exercise and outdoor activities are not only good for the body, but they're good for the mind and soul. Being active and outside in God's beautiful creation lightens the pain of sorrow. God's glory is displayed in nature and I am inspired by it during all seasons.

I go to nature to be soothed and healed, and to have my senses put in order. John Burroughs

I am so fortunate to have a new group of ski buddies who have invited me to hike with them when the snowfall stops.

We're hiking steep strenuous trails twice a week, and there is always a new trail to choose. The inspirational woman, Eleanor Anderson, who first included me, is the youngest eighty-something-year-old I've ever met. There isn't a mountain she won't climb, and she'll never give up. I love her bumper sticker: "God Bless The Whole World—No Exceptions."

Through this hiking group I have made a new discovery. The group changes a little each time, depending on who is available, and is comprised of new friends whom I met after Heather's death. I'm so thankful I have this interesting group to hike with, in beautiful canyons, close to home, in spring, summer, and fall. With every hike there is changing beauty—a new, showy display of God's grandeur.

I now understand why, as I learned in some of the books on grief, that people who have dealt with the death of a child, lose their old friends and often even their spouses, and make all new friends for a fresh start. It's easier, because there are no expectations for help with grief from these new friends. Yet when I invited my new friends on a tram ride and downward hike to view Heather's Memorial at Snowbird, I thought about five of them would come, because that would be above the average number on a typical hike. Eleven people came that day. Their compassion filled my heart. Nine were able to hike the steep terrain to the memorial and continue the decent to the tram deck. (I'll write much more about the Snowbird and other memorials in Part Two.)

I have no intentions of losing my "old" friends or my spouse. Nothing could ever replace them. I have simply made a decision to lower my expectations of all my friends, for help in my grief. Everyone has their own issues to deal with. They can't always be concerned about my well-being. That doesn't mean I can't or don't ever receive understanding and compassion from old or new friends, but I'll just take it if it comes and not expect it.

This concludes the section on: the things that helped most in my grief. It strikes me that each title relates to one or more of the areas for growth that I used to list in my daily prayers. "Dear God I pray that Heather, Emily, Denny, and I develop to our optimum potential; physically (Exercise), socially (Congregation and Friends, Sharing Possessions), emotionally (Shared Grief, Wedding, and Commitment), morally (Bible Study and Service), academically (Writing and Books), and spiritually (Bible Study, Prayers, Doubt and Faith). And I pray, dear God, that we use our talents to your glory."

Hope and Peace

June 14, 2010

None of the books or Bible passages, friends and family, or Compassionate Friends, ever addressed my biggest concern—Is Heather in a "good" place? If I knew that, I think I could be at peace. It seems to be easy for everyone else to assume she is, but not for me. I'm her mommy. It was my job to protect her. There wasn't physical protection for Heather on December 14, 2008, so it makes it hard to believe there was spiritual protection. It seems I have to die to find out for sure, so I don't see myself being at peace until I die. I've accepted that my life has changed and will never be the same. It lacks much of its luster. Heather was the real live personification of luster. Read Part Two to understand that statement.

My acceptance of not being at peace is interestingly helpful to me. There are gifts in all of this: I've already written about a stronger yet not peaceful relationship with God. Another gift is that I truly look forward to death. I'm not suicidal, but I look at death as a gift.

Doubt and questioning are ironically a part of my faith—a part of who I am. It is some of the reason I look forward to death. I look for a revealing of truth. Like my daughter, I have always loved adventure. I look at death as my final and ultimate earthly adventure. I do have hope that my daughter will be there to greet me.

Hope that is seen is not hope. For who hopes for what is seen? But if we hope for what we do not see, we wait for it with patience (Romans 8:24b-25). This is a verse worth repeating.

February 24, 2011

Like I've done many times, today I was again proofreading and editing Part One, and couldn't help but wonder if I will ever find peace. I do have hope that my Heather is in heaven, but will I ever find peace? I then moved to Part Two, and to enhance the chapter on Heather's childhood, I went through a file box that Heather had organized the summer before she died. It contained some special things she had saved from elementary, junior high, and high school. In it I found these poems; the first one written when she was thirteen and the second when she was almost seventeen.

SADNESS
Sadness is a maze.
You try to find your way out,
But your search never succeeds.
You must find the strength
To conquer the trap.

When she was thirteen, Denny and I didn't realize how trapped in sadness she sometimes was. It seems The Devil's Fingernail touched Heather as well. I still often find myself trapped in a maze of sadness, but I know Heather isn't any more. Writing this book is beginning to help me "conquer the trap."

English   Period I
June 1, 1998   Heather Gross

<u>Golgotha</u>

Dear God, we've been blowing these whistles for an eternity in hopes that someone will find us. Do I really hear other whistles, or is that just the echo of our own?
Dear God, we've been lying under this cold night sky, stranded here forever. Could I really be seeing flashlights through the trees, or is that just the twinkling stars above?
Thank you, God. They're here. It's over. We're going to camp, to home, led by our saviors, the Search and Rescue Team.
Golgotha: this little bear with fur the color of brown sugar and a red satin bow. He was a gift from Search and Rescue, a symbol of the feat we conquered and the fear we overcame.

*Golgotha: my tiny friend named after the hike, we survived—
the same name of the mountain on which Christ died, where his
life ended, but where life for all began.*

*I see his arms outstretched to give a hug, like the arms of
God embracing all his people.*

*He is my comfort: the knowledge that I can survive a crisis
without panicking, but instead looking to God for guidance.*

*He is my hope. I had faith that help would come, and it
did.*

He is my triumph. Christ was resurrected. I am saved.

Her experience of being lost and found by Search and Rescue will be explained in her words in Book Two, but for me, finding her beautiful inspired poem today helped my peace of mind. I consider it a gift from God and a gift from both of my daughters. I say both daughters, because the last time Emily spent with Heather, she (Emily, master organizer) lovingly helped Heather clean her rooms and sort her papers just before Heather's trip to China—six months before she died. Some of her papers and other stuff were in a jumbled mess, and Heather felt she couldn't leave it like that out of respect for her housemate and for her own peace of mind. Thanks to the organized files, I found this beautiful poem. I searched and <u>Golgotha</u> was my rescue too. The search isn't finished, but for today I found some peace.

Part Two: Heather Aron Gross

By her mother, Alyce Gross

and by Heather Aron Gross (posthumously)

Outline

Part Two: Heather Aron Gross

Who was Heather?

Before Death:
Childhood
College
Junior Year in Granada, Spain
Mom's Edited Travel Journal
Back in the USA
After College
Two Months of Travel: Down Under and Europe
Back Home
Changes
China
Death

After Death:
News Articles and Reports
Obituary
Celebration of Life
Others Wrote About Heather
Memorials
Giant Tombstone
Spreading of Ashes

Author's Preface

    This is written from her mother's perspective. If her father wrote this, or her sister, or one of her many friends from varied cultures, it would be a different piece. Of course all these people, especially her father and sister, greatly influenced who Heather was; and my writing is not meant to diminish their importance. Yet this book does include the perspective of many; through letters, emails, and Facebook comments. I couldn't include everything written about Heather, but all that I have found and read about her is greatly appreciated and continues to be a comfort to me. I hope all who wrote about Heather were given comfort in the writing as I was in the reading. Heather died too young, so I feel it is up to me to share her with anyone who may read this book. She lives on in the hearts and memories of those who knew her. Through this book, she will come alive to you who didn't know her.

    The chapter on Heather's childhood includes her own words from <u>Heather's Highlights,</u> an autobiography and <u>Keeping Rhythm with the Wind,</u> a collection of poetry and short stories. She wrote them as English assignments in eighth or ninth grade. It also includes poetry written by Heather at various ages, some in the form of Christmas greetings. I used a few quotes from her Foreign Languages Sterling Scholar Portfolio written in her senior year of high school in a rather stilted way, because she was trying to impress a panel of judges. Most of the young adult chapter is definitely not stilted. It is in Heather's own words through travel emails, but I chose what to include. Keep in mind she was writing to her mother and father as well as Emily. If she had been writing to friends or just to Emily there may have been a few more intriguing details included, but I thought she included plenty.

    So again this book is primarily from my point of view. I'm the one who carried Heather in my womb, nursed her, and watched her grow. I nurtured her to the best of my ability. I encouraged her to reach her optimum potential and to be open-minded and nonjudgmental. I kept her close and then let her go—first on little trips with church groups or Girl Scouts. Then to study out of state, and then out of the country, but she always came back home. I never thought I would have to let her go so completely. I loved being her mother and I always will. I taught her and she taught me about loving and life. I keep her in my heart and I'm writing about her to share her through these memories.

Before Heather died, I had no interest in Facebook. It seemed to be for young people only, but when Emily, my youngest daughter and only living child, showed me all the heartfelt comments Heather's friends were making, I saw its value. Emily was able to memorialize Heather's page, and I'm so grateful. Emily allowed me to use her password because, of course, Heather couldn't accept me as a friend. My resourceful son-in-law, Ryan, wrote to Facebook explaining the situation, and they graciously allowed Emily to "friend" Heather posthumously so she set up a new account and didn't have to share one with her mother. I appreciate Emily and Ryan and the compassion of the young Facebook founders. So a big THANK YOU to Mark Zuckerberg. Now I'm able to go there to access Heather's pictures and to feel a connection to her and to the friends who continue to write.

Facebook:
Emily Gross
I had the Facebook people memorialize HG's account, so she will be here forever. My family is enjoying reading all of these wonderful writings! Thanks!
December 31, 2008 at 1:09pm

Alexandra Scott
Heather
still can't really figure out how to deal with you being memorialized... (is that a word). i almost sent you a text yesterday. i have so much to tell you. no hay palabras. wtf.

gom. delta delta. yar is on my leg and i am going to run it 13.1 miles twice in 4 weeks. you are my happy thought.
January 3, 2009 at 9:39pm
(As I explained in Part One, Heather made up words and phrases. Lexy, who was fluent in "G-speak," probably contributed to the evolving language.)

My current thoughts will be written in Times New Roman
Facebook, E-mails, and Letters in Verdana, or scanned as they are
My Journal Entries in Bookman Old Style
Heather's Journal Entries in Bookman Old Style Italic

Alyce Gross

Who Was Heather?

In Part One I wrote about Heather's God-given love for people. I felt it necessary to introduce the vibrant living Heather early on so the reader could better understand the loss. Here I'll continue to share from varied perspectives, including her own, the many facets of Heather

In her senior year of high school, for her Sterling Scholar portfolio she was asked: Tell us about yourself. What makes you unique? What special difficulties have challenged you and describe the effects? She wrote:

One of my most unique qualities is that I know how to get through a tight spot without too much sweat. I've decided that my life philosophy is to "be where I am." That may sound very simple, but it means just that. I need to use what I have and focus on what's given to me at each moment of my life. Then, I'll be able to enjoy whatever I'm participating in and do it fully. In 1994 I lived through three interesting experiences that all coincidentally took place on Tuesdays. They each tried my faith and patience. (The "Three Tuesdays" will be shared in the Childhood chapter.)

Here is what a close high school friend wrote about her:

On-line Obituary Responses: legacy.com
December 18, 2008
Heather was an amazing, and inspirational friend. Heather could always make me laugh, and she always challenged me to think. She knew how to live, and impacted everyone she met.
My life will always be better because of all the times I spent with her. She will live on in my heart for the rest of my life. She was living proof that you could make your life what you wanted to make it. She lived honestly, and fully.
My heart goes out to the family. I wish you the best and guarantee you that your daughter is going to live on in the lives she touched. Michelle Jensen

Now the impressions of a friend she met much later:
December 22, 2008

The Devil's Fingernail

Heather had the kind of warmth, courage, and generosity that most people will never achieve in a lifetime. I am forever grateful that I got to know her over the last few years. She was a great friend and I will always remember how she never left without giving you a hug first. She was an amazing person and will be forever missed. Mary Anne Davies

A few years later—June, 2011, Mary Anne married Jeff Hortin (high school boyfriend of Heather's). One of Heather's gifts was that she was able to keep almost all of her past boyfriends as good friends. In the reading you'll meet several. She had other gifts beyond friendships and boys.

As a retired school teacher, I know almost all parents think their children are highly intelligent, so to show objectively how brilliant Heather was I'll share that she was a National Merit Finalist, thus she was offered scholastic scholarships to several universities. She had an aptitude for learning languages that we didn't discover until she took Spanish in middle school. She learned it so quickly she was able to get a job as a Spanish speaking telephone operator one summer in high school.

Heather studied and embraced life in Spain her junior year in college. With the advice of a friend (former boyfriend) who had experienced and promoted this adventure, she chose to not live with an assigned family, but to go and find Spanish roommates on her own. Because of that bold choice, I have some funny, fascinating emails to share. The first semester, she took language and culture classes at a school geared for foreigners, but her second semester was completed at the University of Granada where she had the nerve to take chemistry (not a good idea) and Italian courses, taught in Spanish. I think that experience gave her empathy for foreign nationals that she later studied and worked with in the United States.

She graduated from Arizona State University's Honors College *summa cum laude* with a double major in Chemistry and Spanish and a minor in Italian. She wasn't right or left brained like most people. She used both sides of her brain. Yes, she was brilliant.

Heather put great effort into her studies, and her work ethic reflected that same boundless energy. I included some copies of letters from supervisors and coworkers to attest to that in Part One. Included here is one more written at a time when Heather was transitioning from science to language.

Cindy Lou Chepanoske, Ph.D.
Seattle, WA
January 21, 2007

Department of Linguistics
University of Utah Graduate School
Salt Lake City, UT 84112-0492

Dear Application Counselor,

I am writing in support of Heather Gross's application for acceptance into the University of Utah Graduate School in the Department of Linguistics. I began working with Heather at Tandem Labs (her current position) in February, 2005 and shortly became her supervisor in the Method Development Group. In our tenure together, we engaged in a number of diverse projects encompassing specific areas of drug discovery and analytical chemistry where she showed superior insight and capabilities well above her peers. In this time I also supported her for a promotion which was subsequently granted by my superiors. Indeed, my last successful projects prior to my departure in 2006 involved an immense amount of work and dedication and were made possible by Heather's contributions.

When I first met Heather, I was surprised to know that she was fluent in Spanish and could also speak other languages; many people from the United States do not bother to learn and practice anything other than English. It was inspiring to hear her converse with our custodians at night since most people don't give them any attention at all, let alone care enough to speak to them and learn about them. After working with Heather for a while, I came to learn about her travels abroad and could fully digest her love for languages and cultures. As sad as I may be for the scientific community to lose someone as gifted as Heather, I know that she is following her true calling.

In addition to Heather's outstanding analytical capacity,

she possesses a very important strength in her ability to bridge communication between scientists in the laboratory. She is very patient while seeking to fully understand the scope of the project, and will not hesitate to ask questions or inquire for help when necessary. Importantly, Heather does not waver in her position when the environment in a meeting or lab instance becomes less-than-conducive. For instance, when there is a deadlock of conflicting ideas or opinions, Heather is the first one to say "Okay, how can we solve this problem? What can we do to get the job done and how can I help?" Her no-nonsense approach in communication among scientists is refreshing and not an easy task.

Heather has applicable experience, knowledge, and importantly, an immense desire that meets the qualifications of admittance. Furthermore, I feel she would be an excellent candidate and would thrive in the environment of this esteemed department at the University of Utah.

Best regards, Cindy Lou Chepanoske

Cindy (who had moved to Seattle, wrote the former letter of recommendation) and Ryan (a former Tandem Labs employee who dated Heather for a short period) had a destination wedding at a resort in Mexico. Heather was excited to attend for many reasons: She would be with friends from her former job at Tandem Labs, sharing emotionally charged moments. She would have a trip to Mexico where she could use her language skills. Also, she would be able to dance and celebrate—all things very important to her. Unfortunately Heather missed the flight that the wedding party was on, from Mexico City to the resort. That didn't stop her. (This was in February, 2008, before the drug wars got so bad.) She took local transportation, changing buses in Mexico City, for an overnight ride to the resort. In route she met some interesting Mexican people and got to the wedding celebration in plenty of time. The wedding party would have been worried about anyone else but Heather.

She had a fearless sense of adventure and experienced life to the fullest. She lived abundantly and knew how to thoroughly enjoy, food, drink, music, dancing, and especially travel. In other words she was interesting and full of fun!

But was it all enjoyment and fun? No, it was balanced with a dark side. I wonder if it always has to be that way—if there are highs, there must be lows—I don't know, but Heather's lows were extreme. We began to learn of them in her freshman year of college, although they started earlier. I didn't understand until reading her journals after her death, and I still don't fully understand.

I've been in a book club for over fifteen years, and by reading many books chosen by other people, I've come to realize I don't want to waste my time reading a book that doesn't have at least one character in it that I admire. My favorite books have a protagonist or even an antagonist with some admirable traits from which I can learn or from which I can be inspired. Being Heather's mother makes my opinions of her biased, but I think she had many admirable traits. Although I want to portray my daughter in the best possible light, it's the flaws that help us relate to or sympathize with a character. We don't want to read about somebody who is perfect. We want a problem or conflict so we can seek resolution. There definitely was a problem, so whether you knew Heather or not; you'll want to keep reading about her and it won't be a waste of your time.

Now we'll move back in time to her beginnings.

Childhood

Life has to be lived. That's all there is to it. Eleanor Roosevelt

I looked through old photo albums to help choose events to write about. It struck me that before Heather died, looking at old photos of the girls made me nostalgic and sad—knowing I'll never get those times back; but now that Heather has died, the pain of loss has gone from a gentle nostalgic sadness to an intense sorrow that seems never ending. In contrast I consider sad nostalgia a gift. It heartens me to look back, because it reminds me that our daughters had a wonderful, enriched childhood filled with unconditional love. I'm so thankful for memories and very few regrets about Denny's and my parenting. It was a privilege to be the mother of Heather Aron Gross for twenty-seven years, five months, and sixteen days. I'm still her mother and always will be.

Heather's first gift to me was the realization that I could no longer be self-centered. I didn't realize I had been selfish, but parenthood taught me that the needs of the child come first, and my needs were secondary. It was a beautiful lesson, because love was the motivation and with it came the understanding that being more selfless is part of becoming a more fulfilled person. Having my firstborn child was an awakening for me that I never anticipated or would have believed, had I not experienced it. The powerful maternal instinct amazed me. How could I love our little baby so completely?

Another gift Heather gave Denny and me was motivation for travel to see relatives and motivation for them to come visit us. We made the effort to take many family trips to California, Montana, and Pennsylvania, to visit grandparents, aunts, uncles and cousins. They all visited us in Salt Lake City as well. Heather's first flight, when she was about eight months, was to my childhood home, Templeton, California, to see and be seen by friends and grandparents. Our girls didn't get to see their relatives frequently, but most holidays were made more special by the effort taken to get family together. Heather's first two Thanksgivings were spent in Kalispell, Montana where she got to be with cousins, and stay at her Godparents' home. Heather's second Christmas was spent in Pittsburgh, Pennsylvania, with her father's family and friends. We flew there several times and in all different seasons.

As an infant Heather hardly ever crawled, she rolled all over the house. I remembered my mother, the teacher, saying a baby needs to learn to crawl as a part of their brain development. Heather was such a great roller, she didn't crawl until ten months, and she didn't walk until fifteen months, so I thought she might be developmentally delayed. I was certainly wrong about that.

At five months she played baby Jesus in a church Christmas pageant, sitting in her car seat which was decorated to look like a manger. She happily sat taking everything in. Someone said, "That baby should be nominated for sainthood." I think her sister and friends would debate that, but she and Emily attended Sunday School and church youth activities throughout all their years in our home.

Heather loved being with me while I was doing any household task. I always spoke to her in complete sentences and explained everything I was doing. I read to Heather every day, and she was such an attentive listener and learner. We were often in the kitchen together. Her favorite place to play was in the lower cupboards taking out pans and bowls, stacking and unstacking them, and then climbing into the cupboard and sitting in there like a little gnome.

On September 5, 1983, when Heather was two years and two months old, she became a sister. The parenting books warned that a new baby can be a big hit to the ego of any sibling, but especially a two-year-old who has been the only child. I carefully prepared Heather for her very important new roll as big sister. I spent a lot of time making Heather understand that she was a role model for and protector to her baby sister. I bought a life sized doll to give to Heather when Emily came home from the hospital. Now Heather could take care of her baby while mommy took care of Emily. Sometimes we would take our babies out for a stroll together.

The Devil's Fingernail

October 7, 1983

Denny and I stressed the importance of prayer with our girls. After reading to them, one of us said prayers with them every night. We also prayed together before meals. Forgiveness was modeled and taught in our little family. The girls learned early on to not hold onto anger toward each other. They made up their own word, "chee," meaning, "Peace, I forgive you. Do you forgive me?" If they had argued at home while getting ready in the morning, on their walk to school, sometimes in the presence of other children; they would use their word, "chee," before parting ways. As the girls grew up, sometimes the role of big sister and protector switched back and forth between Heather and Emily, depending on circumstances. We were and are very proud of the strong bond those sisters had.

In Heather's Highlights her eighth grade autobiography, this is some of what she wrote about her sister:

My sister Emily is better than a best friend. She is a little more than two years younger than me and is three grades below me. Our age difference lets us still be pals. . . .

Emily is fun to be with whether we're skiing, fishing, on a family trip, or jumping on the trampoline. She's smart, athletic, and daring and can always make you smile. I love my sister very much.

When Heather was in high school, her feelings hadn't changed as shown in her Sterling Scholar Portfolio:

My sister Emily and I have always been best friends. She honored me by choosing me as her hero for a school program, but she is my hero because she's the kindest, funniest person I know. She sees me preparing for college by doing well in school. I am her older sister and a leader in her life. The love and support Emily has shown me is long-lasting and solid.

Emily wrote this in 2002 shortly after Heather, Emily, and I returned home from Spain.

Once you asked me why I am so happy.
It's because
I followed the best possible footsteps!
You
Inspired my achievements in school.
Showed me the only way to organize my life, the rainbow.
Revealed my future career of design, by creating miniatures.
Taught me to make music out of life, even when inside a fold-up bed.
Demonstrated that fishing works best when you serenade the fish.
Gave me courage on midnight, spa breaks and ski lift climbs.
Indicated that dessert can be a "beautiful" thing.
Confirmed that I will not die being thrown from a jet ski.
Explained that it is imperative to have a kitchen inside of the fort.
Changed my instinct, to not bring the residents toilet papering.
Displayed that it is easy to get lost on the beaches of Spain.
You proved that I have the best sister in the world!
Step into my shoes and admire yourself.
I love you
Heath.

Some of the lines in Emily's poem need to be explained:

In the condo we stayed at in Grand Targhee Ski Resort, Wyoming, there were Murphy beds that folded up into the wall. Heather always took her flute on the Targhee trips, and she even played it inside the bed, while folded in the wall. She made up a fishing song while fishing with her Dad and sister. (Emily recently sang it to her third graders.) I remember when Heather came home from her first fishing trip, as a toddler. I was fixing the catch for dinner, and Heather said, "That is a dead fish."

Years later I found out that my daughters, when having sleepovers on the tramp in our back yard, on a few occasions snuck into the Cottonwood Heights Recreation Center outdoor pool. They climbed over the fence and then climbed the high platform. I'm not sure if they jumped. (I never should have told them that I used to sneak out and take my sleepover friends to the Templeton Pool, in the cover of the night. That was a small town and a small pool and years ago.)

I believe sleeping parents are "the residents" and the toilet papering was not my fault. That seems to be a Utah thing.

"Lost on the beaches of Spain" will be explained in the July, 2002 travel journal.

In the spring, summer, and fall, Heather and Emily spent hours in our wonderful backyard. It was a time for discovery and carefree adventure for our girls. Some of the backyard toys were gifts from Aunt Ann and Grandma Gross including a small rubbery plastic slide with three steps that they climbed to slide into a small boat shaped pool. They spent hours at that and developed some strong muscles and coordination. Their dad made them a sandbox and Grandparents Gross bought them a swing-set. When Heather was six, her dad built the girls a playhouse on stilts. Their back yard was the place to play in the neighborhood.

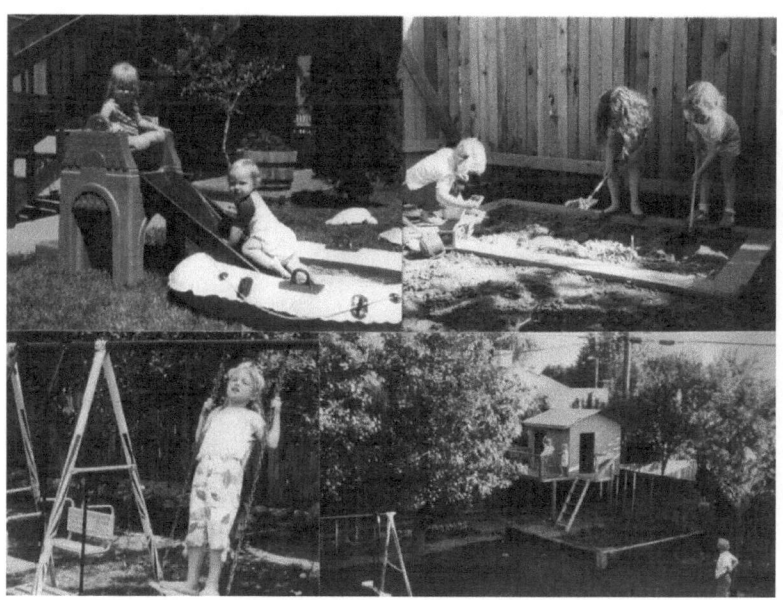

I feel so fortunate that I had time to spend with my children, because I was a stay-at-home mom for five years. When Heather went to Kindergarten and Emily to preschool, I went back to teaching part-time. It was to a job share—half days for three years. I didn't work full-time until Emily started Kindergarten.

Heather's first best friend was our back yard neighbor Danielle Gardner. She wrote about her in Heather's Highlights, published in eighth grade:

The Devil's Fingernail

Danielle
When I was two and you were three,
we would sit in your sandbox, just below your gigantic tree,
and share frozen popsicles.
When the popsicles got sandy, we didn't care.
We ate them anyway.
We would sometimes try to climb your tree.
I finally succeeded when I got tall enough to reach the one long branch.
I even got stuck in your tree once.
Your dad had to help me get down.
Then we'd wander through the gate between our backyards and play in my backyard.
We had tea parties on the patio,
on a little Strawberry Shortcake table.
Our usual meal was apple juice and graham crackers.
When it was hot, we'd play in my boat-shaped, inflatable pool.
We'd put the big brown and orange plastic slide in the pool
and slide into the chilly water coming from the hose.
Sometimes we'd play on the swing set.
We liked the glider,

because we could sit, facing each other, and talk.
Although you're a year older than me,
You've always been a good friend and still are.

    When Heather was five and Emily three, we begin teaching our girls to ski. It was exhausting attempting to ski holding a little one between our legs. We soon moved to using rubber tubing clamped to the tips of their skies, to hold the skies in a V shape, which helped them to snow plow. Snowbird's Chickadee lift was free at the time, so we often taught them there. When Heather started skiing at Snowbird, the thought never entered our minds that, that is where her life would end.

    In February, 1987, with another family, the Emerys, and their two children, Patrick and Lisa; we took our girls to Grand Targhee Ski Resort for the first time. I saw a TV advertisement showing that they offered a nursery and lessons for children, so it sounded perfect for two families who loved to ski. The tradition continued for the next twelve years. The kids progressed in their skiing and were soon off on their own. They could ski to the room for lunch and snacks. After skiing they swam and used the hot tub. Great memories were made on those trips. One year the kids put "stuff" in a tennis can, as a time capsule, and snuck out into the cold night to bury it. I'm not sure if they ever retrieved their encapsulated treasures.

Denny asked his good friend, Randy Emery, to see if his son Patrick could come up with some memories of Targhee to include in Denny's talk at Heather's funeral.

From: Pat Emery Sent: Wednesday, December 17, 2008 4:09 PM
Hey Dad,

    I remember rolling around in the snow and jumping back into the pool at Targhee. I also remember "sploring" [Heather made up that word and many more.] in the woods near the Sioux Lodge. We had some great times skiing at Grand Targhee. Heather was always right behind me, never afraid to go wherever I went. I must have been around twelve years old or younger when she discovered that, for the four of us, our ages lined up for a few days of the year. She would call the house

and rattle off the numbers quick (ie. 10, 11, 12, 13) and then hang up. Over the past five years or so she would always text message me on that day. Since she made the discovery maybe fourteen years ago, she never missed a single year. I also remember riding up to Targhee with her and she always made these fancy bookmarks where she kept track of all the trips she went on and what books she was reading.
Love, Patrick

Yes, Heather valued friends and travel from the beginning. As soon as she could write she started making her traveling bookmarks.

"Don't tell me how educated you are, tell me how much you have traveled." Muhammad, prophet

I'm thankful that I can look back with satisfaction knowing that Denny and I made an effort to do child-centered travel as a family. In June, 1988, we went to the Oregon coast, the Redwood Forest, and to Fisherman's Warf in San Francisco on our way to Templeton, California, where my stepmother, Grandma Dot, and my father, Grandpa Aronson lived. That would be the last time our girls saw Grandpa Aronson. He died November 16, 1988. I'll always regret not taking my girls to his funeral. I went alone so Denny could get the girls to school. They missed saying good-buy to their grandpa and comforting Grandma Dot, and they missed the opportunity of meeting relatives that didn't come again.

Although that experience was missed, our girls did have many wonderful opportunities. They had dance and gymnastics. A recreation center with several pools and an indoor ice skating rink is just two short blocks from our home in a suburb south of Salt Lake City. (My husband and I are still in the house where our girls grew up.) Our girls took advantage of much of what it had to offer: swimming lessons and ice skating after school. Heather even took diving lessons. They had back yard birthday parties with various age appropriate themes, including slip-n-slide, swimming, ice skating, a hobo party where their guests came in costume, ate out of tin plates, and slept in back yard tents. As they got older we took birthday groups to the The Star Theater for a silly melodrama, to Timpanogus Cave, and another time to a Buzz Baseball Game.

In the summer of 1989, our family went to Yosemite and Hearst Castle on a trip to see Grandma Dot, my newly widowed stepmother. Earlier that summer they got to go on their first of several trips to Lake Powel. The first trip included Grandpa Gross and the Emerys. The kids had wonderful times jumping off the side of the houseboat with life jackets securely fastened, digging in the sand, and sleeping under the stars on the flat top deck. As they got older the trips included water skiing and jet skies. Heather wrote about Lake Powell in <u>Heather's Highlights</u>.

The Best Vacation I've Been On

The summer after I was in fourth grade, my family went on a vacation to Lake Powell. We went with three other families: the Emerys, the Robertsons, and the Heinses. The Emerys have a boy my age, Patrick, and a girl my sister's age, Lisa. The Robertsons have a girl my age, Megan, and a boy Emily's age, Kyle. The Heinses have Kate who is my age.

It was fun having so many friends with us. We stayed on a houseboat that had a slide. We went off the slide every way we could. We also jumped off the top of the houseboat into the chilly water.

Megan and Kate were my best friends. We had a lot of fun together. It was like having a bunch of sleepovers right in a row. We slept on the top of the houseboat and watched for falling stars. Patrick was my bud too. Once we got all the kids together. Emily and I taught them a song we had learned at camp called "Pharaoh, Pharaoh." We all put towels on our heads to look like we were from the Middle East. We performed a show for the parents in which we sang the song, and they taped it.

We went water skiing and jet skiing a lot. Sometimes the parents would let us drive the jet skis. It was really fun! The kids also looked for shells on the beaches. We competed to see who could

The Devil's Fingernail

find the most. Lake Powell is a great vacation place. I loved going there and always will.

Heather loved to learn. She thrived in school and couldn't resist academic competition. It was in second grade that she started entering spelling bees. Her sister wrote about some of her awards in an essay that is included later. Again from <u>Heather's Highlights</u>:

I enjoy reading. In third grade, I won in my class for reading the most hours. I also like writing poetry. I have been doing it on my own for a long time.

On-line Obituary Response: legacy.com
December 18, 2008
I was shocked and saddened when I realized that the girl who passed away while skiing was Heather from my very first 3rd grade class at Cottonwood Heights. I have wonderful memories of Heather. She was always smiling, always doing her best. She brought a lot of joy to our class. In the coming weeks I will get you copies of all of the pictures I took of her in third grade and copies of 3 sweet notes I have in my books that she gave me. She kept on being an amazing girl, as I have learned from reading about her life. What a wonderful tribute you have written to her and what a privilege it was for me to be her teacher. May you, Dennis, Alyce and Emily, find peace and comfort now and in the days to come. With love, Lisa Urry Martin

Heather entered several National PTA Reflections (visual arts and literature) competitions. I don't think she ever won, but I loved the poems she entered and was excited when I found some of these elementary school treasures.

In 1990 the theme was "Where Does the Sky End?" When Heather was eight and in third grade she wrote,
The idea for the first line of my poem came to me when I saw some horses.

Where Does the Sky End?

The sky ends where a horse can not gallop.
The sky ends a long distance from here.
The sky ends in hills that aren't known.
Perhaps in that place there is no fear.

The sky ends where the colors are fading.
The sky ends in a place I can't see.
The sky ends where the wind blows above.
And sometimes it whispers to me.

The next year the Reflections subject was: "If I Had a Wish." Heather's was. . .
I Wish to Fly
I wish to feel wind passing by
As I soar and glide through the sky
That is what my wish would be
And that is what would fill me with glee

On-line Obituary Response: legacy.com
December 19, 2008
I remember Heather as the sweetest, smartest little girl in 5th grade. I am deeply saddened to hear of her accident. I have been visiting with JoAnn Warr and Mary Jane Johnson and we all remember her very well. My heart goes out for your loss and my prayers are with you. I know well the anguish you are going through as I lost my daughter 4 months ago and she was only 29. May God bless and be with you. Jean Childs (Salt Lake City, UT)

Sadly she knows the anguish, and she also knows how much it means to have people remember our loved ones.

In the theme of remembering loved ones, our Christmas letters were always a big deal to me, because it was the one time of year I stayed in touch with some of our treasured friends and

The Devil's Fingernail

family. As already stated, Denny and I are from different states: Pennsylvania and California. We met in Germany where Denny was a captain in the Army and I was teaching for the Department of Defense. We were married in 1978 in Salt Lake City, Utah. Our relatives and many of our friends were all somewhere else, so hearing from them at Christmas was and is more important to me than Christmas presents. I knew many people dreaded receiving long braggy holiday letters, so I encouraged Heather to use her talents as a poet to keep ours short and entertaining. Emily was our reluctant yet expert illustrator for many years. Heather would put much time, thought, and effort into her poems, and Emily would whip out cute illustrations with ease. It wasn't until 2002, that I took over the writing of our annual greetings. Of course, we only include what sounds good, and not the whole story, but at least they're short and a good summation of what was happening in our family. I saved copies over the years, and recently reread them to help me to remember highlights in Heather's childhood.

```
Dear Friends:
December, 1991

Dad's helping build a house for Habitat for
Humanity,
Mom's typing a paper and losing her sanity.
Emily's watching cartoons and ignoring it
all,
So I guess it's up to me to send greetings
to all.

Emily's in second grade and doing mighty fine,
She's in a photography club to pass some of
her time.
She's also in Brownies with dad as a part
time leader,
Now she says she'll grow up to become a
```

teacher.
I'm in fifth grade, and it's quite a hoot,
I take gymnastics, Girl scouts, and to top it off, flute.

Mom's very busy since she switched from teaching third grade to fifth,
I'm her greatest advisor, and that's not a myth.
She helps lead my girl scouts, and that's pretty keen,
But, she has some trouble keeping the house clean.
She's working on her masters, which is not easy to do,
But when she is finished, we'll all yell Yah-hoo.

Commercial Funding keeps dad occupied,
He built a new deck, with which we're all satisfied.

We wish JOY to you all for this holiday season,
And always remember that Jesus' birth is the reason.

By Heather (with a little help from Mom)
Illustrated by Emily

The Devil's Fingernail

When I was a child my school teacher mother always planned wonderful family trips every summer. I have fond memories from those adventures. I can still smell the pine scent around the cabins and can hear my mom laughingly banging pans together to scare away the bears. As is normal, I modeled after my mother and made sure our girls got to experience the wonders of many National Parks.

In the spring and summer of 1992, Heather and family had several camping adventures in the southwest as well as in our own backyard. The four of us went to Arches National Park with the Girl Scouts. My memory is of the girls climbing all over those rocks and Heather walking on her hands and doing cartwheels to add to the thrill. We went horseback riding in Bryce Canyon with Kate Heins and family, did a float trip on the Colorado River with a church group, and to top it off; we took a family camping trip to Yellowstone.

That summer we also bought a trampoline. Amazingly, no one ever got injured. We were so lucky and stupid, because I believe our girls reached new heights on that thing, with their gymnastic backgrounds motivating some interesting stunts.

During our summer of 1993 we managed to fit in trips to Goblin Valley, Bear Lake, and just Heather went to Mesa Verde with the Girl Scouts.

On a Bear Lake trip, with our pastor's family, the Klemzes, the moms went rafting, while the dads and four girls, including Andrea, who would be Heather's roommate her freshman year of college, went horseback riding. All was well until Heather's horse decided to be cantankerous and roll over. It could have killed Heather, but she nimbly jumped onto the sand along the shore line, and my guess is that she walked on her hands and did a few cartwheels while waiting for her disturbed horse to right himself. Finally she got back on the offending horse without a second thought. Paula's and my story of rowing against the wind and being rescued by a jet skier paled compared to by Pastor Steve's rendition of Heather dancing off the rolling horse.

Friends who shared some of the trips remember Heather:
Facebook:
Kate Heins [Church friend from infancy who shared Bryce Canyon and Lake Powel trips]
Heather, you are a brilliant person and you have filled my life with amazing memories. You have been a person to look up too and you never failed to make a crowd laugh. You are like family to me and I miss you like crazy.
December 15, 2008 at 11:07am

Andrea Klemz Bagioli [Church friend since fifth grade]
Just missing you lots today. I still can't believe that you're really gone. I miss your honesty and hilariousness that could only be Heather. Love you Heathie G.
June 4, 2009 at 12:24am

Universal Studios, and Sea World got our attention on a trip to see grandma in California. We saw Zion National Park on the way home. Heather later would stop on her own at Zion National Park driving to or from Arizona State University. This early background probably was a stimulus for her to take linguistics students, some from foreign countries, to the southern national parks and show them interesting land forms they may not have otherwise experienced.

In November, 1993 our family made yet another trip to Pennsylvania to be with Grandparents and the Pittsburgh relatives for Thanksgiving. We have wonderful memories of sitting on the front porch with Aunt Karen, Uncle Rick, and Grandparents visiting and watching thunder storms or fire-flies.

December, 1993
Holiday Greetings
The Gross family says hello once again.
In this poem I'll tell you how we've been.

Dad is doin' fine; advancing at his job.
Leasing and financing all day long.

The Devil's Fingernail

Jogging and skiing keeps him in shape.
His help around the house sure is great

Mom has finished her Masters; she is finally through.
She still teaches 5th grade and my Sunday School class too.

My little sister, Emily, is in 4th grade.
She sings in school chorus, and enjoys friends she has made.

We're both in soccer and Girl Scouts too
It seems that we always have somethin' to do.
I'm taking flute lessons, and in band, use what I've been taught.
I'm now in confirmation, and learning a lot.
It's my first year at middle school-grades 7 through 9.
Seven periods and a locker are just fine.

Do not forget what Christmas is about!
Jesus' birth, love, and joy—without a doubt!
With love,
The Gross Family:
Denny, Alyce, Heather (author), and Emily

As stated in the Christmas letter, I finished a Master's Degree in Education in 1993. During the two years I worked on it, as well as teaching full-time, my girls learned to take on a little more responsibility around the house; and my dear husband planned and cooked dinner every Tuesday and Thursday night, as those were my late afternoons of classes after teaching all day. He said, "Just let me know what to fix."

My answer, "No, that's the hardest part. If you want to be of help, you plan it, shop for it, and fix it."

That man took a cooking class with a bunch of women, collected a little box full of casserole recipes, and we all enjoyed his Tuesday/Thursday meals with relish, lots of compliments, and never a complaint.

Much of the class work required that I write papers, and it must have been before spell-check. I started by asking Denny to be my proofreader, but he would get too involved in the content which took too much time. I was working at a fast pace and didn't really have time for much revising of content, thus I turned to my excellent speller who also had an aptitude for grammar, to do my proofreading. That would be my twelve-year-old. Heather was so careful and quick about spotting typos and other errors that I found her skills invaluable.

Also, at age twelve, to explain what inspired the subject matter for this 1994 Reflections poem, she wrote:
I think, if people accept differences and act in their own way, this world would be a better place.

<u>A Wish for Individuality</u>

People, inside, know and feel what is true.
When tasting the dream, the dream becomes a part of you.

To know yourself, your choices, your heart.
You, your dream, shall never part.

Open your mind, see who you are.
Follow your hopes, where? How long? How far?

Differences of people make personality.
Imperfections of character mark you as you be.

People try to act, to seem, as others.
Live with differences; love one another!

The last Reflections poem that I found of Heather's was written the following year, when she was in eighth grade.

THE GYMNAST
Expectancy clutches her stomach
As she waits for the signal,
The judge's raised hand.
The hand moves upward, and instantly
The gymnast's body is in perfect form,
Her arm raised her smile broad.
The gymnast is totally alone
As she turns to starting position.
She focuses everything on her destination
Across the floor,
Waiting for the music.
A nod of her head gives a little assurance.
She is off.
Her body goes through the once familiar,
and now, automatic motions.
Flipping and turning,
Speeding then slowing,
The gymnast dances gracefully,
Only to position herself
For another perilous pass.
This time she needs more speed.
She accelerates with the music,
Her heart beating faster.
A tight landing ends the pass.
She may dance once more.
Her body bends with the rhythm to a slow stop.
Her hands go up, ending her routine.
The gymnast is triumphant.

  The gymnastics experience was important to Heather. She started lessons when she was four years old. When she was eight, she wrote about doing a cartwheel and landing it with both feet on the beam. As a mom watching, it always made me cringe when the girls were on the beam. When she advanced to the point that her instructors wanted her to get out of school early for practice, we had a discussion and decided she had so many interests that she couldn't take that much time for gymnastics. Again from her eighth grade autobiography:

> *In fifth grade, I was good at gymnastics. I tested well enough to be in level five which is the first competition level. This required me to go to gymnastics three times a week for three hours, which I didn't want to do. I stopped taking gymnastics, but I kept practicing at home. I'm still good at tumbling.*
>
> *In eighth grade this year, I made advanced dance. I wanted to make it so much. I practiced the dance sequence we learned for tryouts over and over. I did tumbling in my own sequence, which I think helped me to make it.*

Going back a year to the summer after seventh grade, Heather went to a church confirmation camp in Colorado, June, 1994. It was called Ski Ranch and offered outdoor beauty and challenge. My friend, Barbara Condon, heard about campers lost in the mountains, on a television news broadcast in Denver. She had no idea until later that one of those lost was Heather. The poem *Golgotha,* at the end of Part One of this book, was inspired by this experience. Heather also wrote about it in her autobiography assignment, and Emily wrote about it in a fifth grade Hero Essay. Both are printed below.

<u>A Scary Experience</u>

In the summer of 1994, I went to a church camp called Sky Ranch near Fort Collins, Colorado. Ten people from my youth group went and many other Utahans came too. We went by bus. On the way there my youth leader fell out of the bus. It was parked at a gas station, and she stepped backwards and fell down the stairs and out of the bus. She hit her head on the curb and had to get stitches. She was alright. I should have recognized this as a bad omen, but I didn't.

Camp was fun. We stayed in little cabins. There were kids there from many places in the U.S. We sang songs and had lots of fun. I was enjoying myself very much until hike

The Devil's Fingernail

day. Hike day was a day where everyone went on a day-long hike. There were about five different hikes you could go on, and we had each signed up for one previously. I had wanted to go on the hardest and longest hike, Golgotha. No one else from my church wanted to go, but I signed up for it anyway. I was assigned a hike buddy named Sarah.

The hike started out well. First we followed a dirt road until we reached a lake. From there we had to hike through trees uphill. We stopped for lunch at a boulder field. After that we mostly climbed rocks to get to the top of Golgotha. We reached the top and took pictures of the great view. It was time to head back.

That was when the trouble started. One girl had a twisted ankle and another had a hurt knee. To make going back easier on them, the camp counselors and other adults on the hike reset their compasses so that we would not have to hike back over the boulder field. This was a big mistake. Later the two hurt girls and two counselors split away from us so they could go slower.

The reset compasses led us off course. We were supposed to get back to camp by 6:00 for dinner, but at about 5:00 we came out of the trees into a clearing. This was supposed to be where the lake was. We decided we had just gone too far to the left and needed to go back in the trees to the right to get back to camp. This didn't work. We ended up going through the rain and over fallen trees, tearing our raincoats, just to end up in the same clearing.

It was about 8:00 PM. Kids were getting scared and counselors were getting worried. A couple kids started crying. Back at camp they tried ringing the bell to lead us home. It was a comfort but no help since we couldn't follow the sound. We stopped hiking about 10:00. We were all tired, hungry, wet, cold, and needed to go to the bathroom. We sat in an open space in the trees. I had brought a lot of extra clothes and gave them out to kids who were wet or freezing. I also shared my water with many people. One girl who had stepped in the river while crossing it had hypothermia in her feet. I had to rub her feet for about two hours. The adults made sure we didn't fall asleep because our body temperatures might drop. We sang songs, prayed, and blew our whistles to stay awake and keep our hopes up. Two camp counselors found us around midnight by following our whistle blows. They couldn't lead us back though. They told us that Search and Rescue was on their way.

Around 1:30 AM a three-person Search and Rescue team found us. They had followed our whistle blows also. They found 22 kids and four adults. They led us back to camp in about an hour and a half. We were greeted with smiling and crying faces, warm clothes, a ton of food, and once stinky, now inviting, bathrooms.

The Search and Rescue team came back to camp and gave all of the kids who had been on the hike teddy bears. I named mine Golgotha.

I believe it was after the Colorado trip when Heather returned home she admonished me about being a bad mother. It had nothing to do with her getting lost in the mountains. She was mad that I sent her off without letting her shave her legs. She was so embarrassed because all the other girls had shaved legs. Also her hair was too short and she looked like a boy. I now realized I had a teenager.

May 1995   My Hero   by Emily Gross

My sister Heather is thirteen and in eighth grade. She enjoys soccer, skiing, swimming, gymnastics, dance, playing the flute, camping, reading, and school. In school she is a winner. In second grade Heather won fourth place in the school spelling bee. Since then she has won three school spelling bees. In sixth grade she also won her school geography bee. This year she went to the district spelling bee and got sixth place. She also got first place in the state for a future scenario story about prejudice. Her Future Problem Solving team won second place in the state bowl.

My sister acted heroically when she went away with her confirmation class to Colorado. She had decided to go on an all-day hike called Golgotha. Golgotha was the name of the mountain they were hiking up. Because her counselors' compasses were set wrong, they got lost. They tried to hike back, but ended up going in a circle. Finally they gave up and stopped walking. It had been raining, and some people were wet and freezing. My sister was wearing shorts, but still let others use all of her warm clothes. For two hours, my sister had to rub the feet of a girl who had hypothermia. A three-person Search and Rescue team found the group of 22 kids and four adults around 1 AM by following their whistle blows.

One day my sister was walking to school. She started walking across the crosswalk. She was almost to the school fence, when a car came around the second lane of parked cars and hit her. Heather went up in the air. She must have thought "I have to save my flute," which was in her hand. She kept her flute in the air so it wouldn't break. Heather landed on her backpack which cushioned her fall. She got up and started walking to school, because she had a test to take. People got out of their cars and made her lie down on a blanket by the side of the road. She called my mom on a car phone. My mom had to talk with the lady who hit Heather and a police officer. Heather got to go take her test, but she had to get a note from her principal that said she was hit by a car.

Another time my sister was babysitting two kids named Casey and Amy. They decided to bake some cookies. My sister put the cookies in the oven, and set the timer. She did not know it, but there was a rubber spatula in the oven. When she went to check on the cookies, the spatula was on fire. Casey got freaked and left. Heather asked Amy where the fire extinguisher was. Amy quickly got it and gave it to Heather. Heather put out the fire, but had to clean the whole kitchen because there was green dust from the fire extinguisher everywhere.

Heather is a great influence because she is wise, and smart at every subject in school. Heather is there if I need a friend or someone to talk to. She helps me with my homework and sticks up for me when I am negotiating with my parents.

My question to Heather about the oven fire was, "How could you leave a spatula in the oven?" I don't remember her explanation. She probably didn't have one. She thought she cleaned the whole kitchen, but I do remember Casey and Amy's mom telling me there was a huge mess to clean up from the extinguisher after that fire.

Alyce Gross

After Heather returned from her harrowing Ski Ranch Colorado trip, in that same month she experienced more thrills with white water river rafting with the Girl scouts in Jackson Hole, Wyoming. The following month our whole family took a Midwest trip. I wanted to show the girls my roots. We included Mt. Rushmore, the Mitchell Corn Palace, but the highlight was staying with my Godfather, Uncle Don Anderson and Aunt Lois, in Minnesota and visiting the farm house near Hutchinson, where I was born and spent my first five years of life. On the way home we went through Rocky Mountain National Park, Colorado, not knowing that some day Emily would be making her home in a valley with a view of those mountains. We spent the night in Steamboat Springs, where as a young adult, Heather would drive to visit her close friend and confidant since Junior high, Katie Gracia and Katie's future husband, Paul Dyson. Finally in Utah we stopped at Dinosaur Quarry before driving home. Heather included most of this on one of her traveling bookmarks.

More in Heather's words from the autobiography:
My Narrow Escape
One day in September I was walking to school. I was in eighth grade. It was 70's day at school, and I was wearing a stiff polyester outfit. I had big, itchy gauchos and long, leather boots on. The boots had high heels and were too big for my feet, but I was trying to run because I was late for school.

I reached the crosswalk. The two lanes of cars stopped for me, and I ran (or stumbled) across. I was almost to the school fence when a car came around the side of the second lane of parked cars and hit me. I went up in the air, just a little, thinking I had to save my flute which I was holding in my right hand. My backpack cushioned my fall. I also tried to decrease the impact by putting my left hand down behind me. My weird clothes saved the rest of me. My left hand had a little scrape, and my right leg hurt a little, but that was all, so I decided to get up and walk to school. Many people rushed out of their cars after seeing what had happened. They made me lie down with a blanket by the side of the

The Devil's Fingernail

road. I felt stupid lying there, especially in my weird clothes. I had a chemistry test first period that I didn't want to miss.

Someone called the paramedics. They came in an ambulance and a fire truck. I thought that was very unnecessary and was getting impatient sitting there when I should have been in school. A paramedic examined me. The paramedics wanted to take me to the hospital, but I convinced them I was fine. I called my mom at work on a lady's car phone. I told her I was hit by a car, and she said, "You're kidding!" I also told her I was fine. Then she talked to a police officer.

My mom arrived. I felt better. She had to talk with a policeman and the lady who hit me. Principal Reid came out and walked me and my weird clothes back to school. He got me a band aid for my hand and an excuse note that said I had been hit by a car.

I walked into chemistry class and handed Mr. Burton the note. He looked up at me with wide eyes and said, "What?!" He asked if I was alright and if I wanted to take the test. I did. The rest of the day was normal.

Mom's input: It was normal except that she felt important and noticed because some kids in the hall, with their junior high brains, congratulated her—"Way to get hit by a car, Heather!"

She also shared with me that she was self conscious around the adult rescuers, because she was wearing boots and gauchos with a matching vest that I had purchased in London in the mid 1970's. She felt she had to explain why she was dressed differently—another teenage moment.

Learning my child was hit by a car and lost in the night on the Golgotha hike should have scared me to death, but by the time I heard about both I was first told that she was not hurt. That made all the difference. I thanked God and decided she had a guardian angel like her father's

[My husband, Denny, in his younger years, had been in numerous car and motorcycle accidents and came out almost unscathed. In his more recent history he fell through the rafters of a roof he was building for his pontoon boat. I rushed out to see what the commotion was. The wind had been knocked out of him, but he wasn't permanently harmed. When I realized this, I joked with him saying, "You have the best guardian angel, but I think he's done. There are feathers all over, and he's standing there with a dented halo and his hands on his hips, saying, 'I quit!' "]

The flute Heather saved while being hit by a car reminded me that taking flute lessons was a part of her education.

> From her Sterling Scholar portfolio:
> I have taken private lessons for seven years and participated in the school symphonic band for four years. Playing the flute has taught me to appreciate music. I did well in the Region Solo & Ensemble competition in tenth grade. I have gained self assurance in that I am not afraid to play in front of an audience. This confidence is a quality that will help me become a better leader.

She began playing in church on Christmas Eve, at a candlelight service, starting in 1994, and continued for many years. The professional organist, David Chamberlin, and oboe player for Ballet West, Susan Swidnicki, both played at her funeral. They had accompanied and been very kind to Heather during her flute performances at church. Heather even played it at her cousin Audree's wedding in July of 1995. Her private flute teacher wrote the following.

On-line Obituary Response: legacy.com
December 18, 2008
I had the great pleasure of being a teacher of Heather's. And although I haven't seen her in maybe ten years or so, I still remember her fondly. She was determined, smart, funny, charming, and one of the nicest people I have ever known. I was very proud to have her as a student, and very proud to see the woman she became.
I believe people are measured by the positive, lasting, meaningful impact they have on those around them. By that

The Devil's Fingernail

measure, Heather was one of the best.
        I would like to express my profound sympathy to Heather's parents, Alyce and Dennis, her sister Emily, and to her many friends around the world. I am so, so sorry for your loss. Thank you, Heather. I'll always remember your smile, and that funny little growl you did when you couldn't get something juuuuust right. Whenever I play Bach, I'll think of you. Rest in peace. Kathy Larson

When Heather was fourteen:
Greetings! Christmas 1995

The holidays are drawing near.
Time for the Grosses to spread good cheer.
Here in Utah we're doing fine,
Though the weather's not too alpine.
Eager to ski, we await the snow,
To make the Christmas spirit grow.

Dad's new sport is indoor soccer.
As goalie he's become a great shot-blocker.
Dad broke a few ribs; he plays worry-free.
This year our lights were put up by dad and me.
He was successful in his antelope hunt.
Though next hunting season he hopes for a cold, front.
Last winter, skiing, Dad fractured his hip.
But it didn't slow him down in his church stewardship.

Mom's still enjoys teaching students in fifth grade.
It's amazing her blond hair still hasn't grayed.
With Christmas coming, Mom's directing us all,
As we trim the tree and deck the hall.
She gets us to church every week.
While buying gifts, Mom uses her quick shopping technique.
Dealing with me has given her some stress.
But, Emily's not a teenager, yet thank goodness!

Alyce Gross

At soccer Emily has become a star.
To prove this she has many a scar.
Like her Dad, she's best at goalie, can take a blow.
Emily has jammed a finger and broken a toe.
Her artistic talent gets better every day.
She enjoys drawing as this letter displays.
Emily dearly loves Samantha her rat.
For her, she has built a tri-level habitat.

I'm a teenager. What can I say?
My parents still haven't given me away.
Like Dad and Em, I play soccer too.
Dance and flute, I also do.

I'm getting disgusted with all of this rhyme.
So, let me just list where we spent summertime:

Luther Heights Camp, ID (just me)
Washington, D.C. (Mom and girls with Aunt Karen)
Pittsburgh, PA (all at Grandparents')
Niagara Falls, NY and Canada
Vermont, New Hampshire, Maine
Boston and Cape Cod
Montana River rafting (me with Girl Scouts)
Montana (Audree & Colin's wedding)
Templeton, CA (Mom's HS reunion)
Lake Powell, UT (all of us with Emerys)

The family picture shows my Confirmation.
We hope God's Gifts are part of your Christmas Celebration!
Love,

Denny, Alyce, Heather (author), Emily (illustrator)

The Devil's Fingernail

Facebook:
Liselle Fitzgerald
I remember the times playing soccer. I know you're watching over all of us and your family. At least you were doing something that you loved, when you left this world!
December 15, 2008 at 12:06pm

On-line Obituary Response: legacy.com
December 18, 2008
I had the opportunity of teaching Heather in my ninth grade Honors English and Honors Geography classes. She was a great addition to our class and left a footprint on my life. She was a humanitarian for her fellow classmates; she cared deeply about others. She made positive contributions both academically and socially. My prayers are with her family. She will be missed.
Kathy Anderson (Salt Lake City)

Facebook
Amy Lee Damron Bodell [A junior high school friend]
I'll always remember our Future Problem Solving days...you were so much fun and I loved being around you.
December 15, 2008 at 11:23am

Two excellent teachers, Jeanne Weber and Kathy

Anderson, were coaches for Future Problem Solving Scenario writing, in a state-level competition, in which Heather won first place in eighth grade and second place in ninth grade. (They are short stories that I did not include in this book.) These eighth and ninth grade Honors English teachers did a wonderful job of teaching many types of writing. They had their students keep final drafts in plastic spine-bound books. The books keep everything together and are easy to store and save. Because of this, I'm able to share some of Heather's middle school writing. I've been using <u>Heather's Highlights,</u> her autobiography and now I'm choosing from <u>Keeping Rhythm with the Wind</u> (a poetry collection). Her teachers' professional and loving guidance had far reaching effects for Heather and for me.

WAVE AND DAY
Each new wave that touches the beach
*Is like each **new day** that life will teach.*
A wave approaches then marks the land.
The sign slowly sinks from the surface of the sand.
The next mark veils the last one made.
But, from beneath the face of the shore, it will not fade.
Just like each day that one lives through,
*There is always **change**, something new.*
And to one's life each day will give
Lessons through which one learns to live.

I AM PREJUDICE

i am prejudice
    i pierce pride
        i teach hate

i banish caring and acceptance
    even in places
        where love was once ruler

The Devil's Fingernail

i poison minds
      injure the heart
           and weaken the soul

i work through
      the ignorant
           and the scared

i cause indifference
      then arrogance
           then hate

i create false opinions of others
      based on appearance
           ideas and ways

i live in all people
      but love can prevail
           over me

i am prejudice
      i pierce pride
           i teach hate   Heather Gross

Travel is fatal to prejudice. Mark Twain

I also found this gem from tenth grade, written when Heather was fifteen:

English   Heather Gross
Period 2   November 27, 1996
<u>*My Own Rhythm*</u>
My best friend lives at my house, my sister.
A family bound by love,
Each day, a reminder.
Thriving on fun and running on laughs,

Alyce Gross

Knowing humor is knowing life.
A contrast, my Christian faith provides me with peace,
Creating reverence in a developing spirit.
Like the calming perfection of a rainbow after a storm,
Every color present
A love for all seasons, the best is the one blanketed in white,
Cool and clean, the crisp smell of a recent snow.
On vacation at Grand Targhee, snow to ski on and roll in,
Flakes jumping and twirling, breaking free.
Like the way I dance with the song in my head,
Music, not just sounds, flowing from my flute.
I will play until I find my own rhythm.

Holiday Greetings '96
Dad started a new business; K&G is its name.
Now he's co-owner, but the leasing part's the same.
Mom enjoys teaching, just as before.
With nicer kids this year, she likes it even more.

Seventh and tenth grades are fun for Emily and me,
And of course, we anxiously wait to ski.
Our lives are busy with homework and friends,
But on each other, we still can depend.

Over Thanksgiving our family hiked in Capitol Reef.
There we took our Christmas picture, to Mom's great relief.

So, Merry Christmas to all near and far,
And remember the wise men, follow the star.
Peace: Denny, Alyce, Heather (Poet), & Emily Gross

The Devil's Fingernail

Capitol Reef

At Emily's insistence the girls in the family went to the Utah Shakespearean Festival, in Ceder City, Utah, July, 1996. She had been in the play <u>Comedy of Errors</u> in sixth grade and wanted to see it. It was so much fun to have Emily know more about something than her big sister. All three of us loved the experience and felt so sophisticated that we went again in 1997. Sophistication was not always a word that could describe our girls.

Service Projects

I so appreciate Heather's Church Youth Group leaders, Nettie Priet and Heather LeSieur and her Girl Scout leader, Marsha Gale, for working and planning along with the kids on many worthwhile projects and trips.

In Heather's words:
I like doing things with my church youth group. We do service and fun activities. Some service things we've done are feeding the homeless, and sorting food at the Utah Food Bank.

Alyce Gross

This is Heather writing in her Foreign Languages Sterling Scholar Portfolio about service. There is more to come about the New Orleans trip, including a policeman on a horse. Heather seems to have left it out of her portfolio.

My church has been wonderful in providing opportunities for exciting community work. Twice, I have participated in a long weekend project which we do in the summer. It's called the Urban Plunge and involves many service activities. We collect cans and other various food items from the neighborhoods near our church and then deliver and sort them for the Utah Foodbank. We also work at the homeless shelter, either playing and doing crafts with the children or helping to clean areas like the mess hall and closets. I learned to use a caulking gun in working for Habitat for Humanity. The elderly people in our congregation often need help in keeping their yards or homes clean, so we have done that as well. What's awesome about the Urban Plunge is that we sleep at the church and can't go home for three nights. It's like camp, but the whole time involves service.

I have also done service with Girl Scouts, in which I was involved from the first through the ninth grades. In ninth grade, we visited an elderly home during Christmas. I played the flute in a duet with my friend. My troop also earned our Silver Awards that year. It was a project which we all did together. First, we typed and passed out fliers to the homes in our neighborhoods. The fliers asked for blankets, food, and any hygiene items or clothes that battered and abused women with their children might need. We next returned to those homes about a week later to collect the items and then deliver them to the Marillac House. This is a place where women and their children, needing shelter from abusive husbands and fathers, can stay.

In July of 1997, my church youth group attended a week-long national Lutheran youth gathering in New Orleans.

The Devil's Fingernail

Each day was filled with spiritual growth and group bonding. I never felt closer to my church friends than during that week. One entire day was devoted to a service project. Our particular assignment on that day was to pick up litter in "Little Algiers," a poor part of town across the Mississippi River. We spent many hours under the sun cleaning up the neighborhood. By the end of the day we felt exhausted but satisfied. It was a cultural experience; we were a bunch of white Lutheran kids from Salt Lake City meeting African American Louisiana natives. They talked to us and seemed thankful for the work we were doing. I'll never forget that day, (especially the way I smelled afterwards!).

I am proud to have been an active member of the National Junior Honor Society and the National Honor Society since seventh grade. Through NHS I have participated willingly in numerous service projects including can drives, tutoring, and the Festival of Trees. In NHS, I am associating with other students who understand the importance of service and who are dedicated to using their talents to serve others.

As a part of the experience at the New Orleans youth gathering, participants were to write a story in first person. Following is Heather's story:

I was ready for some good old Rocky Mountain dry air. We had been walking for what seemed an eternity, through the heat and humidity of New Orleans. I felt sticky and sweaty, as I had felt the entire day, from the moment after stepping out of the hotel door in to the street. All I wanted to do was sit down. Suddenly there it was—my oasis in the desert—the fountain. It was pretty big, circular in shape, and perfect for sitting on the side and soaking my feet. Of course, this should have been enough for me, but I became restless and began to wade in the water. Before long, I found myself doing handstands and splashing my friends. I was then banished from the fountain by a nearby policeman atop a horse. This little episode doesn't seem like much, but in a way it represents my entire experience in New Orleans. During the fast-passing week, I spent there, I felt free and refreshed, closer to God, in fellowship with 37,000 kids just like me.

[Those who really knew Heather would not be surprised at all by handstands in a fountain.]

In November, Heather's cousin, Jay Bates, taught us a game using limericks while we were at our Thanksgiving family gathering at Uncle Allan and Aunt Bev's house in Kalispell, Montana. That was the inspiration for the format of the following poem:

The Devil's Fingernail

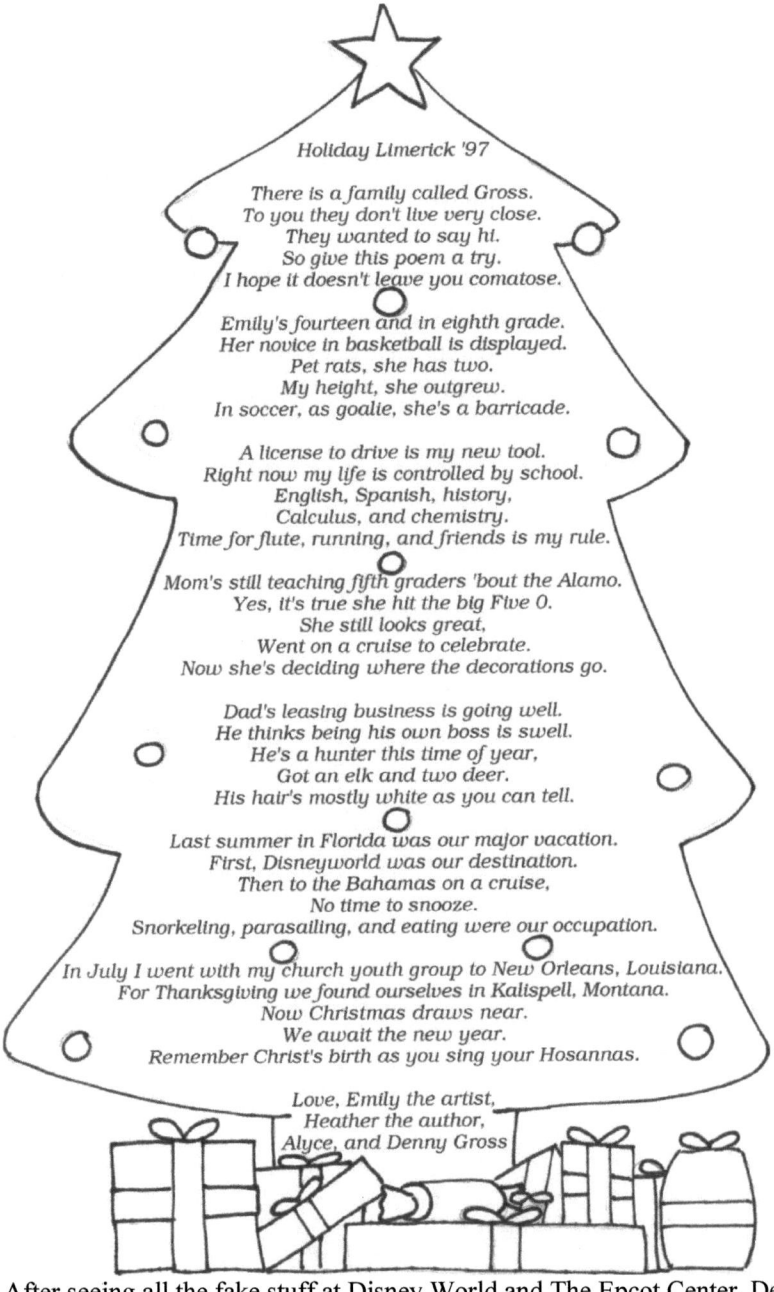

Holiday Limerick '97

There is a family called Gross.
To you they don't live very close.
They wanted to say hi.
So give this poem a try.
I hope it doesn't leave you comatose.

Emily's fourteen and in eighth grade.
Her novice in basketball is displayed.
Pet rats, she has two.
My height, she outgrew.
In soccer, as goalie, she's a barricade.

A license to drive is my new tool.
Right now my life is controlled by school.
English, Spanish, history,
Calculus, and chemistry.
Time for flute, running, and friends is my rule.

Mom's still teaching fifth graders 'bout the Alamo.
Yes, it's true she hit the big Five 0.
She still looks great.
Went on a cruise to celebrate.
Now she's deciding where the decorations go.

Dad's leasing business is going well.
He thinks being his own boss is swell.
He's a hunter this time of year,
Got an elk and two deer.
His hair's mostly white as you can tell.

Last summer in Florida was our major vacation.
First, Disneyworld was our destination.
Then to the Bahamas on a cruise,
No time to snooze.
Snorkeling, parasailing, and eating were our occupation.

In July I went with my church youth group to New Orleans, Louisiana.
For Thanksgiving we found ourselves in Kalispell, Montana.
Now Christmas draws near.
We await the new year.
Remember Christ's birth as you sing your Hosannas.

Love, Emily the artist,
Heather the author,
Alyce, and Denny Gross

After seeing all the fake stuff at Disney World and The Epcot Center, Denny and I wanted our girls to see some real castles in Germany, where he and I first met and dated; so in July of 1998, we had a family trip of a life time.

December, 1998
It's another Gross greeting. Here we go.
Rhymy rhymy. Ho ho ho.

In July, we all went to Germany, Austria, Switzerland, and France.
Next, the girls went to London for the chance

To go shopping and see Cats, Les Mis, and Miss Saigon.
There, Emily's search for Doc Martens became a marathon

Until we found the right color; that was a relief.
Now let's get back to the German motif.

We arrived in Frankfurt, where we rented a V W Passat.
Driving fast on the autobahn, Dad was a speedy hotshot.

In Wurzburg, we visited Mom's old residence.
In Bamberg, we saw where Dad's days were spent.

Dad's K & G Leasing job is the same.
Hunting and now karate are his game.

Mom and the fifth grade still are one.
She wants my college decision to be done.

Scholarship money is Mom and Dad's motivation.
My main concern is a non-Utah location.

Emily's a great student. She has straight A's.
For her art abilities, she receives much praise.

Indoor soccer still is her thing.
Her Confirmation at church will be this spring.

I'm a National Merit and Foreign Language Sterling Scholar.
In June, I'll wear a graduation collar.

I lettered in Cross Country in a California race.
Any opportunity for fun, I always embrace.

This is my last rhymer. Next year I'll be away.

The Devil's Fingernail

Remember the hope that Jesus brought the First Christmas Day.

Love, The Grosses: Denny, Alyce, Heather (poet), and Emily (artist)

December, 1998

It's another Gross greeting. Here we go.
Rhymy rhymy. Ho ho ho.

In July, we all went to Germany, Austria, Switzerland, and France.
Next, the girls went to London for the chance

To go shopping and see Cats, Les Mis, and Miss Saigon.
There, Emily's search for Doc Martens became a marathon

Until we found the right color; that was a relief.
Now let's get back to the German motif.

We arrived in Frankfurt, where we rented a VW Passat.
Driving fast on the autobahn, Dad was a speedy hot shot.

In Würzburg, we visited Mom's old residence.
In Bamberg, we saw where Dad's days were spent.

Dad's K & G Leasing job is the same.
Hunting and now karate are his game.

Mom and the fifth grade still are one.
She wants my college decision to be done.

Scholarship money is Mom and Dad's motivation.
My main concern is a non-Utah location.

Emily's a great student. She has straight A's.
For her art abilities, she receives much praise.

Indoor soccer still is her thing.
Her Confirmation at church will be this spring.

I'm a National Merit and Foreign Language Sterling Scholar.
In June, I'll wear a graduation collar.

I lettered in Cross Country in a California race.
Any opportunity for fun, I always embrace.

This is my last rhymer. Next year I'll be away.
Remember the hope that Jesus brought the
First Christmas Day.

Love, The Grosses: Denny, Alyce,
Heather (poet), and Emily (artist)

On-line Obituary Responses: legacy.com
December 19, 2008
Heather was one of my closest friends while attending Butler Middle and Brighton High School. I still can't believe she's gone and so wish I would've kept in better contact. She had a contagious laugh and a quick smile. She is one of the smartest people I've known and by far the best study partner I have ever had. From Creative Pursuits to Future Problem Solving, to AP Chemistry, she helped me survive many classes and projects.

She was never a rival, always a support. She always had a knack for lightening up a tense moment. I was so happy when she joined the cross country team and we had another common goal. She will be greatly missed, but leaves behind only happy memories.
Janet Ogilvie Stapleton (Saratoga Springs, UT)

Heather, with her cross country team, went to Redfish Lake, Idaho during the summer.

Facebook:
T.R. Brooks [HS cross country friend]
Heather I'll miss you, and your synchronized swimming at Redfish Lake.
December 15, 2008 at 7:59am

    The summer before Heather started Brighton High School (a three-year public school with around 1,500 students) she bravely tried out first for the very competitive girls' soccer team, but she didn't make it. She did play on other competitive soccer teams. Next she tried out for cheerleader and didn't make that either. Both experiences saddened her, but didn't stop her. Track and cross country would accept everyone, so that is where she ended up. She wrote about what it meant to her in her Sterling Scholar portfolio:
    I love being a member of Brighton's cross country team. My coach is Mr. Steve Young, but I know him better as Señor Joven. He is a great influence in my life and has helped me to love running almost to the extent that he does. Our conversations on the track are conducted only in Spanish. I am practicing the language I love while running with great athletes. Our team is the true portrayal of Bengal Pride. It seems that to be good runner, one has to also be a good student, because these accomplishments come only with hard work and dedication. Our team has a special bond that our coach has described as the strongest he has ever been a part of. Spending time together makes people grow close, but running miles together links them closer. Very recently, we

The Devil's Fingernail

completed a 24-hour runathon as a fundraiser for our team to go to a national race in California. I ran eight miles first and then one to five mile segments for the rest of the night and into the next day. I ran a total of thirty miles, earning almost $300 for the team because the pledges we collected were on a per-mile basis. I am proud to be a member of such a devoted team in a sport that requires raw endurance.

Her coach and Spanish teacher also wrote about her:
Re: Heather Gross, Sterling Scholar Candidate
    Heather's academic achievements speak for themselves—they shine off her resume. I have known Heather as her teacher and coach for two and a half years and would like to address what sets her apart.
    First, Heather has excelled in Spanish without the benefit of having lived abroad. Heather has come to her exceptional success in Spanish through sheer hard work. There is not a road trip (during Fall X-C and Spring Track) where she does not spend 90% of the ride pouring through her schoolwork. I wear two hats in my relationship with Heather, and sometimes feel guilty speaking with her in English (as coach), as my "teacher" relationship with Heather—in and out of class—has been exclusively in Spanish for nearly three years. She revels in it! Some of my fondest memories are of Spanish conversations with Heather while running together during a workout.
    Heather is a student-athlete in the truest sense. Heather does not cross the finish line first in races. However, she basks in the only true measure of athletic achievement: measurable self-improvement. A hard earned PR (personal record) in a 3-mile race is as much a victory as first place in the region meet.
    Along with her intelligence and drive, Heather is very gregarious. She is a tremendously positive social influence in class and amongst her teammates. She has been a valued tutor for our Spanish program throughout high school. Additionally, her work last summer as a bilingual, long distance operator showed her linguistic mettle in the most demanding circumstance—over the phone.
    Heather is keen, warm, persistent, and an eminently

worthy candidate for Sterling Scholar.
Sincerely,
Steven R. Young
Spanish AP Teacher
Head Track + Cross Country Coach

Heather's mom again:
    In my thirty-three years of teaching public school, I would sometimes have students who were very intelligent but who really didn't work hard. A few would use the, "It's boring" excuse; but what they really meant was, "This is too much work." In a very few of the worst cases, their parents would back them. I patiently explained to parents how important it was for students to be responsible about completing school work and asked them, "If you were hiring someone for a job, would you hire the responsible, hard worker, or a very intelligent person who wasn't willing to put much effort into difficult projects?" Usually the parents could see my case. A wise grandmother, Judy Patten, once said that when her grandchildren tried to use the boring excuse, she would answer with, "Only boring people get bored." I worked at keeping my classes lively and seldom heard, "This is boring." from students, but I did use that grandmother's quote a few times in my teaching. Heather was never bored with school, and she seemed to thrive on hard work rather than just coasting on her abilities.

More from her Sterling Scholar portfolio:
December 2, 1998
Recommendation for Heather Gross
    It is a great pleasure for me to recommend Heather Gross as one of the finest students I have taught in my class in the last fifteen years. Heather was in my Advanced Placement American History class last year where she showed extremely mature academic skills in many areas. Heather has developed exceptional analysis skills when faced with difficult historical problems. She has a talent for seeing through right to the heart of the argument, and for being able to see clearly both sides of an issue. In terms of writing skills, Heather expresses

herself with clarity and conviction. Having Heather in class was a rewarding experience because she was the consummate student. Her class schedule was the most demanding and difficult of any AP student I taught, and yet her work was always well thought out, creative, and of the highest quality. Heather's academic recognitions are strong evidence of her unusual talents, from her National Merit score, to her being named Academic All-State in Cross Country.

As impressive as Heather is academically, her personal qualities are her greatest asset. She shows tremendous respect for her teachers and other students. She was an outstanding peer tutor and cooperative learner in my class. She showed a generosity of spirit as she helped other students gain success in their AP American History studies. Because of this, other students enjoyed being involved in class work with Heather, rather than feeling jealous of her advanced academic talents. Notwithstanding her demanding academic obligations, Heather has impressed me by the degree of her outside activities in athletics and community service. I have great trust in and admiration for Heather and in her future as she moves on to benefit the community to an even greater degree. I recommend her as an exceptional student and young person who represents everything good about the Sterling Scholar program.

Sincerely,
Kristie T. Pitts Brighton High School

Heather did earn Foreign Language Sterling Scholar at Brighton High School, but not at the state level.

The summer before college, Heather worked for Dr. Steve White, as an Assistant Scientist at the University of Utah in Anti-Epilepsy Drug Development. She injected frog oocytes with DNA subunits and tested samples with drugs in development for treating epilepsy. She had that on her first résumé when applying for a waitress job during college. She was laughing, like only Heather could, when she told us what the restaurant manager asked, "So, did the frogs have epilepsy or what?"

College

Because Heather was a National Merit Scholar finalist, Arizona State University, and two other colleges, offered her scholarships, to their Honors Programs. We visited ASU in February when the weather was beautiful. She was offered close to a full-ride scholarship, and we couldn't pass it up. Although we've enjoyed living in Utah, as did our girls, we had always planned that our daughters would attend college out of state; feeling it would be an important part of their education, to live where there wasn't a dominate religion.

Two milestones that happened before she started college: Sweet Grandma Dot Aronson died April 25, 1999. Heather had mono at the time, causing her to miss the funeral. Our family did get to Pittsburgh in July that year. We didn't know that it would be the last time Heather and Emily would spend with Grandma and Grandpa Gross.

1999 Gross Holiday Greetings

It turns out that last year's greeting wasn't my last.
I'm once again rhyming the Gross newscast.

Dad is still leasing with K&G.
Real Estate also now has him as an employee.

He went deer hunting this fall with much luck.
This season he shot and brought home a buck.

Dad put down a new Pergo floor that's scuff-proof.
He and Mom worked together to re-shingle the roof.

Mom is forever faithful to the fifth grade.
Unlike Dad, her hair still hasn't lightened in shade.

This year, Mom holds a church council position.
She continues her Lois Circle and Book Club tradition.

The Devil's Fingernail

Emily works, making salsa in Produce at The Store.
She loves Brighton High School, where she's a sophomore.

Emily's driving a stick shift pretty well, I must say.
For her artwork, she'll be famous someday.

For college, I did leave Utah; I got out of the bubble.
I'm at Arizona State University where my major is double.

I'm studying Spanish and Pre-pharmacy.
I enjoy life in the dorm, but miss my family.

Right now I'm living near Phoenix in Tempe, Arizona.
Someday I'll be a pharmacist, perhaps in Barcelona.

This Christmas Season, have a wonderful time.
Know that Jesus' birth is the reason for this rhyme.

Love, The Grosses: Denny, Alyce,
Heather (poet), and Emily (artist)

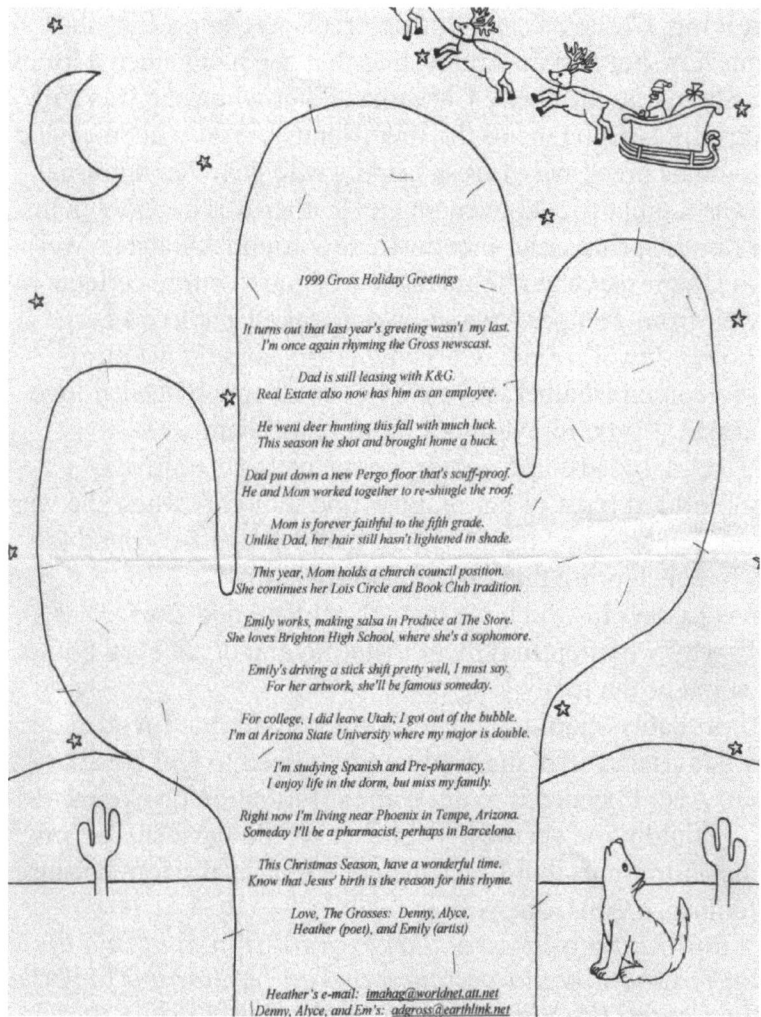

Christmas letters really never do tell the whole story. Much of the first year at Arizona State University, Heather was battling a deep depression that was far more serious than Denny and I realized. We encouraged her to get help at the counseling center, but in retrospect we know we should have made appointments to go with her for help. Out of concern both of us, on separate occasions, visited her in the fall. She came home for

Thanksgiving, Christmas and Spring break. We knew that she was homesick, hot and miserable, and that she had gained a lot of weight. She wrote the above Christmas letter when she was still in a deep depression. One of the few friends she saw in Salt Lake that Christmas break was Teresa Lopez, who gave her a journal. Teresa was a great friend, even when Heather was at a low point. It wasn't until spring, after meeting a new friend Juliana (Jewel) Kling, in Chemistry class; that Heather began to enjoy college life. Jewel, from Tempe, Arizona, would take Heather to her family home. Jewel's mom, Christine Kling, and the whole family welcomed Heather and gave her some much needed love and kindness. I'll be forever grateful to all of them.

I've included some quotes from Heather's journals. Initially I left out most of her feelings and thoughts when she was depressed, but as stated before, I was making Heather sound too perfect. In considering this I had to compare my book to Christmas Letters in which we just tell all the good stuff. That's probably why we often find them irritating and don't even bother to read some of the really long ones.

I probably shouldn't have snooped at all; but I read Heather's journals, after she died, out of a need to feel close to her again. Also I needed it to get some information on events and dates so I could write accurately. I never would have shared any of Heather's Journals, but I feel she gave me permission, because on September 5, 2003, she wrote:

I am thinking that I could do great things in this life and that maybe I would be remembered by many after I die and that maybe this diary would be read or studied or published or not. Ha ha ☺

More than five years later in an On-line Obituary Response: legacy.com, Teresa wrote:
December 21, 2008
Heather's spirit survives through every ones' smiles, crazy laughter, and spasmodic dancing. She touched everyone she met, she was so unique. The language and numbers always had to be precise. Her heart was so full that it finally burst. In every

memory, remember her wild spirit. It is that wild spirit that proves God exists. She now lives in all of us because that soul couldn't be contained by this Earth. In my memories she will always have that crazy laugh and that never-ending glow. TREE (SLC)

Tree is Teresa Lopez who called me from the hospital, in January, 2010, on the day her daughter was born, to let me know that she named her baby Kennedy *Heather*. Teresa was in Heather's Kindergarten class. They became fast friends and remained so to the end. Now Teresa is studying to be a social worker. That seems a good fit, because the journal she gave Heather served as a place for Heather to release some of her darkest feelings. Teresa seemed to know Heather needed that.

From Heather's Journal:
[This was very painful for me, her mother, to read and reread to decide what to include. I feel comfort in knowing she will never be this depressed again.]
January 10, 2000
. . . I need a change, a lot of changes. I haven't spent time writing anything personal since last summer. This journal, a Christmas gift from Teresa, is my fresh start. I hope to write often. I will. Teresa is one of the only friends I've really kept since high school. . . . Anyway, I'm depressed. I gained at least twenty pounds the first two months of college and haven't lost it. I don't even feel like me anymore. I've lost my will to accomplish things. A few nights ago I woke up after a nightmare and a dream. The nightmare was about some ghost girl who lost her love. The dream was a re-lived high school moment. Mrs.C. was congratulating me and of course, Greg, on writing good essays. School used to be my first source of pride. I got two B's and three A's my first semester at ASU. That should be good, but not for me. In college I probably put about one-fourth of the effort that I put into academics in high school. I've procrastinated terribly on papers. That night when I woke up I decided that I have an un-proud heart. I'm

ashamed of my fat body. I'm not smart and school-driven. I'm not happy and friendly. I don't even notice boys, because I know they won't look at me. I'm obviously not running. I'm just blah. For me, "Life be not proud." I have to change. I need to feel like the old Heather. If I don't have a boy, at least I have me. I have a family that loves me. We're going to Grand Targhee in three days. Then I go back to school. It will be better this semester.

January 23, 2000

I'm in Arizona. Grand Targhee was fun. Patty [Patrick Emery] will always be my good friend. I haven't changed. I haven't even run yet while I've been here. Friday night I went out to dinner at Saki's on Mill Street with Megan Ream. I'm going to live with her next year in Best C, the honors dorms. I'm moving down a step to community bathrooms. It's Sunday morning. I didn't go to church because I'm too lazy. I've been in this damn dorm room since yesterday afternoon after I got back from a service project at the Salvation Army. I washed windows and moved dirt. That's the only thing I've done that I'm proud of. I hate my outlook on life. I have probably played Free Cell on my computer more than I have been in class since I got here Monday night. When we were at the airport, Dad said, "I hope you don't play a lot of Solitaire on this thing."

I said, "No." Duh, that's all I do. I shower, go to class, eat alone in the cafeteria, watch TV, and play retarded games on my computer. If I focus long enough on my feelings of self-pity I can make myself cry. My whole life, I have never been this unmotivated or pathetic. I have no friends here because I don't try to make any. . . . Megan Ream got a 4.0. I got a 3.57. I am proud of nothing about myself. I wish so much that it were a year ago. I would be skinny from having the flu. I would be in high school with good grades. . . . I would have my family and my room. I would have my sister. I would feel like me.

February 29, 2000

Alyce Gross

It's 12:25 AM and really March 1st, but February 29th only happens once every 1,461 days, so I decided to write it. Anyway that last entry was pretty depressing, huh? I just read it, and now I'm crying. I miss being happy to be me. I miss knowing that I can look cute in clothes and planning my outfits because people might actually look at me and think I'm cute. I can't even picture myself as a sad wasted away lonely girl in a corner, because I'm too big. I'd be a big blob in the corner. I'm going home in a week and a half, and I'm just as fat as ever. My family thinks I've been running a lot and losing weight. I did that for about a week and then lost all motivation.

I have these damn inspirational pictures on the wall. They're from my dad from a calendar. They're obviously not working. I've stopped crying. My calendar says there's a pharmacy school's open house thing at the Memorial Union tomorrow. I will look nice and go to it. Afterward I will do homework. I will not eat dessert in the cafeteria. I will stop feeling sorry for myself. . . .One of these inspirational things says, "Reflection: Your vision will become clear only when you can look into your own heart." My heart says I need to pray, to sleep, and to love myself. Thank you, God, for the strength to look into my own heart. Help me make it proud. Be with my mom, my dad, my sister, and me. Help me to live today in the name of the Father, the Son, and the Holy Spirit. Amen

April 4, 2000
Spring Break (March 10-19) was fun. I went skiing twice and ran three times. I saw Katie Gracia. . . . I went to dinner and lunch with Teresa. Greg called and we hung out. . . . I've been running regularly since I got back here. . . . Today I ate dinner with Sarah D. She was in my dance class and lives on my floor. I like her. I hope I'll like Megan Ream next year. Last Saturday I went with Juliana from my Chemistry class to a frat party. I had five beers and danced with Ra-shon most of the night. . . . It was fun. I was doing what you're supposed to do in college. Today

there was a note on our white board on the door. Someone wrote, "I want you, Heather. Secret Admir" It would have been nice if he had written out admirer, but at least someone was thinking of me. . . . I'm getting skinnier from running, and I actually felt cute today. ☺ I signed up to run the 1500m and the 800m in the ASU intramural track meet on April 26 and 27, so I have to be in shape and ready to race by then. I also need to feel pretty ok in shorts. I'm doing well in classes. I'll get all A's and probably a B in Honors Human Event. I could try for an A though. Well, this is me happier saying goodnight.

[She did end up with all A's the second semester. Her dad and I wanted Heather to be happy and didn't care if she got all A's, but we knew Heather cared.]

April 11, 2000

It's 12:30 AM on Tuesday. I'm not in a bad mood, but I didn't have a very productive day. I have to be careful. Too many of those really make me depressed. My alarm is set to run in the morning since I didn't today. I hope I do it. I went to my three classes, ate, TV, napped, went to Juliana's dorm to type our chem lab, ate in cafeteria with Sarah, TV, free cell, minesweeper, more food, and I'm going to read now. I'm almost cheerful at the prospect of a good new day. I hope living with Megan next year is good. . . . Change will be good for me.

I should go this Wednesday to the Lenten service. I should run Tuesday and Wednesday morning at least. Then I could go to church Wednesday night and Spanish group Thursday night.

I miss my family. I've changed a lot this year. I'm beginning to understand that it hasn't been all bad. ☺

May 12, 2000

Well, I've completed my first year of college. The nearer the end came, the more fun it got. I hung out with Jewel, Lauren, Tracy, Emi, Amanda, Jessica, and Cynthia a lot. Parents came to my dorm yesterday to check me out. Then they met Jewel at the ASU Bookstore. We U-Hauled all my stuff, and spent the night in Flagstaff, after stopping in Glendale Midwestern University to learn about their Pharm-D program. Today we drove to the Grand Canyon, went to the IMAX theatre, hiked, ate, hot tubbed, and now I'm in bed. . . . I'm excited to see people at home, and I'll be excited to go back to ASU too! ☺

That summer at home, Heather worked at NWB—Northwest Bioanalytical. She did clerical work and lab testing using L C (liguid chromatography).

When Heather was a sophomore in college she moved to the Honor's Dorms. She was happy with her kind and caring roommate, Megan Reem, but she spent most of her time with the Itros.

Taken from her Journal:
Room 302, Jewel and Lauren's room, is where we always are, and where we, just last Wednesday, December 13th, gave each other presents, with Andy too. The girls are Tracy Doyle (Titro), Juliana Kling (Jitro), Lauren Yelen (Litro) and me—Hitro. The Itros are why I love this year and why I can say that college is some of the best times of my life.

I think it was Heather who named the four the Itros. They were/are all brilliant, funny, and talented. I felt so bad for Tracy, because Heather, Jewel, and Lauren went to study abroad in their junior year, so Tracy went back to Wisconsin, her home state, to continue her studies. I won't go into Tracy's struggles here, but Heather was very concerned about her and writes about it in some of her emails from Spain. Tracy is a survivor that I admire greatly. She should write her own book some day.

Facebook:
Tracy Doyle
Hitro

I love you so very much. Titro
December 15, 2008 at 9:43pm [the day after Heather's death]

Tracy Doyle
Hello love, I dreamt about you and Juliana last night—a sad dream that has left me melancholy. However, as if to counter my fears, JEW just sent me an email, thanking all of us for being at the Clarity show in Tempe. I thank you too, for being there, right between my left and Jewel's right cheeks, smothered in tears and joy.
April 7, 2009 at 10:07am

Tracy Doyle
Love you heather, i was just explaining the itros to my new lab.
September 17, 2009 at 10:08 pm

Tracy Doyle [Here she is writing to me, not to Heather.]
 It is so nice to hear from you! I think spreading Heather's ashes around the world is one of the most beautiful things I have ever heard. And you are right, Heather would LOVE that you and Dennis are travelling, meeting people all over, and living.

This past year has been a difficult one for me in some respects, and really great in others. I met the love of my life, Ryan Smith, last November and we are ecstatic about each other. He is sweet, funny, smart, nice... you name it! Then in March he was diagnosed with testicular cancer and it spread to his lymph system. The last many months have been filled with chemo treatments and surgery upon surgery, BUT! He is done with all treatments for now and the prognosis is really good. We stuck together through all of it, making jokes and finding time to love life. We're stronger for it, I know.

Heather's passing and Ryan's illness have been such smacks to my head and heart (motivating me) to live life well, knowing that it can end at any time. And so I try to laugh, to make beautiful things, to dance, and to love.
Happy New Year, Alyce!
Love, Tracy

December 30, 2010 at 10:15am

Lauren Yelen
Oh Heather...I am trying to imagine a world without your interpretive dancing and inspired syntax, without your vivacious, irrepressible spirit. I'll treasure our memories. You will always be loved, Litro
December 16, 2008 at 6:58am

Lauren Yelen
It was a big year for the Itros, Heather G... Tracy fell in love, I married Eric (finally), and Jewel had a baby... we know you were there in spirit with us through it all. Love you and miss you, honey!
December 14, 2010 at 9:02pm

Jewel Kling
It hurts too much to think of the world without our Heather G. I love you Hitro.
December 17, 2008 at 3:41pm

Jewel Kling
You were in my dreams last night Heather—so vivid. It was wonderful, you were wonderful. Weird though cause I knew you were gone even though you were there, but I still didn't want to wake up. Some days it's so much easier than others, but it still hurts so much. I love you.
January 5, 2009 at 9:03am

Jewel Kling
 i had another dream about you. lauren and tracy were there. your laugh is still in my head from that dream. sometimes i do something and i know i stole it from you. i hope you don't mind. its crazy how even things I do that are like you make me think of you and i get so caught in heather thoughts—it's hard to get out.
i still keep thinking you are going to call me and i'll get to see you again.
January 17, 2009 at 9:56pm

The Devil's Fingernail

Now married, Jewel Kling, is a Doctor of Medicine, a Master of Public Health, and a mommy to a healthy baby boy. Heather was to be the middle name if he had been a girl.

Heather's Journal   December 17, 2000 [while she was home for Christmas]

Jon is 21. He lived on my floor, five doors down on the other side of the hall. He was in my Spanish Literature class. We ate lunch together Tuesdays and Thursdays after class. Jon, a senior, is an economics, finance, and Spanish major. He has a 4.0 GPA! He lived in Granada, Spain, all of last year, where I hope to be starting in the fall of 2001. Before that he had been to Mexico and South Africa with a student group, Rotary International, and to London with a different scholarship thing. The kid loves to travel, and he has some ambition. Man, wait, I'm not done with the travel descriptions. He traveled all over Europe, through Turkey, Egypt, even western Russia, while he lived in Spain. Then this year over New Year's, he'll be in Panama. He's coming here and seeing me around January 7th. We will ski and kiss a lot. Then in March he's going to Argentina to school for a year! The boy is amazing. His name is Jonathan. We first kissed the Saturday before Thanksgiving. He took me on my first date ever in Arizona, to dinner at The Olive Garden. I had the chicken vino bianco. Then we went to Zoolights, which was wonderful. They had beautiful music—Christmas, Enya, etc., and awesome lights all over. My favorite was 12 trees that seemed to light with the twelve notes of an octave while they played the "Twelve Days of Christmas."

[It warmed my heart to know that she had a truly nice date in college.]

OK, I have to write our Christmas poem.

Mom wrote the first paragraph.
December 2000
This season we reflect on the legacy we have received and that we are leaving. Denny's father Dick Gross had a stroke while on

vacation in Florida. He died a week later on October 1st. He had been the primary caretaker of Denny's mother Mae Gross. Mae has Alzheimer's and is in a nursing home near Denny's sister, Karen. Although a sad occasion, the funeral served as a reminder of how many wonderful people were a part of Denny's childhood; and it gave him an opportunity to say thank you. We are also thankful for our happy, healthy daughters, for friends and relatives like you, but most of all, for the Advent Promise of the coming Christ.

On a lighter note, Heather and Emily greet you:

The cold mountain air tells me I 'm home.
It's time to spread the Gross greetings with the traditional poem.

Mom and Dad are happy to have both daughters here.
Their jobs and activities haven't changed much since last year.

Mom does Book Club, Church Council, and of course she still teaches.
Dad leases, fishes, hunts, and tries not to give to many Dad-to-daughter speeches.

Mom was in Las Vegas, visiting old friends from Germany.
Dad is recovering quickly from a cartilage-removing knee surgery.

In college, I 'm taking Spanish, Italian, and organic chemistry.
These and three best friends there have kept me very busy.

I just left Arizona. There, it's still fairly warm.
I've had much more fun this year and love the people in my dorm.

In October, Emily visited me at ASU.
She's excited to start her adventures in a year and a half when high school is through.

In August, we all visited relatives and friends in Washington and Oregon.
We scouted colleges there for Em because she'd like a location more northern.

The Devil's Fingernail

Over the summer the three girls took golf lessons together.
I worked in a lab, training toward someday being Pharmacist Heather.

Next year, I'll be studying in Spain at the University of Granada.
Someday, in multiple languages, I hope to be an aficionado.

In AP Biology and AP Art, Emily does persevere.
She has been with her boyfriend Gary for more than a year.

They met through Church Youth Group, where she loves to learn.
Em spends her lunch hour at Bible Study. She has taken a spiritual turn.

At her job in produce, Emily is like one of the guys.
Now, she looks forward to a snowmobiling/boarding trip that
She and her friends have devised.

These snow-covered mountains are God's creation.
He also gave us His Son for our Salvation.

Love, The Grosses: Denny, Alyce, Heather the Poet, and Emily the Artist

Alyce Gross

Heather's Journal   March 9, 2001
   I cannot believe that it has taken me this long to write once more. . . Jon stopped being my "novio" before he even came to Utah, because he went to Mexico instead of

Panama and "God worked on him and told him to have no relationship other than that with God. So pretty much, I got dumped for another love—God. Yep, it's all good. That was a while ago.

Heather had reconnected with her high school love, Greg, so he was the one on her mind by this time.

Heather's Journal   June 27, 2001
I cannot believe that I will be an adult. It is actually very exciting. . . . Tomorrow at 11:42 I will be twenty years old. Man. I want to truly love myself so that I can easily and completely love those around me and love life.

Alyce Gross

Junior Year in Granada, Spain

Heather was wonderful about emailing us during her year in Spain. The first thing I would do when I got home from a day of teaching, was excitedly and expectantly check emails of her entertaining monologues about all that was going on with school, roommates, friends, food, and travel. I printed copies and kept them in order, in a three-ringed binder, as a travel log for her when she returned. I continued this practice while she was on other worldwide trips. I'm so glad I did. Heather knew and appreciated that I was making the copies, so she wrote with that in mind. As she was writing for what she thought would be her own personal journal, she didn't bother with editing and polishing her word choice for publishing. In fairness to her, I deleted a few things that I thought she would not want shared universally. I decided not to correct all the capitalization errors of omission and abbreviations which saved Heather time and money in the internet cafes. (Sometimes she used capital letters but usually not.) Also, I chose not to edit Heather's unique made-up words (G-speak). I found rereading these travel emails delightful, because she was almost with me again. But at times it was very painful, because I realized it is the only way I'll ever get to see the world through her eyes from now on. And oh, what perceptive, caring, life-loving eyes those were.

Life is either a daring adventure or nothing. Helen Keller

A man of superior talent . . . will go to pieces if he remains forever in the same place.
 Wolfgang Amadeus Mozart

Subject: Heather in Granada
Date: Thu, 30 Aug 2001 From: "Heather Gross" <imahag@hotmail.com>
 Hello to my fambily [not a spelling error—just the way Heather recreated words].

I am here and safe. When Jewel and I saw each other, we ran and hugged. The resident director guy, Christian Butler, is way nice. He knew Jon, and really liked him.

Dude, I still can't believe that I am in Europe and Spain and Granada and that I live here!! I am with four other AZ kids from the hostel in a cyber cafe right now. Ok. I love you guys!!!!! Amor, Hermelinda

Subject: Re: Yea!
Date: Sat, 01 Sep 2001 09:31 From: "Heather Gross"

I have had sangria and gazpacho and have many more Andalucian foods to try. Last night we (girls from the program—jewel, marissa, josie, april, and domenica) went dancing at two bars and learned that not only are Spanish women beautiful, the amount of people out on the street at 4 in the morning is crazy.

We signed up for our classes yesterday. In a month after the intensive Spanish stuff, I will take a placement Italian test. I am actually really excited for school to start.

There is a big beautiful park by jewel's apt and my hostel, where I will run once my hip works, so I might want to live by there or maybe closer to the school. Walking everywhere is cool, and I feel like I'm staying healthy because of it. The smoking isn't that bad, just annoying when everyone in the bars is doing it and there's nowhere for the smoke to go.

My hostel is costing about $14 a night, so that is awesome until I find my apt. Some of the numbers we have are for apts. that cost less than $100 a month!! Then I will pay about $30 in utilities for two months. Ok. I will call soon. I love looking at my pictures and being happy but not really homesick. love your little flamenco dancing hermelinda

Heather's Journal   3 de Septiembre, 2001

Today is important as I am moving into an apartment with three españolos. I did not sleep well because of my thoughts . . . , but I am still hopeful and confident that I can do well. Granada—I live here. I love it more each day as I learn how not to be lost at each new turn. It is good having Juliana here with me. Any homesickness for my SLC mountains or Em, Mom, Dad,

Alyce Gross

Greg, NWB (work friends) Spencer, or Chris is lost in my need to know this new adventure.

From: Heather Gross
Sent: Monday, September 03, 2001 12:05 PM
  I might buy a sleeping bag later when it's cold enough to need one. I need to get curtains from the owner of our apt., or I won't be able to take my siestas. I also need to buy a fan cuz dude, it's hot.
  My roommates are Pilar, Carolina, and Mercedes. Pilar is kind of like the mom they said. She cooks a lot. Today I ate my first home cooked Spanish meal. We had, I think, pork cooked in eggs with good potatoes, corn, and tomatoes. There are some language barriers, but usually we can communicate. I go meet the AZ peeps in 40 minutes to see how I did on the test and to have dinner.
  There is so much for me to get used to, and I love it all. I will tell you if there is something I really need that I can't get here, but it seems like this huge dept store Hipercor El Corte Ingles has everything. It's like a nice Super Target with a post office, travel agency, etc. It's two minutes from my room.
  There are some tall trees kind of in the way of my view of the mountains, but then I can see all kinds of city busyness and will be able to see the mountains well when the leaves leave those trees. I felt like I did well on my test today. mmmmmmK. I love you. Dude—Colega so Colegas luego, Heather

Date: Fri, 07 Sept 2001 11:38 From: "Heather Gross"
Dudes!
  Estoy muuuuy bien. I love it here. Fo reals. Right now I am with an AZ girl named Josie. My roommates are awesome. My room is starting to look like a room. They gave me some big white curtains that remind me of our dining room ones. I have a desk, shelves, a cute little closet and a tiny bed stand. There is even a pullout mattress under my bed. They are great cooks, well Pilar is anyway.
  Today is jewel's bday, and there will be good times tonight. Two days ago i went to lunch (alcohol and free tapas) with this cute german guy in my class and his roommate. I told them all about you and your meeting in germanyness. Then i walked all over granada with this girl from Colombia who grew up in

Switzerland. It is great. I speak Spanish all the time, and i'm really getting to know the city.
K. I love you. Yes, big as eurasia. love heather g dawg gross as soroush would say

Date: Sun, 09 Sep 2001 09:56   From: "Heather Gross"
So you guys are at church now I guess. Or maybe Sunday school. I am with Jewel and Josie. We came back from the beach last night and I slept a lot today. Jewel, Josie, April, and other AZ kids all went. April has Mexican parents and already speaks Spanish, but needs grammar help. josie is a really tall blond outdoorsy b.ball player fro NAU. We four girls were together the whole time kind of like the itros were, but I miss them a lot. We were in Almunecar. The water was cold and perfect. We swam out to a buoy, ate paella [a saffron based rice dish with many kinds of sea-food and some vegetables], and talked with this cute Argentine guy who sold us helado—ice cream. I am talking to Chris online now, and haven't heard from Greg.

Mom's Input:
Chris is a nice young man Heather met one night in Calgary, Canada, while we were there for the wedding of our nephew, Andy Aronson. Chris was a groomsman and he and Heather had one romantic night at the reception. He was at the gift opening the next morning with a big smile and some presents for Heather. They communicated through mail and email for a while.
Greg was Heather's "true love" when she was a junior and senior in high school. He ended it just before their graduation. It was a very hard time for Heather. They later reconnected as friends.

I thought Em would tell you about my school. It is like this. I am in Intensive which is just four hours from 9 to 1:00 every Monday through Friday. I did well on the test because it put me in the highest level of the AZ kids; so the kids in my class are native speakers who need grammar writing work, and then a Brasileno, two Germans, and some other Americans who want to improve their vocab and conversation skills like me. It's cool because the native speakers are from Mexico, Venezuela, and Colombia, so we have Latin American consultants as well as

Iberian Spanish knowledge. I really like my teachers, Africa and Cecilia. This intensive schedule lasts three more weeks till the 28th.

I have finally figured out the whole light the water heater thing and make the coffee in the little percolator thinger.

i hope to find a church i like soon and maybe will go next Sunday.

k, I love you, Heather

Subject: en un otro cibercafe
Date: Tue, 11 Sep 2001 08:51 From: "Heather Gross"

hello. I am with my compañera de piso Carolina, or Caro. She took me to this cyber cafe because it's cheap and near our apt. She is sending a message to the mobile phone of her boyfriend, whose whole history I got to hear last night. I went with her, Pilar, and Mercedes shopping. Before that on my own I bought some cute cheap black flip floppies with some little dangly bead things that one couldn't find in los Estados Unidos. Then Caro and I went to this awesome touristy spot called el Mirador de San Nicolas, up these twisty tiny streets in the gypsy neighborhood—the Albaycin. From there one has a great view of the Alhambra and a lot of the city. I can communicate pretty easily with my roommates now, and we had a great boy talk on the way walking home.

Did I tell you about talking to the Mormon Misioneros last Sunday? I was with Jewel and Josie walking from near school back to our houses. The Mormons had a stand set up in this plaza. I knew one had to be from Utah, so I went and talked to these very cute 20 year olds. One kid is from American Fork, another from England, then a guy from Granada and a guy from Peru. We are going to play futbol with them on Saturday.

Oh, DAD! I got your package. It got to my school Monday morning, so in six days. Thank you!

I like this German guy in my class, Oliver, pronounced Ohleeevare in Spanish. He asked for my phone number today so that I can go to el cine with he and his friends tomorrow. dude, so I told him that we were going to the gypsy caves tonight to watch some Flamenco dancing. He might come. Good times.

I love the cafe here, with milk and more caffeine, num.

The Devil's Fingernail

I am now a master of lighting the water gas heater and the stove for making the delicious cafe. I bought a garbage can, hangers, mini stapler, sponger washer thing, and lighter for our apt—all in this Chinese kind of dollar store for about a total of $3.50. I am being smart with money. I have a stash too for if I have my purse or something stolen.

I found out that my rent is really about $147 dollars a month, and not $200, como yo pensaba. Tell Emmy G to write! I loved her long emails of last week.

Now I am going to email an ASU teacher to see if I can do an Honors credit paper for his class while I am here taking his course but through the CLM.

I also will sometime have to take an Italian placement test. k. I think this novel is done. I love you guys!! Heather g dawg grosssss

Date: Tue, 11 Sep 2001 08:51 From: "Heather Gross"
It is all over the news about the planes crashing into the World Trade Center, Hombre!

Heather's Journal   El 11 de septiembre, 2001
Heather wrote this mostly in Spanish in disturbed looking big handwriting. Following is a little of what she wrote:

It seems selfish to now write about my tiny world, my American cell in Spain, when thousands of Americans, thousands of people, are dead because (they say) a Palestinian terrorist group decided this would be so. They are talking about how this is a war against the entire capitalist democratic world, of which Spain is a part.

Date: 13 Sep 2001 12:19   from: "Heather Gross"
Hello, Please continue to give me US based info on what happened Tuesday.

I am in the cheapest cibercafe I have yet found. It's about $.70 an hour. This Morroccan guy I met in the street came here with me. He is twenty. He thought I was German and wanted to talk to me. Then he told me that I was the most beautiful girl he had ever talked to. Great, anyway he is gone now and Canada Chris is instant messaging me.

Last night I hung out with German Oliver and his

friends and one of their girlfriends who is from France. She and I spoke Spanish while the guys spoke German. Oliver's friend is taking Spanish language classes at this school called Carmen de las Cuevas, which means of the caves. It has a perfect view of the Alhambra, all lit up at night, and of the city.

Oliver is 25 and way nice. He is only here for three more weeks, what else? I love you guys, and em reallllly needs to write to her sis. k. love, heather g

Tue, 18 Sep 2001
I just spent the last hour in this internet place reading stories on the MSNBC and CNN websites. Is Bush's ultimatum for sure going through tomorrow? Inform me on the big stuff. ok.

I love you guys and am praying for the people of our country, heather

Date; Tue, 18 Sep 2001 13:40 From: "Heather Gross"
Do not worry. I took a good four hour siesta yesterday, woke up and ate a light cena with Fabiola and Mercedes, did my homework, and went back to bed.

I am reading Michener's IBERIA and want to go all the places he has been. I am doing very well in my classes other than sometimes having the accent of a guiri (pronounced gheeeree, means foreigner). I think I am one of the only students in my class who has been there every day. Today Oliver and I were in group together to work on this thing about providing advice to a person who wants to "be like a rose." Our teacher was like, "oh Oliver y heather once again together in a group es algo fatal," we do good work together cuz the last time was when we wrote this ad about why people should come to Granada and eat tapas [appetizers]. we were in a group with Fabiola, and our ad won the most votes.

Thank you for sending the swimsuit and pliers! Today I siesta-ed for an hour and a half after eating with Mercedes. She made a salad with veggies—peas, corn, carrots, tomatoes, potatoes, eggs, and tuna—very good and then of course one puts lots of olive oil, vinegar if you want, pepper, and salt. Then I went to the twisty tiny streets on the hill, gypsy neighborhood, the Albaycin, with Josie and April. We spoke Spanish whole time though. We then went behind Plaza

Nueva to the street where all the teterias are. These are arab tea cafes that serve delicious millions of kinds of tea. I also bought little Moroccan slippers for about $8 to wear in the apt. My feet always get gross at home cuz there are no carpets and only a few rugs. people here don't go barefoot inside.

Tomorrow is the Manu Chao concert, which will be awesome, my roommate Mercedes, Fabiola her friend, and Jewel, Josie, April and a bunch of other Americans are going. These guys sing mostly in Spanish, but also in English, Portuguese, and French.

Fabiola and I exchanged addresses and phone numbers. I can go visit her in Switzerland sometime. Now I need Oliver the German's address so I can have some more free lodgings, eh?

April, Josie and I were talking about how we have the need to travel bug. We also have the need to study and be in other countries. I want to go on a road trip with them in Mexico next year. They have both been there many times. Then there is South America and well the rest of the world. There is time, eh?

ok. I love you guys, heather

Subject: to whole family
Date: Fri, 21 Sep 2001 05:39 From: "Heather Gross"

Let me say that I am writing to Em about Gary issues, but to all of you about everything else. So, I am in the internet place by my school about a half an hour from my house. Next to me is a girl from Los Angeles with grandparents in Mexico who is in my class. I was laughing reading parts of Em's email because she arm wrestled and rallied and then later was talking about Gary, stuck in one sentence about Bush's ultimatum, and then went back to her boy problems.

We have troops in Turkey, Japan, and the UK. I think this being ready to attack in three or four days seems a little extreme. Yes, we have to do something. We should not explode immediately into war, though. Maybe I would see this differently and want immediate revenge if I were in the US, hearing the stories of lost loved ones on Oprah and watching the Today show. What do you guys think?

We just found out that one of our Arizona group named Brandon [I changed his name] is in the hospital. He was verrrry drunk Tuesday night, walking home alone, and missed his apt. Somehow he found himself later under a bridge clutching a bar thing that was stuck in the ground. I mean he was holding on to something, like he had fallen and landed on it, and then grabbed on to it. He doesn't know if he fell from the bridge or walked down there and then fell, or if someone or a car knocked him over the edge; but anyway he is now in a hospital here with the fifth from the bottom vertebra of his spine smashed to pieces. His mom already flew here. Man, the stupidity of drunkenness.

    Tomorrow I go to the beach with our group. it is a prepaid, already organized by Christian trip. Cool. we go to Almunecar again and to Nerja, where I have yet to go, and where Josie and I have heard that we can do some more cliff jumping. I will write more soon. I love you. heathery feathery

Subject: futbol
Date: Tue, 25 Sep 2001 04:36 From: "Heather Gross"
    Hello. Just finished class. I really like my teachers. Africa, the first one, is very lively and engaging. Cecilia, the Second one, is chill and funny.

    Yesterday Maria came to eat lunch with Mercedes and me. Mercedes made this good fish thing for us—num. Then I went with Josie and April to play soccer with these Americans from U of New Hampshire. They have about 30 kids in their group, of which half are boys, much better proportionals than are in our group. They are good times, and we will play soccer with them every Monday, Wednesday, and friday, when they have this turf court reserved. We have to walk pretty far to get there. It's on the other side of the Rio Genii and up toward the mountains. The court is like an indoor one, but with a chain link fence surrounding it. My hip held up pretty well.
What else? I love you guys, and pray for you *like a mother hen protects her baby chicks.* Heather

Subject: To my sleepy parentals and my sis
Date: Fri, 28 Sep 2001: From: "Heather Gross"
    Dad was typing tired from his office, and then mom was up late writing to me too. Siestas are wonderful. So this is the first time that I have felt that I was in an Internet 'Cafe' cuz I just bought a mini coffee and can drink it while I type to you. I

The Devil's Fingernail

love the cafe con leche here. I think I told you how we make a cup of coffee, and it lasts a day because you just put a tiny amount in—like an espresso shot, and then fill the rest with milk. It is delicious.

I have been alone in my apt since Tuesday. Last night Josie, Jewel, and April came over and hung out. Today was my last day of the Intensive course. We had our written and oral tests yesterday. I think I did well on the oral and got my written test back today. Between classes I was sitting with Christian our director. Some of the students in my class and I had requested photocopies of our tests. Africa my teacher was walking by and gave me mine. She told Christian that I was a great student. Then he was looking at my test and said "Eres inteligente." Then Oliver the German said "Te invito a una Chupa Chups." He bought me a lollipop. Did you know that they are originally from Spain. 'Chupar' means to suck, and Chupa Chups are the brand name.

The end of our class was cute. We all exchanged phone numbers, addresses, and emails. I have the numbers of the girl from Venezuela and the Mexican American girls from LA. We said we will travel together sometime cuz I was looking for traveling companions who won't speak English.

I just lit some cute dark-skinnned German guy's cigarette. I keep a lighter with me and am popular with the socialites of Spain. Don't worry. Yo no fumo.

They play lots of American music in this internet place and in most of the others too. Now it is Enya. I love Enya. The rain is not stopping. I will just keep writing some stuff to you, k? We did not go to the hospital when I said we were going to, but Josie and I went yesterday to see Brandon. He had his operation Wednesday and is doing ok now. We will go again tomorrow. It was weird. His mom took a picture of us visiting him. His ex-girlfriend also flew out here to be with him. He told us that she was in a bad car accident two years ago, and that then he was there for her rehab etc. Now it is her turn even though the girl is missing her classes at NAU for a week and had to fly out to Spain, man.

Carolina and Pilar will be back in Granada on Sunday I think. That will be good. Then when all my Americans have left, at least there will be roommates with me. I am having fun playing soccer with the UNH kids. I am excited to play with the

Mormons tomorrow. It was funny when Elder what's his butt called me cuz I had him stored in my phonebook on my phone, so when he called it said LDS Richard. K. I think I should end my novel somewhere hereish. I love you, my family.
Heatherina

Subject: Me aqui sin mis americanas
Date: Mon, 01 Oct 2001 12:30 From: "Heather Gross"
    I am kind of sick with a throat and ears cold thing. I feel better than I did yesterday and my pharmacist roommates are taking care of me.
    So Jewel and Stephanie left for Germany today. Josie and April left for N Spain. I am here and have been trying to talk to Mercedes to see if I could go see her in Mallorca, cuz I will have no school things after this Wednesday morning till Tuesday night.
    Sunday I saw a 29 yr old, an 18 yr old, and a 20 yr old bull fighter kill 6 bulls. man, I actually didn't hate it. Very different and too bloody, but one of my teachers told our class that the bulls in las corridas de toros are hurt less than those that die in slaughter houses. I do not know, but at least they do use all the meat.
    Sunday night after the bulls, we walked downtown where all of Granada was out on the streets in their Sunday best watching the procession for the patron saint of Granada, La Virgen de las Angustias. Priest guys were singing over and over about how they love the mom of Jesus who came from her womb, who is the son of the virgin, over and over, yeah. lots of people selling fruit, baked potatoes, etc.
    i will get good sleep tonight, study for Italian tomorrow, and call you guys. I love you guys and will talk to you manana por la manana. Heather

Subject: Re: flights
Date: Wed, 03 Oct 2001 03:44 From: "Heather Gross"
    I am corresponding with Dasch about when he will be here before Christmas and before I come home. I will then decide dates for sure for when to fly and will write to you before I buy.
    My Italian test went well and put me in level 2 where I should be. Plus that is the only class that works with my Spanish class schedule, so it is perfect. At this time tomorrow I will be on

my way to Mallorca.
   I love you tons bigger than Mallorca, Menorca, Ibiza, and Formentera. Heather

Mom's input:
   Dasch was a friend (sometimes boyfriend) of Heather's since Junior High School. After she died he lovingly brought Denny and me a framed picture of Heather skiing at Snowbird. He had skied with her there the Saturday before she died, and he went through the mountain photographer's pictures to find the print for us. In the fall of 2009, Denny and I, in Heather's memory, attended a beautiful wedding of Dasch and Megan Houdeshel, in Moab, Utah, along the Colorado River, where they both had been river raft guides.

Subject: in Mallorca!
Date: Thu, 04 Oct 2001 11:44 From: "Heather Gross"
   I am! I do not have much time to write cuz their internet cafes are spenivissimo!! but it is awesome and i am staying at the house of Mercedes with Her parents and older sister. they fed me good fish and now canada chris is writing me and yeah. my health is good. thank you for writing mom. i think we are going on some cool hikes in the mtn's by the sea tomorrow. i am so glad i got this flight and am here. i love you, hermelinda (as my Italian teacher will call me cuz she can't pronounce the "th" in Heather)

Mom's Input:
   When I taught school in Germany from 1975-1978, I went with friends on trips to the Islands of Mallorca and Ibiza. Through various adventures in Spain, I learned to love the carefree atmosphere there. Those past experiences added to my excitement for Heather's opportunity to study and travel in Spain,

Subject: Back in Granada
Date: Tue, 09 Oct 2001 12:08 From: "Heather Gross"
   Right now I am by my school. I still have all my travel

stuff cuz I went directly from the airport to the CLM for my first Italian class. Um yeah, these people speak Italian already, he he.
i will call. I loved Mallorca. Mercedes' family was so nice and cute.

awesome that you got an elk, dad! maybe there can be some jerky smell filling the house when i come home, eh?

write me more about what Bin Laden said on the news, and how many civilians were killed in the Sunday and Monday US bombings on Afghanistan.

Love, heather

Subject: La Alhambra, travels, dah bee bah doo
Date: Wed, 10 Oct 2001 09:10 From: "Heather Gross"
is the name of the building that I have yet to go see. It is up on the hill and a big thing that the Moors built. James Michener wrote some cool stuff about it. You can read Iberia when I come home and give it to you, mom.

I arrived in Mallorca Thursday, messaged Mercedes to her cell phone, and she and her sister came and picked me up. I ate with her and her Mallorquin speaking family. Her sister is older, 22 and cool, hippie-ish. Her mom would speak to me in a loud slow voice, and her dad was mad that she was speaking to me "in Indian," like that was the only way I could understand. Cool with me. So they had to speak Castellano, which is not what they usually speak, and awkward for them, but they only did half the time, so half the time I had no idea of what was going on. Actually, it has lots of similarities to Italian, so I learned a little.

mercedes' mom is a pharmacist in a village and worked the week days, but her dad has his time off from being a big boat ferry driver sailor guy. he and i made sandwiches for me to eat in madrid, and he took me to the airport at noon. i ate lots of typical mallorquin delicious home-cooked food—sea stuff and tomatoes ground into toasted bread with olive oil and salt and special ham and delicious cheese, num.

friday i am going to Ronda on the train, where pilar's family lives. It's a beautiful little town, I hear, near Malaga. jewel, josie and the rest of them should be back Saturday or Sunday.
friday is important in all of the Spanish speaking world, el dia

The Devil's Fingernail

de la hispanidad, y el Dia de la Virgen de Pilar, the patron saint of Spain. parties. Yeah.

write to your heather about gary, barb [from The Gang], nitro [Barb's dog], bin laden, mikey [Barb's son, an Army Ranger in Afghanistan], elk in fridge, everything. I love you! erheath

Subject: in Ronda
Date; Sat, 13 Oct 2001 14:46 From: "Heather Gross"

I am out with my roommates. It's almost midnight here Saturday night. We are staying at Pilar's house. Ronda is beautiful. The Tajo is this huge cool gorge with the white building village built along its ridge and down in the valley. I got some good pictures. I miss being able to say my heatherisms in English. I can communicate, but my jokes that would work in English just aren't me in Spanish.

Being back in Granada and seeing some good old ketchup eating comfortable shoe wearing Americans will be good. yeah.

I love you guys. Thank you Em for the long email, and mom too, heather

Subject: Hi. Sorry. Here is the stuff.
Date: Sat, 20 Oct 2001 04:00 From: "Heather Gross"

I don't have a very good excuse for not writing. I was kind of homesick Saturday to about Tuesday. I was missing you guys while I was in Ronda with my roommates, and then Monday morning Christian told us our school schedules, and mine sucked. I was just thinking about the IPO people telling us not to write home and tell parents how we want to go home when something goes wrong. I wasn't wanting to go home—I just didn't want to be sending you bad news.

Tuesdays and Thursdays at 8:30 in the morning to 10:00, I have the lit class. I then have an hour and a half break till my 11:30-1:00 Oral and Written Production class, which is da bomb diggity. I mean there are 14 kids in there, and we can talk. It is 7 of the same kids from my intensive class last month, in which I received a 9.5 out of 10, which means an A to ASU. The teacher is cool and nice and lets us vent on Thursday,

We read this article about how there are three stages for the foreigner who lives in Spain. The first is fascination with the siesta, fiesta, and easy good times lifestyle. The second is some word like frustration or angriness. The third takes place when the person goes back to their own country and then misses spain. I just went off in class about how I am in the second stage mainly with school stuff and how the other classes are set up etc. It felt good. There are smart Spanish speaking Americans, a new German, and a British lady in that class.

then I have to walk the half an hour back to my house, eat, chill, and walk back up to the CLM by 4:00 for the clapping, knows about gypsy music man class. Jewel is in that, so that is good. I have that till 5:30 and then a break till 6:00 when I have Italian, which is still hard, but which I like, till 8. Then I walk back to my apt. with a very cute Javi, "Hahvee," short for Javier. He is from Ronda and grew up with Pilar. He is taking German at the CLM cuz his major is tourism. I think he speaks English, and some French. He also knows some Italian and uses it with me cuz he lived with two Italian guys last year.

Monday night, I hung out with Josie, Jewel, April, three Australians, a Canadian, and a blond guy from Israel. That was interesting. josie and april met the first ones in Lagos, Portugal, and the Israeli guy in Bilbao.

Tuesday, I was at school all day and just getting upset with the class set up and the fact that I couldn't play soccer on Monday and Wednesday nights. I think this soccer thing that I signed up for will be better, cuz it will be mainly Spanish from here people who don't speak English. Also, we will play on green grass, instead of on the court I play on with the soccer kids. I miss grass. Even at ASU, in the desert, we had a huge field to use for soccer. That was another thing I was getting out of my system in my cool little discussion class.

My apt is pretty cold I think because of this city's need to build everything with marble floors and no carpets and no vacuums and no dryers and no dishwashers, but there are bidets, yes. the one in my and mercedes' bathroom doesn't work cuz it leaks, but i don't care cuz i shower. they all shower almost every day too. if i wanted to use the weird ass bidets i could, cuz there is one in pilar and Carolina's bathroom.

k. those girls have these kind of boyfriends: Carlos is

Pilar's. He is tall and has dark skin and dark curly hair, which Pilar just shaved off, and he looks like he has some Morroccan blood in him. He is often in the apt. I am often surprised to be in the kitchen in the morning when no one else is up, and then think a roommate just woke up, and it is carlos going to the bathroom.

The no dishwasher is fine. It means I have a drying chore to do instead of having to cook more. you see, there are four girls in my apt. i am one of them. There are seven days on our little table of chores, ha ha. mercedes and I are like the kids. pilar is the mom. she and Carolina argue and are always together like a little married couple.

Mom's input:
Not hearing from Heather for a week was worrisome, because she usually emailed so often. We, of course, had recent memories of her long deep depression, so some of the previous email was a cause for concern; although within the email it sounded like she was feeling better, and it was reassuring that she was sharing her feelings.

Subject: i love you and more [same day]
Date, Sat, 20 Oct 2001 04:59 From: "Heather Gross"
so, I didn't realize how much I need to tell you guys. you are my family, but it is also like you are my journal, and i love writing to you. I still write everything I do on my calendar, and i do write in my journal, but i really need to get all the stuff in me out to you.

so there is Carlos who is really tall who is with little tiny freckled loud voice Pilar. then there is quieter, loves to laugh, and has a beautiful face, Carolina. She has her boyfriend Gerard, who is I think from Barcelona, and his name is Catalan and pronounced—Yareehrrd, or something. He is even taller than carlos and a foot taller than Carolina and skinny and way quieter than Carlos or Pilar or Caro and can also be found in my house in the mornings. Thank God Mercedes doesn't have a regular guy over or I would never be able to pee. ha ha.

the thing about carlos is that he eats at our house often. He does not buy our groceries. I do not mind when Pilar's brother is here, but Carlos "tiene mucha cara," according to Caro (Carolina), this means he has a lot of face and doesn't care if he is bugging people or taking advantage of them. Caro and Mercedes like Carlos but think Pilar is stupid for feeding him and letting him be at our apt all the time. Two years ago the roommate Maria had problems with Pilar cuz she hated Carlos and wouldn't let him in the door with the buzzer that people have to use to come into the apt building. Anyway, these are the little soap operas of where i live.

Wednesday morning, Mercedes and I went to get our hair cut. I love Spain. It cost us 1500 pesetas, which is $8.00, to have our hair washed, cut and dried. I wanted to stop the development of the mullet. Once I remembered the words for length, bangs, part, etc., I could communicate with the lady. K. These people tie a little white, looks like a short robe thing on you. Then girl washed my hair in comfy chair and sink. then girl cuts my hair very well. I have gotten many compliments and it is not too short, I just don't have the tail. I think it will grow out to how I want it as well. Then other girl dries my hair, cuz she is the hair dryer or something, while first lady looks on as her creation comes to life. It was weird, cuz then she comes up and finishes drying and shaping my hair, like she had been letting hair dryer girl play with her clay but now she is going to finish her masterpiece sculpture that is my head. ha. it was cool, and all this was for $8.

My day to cook is Friday. Oh yeah, I was going to talk about this a long time ago in the first email. I don't know how to cook. This is why my name is only once a week in the slot for making the lunch, the big meal. That means I wash dishes or clean up the kitchen after lunch more, but that is cool with heather. I made rice with corn, peas, tuna, and peppers. people put salt and aceite, which is olive oil on it. i cooked the rice too long. I was going to call you and ask you how to do rice, mom, but jewel told me kind of. I need some recipes or some advice, so that I am not always having to ask my roommates how to make stuff.

Anyway, Mercedes was at her Barril which is the drink wine thing they have at the University for the students, and Pilar and Caro were getting tapas. they sent me a message that i didn't have to cook, but i did not check my phone.

so, i made the rice thing, and it wasn't that bad, mainly only i ate it cuz caro and pilar got home having eaten, until the

whole world came over; that would be six Andaluz Spanish accent speaking boys who ate my food and loved it. that was cool. they also ate sandwiches and more. they were Quino, pilar's brother, and his friends, some of whom I met the weekend before in Ronda. i have been writing these emails for more than an hour, but i am almost done.
sorry i only write about me, but it would be hard to just ask you a bunch of questions, so write and tell me the new things. I have not heard from Em. Em write.

Last night was very fun. The Centre de Lenguas Modernas had a party too—a barril. There were barriles all over the University yesterday I guess. Barril means bar. They served Tinto and beer, sandwiches and strong drinks too. Tinto is what I often drink. it is like Sangria, or a wine cooler. Mercedes had left for Jaen, a town an hour from here.

Caro and Pilar were asleep on the couch, when I got home from being at Christian's office and being at the outdoor store with Josie and Jewel. Josie signed up for backpacking and had to buy her sleeping bag. So I went with Caro and Pilar to the CLM and met josie, jewel, and dan there. Dan is cool. He speaks Spanish pretty well, and he and jewel are hilarious together. This party was awesome. there were a lot of Americans, but also tons of Spanish, some Italians, germans, and british.

I asked the band to play this song I love "Sigo aqui, esperandote..." I continue here, waiting for you. It is a pop dancy Spanish song. when i requested it, the guy asked me if Heather had a Spanish translation cuz he couldn't say heather. so then when he played it he said, where is my blond Hermenlinda who wants this song? it was fun. they had everyone in lines doing these weird dances, kind of like the picture you get when you see a bar mitzvah and everyone is singing and moving together. Pilar's Carlos was already there with Mike and his New Hampshire americanos, and Caro found her Gerard too cuz he has friends who study at the CLM. It felt good that I could go there with my roommates and then have them already know people.

I love you guys. Write me about you. Heather

Subject: heather la pluma (the feather)
Date; Tue, 23 Oct 2001 11:53 From: "Heather Gross"

Hi. Dad!!! I was sad that every time I called I didn't get to talk to you.

I just left my amazingly hard Italian class. Man, I have to read a book in Italian by December, Um, yeah. Do I even read whole books in Spanish??

I just got your message on my voicemail and tried to call you, but there have to be some consequences to having such a cheap phone card: it's sometimes busy. So, I will call back soon, your noon something.

I got your package today. Thank you for all the gum and now I will be the coolest six blue handkerchief girl in Spain. The gum here is weird, so I am happy to have the little good packs you sent. Hmmm...

I will send this to Mom too. so hi Mom and Em. I want to see Em's dress. I am really happy that I get to see you guys at Christmas. What else is cool is that I will be back here on January 6, which is the day of the Three Wisemen, the big present day in most of Europe. Today and Thursday are my big school days. I look forward to Wednesday, when I can wake up a little later, run, do homework, and only have my one class at night.

Yesterday, Monday, I ran in the Garcia Lorca park, but I am going to start running in the science campus of the university, closer to my house or on the bike path. There are too many bored old men in the park in the mornings.

Thank you for the cookie recipe. Mom! I have to look for oats in Hipercor which is the super big market deptment store version of the Corte Ingles next to my house.

So, my cooking day is Friday. What should I make, Mom? I can get help and suggestions from my roommates, but it would be cool if I could make something kind of American or Utahan or Alycian that they had never had, but liked. They love feeding me because I love everything. Mercedes is always laughing when I love the food and can't find anything that I don't like.

K, I am going to try to call you again, Dad. Hey Em, did you get your essay from me in time? Did you like my suggestions? [Emily sometimes emailed school work to Heather for editing help.]

I still write to Tracy and Lauren. Lauren will be in France starting in January for a semester.

I love you guys bigger than all the handkerchiefs Kmart has in stock sewn together. Heather

Subject: Sunday
Date: Sun, 28 Oct 2001 07:53 From: "Heather Gross"
So, no one has written to me in four days, of you guys I mean, so write.
Yesterday was a good day. I went to the Alpujarras, these little towns up in the Sierra Nevada Mountains. I bought a warm rug for my room in Al Jerez, the highest altitude village in Spain.
The villages up in the mountains were beautiful and quiet. The weather was perfect. I think it was hot in Granada, and would usually be pretty cold up in the Sierra Nevadas, so it was good. I was missing the autumn Utah though. There were about ten trees that were yellow and maybe three with red leaves. I just realized I haven't been in Utah to see the leaves for three years.
Dasch writes to me a lot. He is funny and nice and will be way fun to have here.
Spencer from my work writes too. He told me that they finally finished all the samples in the study that I was working on. It is cool that I am keeping in touch with him.
I think that will be good Mom, you showing me how to cook stuff while I am home. On Friday, April came over and helped me make pasta with garlic and olive oil flavoring, and then mixed with hamburger and tomato sauce. It was good, and my roommates liked it.
Write me something. I love you guys and miss you a lot, Heather

Subject: Monday
Date: Mon, 29 Oct 2001 11:02:56 From: "Heather Gross"
Today has been a much better day. I should run all the time. Do you remember when we were visiting ASU my senior year and you, Mom, said that I get a high from running? Yep, very true. This morning I woke up with a little bit coughy and with some pukus, but still pretty good. I ran on this bike path that starts pretty close to my house and goes along the other side of the highway, with bushes in between the path and the highway and then turns

Alyce Gross

into a road out into the country. I ran out to this milk Puleva factory and then turned around. There was a group/herd of goats and lambs along the road, and it was beautiful weather. Granada has been unusually warm the last couple days.

    I called Christian and we agreed to meet at 4 to go see the doctor. When I found him, he said that he had forgotten that they didn't open till 5, so we went to the Garcia Lorca park and talked. I told him about my culture shock problems with the way that people here party. He is so cool. He told me all about how he had the same issues when he came back from England. He told me all about how he was a rebel kid in high school, and how it sucks that all the kids here drink and pee in the streets and are out until the sun comes up. It is awesome having such a cool director, friend, helpy guy.

    Then we went to the doctor. I got a lady. She is just a general doctor. She told me to go to a pharmacy, buy a sterile bottle, bring my first pee of tomorrow to their lab, and then to make an appt with a gynecologist. I didn't see the doctor about my throat cuz I think I will be better with one more night of good sleep. I have an appointment for Nov 6 with a woman gyno. That will be good; I think she can prescribe pills like the lady did in SLC before.

    Now I have to go to class, my first class of today at 7 PM.
    Thank you all for writing. I love you! Heather

Subject: More pee
Date: Tue, 30 Oct 2001 05:49 From: "Heather Gross"
    So today has been really busy. I peed in my sterile bottle that the doctor's office does not provide, and that I bought at a pharmacy, this morning. I had a class at 8:30, and since the doctor's doesn't open til 9:00, I had to go back to my apt until after 10:00 and take the pee to the doctor lab. so i was there waiting for the lab person to come back with my wonderful cup of pee in my hand. lady took the pee. i paid to get the results and had to wait for her to analyze the pee. all this so they could tell me that i am not pregnant (which I of course knew, but they didn't) so that when i go to the doctor next tuesday, she can give me pills to start the flow of hormones. so that lab waiting took a while and then i had to walk way back to my school.

    now i am on my way home from the second class. i was late to that cuz of the pee place, but i talked to the teacher, and she is way cool, saying health before school and not to worry. I go eat and then walk back to school for the third time today, for clapping happy time and Italian heather is dumb time. It's cool. I actually like these classes.

We are trying to figure out what or where to do this four day weekend cuz Nov 1 is the day of all the saints, and Nov 2 is the day of the dead people, like memorial day but more into the death. Halloween is only here cuz they took it from the US, but it's not a big thing. The bars in Granada just know that there are a lot of foreigners here, lots of Americans, and so they have parties. I will put some weird costume thinger together like dad said and have good times at the party at my school wed night.

Now I go to eat some good food that Pilar is making. num. and then hike back to school, Love, Heather

Subject: jFellz Halloweea!
Date: Wed, 31 Oct 2001 10:45

Today has been a good day, and the rest of yesterday too. My Italian class was not bad. I talked to the teacher after class in Italian, of course, and told her that I was scared about having to read a book. She told me that she would bring me a not so long thing to read instead, and that that would be enough. cool.

So, the damn guy at the computer across from me is smoking, and I miss the not being allowed to smoke in public placesness of Utah.

We decided to dress up and go out and be Americans on Halloween. I am going to be a rainbow. Yay!! I already have little clippies in my hair in rainbow order with my hair all up in little doobins (that's for you, Em), and yeah, Jewel and I have class in half an hour—7 til 8:30 and then we will go get all done and disfrazadas (costumed). We are meeting with Kate and other Arizona kids at Rachel's at 11 cuz Kate has face paints. I will have rainbows all over my face, or maybe just big rainbow stripes. Pictures will be taken. There actually isn't a party at school, just ones at bars that give you a free drink for being in a costume or something.

I hope you guys are having a great candy-filled Halloween. I love you!

Subject: Finally I get to write to you guys.
Date: Mon, 05 Nov 2001 From: "Heather Gross"

I got the envelope with the pictures and the plane tickets and the Halloween card!! Thank you, dad!!

K. I did not go to Salamanca. I went to Huelva with Carolina. This is how it happened. So, I was upset Thursday, cuz as has happened before we ended up not getting on a bus for where ever we said we were going to go, and Heather had already packed. Caro told me I could and should go with her to her family's house in Huelva on Friday, yay!!

We took a bus to Sevilla, and her brother who is 27 and works there drove us to Huelva, an hour toward the coast from Sevilla. Sevilla is three hours from Granada, and I will have other opportunities to see that soon. So, Caro is 24, she has Jose Manuel 27, Maria del Mar 25, and Rocio 17—brother and two sisters. Dude, these people all still live at home. yep. Her brother lives in Seville during the week, but in Huelva on the weekends, cuz his fiancée lives in Huelva where she works as a nurse and also lives with her family. Caro's older sister works as a secretary, and her little sister is still in high school. Anyway, her dad is a butcher, and her mom a nurse, and they are all really nice and welcoming and cool.

Her brother and Lola are getting married in May. Caro's roommates (including me) are all invited to the wedding, yay! I get to see a Spanish Catholic wedding where the people know how to eat and party and dance, and I get to dress up and hang out with my roommates.

Caro and I went with her bro and Lola to the place where Columbus sailed from Spain. There are three life size boats, replicas of the ones Columbus used, and we took pictures of stuff like me being that Titanic girl flying at the bow of boat. The one side of the shore thinger has old Huelva like houses and then you walk around the pond that represents the Atlantic Ocean and there are Native American statue people. They are of course naked, and there were old Spanish ladies screeching with excitement at seeing penises—pretty amusing.

After this we four went to Niebla, a town by Huelva that has a medieval castle. They had it open for four days, cuz it is that town's festival of the year. Inside was a market and juggler, jester type people, and people dressed like the king and queen. i bought some food thing to bring home.

so then, that night caro's parents took out lola, the family, and me to dinner, and dude. num. it was to celebrate

their 28th anniversary that was a week ago. they gave gold bracelets to all the girls, including lola, and caro's dad's gold watch was passed on to the son, and since i was there they bought me turtle neck to wear. the people bought me a gift plus fed me at this awesome restaurant. this dinner which included wine, lacquers (i had a nonalcoholic delicious apple thing), dessert, nuts, bread, and lots of fish thingers; of course did not start until about 11:30. he he. yes, thank you notes are in order.
Love, heather

Subject: to the fam shmam wiggitty wham
Date: Tue, 06 Nov 2001 12:50 From: "Heather Gross"
    today has been interesting, the interestingness started when last night i got up from the computer after having emailed my life to you and realized i had no money to pay the internet guy cuz i had no purse, cuz i had left it at school. it was then 10:30 pm, and i was hungry, had not yet eaten dinner (normally eaten at 9ish here), and was like, "shit, the school is closed." I just went to Trapala, the bar where jewel, josie, april, and I always hang out and spill our weekends cuz josie is always hiking and i am somewhere and we have to know each other's stories. so jewel and april were there and i interrupted their talkings and told them my missing purse problem. they calmed me down about how it would be in the office at the school and that i could get it in the morning. my keys aren't that necessary cuz there is a buzzer thinger at the piso (apt). i was just frustrated that i could be so dumb.
    today i went to the school (the Centre de Lenguas Modernas, the CLM). i went to the CLM and got my purse from the office guys and went to my lit class. I like that teacher, and i like the stuff we read. so after that jewel and i went to the cemetery. dude. the cemetery is interesting and weird, and the tombs are all stacked up on each other. There are these huge statues of jesuses and marys and angels. so i went there cuz i needed to so i could write about what the Day of the Dead is in Spain for my POE class.
    i left that class early to go the gyno and she did an ultrasound of my ovaries, and i have no cysts and so i have to take pills which i started today to tell the hormones to start the period. cool.

Alyce Gross

write me parents!!!! love heather g

Subject: Thursday Jueves Giovedi
Date: Thu, 08 Nov 2001 03:18 From: "Heather Gross"

My travel plans, shiaavel plans. Anyway, I still went somewhere for the weekend, and had fun. Today is a much better day. That is because I have things to do. Jewel and I just bought tickets for the Alhambra for tomorrow morning. YAY! Then I will be able to send postcards of the biggest tourist attraction in Granada, having actually been there. Jewel and I saw it from the outside two days ago when we went to the cemetery. I have read tons about it, and am really excited to finally go.

It is cold here now. I don't know if the heat just hasn't turned on yet, or if I just need to buy a big bedspread, but two nights ago I woke up freezing, so last night I slept in long underwear, t shirt, pajama pants, sweatshirt, socks, and ski hat. he he. it was nice and very warm.

In class this morning, we were talking about this novel from the 1800's written in Colombia. Anyway, it was supposedly about pure love, which to me means, not physical. It is a love based on the virtues of the people involved—their intelligence, how they view the world. nope. Then, the woman didn't think. They were beautiful and good, and that is why they were in love. blah. The lady teacher was like, "um I think this story is aburridisimo—very boring, and I wouldn't ever suggest that you read more than the excerpt you already had to read." yeah. It was a stupid soap opera with everyone crying and no real action other than the pretty girl crying and dying. I like that teacher a lot. She speaks very clearly. I understand every word the woman says. It is nice. I actually do understand all my other teachers too, but some of them have terrible Andalucian accents, not saying their d's, their s's, etc. I think though, that I have really improved in how well I grasp the language.

You guys should send mail, just envelopes, not packages, to my apt. It would be cool to get mail there. You have the address, right?

Write and mail. I love you bigger than all the writings of all the languages in the world! Heather

Subject: tuesday

The Devil's Fingernail

Date: Tue, 13 Nov 2001 03:39 From: "Heather Gross"
So yesterday was a bad day, cuz lately I like to be emotional. It is dumb. So my sucky soccer doesn't exist, cuz not enough damn Spanish girls play sports or signed up for soccer, and of course it would be unthinkable that there be a coed soccer. blah. it is actually not that bad cuz now i can run those mornings and then shower and be out of the house in the morning.

so the problem at the house is Pilar's f_ _ _ _ _ _ Carlos, in both senses of that word, and he is annoying. sorry i am swearing, but Spanish swear words just don't cut it.

I am really excited to be home in our warm house with the new windows, even though it will only be two weeks.

back to yesterday: I think I am just full of hormones and just want my period to come already. so, I had to go talk to Christian about chemistry next semester, and that just scares me. he will help when we go to see some advisor lady tomorrow. So I was at his house/office and about to cry. Christian took me to coffee, which was actually Fanta Naranja (orange pop) for him and hot milk with Cola Cao for me. we were at a cafe in the mall, and I cried. and I don't even know why I was crying, but mainly cuz I am reallly cold and sad, cuz no soccer; and i am ugly, cuz i have zits. so Christian took me and we bought a heater for my room, cuz there is heat in my building, but only from 5 to 10 in the afternoon/evening.

then Carlos: I told Christian about him too. Then Christian told me his girlfriend problems, so it was nice to hear someone else's.

we walked to jewel's and left the little heater there, and jewel and i went to school. after i got the heater and walked to my house. I told Caro and Mercedes I was sad mainly cuz carlos is always in our apt, all over the couch, and i am not comfortable with him always here. so we were discussing how we were going to say something to pilar. we were saying, "at least he is not here now," but of course then the doorbell intercom thing goes off, and of course it is that boy. mercedes is 20. pilar 23. caro 24. Carlos is 27 or 28 and a lazy bum who is taking like 7 years to do a 3 year major, and his socks are in our laundry.

pilar can tell me to make sure i paid the fine for the late video, but can't even tell carlos to get his lazy ass out of her bed, off our couch, out of our fridge, or out of our house.

this email is just full of angst, and i don't really feel that mad today. i am actually much better.

so last night, we, the other three girls decided that mercedes will talk to pilar today; but i guess i will if she doesn't, blah.

i had lit class this morning, and i slept wonderfully with my heater on last night. I miss moving around in cars. I think that is why the cold affects me so much. Yes, cuz i have to always be out in it or in my apt in it.

now I have to go to my written and oral production class which is actually just sit and chill and talk about gypsies or something class. then walk home to find some boy on my couch. he is even there when no one else is, and sorry this email is so random.

I love you more than all the times Harry Potter does magical things. Heather

Subject: package
Date: Tue, 13 Nov 2001 08:04:27 From: "Heather Gross"

I just wanted to say that I did get the package, and thank you!! I got it yesterday, so two weeks after you sent it. I need and love everything and love getting mail. yeah. I will cook some good taco or fajita stuff.

Today when I went home for lunch, there was no Carlos. yay. Also, I wanted to say that I love the heater in my room; and I wear always this greens and cream striped scarf that Carolina exchanged for me at El Corte Ingles, cuz that shirt that her parents bought me was too tight in the neck and wrists. now I have cool guitar playing guy Flamenco class. Love you guys!!! Heather

Subject: to my Mom
Date: Thu, 15 Nov 2001 12:51 From: "Heather Gross"

I am much better, and have been for a few days now. It would be the end of my school week, except I have Italian class tomorrow, cuz my teacher wants to make up for the classes we missed because of festival days. I am on the tenth day of my hormone pills, just have two left to take tonight, and my period still hasn't come. It was supposed to during the ten pills or just after. It best be comin. I just needed to go

The Devil's Fingernail

running. I did that yesterday morning for about an hour, and it was gooood. Christian also helped cheer me up. I love my heater. It is warm, and good. Dad and Em can read this too, but it is directed to Mom.

so Monday night Caro, Mercedes and I discussed that we would tell Pilar that the Carlos coming over business has got to stop. but we were all scared to do this. Caro said that if she started she would just be really mean. so we decided Mercedes should do it. so that didn't happen cuz... Wednesday morning, Pilar was at school studying. Caro and Mercedes didn't have class cuz the stupid U of Granada has a strike day every Wednesday, cuz the Spanish govt has this new law that will privatize the university; so the teachers just aren't teaching every wed. anyway, my school is private and not really part of the public U. so we have school on wed, my one class civ and culture, blah bun dee bun doo.

i have tons more to write, but will continue this tomorrow. i have to tell you the crazy events of last night and carlos and his friends, but now i just have to be going home after being at school all day craziness. thank you for worrying about me mom.

I love you and am happy and hope you are too. love heather g dawgggg

Mom's input:

Heather, as her friend Katie Gracia described it, sometimes spoke or wrote in "stream of consciousness" mode, so put on your seatbelt, here we go:

Subject: Tracy, Pilar and More
Date: Fri, 16 Nov 2001 13:28 From: "Heather Gross"
Hi Family, today is a good day, except for the email from Tracy in Wisconsin that I just read. She is really depressed. Pray for her at dinner for the part I say when you go around in the circle.
[Our family always, on week days, had dinner together. We held hands around our round wicker table from the Philippines, which I still have in the kitchen. I would start with "Dear God, thank you for

the food." Denny gave thanks for health and prosperity, Heather thanked God for something funny, unique, and different every time, and Emily ended with a speedy, "Love you God. Amen."]

She [Tracy] is really really sad, I mean like always, and is seeing a counselor and has an appt. to see a psychiatrist that can prescribe antidepressants, so that is good. She says that she hasn't been happy really since the summer before her senior year of high school, so that is a long time. She met Shawn her senior year and then she met the Itros and Andy at ASU and opened up to these people about how sucky her childhood was with the problems with her mom and drugs. So since she stopped repressing these memories and sadnesses, they've just seemed to become huge in her life and always make her feel terrible.

so, when I am sad, I have to just remember how awesome, awesome, awesome my life is and has always been, and look at all the opportunities I have; the wonderful loving family I have supporting me, and think how fortunate I am to be living in a foreign country, learning its language, and sharing this with my best friend in the world, and with an awesome director friend guy and cool roommates who have little dramas that make for interesting stories and shouldn't depress me.

Heather's Journal   18 Nov 01
So I am writing this as a prayer for Tracy, that the cloud that follows her and consumes her begins to lift and that sun enters her life again. . . . So what does this mean? Tracy has good in the future, and I have good now and always have and have to always know this and take care of myself.

So, the pilar thing—let me tell you my week chronologically. tuesday all day at school, good. Busy—means heather is happy. Wednesday I ran for an hour. I was supposed to meet my first Intercambio guy, Javi, at 11:00; but I had said I would go with Christian and Cyril to talk with the lady who advises foreigners about the U of Granada and will help me register for chem and tell me important stuff. the Elena advisor lady of course was not working because it was Wednesday, strike day.

Jewel met with Javi instead of me. jewel just went to where I was supposed to meet him, and looked for the guy I described, and was like, "Javi?" and it was cute and they only

The Devil's Fingernail

spoke Spanish and he walked with her to the CLM.

Christian was at the law building of the university which is closer to my house than the CLM. Christian likes talking to me and wanted to see if i was happier since two days before when i was crying. it is awesome that this is my counselor guy. we told him that we don't want the other Arizona kids to come in January cuz we don't want to have to share him with more people. He likes being so liked or appreciated. so then I went home to tension land.

k. that morning before I went running, Caro and Mercedes were in the kitchen discussing when the Pilar talk would take place. then Caro was like, dude, his dirty clothes are in our dirty clothes basket. that is gross, and we are not washing his laundry. so we got the shirts and socks out and put them in a plastic bag and put them in pilar's room, for her to see when she came back from studying at school. pilar came back, went to her room and saw the clothes and just didn't say anything about them. it was weirrrd. we were just eating and she was not talking, and usually pilar is the loud talker; although she never talks about her feelings or stuff in her life. so we said nothing too.

then we went to do the midmonth grocery shopping. i took my big backpack which is awesome and very functional. i carried home the milk in it, tons of milk. the milk here is sold in little cardboard boxes that you buy tons of, store in your cabinet, and then put in the fridge one at a time when you open them.

that night i had lit class and then later that night. . . 4 something in the morning, "beeeeep beep" sounds the door intercom ringer thing. It was Carlos, drunk with two drunk friends. These two friends live with Quino, Pilar's brother. They had lost Quino and only he had keys, so they decide to come wake up four people instead of walking twenty minutes to Carlos's house. I kind of went back to sleep and never left my room to see what was going on. Mimi (Jaime) had brought a big tree limb as an offering to let them in I guess. that is kind of funny and so was the next event, but not at the time. so at 5:20 Mimi comes in my room and wants to sleep in my bed. dude. so i made him leave and he ended up sleeping in the other bed in Mercedes room. the other friend slept in the living room, and he must have been freezing, but i don't care.

in the morning i see Caro, and the girl is mad. she is like—my blood is boiling, and when she got back from school she woke up the three and yelled at them, and only the one other friend guy really felt sorry. so then she told pilar why we had put the clothes in her room, and pilar said that she felt displaced or like not one of the group. caro told her how i felt uncomfortable with carlos in the house, and that he is just there too much. this was when they went to their swimming thing. Mercedes and I were at the apt cuz she had to study for a test, and I had my break between classes.

last night i went out with jewel and josie and these english people and rugby people and some boys, from somewhere in Africa that we met in the street, that speak French. one of them is in love with jewel. it is funny and weird cuz they went to get chocolate and churros today, and the guy colored his hair and got an appt. for jewel to color her hair tomorrow. he paid for drinks for us last night, cool. the night started at this cider bar, and then the shot bar, and then a dancing bar—that was fun. the cider bar is our favorite place. it is called the sidreria. the shot (chupito) bar is the chupiteria.

Pilar left for Malaga yesterday, and mercedes today. tonight Caro's sister and her friend are coming from Huelva. it's the 25 yr old sister Maria del Mar that likes me and wanted to rent to me so that i could stay at her house longer and entertain them. so that is cool that she will be here till thursday.

great. this weird guy i know, i am not going to type his name cuz he is looking at my computer, just came in and is sitting at the computer next to me. Dude, i hope he can not read english. that would be good. he is speaking morrocan i think. Um, he is weird. i met him two months ago in the street, and he told me how beautiful i was and thought i was german. and he is annoying. so i am going to leave soon, he he.

so k. i love you and need to get away from the weird guy. and you guys sound healthy and happy. and i am too. and em needs to write, and my zits are better. and i love you a more than all the cigarettes the old guy in my Italian class smokes, which is a lot cuz he has at least two in the ten minute break we have after the first hour of our class. and pray for tracy.
Heather

Subject: Tracy's 21st bday today
Date: Mon, 19 Nov 2001 10:50 From: "Heather Gross"

The Devil's Fingernail

I sent her a snail mail card and an email one too.

Today is good. I ran and then went with Christian to see the advisor lady who likes to not be there, so that will happen next week with a real appt. but i got to sit and hang out with Christian so that was good.

Then I cooked chicken with parmesan cheese, jewel's mom recipe, and dude. Everyone loved it. Caro's sister and the lady that came with her from Huelva were all excited to eat American. I think Pilar is just going to be gone a lot and Carlos is never at our house, so that is kind of sad, but better.

Then did some homework, turned in my third roll of pics to be developed, and am now on my way to civ and culture class.

Mom, I think your email at home must be really slow, cuz i checked my email Saturday, but had only received what em wrote Friday and not what you wrote last Thursday, so yeah. I am glad you are my available adult, and I think you guys did excellently with us as kids. Thank you. I will make a list of warm things etc. that we can get when I am home in four and a half weeks, yay! tomorrow I will go in and talk to that doctor when i know she works, so that will be good.

Write me and pretend I am there for good food on Turkey day and I love you more than all the words in German the German guy next to me has ever written. Heather

Subject: fast
Date: Wed, 21 Nov 2001 09:05

Hey! I have to write quickly cuz Christian is waiting outside to talk to me about the Chemistry advisor lady. Awesome about Trina and Andy's baby!! Will she be healthy and ok?? I wrote to Chris and asked about it.

K. It is cool cuz I have run 3 days this week and am going to get help from my teacher who was my intensive Spanish teacher the first month, Cecilia, who speaks and reads Italian too!! yay. I have done all the reading I need to and am not so scared about Friday.

After that class, we the AZ people, are having a Thanksgiving dinner at the other Heather and Marisa's apt. num. I have to bring some good American food, maybe I will finally make the oatmeal cookies or use some fajita or taco seasoning or i don't know. what should i make? the main

stuffing, potatoes, dishes are covered.
    i talked to the doctor. i start anticonceptives sunday whether my period has started or not. yes make appt. with dr. edwards, please, mom. k. i love you guys, and have a wonderful HAPPY TURKEY DAY! and think of me. love you, bye, wave, Heathey

Subject: Turkey day
Date: Thu, 22 Nov 2001 12:44 From: "Heather Gross"
    Dudes. I will call you. Jewel has her lip pierced. Tracy is getting happier and had a good birthday. My Italian thinger is tomorrow, and yeah. I love you. Pretend I am there eating good things, heatherey

Mom's Email:
Subject: Thanksgiving
From: adgross To: Heather Gross Date: Thu, 22 Nov 2001 13:53
    Hi Heather, Thank you for turkey day card. It's cute. We'll call you from our regular phone. I hope you have festive times with your American friends group. Make the most of it and remember it's a day to be thankful. Also remember you'll be in your red carpeted warm cozy home soon for Mom's cooking, Dad's sage advice, Em's boy stories, and lots of love and companionship. We'll shop for all the stuff you need to make you more comfortable and fashionable. We'll cook together, ski together, and we'll all listen to your stories, and look at your pictures. I'm so thankful for my loving family, and for my capable, interesting daughters. Also I'm thankful to hear that Tracy sounded happier. Love you with whole heart and soon to be full tummy!! Mom

Subject: Re: Thanksgiving
Date: Fri, 23 Nov 2001 12:52 From: "Heather Gross"
    I loved your email, mom. i just finished Italian talking and did well! yay! it's over. now to eat with the AZ's party, and then go to cordoba tomorrow morning, cool, k. i will call or write sunday. I love all you guys!!!

Subject: Cordoba
Date: Sun, 25 Nov 2001 12:11 From: "Heather Gross"
    Now i am a little bugged cuz just wrote a big thing and

The Devil's Fingernail

it was erased, k. but. first of all that broccoli thing i made was delicious, and my roommates and especially everyone at the thanksgiving dinner loved it, and there are cute Italian boys in this internet place talking Italian, so there were all the traditional good foods, except for the cranberries and the turkey, but there were pieces of turkey on pizza. then we did apple pie shots. you sit in a chair with your head back, four people stand over you with the ingredients and pour them in your mouth in this order: apple juice, vodka, whipped cream, cinnamon.

i went home after we walked to a club and had decided to bring my backpack and my empty broccoli pot. jewel had brought my dish heated up to the party so that i could go straight there from Italian. so then i went home and slept enough to wake up and shower and go to the bus outside Christian's house/office with all the az's to cordoba.

there is a mosque, la mezquita, there with the middle gutted out for a Catholic cathedral—interesting. i had read all about it already in James Michener's Iberia, so that was fascinating to see it after i knew about it. We hung out in Cordoba all day and saw the old Jewish quarter and ate good food at this place that i recommended, cuz it was in my Rick Steve's Guide to Spain and Portugal that you guys bought me—Thanks. we got home, after two and a half hour bus ride, in which jewel and Stephanie and i were on the top part of the double decker bus freezing; cuz we didn't know there were seats in the bottom part, and that is where the heat was. It was funny when we came down in all our clothes, me in my hat and gator and coat and gloves. then we were warm.

I slept well when I got home, and woke up and decided to run forever. k. I ran really far today, for two hours!! 12 miles at least!! it was cuz i had my cd player and i never go with music, but i decided to take Manu Chao with me. i didn't get bored, so i just kept going. i went home and stretched well and showered and ate good food that mercedes made. then went with the az's and Christian to soccer game, but granada sucks, so jerez won.

chris wrote and is in love with the baby of trina and andy, and it is not as freezing here as it has been. are you snowboarding yet, em? i love you guys more then how cute this Italian guy next to me is. Heather

[Heather's long run and other extreme behavior didn't surprise me, because she had been like that for years. It didn't surprise me, but it should have been a warning sign.]

Subject: i like my greens and cream striped scarf
Date: Tue, 27 Nov 2001 06:16 From: "Heather Gross"
    from caro that i am wearing right now. it is cool that dad called me yesterday; and i just wrote to em, my itros, dasch, and amanda who is in edinburgh, Scotland.
    jewel and i will have to plan ahead a little more if we think we are going to fly places on spain holiday days, cuz the only flights left—spensive. so we will not fly, but bus it to somewhere that weekend.
i told dad this, i think, but yesterday i went with Christian and finally talked to this advisor lady and got my international programs U of Granada card and can now go to the science campus and start figuring out what i am going to take in feb till July, that will give me credits in the US; and what will be my schedule so that i can still take Italian at the CLM.
    jewel got her first package yesterday, and it was so cute how excited she was. i have totally slacked on sending real mail, so sorry, but i will show you my pictures in real life when i am home cuz the scannerness just isn't worth the time i waste trying to get the pictures small enough to be sendable.
    i loved the listing of the stuff we can do when i am home, mom! I love you all and am so thankful to have such an awesome relationship with all of my family. Thank you for being my best dad, mom, and sister ever!!! Heather

Subject: heather here
Date: Thu, 29 Nov 2001 06:17 From: "Heather Gross"
    yesterday i ran 10 miles. after civ and cult class jewel and i saw juana la loca, the crazy. Juana la Loca was the daughter of Isabel and Ferdinand. She had to marry Felipe, a Hapsburg Flemish guy, Flamenco in Spanish. So that is weird, the word flamenco means from Flanders and also the dancing guitaring singing southern spain often associated with gypsies art form. anyway to continue with my history lesson. This Juana was declared crazy mainly because of how she reacted to her sex fiend cheat on her husband. The movie didn't show

her life other than the parts having to do with him. it kind of bugged cuz it was just a soap opera with fancy royalty outfits and castles, and this is what is representing Spanish cinema at the academy awards. so that is me being siskel and ebert. i know one of them died, so the other guy.

anyway, today is my lots of school day. i am here after my first two classes, cuz i go home to my aloneness, which is cool cuz i listen to good american music and eat the stew pilar made while my roommates are swimming.

mom, i was thinking about the infamous poem of Christmas that i write. may i do it in Spanish? much easier to rhyme. i do not have my english rhyming dictionary, and i need you guys to give me some subject matter about each of you that you would like me to include. did i write about dad starting medical billing in last year's poem? hunting and fishing and stuff, mom: teachy, walking with weight, and going to help me cook stuff. Em: boys, art, u of co, awesome in hard school classes, me in other country and stuff.

whoever is reading this right now. respond to it right now. yep. it is cute to think of parents watching west wing together and being all into it. the people here say teetahhneek instead of titanic, and it is funny. Have good ends of your weeks.
Love from Iberia. Heather

Subject: domingo domenica Sunday Date: Sun, 02 Dec 2001
Hi, Family!
Last night I had fun at this ska concert. Em can explain ska, i think. if she can't, it's like punk but happy fast moving music with trumpets, trombones, guitars, drums, and singer. the group was called la gran orquesta republicana, the great republican orchestra guys. Mercedes had heard a ton. they are from Mallorca. They played at La Planta Baja, the Basement, a discoteca club.

Thursday night i hung out with the J's, and other AZ's: Casey and Rachel, then another American girl from the CLM, and Rachel's friend Eli. We went to a very cool Irish pub and then to the Planta Baja to dance. Techno in the US is still much better than anything I have heard the Spanish produce.

Friday I cooked easiness frozen potatoes, carrots, peas, and green beans, smooshed up with mayo. Then April,

Stephanie, Domenica (her name means Sunday in Italian) and I went to the cathedral—beautiful. It's the second biggest in Spain, and is different cuz of the lime they had to use because of disease back then. the walls are painted white, so it has a more inviting feeling. I like having my Rick Steve's guide to Spain and Portugal. He ends up being my tour guide in the touristy stuff, and then i get just enough info, and don't have to buy a guide book or be wondering about whom is being represented with this statue, etc.

    Saturday i ran with Josie, and Mercedes came on her rollerblades. This was kind of annoying cuz we wanted to go on our road to the milk factory, but there is a part that is just dirt, and then the out-in-the-country road is kind of rocky too. So we kind of carried mercedes across the first part, and then ended up running ahead of her. then just stopped and all walked back. It was all good though. We also saw jewel running. it's cute we have our little running club. i am glad i discovered this road and told my j's about it cuz there is very little traffic, mainly just women walking and bikers; and there is a great view of the city. jewel is running a lot for the first time in her life, so that is healthy and good, she also pretty much quit smoking, wasssup.

    today has been a get up, clean cuz my name is on for today; and then, eat, shower, leave. I went to Christian's cuz jewel and josie were gone and I didn't think to call april. he showed me pictures from his high school days and early twenties when he was living in England. he is nice and a good listener advice giver. now jewel and other az's are here at this internet place, i think we will call javi.

    It will be cool to share the world here with you. I think that if you are coming the second half of July, after Em's youth thinger, you could stay in my apt. By then probably at least one or two of my roommates will be at their houses.

    Dad, man, it would be cool if you could come. Thank you for always keeping up on my school mail and stuff. You are awesome. What is going on with the Steelers?

    This Antonio guy in my Italian thinks Karl Malone is too old, and if he wants a chance at winning a championship he and Stockton should change teams. Tuesday in that class was funny. He and this Maria Jose girl are my favorite people in there. I said, "Wassup!" about something, and they thought it was hilarious cuz they had seen the Budweiser commercials. They didn't believe me that people really say that. I punched Maria Jose in the arm and said Wassup, like I do to greet people. This was entertaining to them.

I love you guys more than all the Sundays there have ever been. Heather

Subject: Re: Dad the hunter
Date: Tue, 04 Dec 2001
heather the runner

I was kind of bored yesterday. I guess more like numb. I decided that is dumb cuz I live in a foreign country. Things should not be boring. I ran, cleaned, ate, showered, then went to meet Jewel. I don't know if I wrote you guys about the guys playing music in the street, but I think I did. Anyway they are really good, and they were in Bib-Rambla plaza today playing good Christmas stuff.

I am actually pretty happy right now cuz the future is getting closer, my midtermish tests next week shouldn't be hard, and today I am wearing my high neck brown, orange, pinkish red, and blueish gray sweater that I bought at a second hand store for 500 pesetas ($2.75).

I am also very happy about the jerky, and that my sister is so awesome at school, and that I have such loving parents. Yeah. It will be good to be in a car and drive through my mountains.

Is there more Bin Laden-the war or pre-Olympics stuff on the news?
K, I love you. Heather

Fri, 07 Dec 2001 17:12
[Heather wrote in reply to Christmas Letter ideas from Mom]:

Monday sounds soon, but I can try. Sugar plumbs and poems are in my head. Hortin wrote about his life in Chicago and that he and Mike want to come to Spain, which would be awesome.

Today was run and go to cafe with Christian and see beautiful festive lights all turned on in the city and over many streets. I need to study a little for tests next week and then be ready to go to Madrid and then to our house. I love you guys!!
Heather

Subject: Heath and Jewel being touristy
Date: Sat, 08 Dec 2001 14:33 From: "Heather Gross"
    Thanks for giving me stuff to put in the poem. Last night and today were good. Jewel's [Spanish] family is in Loja, a pueblo outside of Granada where her mama's family lives. Her shower is broken, so she slept over at my house and took a good shower that actually has pressure after we went to a discoteca.
    So, this morning/afternoon Jewel and I went to la Capilla Real, the royal chapel. There we saw the tombs of King Ferdinand and Queen Isabel, los Reyes Catolicos and Juana la Loca and her husband Felipe el Hermoso, and also Prince Miguel. There is the best art collection in Spain put together by a woman, Isabel, of mainly Jesus pictures—very cool.
    Then we went to the free Flamenco show up in Sacromonte, the gypsy neigborood. Two guy guitarists, a drummer guy, a singer/clapper guy and singer/clapper big lady, and two very cute skinny with strong legs and dark greasy, one long one short, black hair flamenco guy dancers. If we had arrived about two minutes later, we would not have gotten tickets. So our seats were in the way up there, but it was still really amazing to see these guys stamp there feet with such precision and so in rhythm with the clappers and drummer and guitarers.
    Tomorrow we are going to the Mercadillo with Christian in his car. Being in a car is a privilege, and that Christian likes hanging out and wants to drive us is too. I will do the poem tonight and email it tomorrow, and I'm not going out tonight so that I can study well.
    I love the lights all over the city here. There are some beautiful views, especially from up where we saw the flamenco. We were there at 7 to get tickets for the 8 show. I think we will have to go at 6 if we want to be able to get into the lower seats. That would be better cuz from there you can see the background. The stage has windows behind it, from which the audience at the lower level can see the Alhambra in the distance, all lit up. I can't believe they put that thing on for free.
    I am so excited for the next weeks. I love you guys more than all the tappies the Flamenco guys do. Heather

Subject: since Saturday to today, Tuesday, and other stuff like dasch
Date: Tue, 11 Dec 2001 07:23 From: "Heather Gross"

K. I wanted to update the happenings even though we, mom and I, were instant messaging all yesterday morning on the poem, and so now, is the other infos. Sunday morning we went to the mercadillo where I bought a blue throw blanket for $6, to bring some colors together in my room and hide the ugly but warm blankets on my bed. then i bought a CD from the Senegal guy. There are very-black-skinned guys that look really different than African Americans, cuz they come from Africa and sell their illegally-burned CDs. These CDs cost $2.50, which is awesome, unless you buy from the Senegal (which is right below Morocco) guy from whom i chose to buy; and he sells you a case with the Pitufos on it, but a CD with some crappy flamencoish pop guy. I will buy no more of these CDs unless I bring my discman and test it out first. I do not want to have a prejudice against the Senegalese, but yeah.

I am very happy we finished the poem, and that mom found some awesome rhymes. I would be sad to go home and see what you sent to all your people without me having written it.

So this morning, I had my lit test and did well. I analyzed a poem I had studied and had a choice of two authors, about whom I had to write. I could have done either of them, so it was cool. I have my Flamenco test in an hour, and then Italian.

Oh yeah, Sunday after the market, Christian as planned; did drive Jewel and me outside of the city to a beautiful neighborhood and lake. It was so good to get outside of the city and see nice spread out land and quietness.

I cooked those fajita thingers with the spice that dad sent yesterday, and it was good. I didn't really explain to my roommates how to put not too much meat on the tortilla, so that they could fold them and eat them without forks. that is ok. were still good.

Now I be going back to school and tests. In between at 5:30 we meet in the Cafe of the CLM, like we do every Tuesday and Thursday. Today we are going to give Christian a gift of a nice frame with a picture of our whole group from the first week we were here. Kate, a girl in our group, collected money for it; so we could all give him something together. It will be cute for Christian to have a picture of his first group from the first time he was a director.

I love you more than all the money this internet place is making cuz it is always full and always open and yeah. Heather

Subject: Santa Lucia
Date: Thu, 13 Dec 2001 14:21 From: "Heather Gross"
Hi fambily!!!
    After my Italian class we all stayed to see this thing that all the Swedish students did for Santa Lucia. It was beautiful. They turned off all the lights in the CLM and had floating candles in the fountain. All the girls were in white long skirts and shirts with silver tinsel belts and wreath hats. Santa Lucia walked in front with the advent wreath on her head. The boys wore long white things too and white point wizard hats with silver stars on them. They walked in a procession all along the balcony and then downstairs where they sang tons of traditional songs, all in Swedish. There were also some girls dressed as Santas who danced around elvishly. The whole thing was lovely.
    Then we walked through holidayish lit downtown Granada. Dasch did more tripod picture taking. Now we be here at the internet. Tomorrow I buy more Christmas presents, show Dasch more Granada stuff, and pack. We leave Saturday morning on the bus five hours to Madrid.
    OH! Tuesday night I made my famous oatmeal cookies and have never been a prouder cook. This would be because when I woke up the next morning, there was a note from Caro saying ummm, ummm, ummm, congratulations, Heather, these are the best cookies in all of Granada. I gave a little thinger of them to Christian with a note about thank you for making these months awesome. Caro wrote down the recipe and is going to make them at her house once she finds some vanilla. The stuff I bought isn't real; it's sugar water, but it worked. The thing is that the Spanish do not measure with cups and teaspoon volumes; they do it my grams and mass. anyway i guessed well.
    save me lots of jerky. so now i am taking dasch to some gooood nummmy tapas. I am so excited to see you guys, and write to me!! and yes. I love you!!! Heather

Subject: MADRID
Date: Sun, 16 Dec 2001 04:29 From: "Heather Gross"

The Devil's Fingernail

    I am here in the capital of Spain with Jewel and Dasch! Yesterday we got here at about 1:30 PM. We then went to our hostel, where we had reservations; and then to the Prado, the most famous museum in all of Spain. We will go to another museum with more contemporary stuff, the Reina Sofia, today. Jewel flies home tomorrow, and Dasch and I are talking about Salamanca, El Escorial, Segovia, and Toledo.
    Walking to this internet place I saw this Antonio, from my Granada Italian class. Pretty cool, eh? Madrid is all lit up beautifully for Christmas.
    Friday night Jewel, Dasch, and I were shopping and Christian called. We went to Tapas with him to say bye. Dasch had bought a bottle of red wine and decided to open it for my roommates to try. We had a kind of traditiorial Spanish cena, dinner, with little clams and arid good wine.
    I have lots of extra room in my big suitcase, which I filled with newspaper, so coming back with other stuff will be fine. This internet place is good cuz you get a ticket and use up minutes till your credit runs out. Write me about your weekends.
    An alert to keep my valuables with me at all times just popped up on the screen. Elton John is singing. I love you guys more than how famous Marilyn Monroe was being a candle in the wind. Heather

Heather didn't know that she too was "a candle in the wind."

From: Heather Gross Sent: Monday, December 17, 2001 2:55 PM
Subject: Re: flight info
    This morning we took Jewel to the airport and left my big suitcase, which is like a Santa bag for you guys, in a locker at the airport in Madrid. Then Dasch and I took a train to Salamanca, where I am now. I have not seen much of it in the daylight, but la Plaza Mayor is beautiful, and I am way excited to tour tomorrow. We called from Madrid and made reservations in our hostel.
    Salamanca has a Granada feel to it cuz it is a university town and is full of students. It is midterms week, and one can tell they are busy. Dasch is being mr. photographer with his tripod while i wander and stare at statues. we just ate some good dinner with wine. num. Skiing will be da bomb diggity. I

am glad you like your skis, mom.
    K. My best Christmas present will be getting to see you guys!! I love you guys more than how cold it can be in this part of Spain. (I am wearing all my coats and my long underwear under my jeans.) I am excited to have nice extra warm water that i don't have to light before i shower!
    Heather
    I will send flight info when i check the exactuals soon, by wed.

From: Heather Gross Sent: Wednesday, December 19, 2001 2:21 PM
Subject: flight and me be coming home!!
    Dasch just got here after shopping for his girlfriend and himself and now we have to go to a movie, yay! then i come home!!! so, this morning dasch and i left our hostel at 7:15 AM to make it to a 7:45 train back to Madrid. We had to book and barely made it. I have too many awesome presents for you guys.
    This internet place is the same one i was at before in madrid. i have leftover credit from my and jewel's cards, dasch is not the internet maniac like i am and so is admiring his recent purchases from el Corte Ingles.
    Today we saw El Palacio Real—lots of expensive fancy rooms with explanations from my Rick Steve's Spain and Portugal guide, and an awesome museum of art—much more contemporary than that of the Prado. like Picasso's Guernica, very cool.
    another neat thinger is that i was reading the Salamanca chapter and finished it in Salamanca of Michener's Iberia. I like traveling. i love it.
    hey, too, i had my period, so maybe i can give you guys grandkids many years in the future.
    do not put any ornaments on the tree, especially the EVIL SANTA!!! I love you guys more than all the names and characters there are for whoever it is that brings the presents to the kids in the countries all over the world during Christmas time!! I will see you in 32 hours!!! i cannot wait!   lOvE,
heather

Heather's Journal   *20 December 2001*   *While in*

The Devil's Fingernail

route coming home
.... I will treasure being with my family in our house with carpet and always warm heaters and our Christmas tree and deer jerky and seeing Teresa and lots of other people. . . . Perhaps I will ski in my mountains. I will talk to Jewel, Tracy, and Andy on the phone; hopefully Lauren in Michigan too. Tracy is flying to Arizona. Jewel will be home for three weeks. It will be an awesome feeling to be going back to what I have in Granada. Christian is maybe the best new friend I have made there. He is our director and has taken to me like an older brother. I think especially because one day I cried to him. I was pretty depressed . . . just normal waves of emotions. We 14 AZ kids are his first group. Christian grew up in Granada and is the best in being an information resource and friend. I am excited to give my fam all the good presents I'm bringing from Spain, also to run on the treadmill and play in Utah nieve.

We loved having our Heather home from December 20th to January 4th.

Christmas Greetings 2001
I'm studying abroad, so this year I'm writing from Granada, Spain.
E-mail keeps me connected to my Mom, Dad, and Em on Coventry Lane.

They are excited to have Montana relatives for the 2002 Olympic Games.
Mom's teaching and on church council, while dad is leasing and billing medical claims.

Emily, a senior, is doing well in English, Calculus and Art.
In the fall Colorado State University is probably where she will start.

I have courses in Spanish, Italian, and chemistry at the university of Granada
And am working on becoming a travel aficionada.

Last August our family enjoyed an Aronson reunion,
At the wedding of Andy, our Canadian cousin.

Soon, I will be home for Christmas, deer jerky, and pumpkin pie.
Then back to Spain where Mom and Em will visit next July.

We hope you find peace in this difficult time.
We send you our love through this well traveled rhyme.

Love, The Grosses
Heather (author), Emily (artist), Alyce, and Denny

Christmas Greetings 2001

I'm studying abroad, so this year I'm writing from Granada, Spain.
E-mail keeps me connected to my Mom, Dad, and Em on Coventry Lane.

They are excited to have Montana relatives for the 2002 Olympic Games.
Mom's teaching and on church council, while dad is leasing and billing medical claims.

Emily, a senior, is doing well in English, Calculus and Art.
In the fall Colorado State University is probably where she will start.

I have courses in Spanish, Italian and chemistry at the University of Granada
And am working on becoming a travel aficionada.

Last August our family enjoyed an Aronson reunion,
At the wedding of Andy, our Canadian cousin.

Soon, I will be home for Christmas, deer jerky, and pumpkin pie.
Then back to Spain where Mom and Em will visit next July.

We hope you find peace in this difficult time.
We send you our love through this well traveled rhyme.

Love, The Grosses
Heather (author), Emily (artist), Alyce, and Denny
adgross@earthlink.net

Subject: Heathy writing from the Spain in 2002
Date: Mon, 07 Jan 2002

    I am so happy to have an email from everyone in the family. You guys are so cute and nice and loving. And I think our family gets along way too well. I love that you wrote right after I had left, Em. And Dad, it is cool that you got a little teary eyed and that you told me. you saw how I did, right?

yep. so, i am good now. this is the first time I made it to the internet. I slept 12 hours the first night, after Josie and I watched Charlie and the Chocolate Factory. Em, how are you the most awesome sis that just lets me copy all your clothes and packs my suitcase so well for me?

The Cabalgata de los Reyes Magos (the parade of the wisemen or magic kings) was a bunch of sparkly floats and little kids and some old guys throwing candy to tons of scrambling Spanish people trying to grab the candy. the old people will even kind of dive for it. twas interesting.

Josie slept at my apt Saturday and last night (sunday) too. we ran Sunday afternoon and today morning. i am eating well too, so I feel healthy and time adjusted. she feels weird living with her family and brought her guitar over to play at my house cuz she feels like she can't play it at her house.

so I cleaned the whole apt, swept, mopped, and dusted, except for my roommates rooms. Pilar and Carolina got home today. I think Mercedes tonight or tomorrow. Jewel got here yesterday afternoon, but I didn't see her till today because she went to sleep forever because unlike always prepared and packed (this is sarcasm) heather, jewel started packing at 1 AM the night before she left, then dyed her hair at 3 AM. and then had to leave for the airport at 6:30 in the morning.

so she and Josie and I are just full of stories and it is fun. Oh yeah, I saw Christian even before Jewel cuz he came over cuz i didn't hear my phone when he called. He thinks Em is reallly cute from the pictures of us and the tree. he he. Jewel brought her pictures over. I hadn't seen any of them because she waited to be in the US to develop all of them. It was like getting Christmas presents because she gave me all the doubles I wanted. She has so many cute ones, lots from when we had parties and I wouldn't bring my camera, yay!

School starts tomorrow!! at 8:30 in the morning with one of my favorite classes, literature. I will give my roommates the Olympic animalies. I think it is a little sad that I am missing the games, but according to Katie Gracia, I should be very grateful.

I just I realized that I did have an awesome break. I even went to dinner with Teresa and Roland at La Puente. He asked about how you guys were doing, and if you were still friends with that Randy guy, dad.

    I meet all the new AZ kids tomorrow, and we all have a dinner at 9 with Christian. K. I love you guys. I will go to the post office tomorrow and look for my package from you guys. Thank you for offering to send more, dad. mom, thank you for doing so much shopping with me. i love my pajamas and pants and am wearing the boots, and they are fine for walking around here. the blue pants are hemmed well and cute.

    Write more newses ! ! ! ! I love you more than how relieving it is to just be able to know exactly where I am going all over this city. Heather 'Hermelinda Asquerosa' Gross

Heather's Journal   9 Jan 2002
*   Um, I didn't even talk about how awesome being home was, but it was. The best was my dad and my mom and my Em. I also had lots of fun at Greg's cabin, and with Katie Gracia, whom I brought up there, and whom I had only seen about once each Christmas and summer after my first semester at ASU.*

Subject: Jueves
Date: Thu, 10 Jan 2002
    That is awesome about Tristan!! [She got Olympic gold for the skeleton.] My roommates loved their Olympic mascot thingers. I also gave each of them the poem, a fam picture, and an Olympic postcard with a note from me on it. Hey, will you guys send me an Olympic postcard with some Salt Lake picture on it or something while there still are some?

    The euro thing is interesting. People can use pesetas up till February 28. The exchange is something like 6 euros is 5 dollars—easier than pesetas.

    I keep thinking of the stuff I will show the mom and the Em when you guys come. I can't get my package until I get a notice, and that hasn't happened, so I hope it is still coming.

    Going home to eat. Write, please. I love you Heathy

Heather wrote emails about every two or three days. Although it was difficult to decide what to leave out, I did not include them all.

Subject: Heathey happier

Alyce Gross

Date: Tues, 15 Jan 2002

Hey, you guys. You are great. Yeah, I am so fortunate to be here. and I am in a way better mood than when I wrote and when we talked. Thank you for the perspective giving story of the guys in the army in Germany, dad.

so I went skiing by myself yesterday. It was just good to get up in the sun and out of the city. I made myself a blue cheese and bacon sandwich, in our sandwich grill and another of hardboiled egg and mayo and packed them, num. these should not be the most important things of the day. k. I rented skis which i found just before I got on the bus at the bus station that are cheaper than the ones at the mall that Christian recommended and tons cheaper than renting up at the ski resort. anyway, the snow sucks. it was ice with powder crap over it. but i still had fun. there are also no trees, so i miss that. there was tons of wind at the top of one lift, the highest, point, from where you can see morocco! it reminded me of the top of Bannock. did they change that lift name at Targhee? so you guys sound like you are having good times skiing too.

thanks for the more cooking ideas, mom, hey!! I finally got my package! my portero the doorman had it and probably did since early december, but anyway, thank you!!! the beanie, fits like a swim cap, but I really like the colors, can you return things 8 months after they're purchased, like next July? if not, i can mail it back, or make use of it here, i also loved alIII the pictures.

after skiing, i went running and then showered and went to my 7:00 class. today has been all school and the first day of Italian. I told my teacher about the going to Italy and she will give me ideas of special stuff to do.

Hey—and that money that I thought I had to pay twice for my phone mistake ended up being taken off. i mean i only paid once—so that is cool, even though i know i shouldn't get upset over dumb stuff like that.

I am thinking that my next semester doesn't have to be so scary. I can take one chem class and maybe some translation classes, but at traductores—the university campus building near my house. as long as i am filling the 12 hour full time exchange program scholarship requirement.

i love that i have active awesome parents, and my sis. she's da bomb. Chris is telling me about the last time he can

The Devil's Fingernail

remembered being homesick, cuz i was telling him about my emotionals until recently. it is cute. My roommates are awesome too.

oh, no. this strange AZ guy just got online, i need to get off the internet sooooon.

um. yeah. so i am really much happier and know that i have tons of things to be happy for and can always remember them when i am sad.

if you guys see tree or tristan, say hi! ! I love you guys more than all the types i have ever typed with these fingers. Heather

[So, again Heather was having her ups and downs with emotions, and was doing her best to focus on the positive things in her life. She did have bouts of depression in Spain, but not nearly as severe as that first year in college.]

Subject: good cooking and travels
Date: 20 Jan 2002

Hey!! I have lots of newses. K. Thursday at the arab baths was awesome. That night I was walking to the sidreria, the cider place, and saw my Moroccan dude friend who was working at the Shawarma place. Shawarma is like the muslim countries' version of gyros, num. Anyway, I had talked to him a lot, so he invited me to have an Arab sweet thinger and talked to me in his weird non-conjugating of the verbs Spanish.

I had to leave to go see Jewel and Josie. Josie's real dad and her step-mom, who are in Granada, were at the sidreria. Then Jewel and I went up to the Arabic baths with Stephanie and Mark. Mark is gay and like one of the girls. They smell kind of weird, with Jasmine oils in the water. There are two shallow pools, a hot one and a cold one. You keep switching between the two and get called sometime to get a fifteen minute massage. Then we four went back to my Shawarma dude's place.

Friday I ran and cooked the chicken thing recipe you gave me last week, mom! It worked. I used mushrooms in a can we had with bechamel, which is the creamy flavored stuff people used as filling or flavoring. I did the chicken with olive oil in the micro first, and broccoli that I bought from the fruit man the night before. I fried the mushrooms on the stove, and Caro helped me do the bechamel on the stove too. Then I put all that stuff with chunks o cheese in the oven for about 25 minutes. The only thing I messed up was the rice, cuz I put too much salt in it. but my roommates loved it.

We (Jewel, Stephanie, Dominica, and Leah who came with the new Arizona group) met at the bus station and left for Malaga at 9 PM. There we got to our hostel that I had reserved a few hours before.

So, yeah, I have been gone all weekend, but before I didn't want to write that we were going to go, cuz last semester we tended not to end up going; but now I am the traveler. That night we ate at a delicious pizza place and decided to not go out so that we could get up and get on the bus. The next day we went to Gibraltar! Four of us got a bus Saturday morning to the Rock on the Prudential commercials, the most southern tip of Europe, and not Spanish. It's owned by Great Britain. The bus schedule ended up letting us only be there for four hours, but we got a tour guy who took us everywhere in an hour and a half; so he was very worth it. Gibraltar has some cool stuff. There are monkeys that live on the top of the rock and are just in the road when the car stops. The guy had to shut the doors immediately, so they wouldn't get in. I walked around to the back of the van and all of a sudden there was a fat heavy monkey on my head. The tour dude told him to jump off the van and onto me. I have a picture of this.

[I, Heather's mom, laughed at this picture, which I saw later, on Heather's refrigerator in her last home in Utah. I'm not sure where it ended up, but I hope someone who loved her has it.]

Then a monkey stole a Winnie the Pooh key chain off Dominica's back pack, and the tour dude tried to tempt him with my gum for five minutes before he gave back the Winnie the Pooh. the monkey had taken the Pooh's shirt off and sucked on it. It was hilarious. We saw the inside of a cool stalagmite/tite cave and then the tunnels British soldiers started digging in 1789, to defend Gibraltar from the Spanish and French trying to win it back. They used the caves in the World Wars too. There are more than 35 miles of tunnels in the rock which now house military offices and stuff. We had an awesome view of the Atlantic, the Mediterranean, and Africa all at once. Gibraltar is supposed to be one to the Pillars of Hercules and the entrance to Hades. The monkeys were the coolest part of the tour.

The Devil's Fingernail

Later we had some, good fish and chips, and went back across the border to our bus back to Malaga. We napped and then went dancing. We are thankful for the going out crowd of Granada. Most of the people seemed to be older than college kids. We didn't get the accepting of Americans vibe that Granada bars give, but we still had fun.

Today we walked around beautiful Malaga parks and got on the bus back to Granada at 4 PM. Piler's brother Quino was on the bus with us. He had been in Almeria, playing handball. Now I am here. I have so much to be thankful for here. I mean my apt and roommates. I have seen Amanda and Leah's apts, and I am so lucky to have a big room with lots of light, and roommates that do all their laundry and cooking and food buying and cleaning together.

I just bought a small bulletin board from the Chinese people dollar store to put more pictures up in my room. Tonight I am going to the movie with Amelia.

Hey, mom, will you keep sending recipes like that? That would be perfect, something with meat in it like once a week, cuz I only cook on Fridays. Then I can plan if I need to buy anything extra and not be making random, grilled cheese sandwiches and omelets like I did last week. I was proud that I had bought the broccoli the night before and taken the chicken out of the freezer, and had thought about what I was doing, so that it wasn't a rushed.

Michelle and Chris wrote. Michelle is such a young, party kid like me, while Chris writes with such maturity and is so all adulty but still fun.

I will call soon. I love you guys more than how good the monkeys in Gibraltar are at stealing stuff from tourists!

Subject: rain Wednesday
Date: Wed, 23 Jan 2002

There was tons of rain yesterday and some today. so I hope this means there is snow up in the mountains. I will check it out soon.

I am here with Caro helping her internet. Spanish people don't grow up learning to type in school or with computers in their houses. She is cute and some Spanish dude in this place thinks so too. I got her email address from her and put it in my address book. so now he is writing her about how

he likes her sweater and her dark hair. tis funny.
    I think I have my classes for the next semester figured out. Christian and Julie of IPO are really helpful. I ran 5 miles and did my leg thingers and pushups today, then went and talked to the science register lady with Christian.
    thank you all for writing. i love hearing from each of you guys. even though the stir fry should be pretty easy I printed it off, mom. your day off sounded fun. i am glad you guys have found porcupine grill and their spinach salads that you love.
    Granada is now not Spain's candidate for the winter Olympics of 2010. Christian is sad. He wanted to build cabins for them and work for them too. I think it is good, cuz the one ski resort here is nothing compared to the awesome skiing in UT.
    This internet place is not that far from school, but it's raining and i don't have my hat. I will be ok. I love you guys more than all the times this song has weird noises in it (that would be a lot) Heather

In a post card written on Jan 28, 2002, she shared: *I pray, "like a mother hen protects her baby chicks" prayer for you guys every morning.* It made me feel good that she was modeling after me.

In Venice one never loses the sense that life is being staged for the onlooker." Jonathan Raban
Following are two perspectives (Heather's and Jewel's) about "life being staged for the onlooker."

Subject: the Heath in the rome on il Giorno di San Valentino
Date: Thu, 14 Feb 2002 12:09 From: "Heather Gross"
    so I have little time on this way expensive Italian internet card I bought in Venice, and am using up at one of their other locations, in the train station in Rome. Today was pretty cool, and I am so excited for tomorrow. We saw all the Rome stuff outside of Vatican City, like the Colosseum, the Pantheon, and tons more. Tomorrow I will take pics of St Peter's Square, like you have, Mom. That will be da bomb. Venice
    k. so the best story about this trip happened in Venice with Jewel. We were just walking around the first day we got

The Devil's Fingernail

there.

That city is so unique cuz there are no cars, and just lots of water and bridges. So it was the second to last night of Carnevale. There was some dude with a boom box in the huge square by the bell tower. He had some good technoish stuff going. Jewel and I stopped and were just dancing. Then it was just me, and all of a sudden this circle had formed around me, and there i was in my beanie dancing and people taking pictures, like i was a street performer. it was awesome!!!!! and then jewel danced with me too, and we did this for a half an hour, with people watching the whole time. man.

k. and i love you all more than all these weird astronaut looking glasses all the hip peeps in rome are wearing!! heather

Jewel, kindly wrote about the Venice dancing as well, and much more, when asked to share some memories for Heather's memorial service.

During another one of our trips we had probably one of my favorite study abroad stories ever. We were in Venice, Italy during carnival and there were loads of people dressed up, enjoying the festivities. During the second night of our stay we were on the way back to meet our 10 PM curfew at the nunnery (we hadn't booked a hostel and it was the only place we could find!), when we saw a dude with a boom box and some great dance music by the bell tower in San Marcos Plaza. Heather and I stopped to enjoy the music but did not understand why no one was dancing. Shortly after in true Heather style she busted out her infamous dance moves. I could not resist and joined in on the fun. A large crowd of tourists began to crowd around us, multiplying by the second (who wouldn't stop for Heather's unique moves!?!). Soon there were loads of people filming and taking pictures, thinking we were a part of the carnival festivities. It's too bad we had a curfew because I think we could have danced all night (and probably put a hat out and made some travel money too).
By Jewel

Heather's Carnival mask is displayed at our home in Utah on a dresser top along with pictures of her.

In a February postcard from Roma, she wrote about the

Alyce Gross

huge museum crowd to see the Capella Sistina (Sistine Chapel) and, *to go up the dome of le Basilica di San Pietro, you can pay less to take the stairs instead of the elevator, which I did running.* ☺ *I want of come back to Italia very soon. K. I love you guys more than all the tourists in all i musei (museums) in the world.*

Subject: 3 days after Valentines me in spagna
Date: Sun, 17 Feb 2002

I am in Granada. got here last night. I am just writing a little thinger and will call when i leave.

Here is how our trip was. We flew to Rome from Madrid on the 8th of feb. We slept there that night in a HI hostel, Hostels International. I got a hostel card for these places before I left, a good thing I bought from Council Travel. anyway, that place was huge and had dorm rooms of sixteen beds and breakfast included.

the next morning jewel and I got to the train station and bought a kilometric ticket for the trains, which gives us free or a discount on tickets for all the trains in italy, with 3000 kilometers of distance to use. we went from there to Florence Saturday. There we stayed in the bomb hostel. We did tons of tourist stuff there. The David is at la Gallerian della' Academia, a museum whose only cool thing is he. but dude, he is perfect, and it is crazy that someone could sculpt something so well. He was done in 1502-1504.

we stayed in Florence Saturday and Sunday night. on Monday morning we went to Venice. There we stayed Monday and Tuesday night in the hostel run by nuns. lots of water, no cars, masks and carnevale.

Wednesday we trained to Rome—were there wed, thu, and friday night in a different smaller hostel than the first, with our own room and a kitchen, and in a location much closer to the city center; like four minutes walk from the train station. we flew to madrid yesterday morning and bused to granada getting here at 8:30 pm.

So when does Olympic company get there tomorrow? Did you guys go to church this morning? I still have not seen anything on tv about the olympics cuz i haven't been around one, but also cuz it is not a very big deal here. I read the sports section of an Italian paper on the way home. There was more about soccer than the games – just one story about a scandal between the Canadians and Russian figure skaters who should have won or something. i still don't read Italian fluently. hey, but i did speak it a lot, and well. twas cool.

k. i love you guys more than all the screaming nine year old girls at all the Blink 182 concerts. Heather

Subject: me really frustrated
Date: Wed, 20 Feb 2002 04:13 From: "Heather Gross"

My classes supposedly started Monday. The inorganic classes I had chosen do not work to just come into half way through the year. Yesterday after the second class, I talked with the teacher. He was very nice and kept telling me how awesome my Spanish is and how he knows this dude in the chem dept at the U of U and helped me find some classes that are just this semester. So I am going to go talk to those teachers if I can find them.

Anyway, Monday I was really upset and have been crying, because I feel like it is a waste of time that I am here for two semesters taking dumb classes that don't help me with my major. I should be in Italy or at ASU. And then when I want to tell someone about this, I can't call them cuz I don't have my damn phone. anyway, I am going back to the sciences building now. and you won't have read this till after i know more, but i will pretend that you have and that you are praying for me, cuz this is a huge mess. and then all the news stations for the sports, put 20 minutes of soccer and a clip of Olympics, so I let that get me all frustrated too. and Christian can't do anything cuz he has no idea what classes would work for me, and the whole problem is that the exchange program here just shouldn't exist.

and thank you for all my packages!!! you sent a lot of postcards, mom, thanks, and for the news clippings. and i love the cd, dad. I just need a hug or something, but listening to music from you is good. sorry this is just a big complainy email. did you guys like all my explanations with the pictures i sent?

I love you. i am glad you're having fun with Olympic guests in my room. Heather

Subject: Thanks
Date: Thu, 21 Feb 2002 12:31 From: "Heather Gross"

for listening to me.

I think I am straightening something out, but still have possible classes in the air. I found a semester long inorganic chem class that is taught in the chemical engineering dept, so I think I am taking that and one other class to be determined.

My phone is on the way from the nun. I am not obsessing over the Olympics mom, I would like to know about Tristan Gale and the events that you guys see. Say "Hi" to the guests, especially Aunt Bev and Uncle Allan for me. I love you guys.
Heather

Subject: monday better than last
Date: Mon 25 Feb 2002 10:28 From: "Heather Gross"

So, I talked to mom yesterday on IM, but did not talk to the rest of you. I am using the computer at the library in the building where my translation class is. There are signs on all of them that say that they are not for email or personal work, only for bibliographic consultation, so this will be quick.

This weekend was cool. I was so happy to not have to worry about school. Friday morning I went to two more classes, this complement to inorganic, and some very specific organic class about heterocycles that are both for 3rd yr students and which i think i am not going to take. I have to still find out if I have 12 hours with just the three classes I'm in now: Italian, Translation, and this inorganic chem in the chem engineering dept that just started this semester; so that is according to what Julie Williams of IPO writes back, and what i found out from the people in the office upstairs who go home at 2.

friday night i went to a café with dominica and jewel. then watched the Olympics live from 2-5 AM. i got to see the gala of the ice skaters, twas cool.

Saturday i ran for the first time since before Italy cuz I'm healthier. I went a new way on this trail along the freeway. i told mom this little story. there was some homeless dude's shack and this wolf guard dog who chased me barking. i turned around with my hands up and he decided to not bite me.

that night jewel, stephanie, and dominica came over and hung out at my apt. then I went out with my roommates to a plaza and to a bar. sunday caro's parents came to visit, they took us all to a delicioso ristorante italiano. num.

The Devil's Fingernail

today after lunch, before my chem class, josie came over. she is very cool and a great friend. she is good at cheering me up and helping me be excited to be here. we will probably be the only people, of the AZ group, who will stay to the end of July.

right now it is easy to have feelings of wanting to go home or of just not be feeling right in spain cuz it is transition time. it will be cool to have her here during June to travel with and go to the beach with and stuff.

i will write back to you, em, soon. i love you guys a lot, and it is really easy for me to want to go home and cry about missing you cuz you are so wonderful. so i love you more than all the dumb tears i like to cry about that. Heather

Heather did struggle with depression in Spain; but she did her best to self-analyze, to try to focus on her blessings, and pull herself out of it with exercise. Through it all she still managed to be a good friend and relied on good friends like Josie and many others.

Subject: stuff and my trip
Date: Mon, 04 Mar 2002 12:59 From: "Heather Gross"
I was already here this morning writing to you guys and then realized that I didn't even write what I was supposed to—my journal entry type stuff—the stuff you, mom, like to print and save; but before that, Katie Gracia wrote back to me. Yay! I figured out her email address and wrote her last week and she just responded. She said she had been so busy, and you guys sound busy, and I think that is what I miss, and people. Josie and I had a good talk. We have a lot of the same problem. This whole, "why are we here right now? Frustration!!" so I am ok—I just want to get through this semester of dumb classes. I do not like chemistry. I am falling asleep cuz it is at 4 every day after big meal time, but when I am awake I do not know half of what I should be taking notes on, cuz weird mumbly Andalucian Spanish is not my first language. blah.

but k. so Katie Gracia wrote that the Olympics were verry cool, and that part of me went to the opening ceremony and one of the luges and a hockey game and something else cuz she wore my ski pants to all those things, so that is cute.

Alyce Gross

My trip: Thursday morning, I got to the bus station to leave on the 10 bus, but we couldn't get tickets for it cuz everyone in Granada was leaving on a bus; cuz of the puente, which means bridge—
the holiday that laps over to the weekend. So Josie was there too, cuz she was going to the beach and also couldn't leave till 1:00. She, Domenica, Marisa, Jewel, Sydney, and I went to a cafe across the street for breakfast. Josie and I walked around and sat on some benches. We are good talkers for each other. Then I got on the bus with the other four girls to Madrid.

We found the Hostel Internacional, where I get a discount cuz of my HI card. It was up on a hill in a castle! The room with breakfast was 10 euros. we had a cute little window from which we could see Toledo. This city is up on a hill surrounded by green mountains and a river.

friday morning we went to the Cathedral there, the bomb, the coolest art thing was this hole in the ceiling with angels painted that tumble into the main part and then become statues. it is described in Michener's Iberia, and was cool to see while reading about. He took twenty pages to describe the stuff in la Catedral de Toledo, so I had fun speriencing it.

We then went to the Alcazar, which means fortress or castle. In Toledo it was a big fortress, just a big square block with a cool square and a statue of two dudes fighting in the middle. I had Jewel and Sydney be the two dudes and took their picture. There were rooms filled with armor and minitures of soldiers, not too interesting. The nice thing about all this is that it is a ton cheaper to get into all the tourist things in Spain than it is in Italy. We went back to the Cathedral to see stuff we had missed and ate at el Delfin, a cafe. Outside la Iglesia the church de Santo Tome. I asked this dude where to get some good Mazapan. He recommended some delicious stuff nuns make. Real marzipan, as spelled in english, is made of just almonds and sugar. it is num. we had that and some made with eggs too. Toledo is famous for its mazapan.

that night we took a bus north to Madrid, and then left on the second to last bus at 10 pm, for an hour and a half north to segovia. it was snowing the last half hour of the ride, and this was jewel's first sight of falling snow. Then we stood in it and got a taxi to where we thought we could stay at a hostel. dude had given 8 beds to american girls, so no room. we were like mary and Joseph and jesus or something cuz we tried about five other places with people not answering doors or not having room. so we ended up at a hotel for 21 euros a night. not so bad. in Segovia, the next morning, we got breakfast cheap at a supermarket that we found with the help of a nice segovian man who walked us most of the way there. the aqueduct is tall and big and has lots of arches and no mortar—Impressive.

next we went to the alcazar, where the cathedral looks like a disney castle. we climbed the tower there for an awesome view of the city and snowcapped mountains in the distance. the taxi driver told us that there is skiing 20 kilometers away.

we did that tourist stuff in the morning so that we could get to madrid for Saturday night. that evening in Madrid we met marisa, domenica, paul michael, meredith, and jaime to go to the centre de arte la Reina Sofia. i went there with Dasch in December, but that is ok. Picasso's Guernica is the bomb. That is the main thing i looked at. We were there for a couple hours till 9 at night when it closed.

Sunday morning we went to a bus stop to get tickets and left for granada at 1:30. they showed Sgt. Bilko, a dumb steve martin army movie, made dumber cuz in Spanish, on the bus. but i had my music and the Italian novel i am slooowly reading.

now am here. i think the rain is doing a number on my spirits. it is nice that josie and i feel the same and have each other to talk to. sorry if i email you too much. i love you guys, heather

Subject: Re: feel better
Date: Wed, 06 Mar 2002 13:42 From: "Heather Gross"

Hi, family. I am still kind of in a slump, but tomorrow is a new day, and that will be good. I went skiing yesterday with Josie. She snowboarded. I had fun with her, but kind of didn't cuz we saw Casey up there around noon. They were both snowboarding and liked runs that weren't so awesome for the skier me. Anyway, it was still very nice to be out of the city. There was a ton of powder, sun, and few skiers, but the good part of the mountain wasn't open because of avalanche danger.

I need to get over myself and this crying thing I like to do. I will find out about doing community service, and I could do that even if it doesn't help toward my scholarship. I hope

your sore throat is better, mom. I got your thing in the mail, dad, about the Olympic athletes who lost medals because of doping. thank you. i really love mail. i am running with josie in the morning and then meeting that nice Julia girl from my translation class for breakfast.
    i love you mom. i love you dad. i love you em. Heather

Again Heather is doing all she can to control her emotions—this time adding community service and showing compassion for her friend Tracy. Heather shared that Tracy emailed her with good advice, and Heather shared with us some of her response to Tracy:

Sun, 10 Mar 2002
    so this is a lot of stories, but i wanted to tell you them. and i love you tracy. about a counselor—I think i have Christian and caro for that. Caro is Carolina my roommate. I really like her and can talk to her forever and that is good.
    and i just smile and love you saying how you told your friends about me crazy dancing. in my Italian class, we were supposed to bring an object really special to us, so i brought, of course, the itro necklace, and explained all about us. and in toledo, jewel and i yelled out to you from the bridge, we love you tracy, and i just love this thing we itros have.
    k. hugs, and i am hugging you so hard right now. i love you tracy, heather

    so, yes, family, all those things. i really do love caro. and so hope that she, Mercedes, and pilar too, can come to the US. Evan wants caro to visit him too, cuz he is in love with her i think; but they have established that it is just friends—whatever.

Heather's Journal   12 march 2002
    I am sitting in the sun. . . . The birds are chirp, chirping here, and being outside like this is all too beautiful for me to be writing about problems. But, a

thing I so need to write is that the 2002 Winter Olympic Games in Salt Lake City, Utah had the women's skeleton as an event for the first time, and that my friend, Tristan Gale, won the Gold Medal! Pretty cool, eh?

Subject: Re: Dad counseling and it's ok, mom
Date: Tue, 12 Mar 2002 13:34 From: "Heather Gross"
You did not numb me with your lecture, dad, and it was ok talking to mom, you talk sense which I need more than niceness. I mean it is good to hear that I am in charge of my happiness.

Mom's input: Sadly it took four years for us to understand that we were wrong—she needed kindness. We didn't realize that Heather really couldn't control the depression problem. She tried so hard to help herself by appreciating her friends and family, focusing on what she was thankful for, getting plenty of exercise, and working hard in her classes in spite of being depressed. Probably the most important thing is that she continued to communicate openly with us.

So today I ran and then went to the park with my Italian novel. I finished it and understood it. I have my oral exam on Thursday, where I tell the whole class about the book for ten minutes. Tomorrow I am practicing with Mario, so that should be good. At the park too, I wrote in my journal about jewel stuff, kind of like a letter, with all of what I needed to say to her. Then after I went to her house and we had a good talk, and I read her what I wrote. So we are planning to go together to see Lauren and Amsterdam.
I saw on the news about how they commemorated 6 months after September 11. My problems do matter, but I need to know how awesome my life is, and know that much more serious stuff goes on.
Today, I focused in chemistry and understood more. I will talk to the teacher about what you said, mom. that will be good. You don't have to call, mom, unless you have a cheap way of doing it. but it would be cool. Now I am going to play soccer with that Julie.
Thank you for being a supportive good advice awesome

family. I love all you guys more than how excited everyone here is cuz the girl Rosa, from Armilla, a town in Granada, was chosen from that singing program to go to Eurovision. Heather

Subject: la Fiesta de la Primavera
Date: Fri, 15 Mar 2002 05:32 From: "Heather Gross"
    Hello, family. I love reading your emails. I need Em to write back, por favor. thank you, Dad, for taking care of all my stuff—driver's license, taxes, and all that paperwork school stuff you always inform me about. It is so nice to know that I don't have to wonder about the stuff being sent to me in another country.
    Mom, thank you for calling me. I have your message saved. It is cute. It must be nice to have no school today and to have all your conferences done after long days at school. My phone is testy and likes to turn off if I put in my purse. I think the battery easily disconnects or the antenna being touched makes that happen. Anyway, if you get a cheap way to call me, probably let me know around when you would call so that I can have my phone working and on.
    so Tuesday night I played soccer with these Spanish girls who are good and have played in a league. The only grass the U of Granada has is for rugby. We played on a cement court outside, but it is cool. Julie is an American girl from the CLM. I had tea with her last Sunday at her house. She saw these girls playing once and just asked to play. Anyway, I had lots of fun and am going to keep playing with them.
    It has been rainy, but today is sunny with approaching clouds. Mario is the Italian guy I liked and who now is just my helper for my class. He helped me figure out what to say and what to focus on in telling about the 90 pg novel I read on Wednesday. I met him Thursday again and had him listen to my speech. I also did it for Josie and Christian. So the real thing went really well. I like the story. The story was about this dude who gets cut in half in a war against the Turks, but how one half of him survives and goes back to his hometown. Then the other half of him comes home a year later. The nephew of 8 years tells the story. The two halves of the guy have a duel to win the hand of their love and end up getting sewn together into one dude. It was a good story, so I had fun telling about it, and my class was laughing and didn't look too bored.
    in chemistry, I have talked to one student, Jesus. All the

kids are Spanish and maybe 18-25. For some of them, it could be their first year in college, and others, that are taking this class over—they are old. Jesus told me that I am the first foreign person he has had in a class before.

I will talk to the teacher next week, now that my Italian talk is over. I think it will be ok.

Today I woke up with a kind of sore throat. It feels better now after juice and these suck on them medicines from our drug cabinet. I haven't exercised since Tuesday, because of the rain and will maybe go swim later. I don't know if my roommates will eat at our apt, but I will go make pasta and broccoli that I bought.

I was kind of bumbed, cuz tonight is Mario's birthday party at a bar and then dancing or something, but we—Jewel, Sydney, Stephanie, Mark, and I are leaving at 11 on an 8 hr bus ride to Valencia on the east coast to see las Fallas! so that will be cool, we get there 7 in the morning and are staying all day till 2:30 AM Sunday to come back to Granada on the bus. This is because there are no available places to stay. Las Fallas (Fighyahs) are a big fire and fireworks display party that Valencia is famous for.

This trip to France or Amsterdam is still not set, cuz I can't find open train seats and don't know if it will be worth it to leave Sunday or Monday and then try to come back to Spain by Friday to see the end of Semana Santa.

You guys have fun skiing Saturday. Em, what is up??? I hope to see spring flowers soon. There is lots of rain, but they are coming.

I love you guys more than how many times I had to turn on my phone yesterday. :) Heather

Subject: feeling better kinda
Date: Mon, 18 Mar 2002 02:34

thank you for writing. Yes, the dr thought it was some kind of an allergic reaction and told me not to eat certain kinds of foods after asking me all the food i had eaten recently. I hadn't eaten anything weird, so I don't know what caused this rash. it is fine not being able to eat stuff cuz it hurts too much to swallow anyway. so I still have the rash, and it is actually worse – red puffy all over my body except my hands, feet, face, and part of my stomach, but my throat feels a little better. I have fuimicil, which is a powder you mix with water, and antibiotics for my throat, and then pills for my rash and tylenol they gave me for if i have headaches. at 1:00 Pilar and i think Mercedes are going with me back to the doctor's for a higher dosage of the shot. Yay, in my butt again.

    so i should not have gone to Valencia. my throat started feeling kind of bad on thursday, and still hurt a little friday, but we already had our bus tickets and i wanted to see las Fallas.

i think i said this on the phone, but anyway we didn't see the big fire show because they burn all these huge paper mache wooden structures on tuesday. it was still very cool.

    we wandered the streets and got to see these huge structures depicting societal faults (fallas). we ate lunch out on the grass there and tried to nap. this is when i went to pee and realized this rash was not just little red dots on my forearms. anyway we saw more fallas, had tea, got paella, and then it rained. a lot. i had my hat, but there were only two umbrellas among the seven of us. we went back to the bus station, and three of us got on the 11:30 instead of 2:30 AM bus for which we had our tickets. that bus ride was hell. i was cold and couldn't use my coat as blanket cuz it was soaked. anyway i made it back.

    so yesterday i got home, showered, and then slept from 8:30 to 3:30. i woke up and gave a note to my roommates saying that i had gotten home at 8, that i had a rash, and that it hurt to swallow and talk. they immediately had me get dressed and took me to the doctor. i didn't wake up earlier cuz i thought that there were no available doctors on a Sunday, but they knew where to go.

    Heather's mom interjecting: I love those roommates!!!

    now i will see about getting a new phone and then go back to that clinic. i think i will be better soon. i have my Italian final tuesday night. i will go talk to my chem teacher soon. i think i am not going to buy any plane tickets for semana santa cuz. Portugal sounds good. I wrote to Jon asking what he thought, and he said i had to be in spain to see Semana Santa, so i can do that if we go to Portugal for the first part of the break, and if i am healthy.

    how was your Sunday? did mom and em have fun shopping? were you at your office, dad? thank you for writing your big email, em. i love all the details you write me. you sound like you are having fun and are so responsible. i will keep you updated, if i have a working phone, about how my health is.

i love you more than all the red dots merging into one big weird looking thing called my skin :) heather

Subject: rash
Date: Wed, 20 Mar 2002 01:45:12 -0700 From: "Heather Gross"

this rash is not cool. i already told mom about how upset i was yesterday because of my awesome chemistry teacher telling me that i should know more Spanish for the years that i have studied it. so i have missed this morning's translation class. i just called the julia girl in my group and told her about the rash on my face. she met me at the door of the building. she said i should just not go to class since i am so uncomfortable, that it is fine to miss and that she will give me the notes from today. tonight our group will meet at my apt to finish our presentation we have the week after Semana Santa.

i have the rash on my face. i look kind of freaky. so now i will call Christian and see about going back to the doctor, because my roommates have tests. the rash just seems to stay about the same size and change places where it shows up on my body. it sucks. i will go to chemistry this afternoon, because i said i would meet with a girl to photocopy notes.

my Italian test last night went pretty ok i think. i can make it through today and tomorrow and then will have no more school for a week and hopefully this rash will leave.

k. i love you all more than all the embarrassment I am feel going out onto the street with this face, heather

Subject: Semana Santa is here
Date: Thu, 21 Mar 2002 14:13 From: "Heather Gross"

yay. thank you for calling again, mom. It is so good to know you care so much. i did well on my Italian test, better than i thought i had. i will study hard for my chem test. tomorrow we leave for Portugal, in a car. Lagos on the southern coast and then up to Lisbon, yay. I will take care of me and my health, not be in the sun, and still have fun.

K. dad. I rented the car on your card. It was 278.86 euros. This should be around $250.

I need to go home and eat. I am hungrry. sorry this is

so short. I love reading all your guys' newses. thank you. you sound really busy with all your claims stuff dad. i am so excited that you girls are coming!!

    i love you guys more than all the times i have pushed a key on a keyboard, heather

I don't think Heather ever knew what caused that nasty rash, but it went away. Interestingly, I slept in Heather's room four months later and I got a rash.

Subject: Tuesday
Date: Tue, 02 Apr 2002 09:43 From: "Heather Gross"
    hi, family. i am pretty frustrated with this chemistry, but i am studying and will go study more after this email. i just wanted to say that i got your folder with the tristan articles and card and then the separate card, mom. the easter package still hasn't come, and i hope it was not sent back to you or something because the Centre LM was closed all last week. my throat is getting better.

    i will write about Portugal later, for email journal purposes, [She never did write about it, but she later took Emily and me to Portugal, and I'll write about it in coming pages.] but Easter church with Jewel and Sydney, at their Catholic place where they go, was pretty depressing. There is no book to follow. There was no music. Sydney said that normal Sundays were better than that one. The only good part was the sermon. the communion was only a wafer. this all must be due to the govt keeping churches going, and the fact that the offering was random change people throw in the collector thing. I could not believe that we were supposed to be celebrating the most important day of the Christian year. man.

    so i do like my translation stuff. we prepared our presentation today and do that tomorrow morning.

    i have to be registering for ASU next semester, but can finish it after my test friday. Lauren comes next thursday. I got a 9.0, an A, in my Italian for last tri, so that is cool.

    you parents sound busy with the church preschool, and book club, mom, and your golf weekend, dad.

    oh yeah, i registered myself for tai chi for tuesday and thursday mornings, so i will see how that goes.

i love you guys more than how famous tristan is becoming. did you ever find a cheap way to call me, mom? maybe i will call soon, heather

Subject: thank you!
Date: Wed, 03 Apr 2002 11:10 From: "Heather Gross"
 so, i just wanted to say that i got my Easter package! Thank you! Mom and Em, you guys are good, know what Heathy wants, shoppers together. I have yet to get the package home and take out the shirts, but they looked cute when I peaked at the CLM.
 The notes that I have photocopied—my chem study ones—are good and reliable. I hope I can at least show the teacher that I am trying. I will be happy to get through Friday. Then tai chi and Lauren and planning when you guys are here and stuff. What do you know about tai chi, Dad?
 I love you all more than so many ways there are to name a chemical compound when you start doing it in other languages, Heather

Subject: Re: Test
Date: Fri, 05 Apr 2002 10:46 From: "Heather Gross"
 Hi family, but not dad till Monday, i guess.
so i am pretty sure that i did not pass my chem test. thank you for praying so much, mom. Man, tests in Spanish universities—to be well prepared you have to be studying for at least two weeks before. this is what i would have had to do to be able to have had in my head the specific reactions that this teacher wanted. so i don't know what will happen, see, this was the first parcial—like midterm, but you have to pass the test to be able to take the second parcial, or wait till the end of June to take the final all in one test. this is what i would/will have to do. i think it will be ok if i fail the class. Julie is figuring this out for me.
 now i am at this internet cafe. jewel and Sydney met us at the other place and we all came here cuz i need to finish my pre-registration for ASU for fall semester. yay. i am signing up for chem classes in my mother tongue, wassssup.
 the clothes are all so cute and fit well! em, you just gave me your shirt, dude. thank you. em, you sound bussssy. your dress sounds awesome. i will keep my phone on all the time, so call whenever, but i most likely would have it with me and here in my

Alyce Gross

daytime. (which till Sunday, is nine hours ahead of yours.)
    i love the song on now. jewel and i are dancing, wassssssssup. i love you guys more than this song. Heather

Subject: chai tea
Date: Mon, 08 Apr 2002 From: "Heather Gross"
sounds like tai chi, eh? well that starts tomorrow.
    this was a rainy weekend. i slept a lot and got almost all better, just have some boogies. so i swam for an hour Saturday morning, and then ate some spinach with caro. then mom called, and i loved that. i swam 20 laps in an hour. i usually just do 45 min of 15 laps. i ran sunday morning, after not having done so for two weeks since portugal, so my body is getting back into this use my muscles stuff and it is good. the muscle from my shoulder to neck hurts from swimming. mercedes gave me a massage for this last night. after i went to church with jewel and Sydney. non easter Sundays are happier and more praisey.
    so today i only had my chem class. we won't know grades for a few weeks. i didn't have my translation class cuz today was the patron saint day of the facultad. Spanish people have saints for the colleges within their universities. yep.
    so how was the golf, dad? and your potluck with the wives, mom? and em, i want to know about pauly shore, and when is prom?
    i love you guys more than all the golf balls in the world, the ones in bodies of water too, heather

Subject: chi
Date: Wed, 10 Apr 2002 From: "Heather Gross"
of tai i started yesterday morning and love it!!! it is very cool. the instructor is from argentina or somewhere where they say there double L's like SH's. The people in it are all girls, about ten Spanish ones and two other foreigners, one Swedish who is telling me where would be good places to go there, mom. :) then i swam 20 laps in 53 minutes, how fast do you swim, dad? what is good pacing?
    this not travel and study my head off advice...nope. i mean i think i am not going to take the final exam. this is how that works: today Christian and i talked to Elena, the advisor for the university at the international relations office. she

suggested that i get a certificate of attendance, as a no-show for the test—looks better than a failing grade. i am talking the honors college and ipo about this, but this would lift some stress. i would keep going to the class and learning, because now that i can take decent notes i kind of like the class, and the Jesus dude i sit next to is nice.

my translation class's final test is June 17. then i would have some time to travel, cheaply and smartly, before you girls arrive.

so that is what i am thinking. tomorrow lauren arrives at 2:05 PM at the train station where jewel and i will meet her. yay!!
i love you guys more than all the chee's ever said, heather

Subject: rainy granada and 3/4 of the itros
Sent: Friday, April 12, 2002 10:49 AM From: "Heather Gross"
or the "tetros" as jewel's mom wrote to lauren. hee hee.

    i went to tai chi, swam, bought chicken breast and more broccoli, and went home and started cooking. then jewel met me, and we went through the rain on the bus to get Lauren. next more being in the rain and crowded bus back to my house, where we and josie the four americans ate with Carolina. Today at lunch with my roommates, Caro just kept saying stuff to her with hand gestures, expecting her to understand. Then I would translate.

    it is working well having lauren stay at my apt. I am glad I have room for her and that the extra bed fits not too crampily. The bad thing about her being here now is that there is rain predicted till Tuesday when she leaves. We'll do the Alhambra and the chapel where Ferdinand and Isabel are buried. Last night we took her to our cider bar and were the only ones there, cuz this weather is not conducive to people going out. We are still having fun.

    My honors college advisor is helping me, and says I can keep my scholarship by adding the credits from first semester to make 24 hours for the full year. I won't lose it; don't worry. I won't have to finish my undergrad at the U, but I might want to do pharmacy school there.

    i love you guys more than all the umbrellas (as dad pronounces it:)) out all over the world.

Subject: friday yay
Date: Fri, 19 Apr 2002 11:42 From: "Heather Gross"

Hi, family!
>   This morning I met Jewel at the travel agency. I am flying with her from Barcelona to Budapest on June 3, and then from Frankfurt to Malaga, Spain on June 16. I put this on the credit card, dad. It was 316.04 euros, which should be about $285-$290. We will stay with her foreign exchange student girl in Budapest, then go to Prague, through Berlin, to Aucken, Germany to stay with her other old foreign exchange student. We hope to go up to Amsterdam from there, and then fly from Frankfurt back to Spain, so jewel can fly home and i can do my translation test.
>   so my chem situation is that i am translating the chem syllabus so that the chem equivalency provider guys at ASU can tell me what class i can take there to make up for the one here. so i think i am ok, and will tell you when i am sure. :)
>   guys. I love you more than all the different temperatures going on at the same time in the universe right now. Heather

Subject: translationals
Date: Wed, 24 Apr 2002 10:57 From: "Heather Gross"
>   twould be cool to be going to Em's Art Show. I miss you guys. I am so proud of you and your talent, Em, and wish I could see it.
>   About having my apt in July, there is no problem. My roommates don't usually pay the rent for July or August, just the minimum water, light, and comunidad—the whole apt building upkeep thinger. so they will use my down payment to pay for what extra water and light expenses we run up, which will be more than enough to cover that. I will leave my keys with Mercedes' friend Carola who lives in Granada.
>   I love you guys more than all the keys ever made or copied or falsified or whatever, heather

Subject: friday
Date: Fit 26 Apr 2002 05:26 From: Heather Gross
Hi, Family,
>   So the best news—yesterday: I did some tai chi with just the people cuz my teacher was in madrid and could't get a sub, but the tall Spanish guy in there taught us, and it worked. He even had tai chi-ish music with him, and a girl had incense

with her, just like we always have, so it worked.

then I talked to my chem teacher, and he was helpful, and nice!?! We went over my test, which I totally failed as I knew I had, but that was good. He reads English, but doesn't speak it, so he looked at the translation I had done of his syllabus and helped me find some terms that I wasn't sure of in English in his chem books, that he has in English. It was good. Also he said that he would give me the attendance certificate. I told him that I am not sure if I am going to take the test. If I take it and don't pass, he won't give me a SUSPENSO = fail, he'll give me a NO PRESENTADO = no show, the same he will give me if I don't take the test. then if somehow I do pass, he will give me an APROBADO, passed. so this is cool.

next i made some pasta with tomato sauce and pineapple that I cut up. i do not know how to cut pineapple. i think any of you would have done better and accomplished the task in a fourth of the time it took me, especially Em.

So dudes, no one told me about the art show as was promised.

Thanks for calling me and paying too. Yeah I needed you to call, and I am glad you worry about my health and stuff.

you are funny mom, and should write that you love summer in your teaching philosphies.

i will go look for a dress soon. what is up, my sis?

k. I love you guys more than all the internet cafes in the world, cuz now i am at a new one. Heather

Subject: Jean
Date: Sun, 28 Apr 2002 12:39 From: "Heather Gross"

hi guys, it is Sunday and 1 pm there, 9 pm here and still light out. we got back from our very fun trip an hour ago.

i am talking to mike peterson online and printing out info thingers on hotels in London so i have some examples of british english hotel lingo. i also have monument pamphlets on granada in english and info on the food here, cuz these are the things our teacher told us would be in the translation on the test i have in 12 hours. mike p told me that hortin is coming back to UT to go the U in the fall. that is good. I'm excited to see the people there.

so Friday, evan (who is the American who is kind of with Carolina) and his friend mark (visiting from AZ), josie, caro, and i ate lunch together. we used the last of those flavor packets you sent, dad, to make delicious fajitas. evan had been missing good mexican food he could get in az and said this was the best he had eaten outside of north america.

    that night i went out for april's birthday to Chinese food. then we went to a karaoke bar which wasn't that cool, from there I went and got Carolina to come with me to Josie's rugby party at another bar. then we went dancing at the Meeting Point, for which you don't have to pay to get in, if you are with rugby guys who know people. so we got home at 7 AM. this rugby guy who liked caro and his roommate walked us home. they had to wait for the buses to start running so they came up to our apt, and one of them made me a Spanish tortilla with potatoes, eggs, peppers, and onions. this fell apart but that was ok, cuz i took it in a small tupperware thing and pieces of bread to eat for the lunch i packed.

    the bus left at 8. jaén is beautiful, cuz there are tons trees. Anywhere you look, it is spotted geometrically, hills of olive trees, which look like big bushes with a little trunk. the Guadalquivir River starts there and makes an awesome valley. Saturday, we weren't in the cities, but rather went to this beautiful natural park. i was not too tired, cuz i slept some on the bus. we ate there and then hiked for three hours. i got in the river a little bit. we found a big toad and there was also a little water snake guy. we saw deer, trout, and animals that remind me of dad and good food. so the trout were hilarious. they were in this nice pool area and some went over the three foot tall waterfall. then they were trying to jump back up the waterfall.

    from there we went to úbeda to our wonderful four star hotel. this is the second hotel i have stayed in spain. the other was in segovia with jewel and Sydney when we were trying to get a hostel in the snow and settled for paying 21 euros each for a hotel. Christian made the room assignments and put me with jewel and Sydney, but we all ended up hanging out together in one room. first we went to the huge target like grocery store behind our hotel to buy food for today's lunch and then most of us went to an Italian pizza place for dinner. this morning there was a good breakfast buffet, then on the bus we waited for tons of sheep to cross the road. Next we went to the center of town walking and touring renaissance old style nice buildings of úbeda. Finally we bused to baeza to hang out in a beautiful plaza and see more old buildings.

i love you more than the millions of olive trees in Jaén, (the region that produces the most olive oil in spain.) heather

Subject: las Cruces
Date: Thu, 02 May 2002 04:52 From: "Heather Gross"
that means Crosses, pronounced Lahs Croothays. There are a lot of them up in different neighborhoods around Granada, cuz tomorrow is the Day of the Cross; commemorating the day a dude's wife in Italy in the 4th century supposedly found the cross on which Christ died. so there are bars out in the street too. this means partying will be going down, and it's not just the college age kids, but everyone. the party is supposed to be just tomorrow, when i am leaving with pilar, caro, and her brother to go to Huelva, but it starts tonight, so i get to see some of it.

My test monday didn't happen. That is cuz our teacher was out of town, and was having a sub teacher come at 9 to give us the test. She slept in and arrived at 10, with one hour left of class, which was not enough time, so we postponed it till next Wednesday. Yesterday, Wednesday, was labor day, or the Day of the worker, so I went to the beach with my roommates. Now I won't be so white in my dress.

Oh yeah, I bought a dress on Monday. The first time I went shopping for one! Caro helped me look. It is two pieces. A dark teal thing that goes in an A shaped and ties around my neck with the top of my back open. There are two little sewn on rose-ish flowers at the top at my neck. then there is a kind of fitted skirt with a seam that makes a wave ruffle at the bottom. It came with a shawl all for about $85. The place is taking in some seams so it fits right, and I will get it tomorrow morning. I think I am borrowing shoes and earrings. This wedding will be fun.

I hung out with that English dude, Gavin, for a little while on Sunday night. He is funny, but like the rugby people, he likes to drink. Tuesday night I went out with Josie and hung out with Spanish and then Americans and then Spanish—fun. Yesterday was mostly spent at the beach. We brought sandwiches, and I swam in freezing water.

Today I had tai chi and went swimming. We did tai chi outside with the birds and sun and light breeze, was cool.

I am better, yes, cuz I am not worrying about chem. It is

fun being here and sad that I am going to leave it. I am excited for traveling and then having my girls here!!!

So what is up with you, Dad? Emmy G, dude, where are you? Uncle Rick sent me a typed letter with money for my coming birthday. It was long and nice and funny. I will email him. Now I need to go make some food for people to eat. Then tonight I don't have chem, but do have Italian.

K, I love you guys more than all the sun bathers on all the beaches everywhere. Heather

Subject: tuesday and yeah
Date: Tue, 07 May 2002 08:42 From: "Heather Gross"
i had a dream that i looked out my window and there was snow everywhere. i think i miss snow. well that, or good weather, cuz now it is rainy cloudy here, but that is ok, cuz it is interesting. i don't have much newses. i bought my barcelona ticket for the train overnight with jewel today. i did tai chi, but it was not relaxing cuz the teacher was getting all demanding and mad—we hadn't memorized the sequence.

i will buy a hair dryer for us while you girls are here. good idea, mom. em, you are in your calculus test. i bet you are doing well. that is awesome that your english one is over. the blink concert sounded like the bomb. i am jealous.

hi dad. love heather

Subject: meditation
Date: Thu, 09 may 2002 11:52 From: "Heather Gross"
is cool especially when a guy with light brown curly, kind of long hair, tells you about your internal smile and breathing out the bad energy and focusing on the light from the stars in his argentine accent. that was the second half of tai chi today.

also my throat is a little puffy, but i am taking amoxicillin, and that is good. i ran a quick 2.5 miles and went with josie to get her earring changed. last week she pierced that thing in front of the hole in the ear, next to her face, like that girl on your soccer team, em, arianne had; and april pierced her nose. i am one of the only peeps from the az old group (the all year longers) that hasn't pierced something while we have been here. it is really cheap. that is why many do this.

so yes, dad, i am happy for the end of school. this trip

with jewel is going to be awesome. do you know why? because for more than half of the time we are staying with people she knows in budapest and then, in auchen. jewel emailed the budapest people and the guy wrote back in funny english about how they will pick us up in the airport. the german girl wrote about how it will be Tim's birthday (this is her boyfriend or husband guy she lives with) while we are there, and how her dad will take us to the airport in Frankfurt, and stuff, yay. anyway, we have our train tickets to leave to Barcelona in three weeks from tomorrow!!!

[Some of this trip will be covered, from Jewel's point of view, in the Celebration of Life chapter.]

so tonight i am going to the Arab baths with josie and will get a massage, and that will be the bomb. I will take the mom and the em there when you are here. josie's neck hurts. How is yours mom?
em needs to inform me of how her life is now, cuz there is no stress about A.P. tests, or is art stressy? or what else?
mom write too. thank you for writing, dad.

Pilar went to Malaga to see the concert of that show i wrote about—Operacion Triunfo. Mercedes has her pharmacy promotion dinner. I will go home and see Caro.

I love you guys more than all the times roommates have seen and not see each other. Heather

Mom's advice:
Subject: neck   From: Alyce Gross   To: Heather Gross
Date: Fri, 10 May 2002
Hi Heather,

Your trip sounds interesting. Be sure to not be a burden to those people and pay for stuff—like the gas for the trip to the airport and back.

I'm already looking forward to the Arab baths. I've never had a massage, except by my physical therapist on my neck. This morning my neck feels better. He's given me stretches to do and I guess they're helping. I was on the treadmill after school, yesterday, and my neck was hurting. I think it will be a slow process, because it has been hurting for a long time.

We're painting pop bottle fish at school today. Next

week is the Hero Program. My students are still the best, but I'm anxious for summer like always.

This is short. It's 6:00 am. I'm going to go make coffee and shower. I love you more than all the drops of water in my shower. Let me know about your throat. You seem to get that a lot. I wonder if your tonsils should come out.
Mom

Subject: on the day of the Mom
Date: Sun, 12 May 2002 08:24 From: "Heather Gross"

Thursday after the baths, which were sooo relaxing, Josie and I ran into Minoru, the Japanese kid who goes to school in England who likes me and Casey, and then some more AZ people. We went to the Irish bar Hannigan's. It does not feel like you are in Spain there. There are a lot of foreigners and music in English.

Friday I met with my translation group girls to finish our text that we present in class tomorrow. Then at the CLM, I had an Italian makeup class where we watched a movie. I saw Jewel and Dominica's play. It was funny and entertaining. Caro, Mercedes, and Caro's friend Vero came too. We went to tapas with them and Americans. Saturday I ran and swam and hung out with Rachel, Marisa, Minoru, Josie, and rugby people.

It is beautiful weather here. Yah, sun.

I hope you all, especially Mom, have a wonderful Mother's Day!!! I love you more than all the moms there are and have ever been, Heather

Subject: hi on thursday
Date: Thu, 16 May 2002 04:12 From: "Heather Gross"
Hello family,

so i have't been to the internet since last sunday. your mother's day sounded nice. Beni Hanas, num. i am glad you liked the card, mom. congratulations on being on council for so long and doing a good job as the Christian Ed person.

i wish i could feel like school was done. i would already be finished with my spring semester and be back in SLC if i hadn't studied abroad—weird.

this week I've been nice and productive. i got up before 8:00 on monday to run before my translation class. i did that

The Devil's Fingernail

tuesday and today before tai chi. it is already like summer here, so it is nice to run before the sun gets me. i am sure that 8 doesn't seem that early to you people, but it is for people here.

so, em, you are applying for engineering scholarships? is that through CSU or something else? what is the date of your graduation? is it at the E center? When and where is your senior dinner dance? are you excited for all that stuff?

My group did our presentation in my translation class on Wednesday. It was a short translation. the class was fun, though, because we did well. the texts were all off of a Spanish newspaper website. our thing was a little biographical blurb about the secretary general of the Spanish Partido Popular, Javier Arenas. He used to be the work and labor minister, so the translations have to be in British English. The teacher always makes references to North American English and looks at me or the other girl from CA in the class. So she was talking about our decision to use employment instead of work or the American term "labor." labor in British is spelled labour. She said this was good so as not to confuse the reader with: the "Labour Party" in Great Britain. but I was in the back of the class and immediately i said (just so those—a bunch of English and Irish people around me heard) with "having a child." i was not even intentionally making a joke. I always think of how mom was in labor on Labor Day with Em. anyway, they thought that was hilarious and a little corner of the class was busting up for too long, so the teacher let us have our break. hee hee.

last night, i watched the European league football (soccer) championship. It was exciting. This is the club teams league. Was this on tv in the US at all? Real Madrid beat the German team 2-1. The second goal by us was awesome. After the game, walking home, there were so many people in the street with Real Madrid banners and honking and screaming. It was as though Granada's home team had just won the superbowl. The real rivalry here is between Real Madrid and Barcelona, so the Barcelona people wanted the German team to win.

I hope you guys are good. I love you more than all the crazy soccer football fans in the world!!! Heather

Subject: travels and thingers
Date: Mon, 20 May 2002 02:51 From: "Heather Gross"
Hi Family!

Alyce Gross

I am excited for traveling, but need to keep my head in school right now. Did the girls say I am thinking about going to Japan to see Minoru in two summers? I have a problem called the travel bug. :)

This is my pretty set travel schedule so that you guys know where I will be: May 31 night, on train to Barcelona, with Jewel. There till June 3 when we fly to Budapest. There till around June 7, then to Prague the 8th and 9th. We should be in Berlin around June 10th, next to Auchen, Germany by June 11 or 12. From there for one or two days we will go up to Amsterdam, but will be mostly staying with Jewel's Alexandra friend in Auchen till we fly from Frankfurt on June 16 to Malaga, Spain. That day we take a bus back to Granada. I have my translation test Monday, June 17. Chemistry is Friday, June 21.

Then I fly from Madrid on June 25 to London and then to Edinburgh, where I stay with my AZ friend from the dorms, Amanda. I fly July 1 from Edinburgh to London, switch airports, and then from London to Genoa, Italy that same day. July 1 to the 5th or 6th I am by myself in le Cinque Terre (cheenkway = five) village things on the northwest coast of Italy, just southeast of france, and then in southern France to travel by train back to northern Spain, where I meet Josie by July 7 in Pamplona. Then I continue south to Madrid, where my mom and em arrive on July ll, in the morning, i bet. So send me the flight info when convenient.

My weekend was fun because it was different—we had a car, and I was with fun people. Josie is the best friend I have made here this year, so I am really glad she will be in the US with me next year, usually in Flagstaff, AZ or in Ft. Collins, where her family lives and where my Emmy will be. Her rugby dude Salva is nice and wasn't bugged to be dragging around three foreigners, two blonde American girls and Minoru, my Japanese British accent friend. Thursday night was really cool too because Minoru's Spanish friend, Danny, who also was amazingly nice to we foreigners, treated us to see an awesome flamenco show up in Sacromonte, the gypsy neighborhood.

Josie and I hiked up there and higher to the abbey/monastery on Friday. AZ peeps went to our cider bar Fri night. Saturday was to the beach near Malaga with Josie, Salva, and Minoru, and kind of camping that night.

Em, in a limo to your dance—cool. That will be nice—dinner with the Holbrooks for graduation. Congratulations, Em!!!

The Devil's Fingernail

Man, we are both coming to kind of endings now.
    I just came from translation. There are so many terminologies for politicians, in all cultures, that have totally different meanings when translated literally.
    Did dad bring home some fish for you to eat, mom? You guys have nice weather now? It is already too hot here, but i like it. Now i am going to write to my German Oliver friend who was in my intensive class here last September. He lives somewhere near Berlin, so I will see if I could see him while we are there.
    I love you guys more than all the possible travel routes one could take to see all the countries of the world!!! Heather

Subject: leaving
Date: Fri, 31 May 2002 12:17:32 From: "Heather Gross"
for barcelona in an hour!!!
    k. this week has been busy and sad and happy and fun. full of goodbyes and changings. i said bye to josie yesterday. i will see her in a month in italy. Wed night we (as in AZ people and minoru and Italians and mercedes) were at the fair. we hung out in the mostly foreigners caseta tent thing, which was like a discoteca. today i ate with Sydney and her parents, jewel, and Christian. jewel and i bought little granada-ey type gifts for the people in whose homes we are staying. then i hung out with minoru and casey and dan and said bye to minoru. he was really sad and told me how much he will miss me. I gave him a kiss. he is a good friend.
    k. family! i will be in barcelona and can use my spain call card till, monday. so i will do that. i love you more than all the rods and reels thrown into lakes!!!! heather

Subject: barcelona
Date: Sun, 02 June 2002 From: "Heather Gross"
is the bomb!
    i am in the hostel on their free internet. yesterday jewel and i saw the cool weird Gaudi church—la Sagrada Familia, and then went to Pare Guell—this weird Gaudi architecture place. What was awesome is that they had an art school exhibit going on. There were people painted different colors—each color had a girl and a guy in just a thong and the rest of their bodies covered in one color of paint. first we didn't realize that this art thing was going on. jewel and i were sitting on a bench eating strawberries

and see this lady acting like the people in that movie—benny and joon. so she was in a bright pink dress thing and goes up to this tree and starts rubbing her face in its leaves. but really slowly like she was trying to get to know the tree or something, then she twisted herself all through it. it was weird dancing like i would do. so then we see these color people and realize that there are art people doing trippy things all over the place. very cool.

    our hostel is so great. We (mom and Em) could stay here— It's not just kids. there are these, we love jesus Christian kids from DC. they are our friends and tons of others we have met—almost all native english speakers from the US or Canada or Ireland or something. i forgot how attractive american boys are to me. :)

    so today we will see more stuff like mont juic and the gothic cathedral. las Ramblas is—what Hemingway called the most beautiful walkway in the world. our hostel is right off of it. it goes down a main street to this columbus monument thing at the end at the ocean. that is cuz columbus came to the port of barcelona when he returned to Spain from what he thought was the indies 500 years ago.

    tomorrow we fly to budapest! yay. the metro in barcelona is nice. europe is just so much more welcoming to a backpacker than the US would be.

    so how are you guys? having a nice sunday? excited for school to be over, girls? thanks for offering to look for apt listings for me, dad. i will have to think about that more and figure out what i am doing!!

    k, i love you guys more than all the flowers ever sold on las Ramblas! Heather

Subject: hungarians
Date: Mon, 03 Jun 2002 From: "Heather Gross"
have the z in the place where we have the y on the keyboard, but other than that they are the bomb!!!!

    we are in the house of these people, friends of jewels's grandpa. they are so nice and helpful. All is good in the travels today, except that our luggage was left in amsterdam (where we had our layover), and we should get it tomorrow. It's all good. K, you guys sound busy and excited. if I don't write before em's graduation, CONGRATULATIONS!!!

    these people have cute cats and a dog. i am so lucky to be staying and eating here for free! ! ! we will give them spain

presents once our luggage comes.
   so i love you more than all the poppy seeds ever used to make nummz hungarian desserts!! heather
   ps—mom, I am never traveling alone. Scotland with Amanda, then I fly to Italy where i am with josie and jerry—to pamplona with them, and then just to madrid. no worries. k. love you bye wave.

   The part about "never traveling alone" turned out not to be true. It became significant in sending Denny and me on a quest to Italy. There was yet another trip inspired by Heather. After the previous email about Hungry, Heather sent us a series of postcards from Budapest, Prague, Berlin, and Amsterdam. This was also significant, because eight and a half years later, December, 2010, Denny and I chose Prague as a place to spread some of Heather's ashes. Our journey also took us to Budapest, Hungry.

Subject: Re: waiting
Date: Wed, 12 Jun 2002 10:50 From: "Heather Gross"
   i am sending postcards about those places. i am in amsterdam with jewel right now, and we love it. this internet is expensive, so i will write more from spain in four days!!
   i love you more than all the bikes and dikes in the netherlands. yep. Heather

Subject: me back
Date: Sun, 16 Jun 2002 09:30 From: "Heather Gross"
   Yes—I am glad there is a Germany, and that you guys met there, and that Em and I exist because of that. so it is Dad's Day, so HAPPY FATHER'S DAY!! I will call you guys soon. I had so much fun on this trip. It was great staying with people.
   I now am preparing for my translation test. It was rainy and almost cold in Amsterdam. then okayish and sunny the last day in Aachen, and now it is hot, i mean like Arizona HOT here in Granada.
   i just talked to josie on her month long hike. she is having fun and walks with people, so is not alone. she is talking about buying a plane ticket when she gets to the next town—to meet me in italy—instead of taking a train. jewel is very excited to be going home. i will miss her. Amanda, in Scotland, wrote me and

is happy for me to come.

Germans are cool. It is wonderful that they know some English. I learned little bits more of German.

I love you more than all the heinekens consumed each day, which is supposedly millions. Heather

Subject: wedding
Wed, 19 Jun 2002 12:55

Hi parents. Translation test went ok. That is all I know. So I am studying a lot, and I think that if I had to do like the Spanish university students do—study pretty much all of June—I would go crazy for reals. my test is friday morning—1:30 AM UT time, so you can dream of me doing well then. :)

So, sounds like Minnesota was good times. Yes—we should be thankful for our awesome weather in SLC. I miss it. I guess more I miss AC or swamp cooling, or anything, better than the not-hot-air function on my heater. Have you guys gotten some postcards? I got a letter from a girl in Kalispell, whom Aunt Bev told I was in Granada. She is thinking of studying abroad, here next year. I will tell her—yes, yes, yes!

Man, Dad, thanks for doing all this pre car stuff for me. So, when is Em in UT? Does she go straight to Templeton or her youth thing from her girls' trip? I am so excited for it to be two days from now. Yay!! It is good I will have some time to do stuff in Granada before leaving to Scotland. Amanda is emailing me about us going to see the highlands for some days! Josie keeps calling me from her pilgrimage walk in w Spain. She just got to a city and found a ticket to Genoa to meet me there.

Carolina had to say bye to her Evan Tuesday. He is the guy from ASU that I introduced her to. She is seriously thinking she will come to the US to live for some time in a year. That would be wonderful!

I will write more after the test. I love your emails. Heather

Heather's Journal   22 June 2002

Hello. I just read the last entries and realized that I have let so much go by without my blabbering about it in here. "Hello, Again" (That is a movie with that actress from Cheers—Where everyone knows your name—Shelly, what's-her-butt-Long--I think. Anyway I loved that movie when I first saw it when I was little. She dies and her witch crafty sister brings her back to life a year later.) So now with that long aside, I was thinking perhaps that is a little like what this year has been for me—a revival. I have been alive the whole time, but man, now I am . . . different. Right now I am thinking of how much I have loved living with my roommates. Pilar: I love living with her—maybe cuz she is an awesome organizer, bill payer, cleaner, and cook! ☺ ji ji (hee hee in Spanish). So Mercedes is a little scatter-brained and the hippy of the piso, and I can really tell that she is good-hearted by the way she sings when she plays her Silvio Rodriguez tape. I will miss that. And Carolina . . . I love her and love our talks and love that I can cry and she will listen. I loved that I went to her house twice and her brother's wedding and went running with him on the morning of his 300 people wedding. . . .

Yesterday I had my química inorgánica *final—which I did not pass—and for which the teacher will give me a* no presentade, *which is better than a* suspendido.

Subject: Re: Test
Date: Sat, 22 Jun 2002 04:54 From: "Heather Gross"
     Hi parents! Thank you for writing so much and being so nice and caring about me and my test. Well, I did ok, but I do not think that I passed, and I was mad after cuz I realized that i did one thing backwards, and that really bugs, but it is over, and i will not lose my scholarship if i talk to the right people back at ASU. i hope.
     so you guys are just busy people. it would be fun to be in our clean house with the swamp cooler and slushies, mom. short haircuts are good dad. i do not know how these girls here, with all their hair, can handle it with the weather. so it will be different in Scotland. Amanda and I are going north of Edinburgh to the Highlands. They are supposed to be beautiful. She told me to bring a raincoat and that she still wears pants and sweaters! Hmmm...so i am bringing winter clothes and then flying to coastal nice weather in Italy. I am now a good packer and can fit all this, for two and a half weeks, in my backpack, to last until madrid. (yay!! i see my mom and sis so soon!!)
     i watched spain lose to korea this morning. it sucked cuz it was clear that the refs just wanted to be jerks to us. we had

two balls in the goal that were called as not counting!! one was for sure not fair. my roommates all call anyone who looks asian a chino, Chinese, so whenever Carolina would talk about Minoru, she would call him Miyagi, like from Karate Kid, or chino, or something; and i would be like, Japonés. so then today they kept calling the Koreans, Japonéses, and it was just funny. by the end they were all just putos chinos, damn chineses cuz we lost. but I am excited to go there someday cuz Asia does just seem like a huge land of people with dark hair and squintier than us eyes and I would love to see it. Minoru wrote me and misses me and says he just watches lots of world cup games cuz it rains there, and he can't play golf.

    yeah, I better have a good job for all these travel plans, eh? so yesterday after my test, Carolina made me feel better, and then i ate my last meal cooked by pilar. i had a nestea with Christian, while he had a chocolate shake. this is like liquid flavor. americans know how to make shakes. anyway so we talked forever and then we went to a travel agency to see about car rental and stay in places around spain deals. i think we will do hostels, cuz the reservation thing will not work too well, especially if we are not sure how long we will stay in each place. so, there i bought my bus ticket for monday night to Madrid, cuz i fly from there. then Christian and i studied a map of spain, and he made me a list of where we have to go, and the route to take, and it was cool.

    i was happy to talk to you and tell you about what to read in michener, mom. there is the part of the drive where we have to go out of the way through sevilla to get from cadiz to where Carolina lives in huelva. this is cuz of Las Marismas—the marshlands that you will read about.

    so then i took caro to the internet last night, and I was trying to write to you and tell you my test was ok and that i am almost not sick. i don't think it is allergies, but my own throat issues or something, so yeah, we fix that in august. i don't know about the dentist. i'd rather not go, so that the dude doesn't grind away any more of my mouth. so i had to help Caro do msn messenger, and it was funny. she was writing to soroush in her terrible english. he he.

    so i just got tons of film developed and am excited to go home and see the pics and give some to my roommates. on the way here i saw jewel's Spanish mom and showed her some of us in portugal. she is so nice and misses jewel. Jesus

Fotos is happy to have my business. I had seven rolls of film cuz i was waiting to do them in the US, but I think it was worth it to do them now.

I love, you guys more than all the dumb referreeing that has ever gone on in sports! **Heather**

Subject: Re: registration
Date: Sun, 23 Jun 2002

so I am at Quino's piso, Piler's bro. I was helping Pilar do this thing for one of her labs. She had to go to websites that were all in english. They were from the U of Washington and Tulane U and such. it was stuff about leukemia and anemia. I learned many medical words in Spanish, some organ names. Pilar is very thankful.

So, I have to tell you the cutest thing. Yesterday I went to the pool until 7 and then later went with Pilar here to start her lab project thing. (We just finished today.) so, we got home around 11. All the lights were off and there were candles lit on the table in the entryway and on the heater and walking into the living room of our apt. I said, maybe the power went out, but Pilar was already running off, ahead of me into the living room. I was like, this is weird Pilar always responds to me. This is what I thought as I went to the living room after her.

So, there were my three "Spanish Compis" (companeras for short, which means roommates) with a cake they made out of these sweet cracker things, cream, and chocolate, and a candle on it singing me happy birthday! aaah. man. why am i leaving such great roommates?!! I love them. It was so cute, especially cuz we didn't do anything for their birthdays before. cuz Caro and Pilar's are in August, and Mercedes' is New Year's Eve. I love them. K... so the best thing is that they gave me presents too!! an apron with the Spanish toro on the front and an awesome paper green teal blue and purple star lamp that folds into a flat little box!! and yesterday i had asked all of them to write down some of their best food recipes for me. so it was just a coincidence that they had already bought the apron. they made this cutest ever book of recipes with little drawings of all the dishes and funny side comments like: here you can add what ever else you think of, but don't add anything that doesn't fit, heather, as i know you like to make weirrrd mixes. i love them, and will miss them, so much.

tomorrow i prepare to leave and will call. i swam laps today before the crowd got to the pool. i am organizing my pics. and am glad i developed them already. there are some really good ones from caro's bro's wedding.

i will get us tickets for the alhambra, the arab baths, etc. do you think i should set a date for the rental car? is that ok if i plan all that out?

jewel wrote me the cutest nice email. i am so lucky to have her as a friend and to have, shared spain with her. yep.

I love you guys more than all the different delicious recipes from all cultures! Heather

Subject: off to Escocia e Italia
Date: Mon, 24 Jun 2002 12:35 From: "Heather Gross"

Hey guys, Just wanted to say, "Hi." Oh, and money business: I told mom on the phone—I rented our car on the parental credit card. It was 407 euros, like $375. I will tell my roomies they are welcome in UT. Caro will visit for sure. I can't wait to see you guys!! Love, Heather

Subject: Re: Spain
Sent: Wednesday, June 26, 2002 8:39 AM From: "Heather Gross"

Yep, Scotland, well edinburgh, is beautiful. green is my favorite color. amanda lives in an awesome apt, with high ceilings and big rooms. i have my own room and big bed. all her roommates are out of town right now, so this was a good time for me to come. it is cold. the opposite of spain. he he. i ran through The Meadows this morning—tons of fields of grass that you can walk on!! yay! we will go the Highlands on my birthday, I think.

k, mom, spain: read about almost any place that is along the southern, western, and northern coasts, and then down into barcelona and the costa brava. we will do madrid, granada, pilar's beach near marbella, cadiz, sevilla, Carolina's beach near huelva, portugal: lagos, sintra (near lisboa), coimbra, porto, then spain more: santiago de compostela, oviedo, cangas de onis, santander, bilbao, san sebastian, pamplona, jaca, andorra, barcelona, figueras, the costa brava, then drive south to cabo de gata, Granada, and finally madrid. cool? we will not do all those places, but that is an

idea plan thing i have.
    josie's rugby boyfriend guy, Salva, drove me to the bus station monday night. I called him to say goodbye, and he just offered. I cried saying bye to Mercedes cuz i won't see her for some time. I was in the airport in Madrid with two Americans from the CLM for coffee Tue morning. I was in the London Luton airport for some time yesterday cuz Easy Jet is pretty easy—I mean cheap but not efficient. Amanda was there when I arrived.
    So, I love you guys, and I will try to write again before Italy or from there!! Heather

Subject: Re: Happy 21st Birthday
Date: Mon, 01 Jul 2002 From:"Heather Gross"
    thank you!! bday was good times in the Isle of Skye in the Highlands of Scotland. i'm in london. missed flight to genoa. fly there tomorrow. it's all good. i love you guys, and can't wait to see you. Heath

Date: Wed, 03 July 2002
    Now I am in Genoa, Italy. I am doing internet so that I can try to find Josie somewhere in the Cinque Terre. I am taking a train to where she stayed yesterday, so I hope that we can meet up. Thanks for emailing, Dad. How was California, Mom? That is cool that relatives are sending me bday money. I will write them "Thanks."
    I love you guys and can notttt wait to seeee you!!! Heather

Date: Wed, 03 Jul 2002 10:35 From: "Heather Gross"
    Hey! I am not writing much cuz i don't have much time when italian internet places charge 2 euros for 15 minutes!! In london i met this Chris guy who also missed my flight. He is Irish and nice and a student and tall and skinny and harmless, so I thought it would be ok to take his invitation to sleep on the floor of his flat. We saw some of London yesterday day, and then flew to Genoa last night. I put the cost of the ticket, which should be about $95 on the parent credit card. Thank you. So today I took a train to Levanto, to where Josie had been this morning but already left. I did the hike from there to Monterosso by myself and now am staying here and speaking

Italian and hoping that Josie writes back before Pamplona. dude. There were some awesome views of the mountainy village spotted coast.

I am so lucky to have parents who like having each other around. if you hike on 4th of July, i will be doing the same. i love you more than all the touristy resort towns all over the coasts of the world!! Heather

Subject: monterosso de! mare
Date: Thu, 04 July 2002 01:43 From: "Heather Gross"
is the village town where i am.

My hip is good. My throat is too. I saw 8 people in four hours when I did the hike yesterday. if i hadn't seen these Danish women who told me where to turn at a cross place, I would have, gotten lost. i have a good trail map though. I discovered that I don't like this alone thing too much, and that I can't wait to talk to people. When I find an English speaker, I talk, or an Italian—which is a problem, cuz the old men and the Morroccan Italian speakers love to talk to girls. A 19 yr old one gave me a blue rose yesterday evening, but I told him that he is just like all the old Italian men and all the Morroccan guys in Granada, and that he needs to be not so direct, and he told me that he was looking for his fiancée, so I made him leave. anyway, today i have been talking to this nice Canadian girl, and maybe will leave my bag here, hike to a town and then take a train back.

i am still waiting for josie news, but yeah. i ran around this town this morning. it is tiny and cute. the beach is beautiful. [Now a small amount of Heather's ashes are on that beach.] maybe i will hang out there today, or go to Nice, and find josie in pamplona or something.

k, i love you guys. have a good 4th of July in our country. hopefully i find some americans to party with. love, heath

We didn't hear from Heather until she finally called us on July 8th. We had four very anxious days, knowing Heather was alone. Those long days of being worried to distraction, and Heather's description of the Cinque Terre, led Denny and me on a beautiful but difficult journey, seven years and four months later. I'll write more about it in the "Spreading of Ashes" chapter at the end of this book.

Here is Heather's Dad writing about his action during those four days:
Subject: Dad back
To: Heather Gross   Date: Mon, 08 Jul 2002 22:27

We somehow decided that you were in trouble when we didn't hear from you by Saturday and our concern only increased when we still hadn't heard through Sunday. Since you were traveling alone, that added to our discomfort. We got into the planning what to do if we didn't hear from you, mode. I looked up information on the US Consulate in Milan and sent them an email. They have an office for Americans in trouble. I later talked to a guy in the same consulate and he suggested that going from Monterroso to Pamplona would be a long trip and it could take more than two days.

Mom had sent emails during this time and you hadn't responded which we decided just wasn't like you. At about 1:30 AM someone else from the consulate called us at home and told us if you were in trouble, it was still too soon to notify the police because they must have a period within which they won't do anything. So mom and I started calculating what to do if we didn't hear from you. We couldn't wait until she was on the plane so I started calling people. I called Julie Williams and got Christian's phone. She gave me his home phone and she thought it was his cell phone. I was lucky to catch him at home because he was supposed to be at the beach. He made some calls and sent a text msg to you and Josie. He also called me back to say that he didn't think there was a problem. I also had called your cell a couple times without getting an answer. I called Julie Williams again to see if I could get Amanda's email address. I was in the middle of writing to her when you called.

Mom and I had had other discussions about what to do if we didn't hear from you and you were not at the airport when she arrived. As the day went on, all the possible bad scenarios went through my head and I was just upset. It must have been very strange to hear me cry from relief at you being on the phone. I even thought it was strange, but as I write this email I still feel like crying. So you know how much you are loved. I don't have to sell your car or remind myself how fun it was to go to Lake Powell and Targhee with you. That may sound crazy, but that is how far our thinking had gone.

Randy called me this morning to buy lunch and I told him I had an appointment, but also that we were concerned about you. He called me at the end of the day to see if we heard from you. After you called, I called him. He thanked me because, "he'd now sleep better this night." I'm sure our concern got out of hand, but that is what parents do. Mom and I went to Cottonwood Mall tonight. She bought a travel bag/big purse and I bought two shirts. We also treated ourselves to ice cream cones. She is very excited, and you guys will have a ton of fun.

Love you bigger than you can imagine. The Dad !!!

Subject: San Fermin
Date: Wed, 10 Jul 2002 03:31 From: "Heather Gross"

Hey, guys!! I am in Pamplona and seeing all the emails since the fourth, for the first time. I am sorry I didn't tell you where I was. I really am, cuz I should have realized that my being alone means extra precautions should be made—like giving my family my travel itinerary and letting them know my actual whereabouts and how i am. So I called you from San Sebastian. The next morning I got out of that hotel where we had three Canadian girls and four American boys and me in two triples. So, this nice Charlie guy from Sacramento came with me. He had kind of latched onto me since Irún, the place the train from Nice took me. Irún is right on the border of Spain and France, and 20 min from San Sebastian. Anyway, he liked that I can speak Spanish and could help him get to Madrid, where he was staying with friends. So he did that, and I was on my bus at 11 am to Pamplona !!!

k. I cannot begin to tell you how much i love the fiesta of San Fermin here. that is the Spanish name of our running of the bulls. i will be coming back. the running is just one of the events of the day. i got here at noon. amanda found us a room for 45 euros, which is an awesome price. then we met this alex guy form LA. we didn't know that we could still get tickets for the bull fight yesterday; but we could—for 30 euros, not bad for buying two hours before the thing.

so that was a terrible bull fight—the second matador stabbed the bull four times half way, before getting the sword

The Devil's Fingernail

all the way in. i can't believe that i can watch 6 bulls die, actually 8 yesterday; cuz there were also problems with having strong, long-lasting bulls. anyway, this is not the serious formal torero-ing that goes on in sevilla or madrid. half the people here are foreigners, 2/3 of the people at the fight were drunk, so the wine pouring on people and the pillow throwing gets out of hand. i love it.

k. so we got up at 7 this morning to find the whole town still partying, half-drunk and ready to see 6 bulls, 4 steers, and tons of crazy people run for two minutes to the plaza de toros ring.

here is the news: I ran with the bulls!! this morning, yep. Don't worry. I wasn't in the danger area at all. All I did was wait about 100 meters from the entrance to the ring. They have wooden stand gate thingers that everyone sits on to see the runners. then there is another row where there are police and paramedics behind. so when the people at the front—who the police hold back, started to run, i slipped through the two rows of the wooden things and ran into the stadium.

Bulls were far from me. So i should actually say that i ran with people, behind many of which there were some bulls. Amanda was up in the stadium on the balcony and took a picture of me. That is an awesome way to do it, though, cuz you get in there and then are in the ring to see the real action—the people who haaaave to run. man. so the running today was pretty calm, and unless other people got gored when the bulls were in the street, no one was too hurt. (a comment on the Spanish terminology for this stuff: they call the bull fight the "corrida" which means running. and they call the thing we call the running, "el encierro" which means the closing-in. just thought that is interesting.)

after the bulls, they send out four smaller toros with corks on the ends of their horns, one at a time. i was on the five-foot wall of the ring, in front of it and jumping over it, the whole time. once i really had to jump head first and caught myself with my hands on the pavement and got wet dirt all over me and a tiny cut on my elbow, so that is my bull battle wound.

i am still in my white dirty outfit with my red Pamplona handkerchief around my neck and my red sash on my waist. i love this. you just have a uniform, wear it all the time, and it

just gets dirtier, and it's supposed to.
     so, today i have a bus to Madrid, and get you girls at 8:55 tomorrow morning. i am so excited!!! are you guys?!! dad, thank you for your explainy email. i feel so loved and feel like crying. probably the fact that elton John is singing "like a candle in the wind" right now in this internet place has something to do with that too. :) mom, the you not eating any thing—that scared me too. i don't know how it is to be a parent and think about your kid, but i know the feeling of thinking you guys could not be coming home, and that is terrible.
     i talked to Christian right after i talked to you guys. he had left a message to call him collect if i had no money and to call you. he is great. and you guys are wonderful; and i will call at 2 or 3 this afternoon, your 6 or 7 am. i think you should be up.
     mom and em, have fun on the plane with the movies and the endless good food, and then i will be there to see you !!!!
     k. Thank you for being my wonderful family, and I love you guys more than all the people who have ever felt fear cuz a big ton-weighing animal with sharp horns was in the near vicinity!!!! :) Heather
ps. doctor apt thing sounds good. i don't know if you made it already, mom, but i will talk to you on the phone, heathy

    Only Heather could say she was sorry for making us worry and that she "ran with the bulls" in the same email. She truly was "a candle in the wind." We had been so worried about her being alone until she called us to let us know she was fine. Then two days later she definitely wasn't alone, although that would have been safer, because in her words; "she ran with people, behind many of which there were some bulls."

Mom's Edited Travel Journal

11 July 2002   Reunion with Heather
Heather was expectantly waiting for Emily and me at the Madrid Airport. (Before taking the underground to our bus, I stopped at an ATM and was so thankful that my card and pin number actually worked. I got 300 Euros, and gave 100 to each of us, to lessen the chances of it all being stolen. Heather was admonishing me to stash the money immediately, but I chose to divide it. That is how I got cash throughout the whole trip—300 Euros at a time, and divided it. Thankfully we weren't robbed or mugged, which travelers know, is always a concern.)

Heather was as thrilled to see Emily and me as we were to see her. The love and excitement were pouring out of her. She talked nonstop on the five and a half hour bus ride to Granada. While listening to her rendition of her travels and the Pamplona festivities—how she was never in danger from the bulls, but she was breaking the custom that only men run; I was noticing the brown and yellow rolling hills, Spanish tile roofs, and olive trees, all reminding me of San Luis Obispo County, California, where I grew up. No wonder the Spanish settled that area. It looked like home to them, as Spain looked like home to me.

Heather fed us Pilar's paella and cookies with delicious iced coffee with condensed milk, when we first arrived at her apartment. She was bursting to show us Granada and all her stomping ground for the past year. Her apartment was perfect—marble floors, tile walls, four bedrooms, and two bathrooms.

That same evening we took a taxi through narrow streets to Venta El Gallo for Flamenco. I loved the rhythmic clapping of the dancers who were waiting their turn. The movement of the dance was striking and dramatic. The owner, who knew Heather, was so friendly that he greeted us with two air kisses. We ate at his restaurant with a view of Alhambra perfectly lit to give it a warm inviting glow. The winding cobble streets and houses on the hillside were charming. We had sangria, tortilla (egg and potato), fried peppers, and bread to dip in olive oil and vinegar. Em had melon. The walk home took about forty minutes. The city was alive and fascinating. I was exhausted yet excited for tomorrow as I went to bed at 2:00 AM. The time change made it easy to stay up half the night, which is common in Spain, especially with young people.

12 July 2002   Christian

We slept late—until 10:00 AM and got ready leisurely. We walked to Heather's Language School and then met her beloved, Christian. We had gazpacho, sangria, and pork at a fancy restaurant, as my way of saying "thank you" to Christian for helping our daughter. Christian then drove us out to neighborhoods outside of the city, and showed us his parents' lovely home decorated in what I'll call classic style. He also showed us his very nice flat. The rest of the afternoon, the girls and I shopped in Granada. We then enjoyed a sidreria (cider bar) for cider and tapas (appetizers that that are sometimes free with drinks).

13 July 2002   Alhambra

The Alhambra—the last stronghold of the Moors until Queen Isabella and King Ferdinand forced them out in 1492, ending the 700 Years War, is the biggest tourists attraction in Granada. With Heather as our guide, Emily and I could understand why. We were amazed by the intricate carving in stucco. The tranquil pools and gardens were beautiful. I should be writing much more about the beauty, but some things must be seen to believe.

To: Dad
Subject: Girls (Grillls) in Espania
Date: Sat, 13 Jul 2002 12:42 From: "Heather Gross"

The Devil's Fingernail

    Dude!! Here we are. the em is to my left. the mom to my right. we have been having good Spanish times. Thursday night we went to an awesome flamenco show. Friday we went to my school and to a good lunch with Christian. Mom said "thank you" many times. Then we shopped. you would have been bored. this is a pretty girly type trip. We ended with tapas at my cider bar. this morning we discovered the beautimous alhambra. mom took some good, girls not looking at the camera, pics. [I always tried to get some pictures that weren't posed.] we napped during hot siesta time, while em played 20 games of solitaire. now i hope the mom and em are on Spanish time. now we go to Chinese food cuz em knows she likes that, and she's sick of ham tapas. mom found some cute inexpensive handcrafted earrings for all her cute travel outfits. Yep—we are doing girly stuff. tomorrow we do Arab baths and the royal chapel to see the tombs of Ferdinand and Isabel. Monday morning we have our rental car and will take off for pilar's beach town, south of Ronda, west of Malaga. then to Sevilla. Next we go to Carolina's beach just west of Huelva.
    it sounds like you are eating well and doing some good housework. i can't wait to see the yard when i get home in 18 days!!!! sorry about the heat. It's about the same here. we love you and will call soon!! have a great sat and good fishing sun. love you more than all the tight Spanish man shirts!!!, heathy, emby, and mom.

Sunday, 14 July 2002   Royal Chapel/Arab Baths
    We attended an actual church service in an awe inspiring cathedral where the tombs of Ferdinand and Isabella are on display. Emily slept almost as soundly as the entombed royalty, during the sermon. That evening I learned that travel with Heather is not for the wimpy. The previous night we took a taxi, but this time we climbed the mosaic streets to a high point, El Mirador da San Nicolas, to view the Alhambra at sunset. From there we made our way to Arab Baths with soothing music, low lighting, bath oil smells, and a small fountain which sent water in a little grove on the floor. There were small tile mosaics everywhere of many designs and colors. After showers we

cautiously entered the hot pool soon to move to the cooler water. From the smaller cool pool, one could turn to enter a lovely large hot pool with underwater walkways and benches. There were about eight other people in the pools. All was tranquil and peaceful. It was relaxing, and the warmth helped me get the most out of my stretches as we waited for our massage. The masseur knew his trade and spent a lot of time on my feet. After the baths, we walked a bit and stopped for showarma (chicken gyro). We then moved to a many leveled Tea House where we climbed to the very top floor—the jungle room. The girls had delicious fruit shakes. I had plum tea. Yum!

15 July 2002   Tuna and Tomato

Heather and I did a brisk half hour walk to get the rental car she had reserved. I drove it to the gas station by Heather's apartment. Back inside the apartment, she carefully shut everything off and locked up, but we planned to return to her apartment in two weeks. It was nice to be able to leave a few things and borrow her roommates' towels. We drove southwest toward Pilar's grandma's flat by the beach, on the Mediterranean.

We stopped for a picnic of fresh long skinny Spanish (French) bread and Tuna with tomato sauce poured on it. We were on an exclusive dock with huge boats and yachts of Marbella. We then got into very slow traffic because of construction. We mistakenly drove through Pilar's town, but turned around and found our destination. Heather's cell phone was wonderful for planning and finding people and places. Pilar was excited to see us and introduced us to her brother, Joaquin, cousin, Quíno, and her Grandma. All but grandma spent the afternoon on the beach, which was a bit rocky with some sea weed, but nice. On the way back from the beach, Pilar stopped and bought two fresh loaves of bread as well as eggs. While she cooked we were able to freshen up. I should have showered, but took just a sponge bath, to save time and water. The efficient and excellent cook, Pilar, fixed us the delicious staple—Spanish tortilla with eggs and potatoes. They also served sausages, salad, and bread. The young men (unusual for the Spanish) set the table and served beer to Emily and me.

That evening, again, all but Grandma, walked to a night spot with fine restaurants and huge boats. We had ice cream. Em and I slept in the young men's bedroom. I'm not sure where they slept. The traffic was noisy and I was sticky. I really should have showered while I had the chance.

16 July 2002   Ronda/Cadiz

We drove north following Pilar and her cousin, Quíno, up a windy road to Pilar's childhood home, in the tourist town of Ronda. Her parents were at work, but she showed us her lovely high ceilinged classic style (like Christian's) childhood home. The mostly white city sits on a high bluff over a gorge. It's a beautiful site. Unfortunately, a woman taking photos had died from a fall into the gorge that very morning. Quíno, a lawyer working for the city, had to check in at work, and was late meeting us because of the tragic accidental death. This was definitely not the first death at that location nor would it be the last. Hemingway wrote of murders taking place during the Spanish Civil War, and they allegedly took place in Ronda at the cliffs of El Tajo.

While we waited for Quíno, we walked around Ronda, and got to see Pilar's old elementary school building with its courtyard. We were hot and tired, but we managed, even with Pilar's protests, to find gifts for her to take back to her Grandmother, who had so kindly slept on the couch while Heather and Pilar slept in her bed. We also stopped at three different places to cool off with drinks and topas while we waited for Quíno. He met us at our final refreshment stop, and then insisted we follow him to his parent's home, where he ran in to collect the perfect gift for our trip—a set of three or four various sized soft coolers for food or drink. Pilar and her family were wonderful to us. I'll never forget how cute, little, and energetic she was with her red hair and freckles.

That afternoon we drove southwest to Cadiz. Heather's cell got us a youth hostel in the town center. The bathroom was separate, but close to our room. We took a short nap then walked to a tower with a wonderful view of roof tops, a sea port, and a fortress. Columbus left Cadiz on his second and forth voyages. From our vantage point, we could look out to sea and imagine his sailing ships leaving for the Americas.

We shopped at a market and got yogurt, whole grain cookies, almond cookies, toasted bread, cheese, and fruit for a tasty picnic in our room. Before I could enjoy the meal, I had the most refreshing shower of my life—after the previous day at the beach, and the morning in Ronda. We got dressed and went out to the town square for sangria. All three of us were tired and went to our room early.

17 July 2002   Hot/Hospitality
In the morning we walked to the beach and saw nothing but old people. The college kids were all gone for the summer, but if they had been there, they probably would be sleeping in. The elderly enjoyed walking on the sand and in the shallow water. I noticed all had skinny legs with solid looking heavy torsos. I'm built just the opposite, so I couldn't help but comment about it to my girls. We walked through the market and it appeared to be a gathering place for visiting as much as for daily shopping. It made me feel a little sad thinking how isolated my U.S. life is in comparison.

We left Cadiz and drove to Sevilla, which was recommended as a most beautiful tourist spot and a must see, except in July and August. We arrived at about 1:00 PM, the hottest part of the day in the hottest city, but Heather insisted that we walk to the Plaza de España, which was a filming location in one of the later Star Wars movies. It was amazingly beautiful. She also showed us a spectacular cathedral that she couldn't let us miss, before heading southwest toward Huelva to La Antilla; where Carolina and her family were waiting for our arrival at their beach house. Emily drove (Heather couldn't drive a stick shift.) while I enjoyed the air conditioning and a car picnic in the back seat. I now understand why so many Spanish families own beach houses near the cool ocean breezes.

Carolina had (and I'm sure still has) a natural beauty and grace you wouldn't believe unless you saw her yourself. She introduced us to her warm and welcoming mother, her cute and funny aunt (who was just there to check out the Americans), her sweet sister, Rocio, and an eighteen-year-old young man who was staying there while going to cooking school. (I wonder if he and Rocío are married by now.) We also met little dark-skinned, Che, a twelve year old Sub Sarahan Moore, who came from a refugee camp to live with them every summer. I found out later that his stays ended when the immigration laws got too difficult. (I wonder about him too, but in an uneasy sad way.) All tried to talk to us even though they spoke no English. Heather was very busy translating for both sides of the conversation.

We got to shower after sauna Savilla, (Showers were much appreciated and needed on this trip.) and get ready for a many course meal at seafood restaurant at the beach. Our table was outside and very large to accommodate all the people. The dad, who was a local butcher and seemed to know everyone, was the perfect host of the evening. He kept saying, "Hatha, Hatha," and would tell Heather what to translate and kept talking and telling funny stories to Emily and me all evening. He was so jolly and full of fun. The wine was mixed with lime Fanta, and the seafood was delicious and much of it still had eyeballs. Emily, who didn't even like fish, was a real trooper and tried and did her best to enjoy everything. Heather and I, on the other hand, have never had a problem with eyeballs, and thoroughly enjoyed all there was to sample. Heather actually did get exhausted with all the translating, and that is saying something, because that girl could really talk.

Alyce Gross

18 July 2002   Teary Good Bye/Hello Lagos

We slept late the next morning and were offered coffee and breads for breakfast. Emily even drank coffee for the first time. I was so proud of her. All the young people and I went to the beach, while Carolina's mom stayed home and cooked a huge meal. I asked several times if I could stay and help, but she insisted I go. My new little friend Che and I used shells to dig in the sand, and we body surfed; but much of the time I tried to stay out of the sun, under a parasol. (Heather called it a sombrilla umbrella.) We came home in the early afternoon, for a quick shower, and a huge meal of meat, gravy, potatoes, ham and cheese, gazpacho, fried fish (Em ate some), watermelon—all delicious. We had a long teary (especially for Heather and Carolina) good bye. The sweet dad needed to get back to work, but he drove his car out of the way to have us follow him, and show us the best way out of La Antilla toward Lagos, Portugal. As a Spanish man, he couldn't understand how three women could be traveling alone in a foreign country.

Heather's cell got us Residencial Solar, a great old three-star hotel with a bath in the room. We drove in circles to find the hotel, and there was a reservation cut-off time which added some tension. I did everyone's hand wash, while Heather got ready for about two hours. It felt so good to get all our stuff in the room and organize it. Also the TV was in English. We watched "Bewitched" with Portuguese subtitles. That explained why most of the Portuguese could speak English so much better than most of the Spanish. I didn't realize how much I missed hearing English. Heather was always playing Spanish radio stations in the car.

Lagos has the best night life—not with your mother, but we all had fun. Heather shared a little about a previous trip here, with her American friends, but I'm sure she didn't tell all. We did some shopping and bar hopping. A cute young guy gave me a free coconut drink in a hot sweaty bar, Jo's Garage. It was probably because I was one of the oldest people he had seen there.

Heather wanted us to move on the next day, because she had so much to show us. She really wanted us to see Lisbon, but I told her I needed a rest from driving and besides, our hand wash needed time to dry.

19 July 2002   Beach Grotto

Breakfast was included at our hotel. It was a hard on the outside and soft inside roll (like one would get in Spain) with coffee, hot milk and sugar. On that cool overcast morning we walked about a half an hour, part of which was climbing through narrow passage ways through rugged, cream-colored rock formations (again, not for the wimpy) to a beach with more jagged rock formations jutting up from the water. We sat on a private beach of a hotel. It had thick grainy sand. I leaned against a rock, listened to the waves, and wrote in this journal to catch up from July 12th. Em and Heather drew a USA map trying to remember the shapes of all the fifty states. It actually looked pretty good. At 2:00 PM the sun came out!

We went to the market and bought linner for another room picnic. Em laid out plastic bags on the beds, as place mats. We ate Heather's tuna and tomato sauce on hearty bread while discussing our destinations, and realized we had to skip some of what Heather had planned. We decided to drive early the next morning, north past Lisbon all the way to Northwest Spain. We talked of coming back to Portugal together some day. (Maybe Emily and I will do that, but it won't be the same without our personal tour guide. Nothing will ever be the same without Heather.)

That afternoon we drove back to the famous grotto, past "our" private beach. We made a decent of about two hundred steps, so we could take pictures with us in front of the interesting rocks. We shopped a bit that evening, and went to bed early for southern European and my daughters' standards—11:00 PM.

Alyce Gross

20 July 2002   Whole Length of Portugal/Santiago

Breakfast at 8:00 and we left at 9:00. Again, early for my daughters' standards. I drove from Lagos past Lisbon, Coimbra, and Porto. I was amazed at all the motorcycles that would pass me, speeding up the center line. Everyone was speeding. I drove 85 or 90 mph. The girls were sleeping part of the way, but Heather's moans were audible as we passed cities and sites she didn't want us to miss. The length of Portugal took seven hours, from 9:00 AM to 4:00 PM (3:00 Spanish time).

Portugal was green and brown and felt a little more rustic than Spain. Most of Spain was green and yellow in July, but in the NW it was just green. The roads were wonderful and the engineering that created the long bridges was amazing. The cabled bridges looked artistic—like string art, yet were solid and strong and gave one confidence and respect for human abilities. While crossing them we were looking down on green lush farms and an abundance of rivers. In this fertile area there are pines and eucalyptus. In Galicia, Spain, where Emily started driving, I started writing. It was a white city on a hillside above the sea—sensational!

Em drove one hour and entered Santiago de Compostela. It's a famous pilgrimage destination from early Christian time and still today. In fact hundreds of pilgrims coming on hiking trails from the east were arriving on foot as we were arriving from the south in our speedy little rental car. We stayed in a nice Hostel, Girasol, with two rooms sharing a bath for 42 Euros. The temperature was cool compared to Southern Spain—perfect and humid. We went to the Plaza to be surprised by a parade and pilgrimage festival led by about fifteen to twenty giant characters with giant heads, who represented pilgrims from all over the world. People were in costumes and there was a kind of Celtic music with bagpipes and drums. We couldn't believe the serendipitous perfect timing of our arrival. The celebratory atmosphere was infectious, making it fun to poke around the town.

Heather insisted that we have octopus, a specialty of the area. It didn't look like the calamari we get in US restaurants. Emily didn't partake this time.

As we walked back to our room past the Cathedral we ooed and awed over a light show that lit and highlighted the stone facade. The cathedral was far too massive for my camera to capture.

Subject: Santiago de Compostela
Date: Sun, 21 Jul 2002 05:35 From: "Heather Gross"
Hello, Dadder.

Here we are. We got to an internet today, as you can see. so this town is beautiful. we were at the huge cathedral this morning for a mass in Spanish that em was totally not bored at. he he. then we saw the tomb of st. james. mom says that that is for sure his body in there, he he. i think we drive to Cangas de Onis today. that is a town near the Picos de Kuropa—little mountains in the central NW part of Spain. then to San Sebastian for two nights, and next to Barcelona the 24th and 25th, finally back far south to Granada.

Yesterday we drove the length of Portugal north to get here. Mom drove for 7 hours!! and Em for one. We have been finding some awesome cheap hostel accommodations with the use of my cell phone. it is all pretty convenient. mom likes the flowers growing out of the walls here. we saw some orange and tons of yellow marigolds that you would like. this city is cool, cuz it is the end of the pilgrimage that people do from france for 750 km!! keep writing and we will write when we can find internets. i think i have a roommate prospect for AZ—April, this girl that was in Granada with me this year. She is in that picture of me, Jewel, Josie, and dark haired April, on the bus, that I sent you guys last fall. mom says it's on the fridge. How was the ball game? Did you go to Greater Zion Day? Is that today? it is nicer weather up here in the north. we like it.

we all love you more than all the pushy germans that we have ever stood in lines with to see the tombs of supposed saints' bodies!!! Heather, Ember, and Momber

21 July 2002   Mass of the Pilgrims/Costa Verdé

Alyce Gross

On Sunday we attended the 11:00 AM mass of the Pilgrims and entered the massive sanctuary from the side to hear what sounded like an angel. A nun was singing "Raise Me Up" in Spanish. The pillars caused my eyes to lift up to the ornate gold altar. We were inappropriately dressed in church clothes and received a few condescending stares from the rugged back-packing, exhausted, pilgrims. There were hundreds of them. We should have put dirt on our faces and worn shorts and hiking boots, but that would have been cheating and even more inappropriate, especially in the presence of Saint James; who's tomb we lined up to view, touch, or kiss. I didn't kiss it. It would be an understatement to say there must be a lot of pilgrims' germs shared there. My tour book said tradition teaches that St. James' beheaded body was brought to Santiago de Compostela in a stone boat.

We bought postcards and groceries for our drive and pressed on heading east, at 4:00 PM. I drove until 7:00 PM and Emily until 11:00 PM. The coast was on our left as we twisted and turned on a two-lane road past farms and through small towns. The farms looked old, productive, and small. The houses were stone and white stucco. It was absolutely beautiful—very hilly and a lush green, thus aptly named Costa Verdá. The pilgrims' trek (which Josie had recently done), going the opposite direction, must have been even more beautiful not to mention more exhausting. We stopped at a sort of convenience store and bought 9 Euros worth of junk food to help pass the time on the long drive. The cashier couldn't hide her amazement at the amount of treats we purchased. She didn't know we still had six days left of our car trip. We finally arrived in Cangas de Ouis and found our hostel, Hospedaje Principado for 36 Euros, in the providence of Asturias. It was wonderful to drag ourselves out of the car.

22 July 2002   Contrast: Country/City

Two mountain lakes, Lago Enol and Lago de la Ericina, was our morning destination. We drove about 24K

The Devil's Fingernail

to the low key tourist attraction. On the way we saw mountain goats and long-haired sheep. When we got out of our car, at a little parking lot, we gave some bread to a skinny old bagger man. Lush green hills with mountains in the background were all around us. We felt free to walk across the pathless hillsides toward the lakes. Moving slowly about or lying down off by themselves, were healthy, contented looking caramel colored cows. Although some had long sharp horns, they neither showed nor caused any fear. I felt in touch with nature and made a point to think of all five senses which were heightened, but in a calm way. I made note of the taste of dry toast which I had munched to keep from getting carsick on the windy narrow roads.

The smell of manure in the cool damp air was pleasant rather than pungent. Hearing the deep melodic music of the various tones of cow bells was calming for us as well as the cows. Heather's tour book taught us that each cow had its own sound, and the farmer knew every cow by its individual bell sound. We saw green grey rock outcroppings, bluish purple thistle flowers, pink and purple lupine, and little yellow daises. There was a mist raising or settling, I couldn't tell which, around the lakes. Although there were a few other tourists around, it was a tranquil country feeling that was a total contrast to the city atmosphere into which we would arrive that same that afternoon.

With the Bay of Biscay to the north, we continued east into Santander for an early dinner. Heather's friend, Dash, had lived there, and she had something in mind to show us. It was 4:30 PM and nothing was open, no shops or restaurants, so I drove on to industrial Bilbao where we had reserved a room. Our inadequate map caused us difficulty in finding our hostel, so I had Emily drive while I helped Heather navigate. Maybe I was just going nuts, and was no help at all. I really can't remember, but I wrote in my journal that it was way cool the way Em drove through the streets and parked right in front of our hotel. Also, it was much appreciated by Heather and me, because it was raining. Later as we walked around looking for a restaurant, we knew we were in a bad part of town, because we had to avoid a small begging group of creepy looking young druggies, with weird hair, strange clothes, and lots of black make-up. Unlike the skinny little begger man from the country, I wasn't about to get close enough to these kids to give them anything. I was afraid for my girls, and at the same time, glad they were with me; because I knew they would protect me as I would them. We found a welcoming Chinese restaurant with delicious food. We made it back to our hotel safely, but did walk a roundabout way, because I saw that scary group again.

23 July 2002   Guggenheim

The Guggenheim Bilbao opens at 10:00 AM, so at 9:30 we were checked out of our hotel and using a map that wasn't detailed enough, going in circles on one-way streets, trying to find a bridge which led across town. We could see it, but couldn't get to it. Because we were going the wrong way on a one way street, I stopped the car in frustration. A police car with two Spanish policemen also stopped. One policeman approached our car with a pad in his hand. I thought I was definitely getting a ticket. He looked into the car and Heather translated, telling us that he said, "You really don't have a clue, do you?" She explained where we were trying to go, and those police kindly escorted us a good 15 to 20 minutes through heavy traffic all the way to the Guggenheim. I know I wasn't driving fast enough for them, but it makes me nervous to drive fast near the police. They blocked traffic so the passenger cop could run back and ask us if we needed parking. They blocked traffic again in a round-about and directed us into an underground parking garage. I wanted to hug them and tell them I love Spanish policemen, but the traffic flow was hectic, so gestures had to suffice. We never would have found that parking garage with our map. I had so much love and appreciation for the Spanish accommodating law enforcement that I was walking on air.

The Devil's Fingernail

We had a beautiful museum entrance, through a little park, past a fountain with the rising sun behind it. The best piece of art, in my opinion, is the huge building itself, with its titanium scales shining in the sun. There are almost no straight geometric lines on the outside of the Guggenheim Bilbao. It's all curves and slopes, giving it a textured metallic boat-like appearance on one side. Staircases and lifts are an integral part of the architect's interior design. Inside we walked along a system of bending pathways next to the swerving exterior walls, but the interior side is a three story stunning structure of geometric lines with glass and metal that holds the curving walkways. These lead to the nineteen galleries, organized around the central atrium. The exhibition areas each have unique irregular shapes as well, and pleasant natural lighting is controlled by protective fabrics fixed on the glass.

We spent from 10:20 to 3:20—five hours in that art-filled structure. We started with some coffee (Em had juice). After doing the first and second floors we went back to the little café for Spanish tortilla and then did the third floor.

You can see what I focus on—food, not art. Actually I thoroughly enjoyed the art I saw, but Frank O. Gehry's avant-garde architecture and my enjoyment of observing the character of my wonderful daughters, overshadowed any memory I have of the art displayed inside that extraordinary building.

Emily bought a beautiful sketchbook and sketched the whole time, so you would think she held us up; but it was Heather who did that, by reading information next to almost every piece of art in several languages. She was comparing the translations. Emily moved through much quicker, so I was back and forth between girls, seeing what Emily was sketching and trying to get Heather to move along. I loved it, and I was so glad Denny wasn't there. He'd be going nuts. Heather and I walked around the whole outside, while Emily sat and sketched. We realized the exterior looks different from every angle. The interconnected shapes vary in the most daring designs, but a common feature is the stunning reflective titanium.

To reach our next destination, I drove about one and a half hours, in rainy and windy weather and fast and windy freeway traffic; to beautiful San Sebastián, near the French border. The half moon bay with boats, beach, walkway, wind, people, shops, tons of bars, and a statue of Christ high on a hill with arms held up, to welcome us; all reminded me I was there years ago in a different lifetime, when I was single and free. Its beauty is unforgettable. While walking and taking in the sites, it surprised me to see a stunning cathedral at the end of a busy city street. The city looked more like France than Spain.

A parking garage was our first stop, so without luggage we walked, to find our hotel. We poked around a bit and ambled onto the beach. Heather and I got our feet wet in the ocean. Maybe that gave her some ideas for her event-filled evening. Back at the parking garage, we got some of our stuff from our larger luggage and just brought smaller bags to the room. For our evening meal we first had excellent Basque tapas at a bar, then delicious salads at a sit-down restaurant. I was tired and went to the room at 11:00 PM and wrote in this journal. The girls went out to bars.

I haven't mentioned yet, that the evening meal in Spain is generally eaten around 9:00 or 10:00 PM. After 35 years of harsh dictatorship under Franco, who died in 1975, the Spanish broke out of oppression and began to party. The cities seem to be alive all night, so 11:00 PM is early in Spain.

[The next paragraph is in present tense, because this is an unedited quote from my travel journal.]

It feels great to be in bed. This is the most expensive (75 Euros a night) and the worst room yet. The beds are right next to each other. There is no sink or bathroom. They are down the hall, but it feels wonderful

The Devil's Fingernail

to be in bed writing after a very full day. Again, this traveling is not for the physically weak.

Subject: Donostia
Date: Tue, 23 Jul 2002 12:11 From: "Heather Gross" To: Dad
is Basque for San Sebastian where we be. it is beauuuuuutiful.
    this morning we spent 5 hours at the Guggenheim museo in Bilbao. good times, yet grueling on the one-contact eyes of the mom and the legs of the em. i am a good backseat driver and tour director mom says. or maybe too good. em wants to know how much money she owes gary. did you call him? sounds like you did tons of awesome work on the house!!! cool. i can't wait to be in our home. we're still excited to see barcelona and Madrid. April will be my roommate—yay!! we will rent a bigger car in granada from a bigger than Andalucia rental company to take my luggage to Madrid. we are doing well on the inexpensive accommodations and grocery store eating. we love you more than how weird the basque language is and pray for you every day!! heather, ember, mommbery :)

24 July 2002   Lost Key/La Rambla
    The girls were out all night. You would think I would be awake worrying about them, but I was sleeping soundly when, at 4:40 AM I heard three loud buzzes and a quick fourth. Em woke up the whole hotel! She came in, asked me if I had seen Heather, told me not to worry, and left. I should have worried, but I was too sleepy. At 5:15 AM, Emily came back. This time she was visibly concerned. She had gone back to the beach looking for Heather, but couldn't find her. At 5:20 AM, the agitated Emily spotted Heather from our balcony. They were supposed to meet at the beach, but couldn't find each other. Well, that was silly, because it's a big beach. At one of the bars, Emily had met a boy from Ontario, Tyler, and Heather met Chris, from Dallas. Heather had the key to the hotel and room and lost it somewhere on the beach. This story would have been much more interesting from the perspective of Heather or Emily. Chris and Tyler could

probably add some enlightening detail as well. But my story is: We slept until 10:00 AM. Had a pastry and fiber bread that we shared with our coffee. We left 5 Euros for the lost key, with a nice note Heather wrote in Spanish. At the market we bought Basque cheese and a bag of oranges for the road. Chris and Tyler were never seen nor heard from again. It was overcast, and time to press on.

We left at 1:00 PM, driving from green mountains toward dry rolling hills, to arrive in Barcelona at 6:00 PM, but I was still driving in the sprawling city at 7:00. The traffic was crazy. It felt and sounded like the car was surrounded by bumblebees. Buzzing motorbikes were passing on either side and up the center line. Again, to save my sanity, Emily had to drive to the hotel, Barcelona House, junto a Las Ramblas. It was an ugly bright blue room, down narrow maze-like bright yellow halls, with purple doors. The room had its own bath, and that luxury was enjoyed for two nights!

Strolling along La Rambla is where it's at in Barcelona. We found a great outdoor restaurant, with a good vantage point to people-watch. An anything-goes atmosphere, cosmopolitan crowd of rich and poor, street music and other entertainers, made for a fascinating evening. And the weather was perfect.

25 July 2002   Barcelona

We enjoyed the first breakfast cereal of our trip. While touring we walked past a cathedral with a street entertainer, "Jesus," out front and on to a Picasso Museum. We were done in two hours or less. [Nine months later, in Arizona, Heather and I bought some Picasso prints for her apartment that reminded us of our time there.] The metro got us to La Pedrera, a Gaudi house with his swerves in concrete—another piece of architecture without straight lines.

We walked! We shopped! The girls bought pants at a Zara clothes store. The open market, el Mercat Plaza Boqucira, was my favorite with beautifully displayed fruits and vegetables. We bought apricots, pistachios, and tropical trail mix to snack on while we walked over a bridge to the interesting dock area. [In case you haven't noticed, this was a low budget trip—my favorite kind, because one experiences the culture more intimately this way. We only bought one restaurant meal a day.] There was an impressive Columbus statue up on a high pedestal; he with his bulky clothes, was pointing out to the Mediterranean Sea and beyond.

Emily got it in her head that she needed some Miró post cards that were waaay back at the soon-to-be closing, Picasso Museum arty stores. When we finally made it, the store Emily wanted was closed; but Heather and I managed to reach through the steel grating to get Emily's post cards. We left more than enough money with a nice note. At another store I bought a little mosaic mirror (that I still have in my bathroom today). Heather led us to a plaza, by a Hostel where she had stayed before. There we had sangria and paella. It tasted delicious, and it was delightful to sit at an outdoor café with so much to visit about, after a long day of walking and shopping.

To: Denny
Sent: Friday, July 26, 2002 12:39 AM
Subject: in Barcelona
but we be leaving soon, we loved it here and now have a long drive to granada today. i am excited to see our new house you have created! mom likes the idea of astro turf instead of a front lawn. this is mom writing:

Hi Denny, I had to see if I could still think for myself. Heather has been in charge and doing a great job. Em is back in the room waiting for us to go to breakfast. We have a long drive, but the roads are great and the police don't care how fast you drive, or about much, except that they were very helpful in Bilbao. Tell you all about it when I get home.

Love and miss you, mom, heath and em

26 July 2002   Driving Day

We were in the car for nine hours, driving on C32 west and E15 SW along the Costa Dorada (Golden Coast) past Valencia. The Balearic Sea was east of us. As we passed Valencia Heather reminisced about her hellish trip there where she and companions were in the rain and came home on a cold bus, in wet clothes. After that trip, Heather ended up with an irritating rash all over her body. [Years later Heather's Uncle Allan and Aunt Bev were robbed in Valencia. Their passports and much more were stolen, so that city has no fond memories for us.] We then headed south. After Lorca, we went west on A92, to Granada and Heather's apartment. Home at last.

None of us wanted to go to a market, so for dinner we enjoyed Port wine, hot dogs, and old bread. I showered before bed, and it felt sooo good. I was in bed at 11:00 with swollen legs.

We had circumnavigated the Iberian Peninsula in a little less than two weeks, 4,164 K in 12 days.

27 July 2002   Granada

At 10:00 AM, we returned our sweet rental car. The charge was $365 for 12 days. We made arrangements for a larger rental car to get us to Madrid and to accommodate Heather's two huge suitcases, holding all her possessions from a year in Spain. On the way back to the apartment we bought five decoretive pillowcases, and a blue and white tile and half vase to hang on the outside wall by our brick patio at home in Utah. All were things I could easily pack. We shopped a last time at Heather's beloved Hipercore for salad, fruit, and beer. We ate at 5:00 PM in Heather's kitchen, did wash and watched <u>Willy Wanka</u> on TV.

28 July 2002   Packing /Emotional Day

All I wrote in my journal was "packed," but even without the reminder of the journal notes and details, I remember this emotional time very well. It revealed a lot to me about both of my daughters. We all had serious packing to do, but especially Heather. She was getting stressed and upset, partly because it was hard to fit everything she wanted to take in her suitcases, but mostly because she always had a terrible time leaving any place. I first found that out when she had to leave for college. Here she was again, going through emotional turmoil. I really wasn't very good about dealing with it. I was trying to reason with her, and talk her through it, but Emily was the trooper. She just started organizing Heather's suitcases in amazingly efficient ways. Instead of talking, Emily was doing, and got all that was important to Heather into those two large rectangular black cases.

I'm jumping ahead in time, because it made me think of when Heather was leaving her apartment near ASU after graduation. She was a basket case, and there I was again, trying to talk her through it; but her boyfriend, at the time, Aaron, got on the phone and started taking care of shutting things down. Then he, Denny, and I talked her into getting rid of a few things, like volumes of college notebooks. This time we didn't have to fit everything into two suitcases, because she had a car. I included this because it was that same separation anxiety and intense emotion that boiled up in my sweet Heather. Aaron may not know this, but I'll always be thankful to him for being patient with her and helping her. Maybe he'll read this book one day.

Back to the Journal and Granada
   It was hot; so we went to the public pool, past the University of Granada's Engineering Building. We happily ran into Heather's lovely Italian teacher at the pool, and unpleasantly happened to sit near a small group of drugged-out people. Also there were cigarette butts all over the ground. I was grossed out, but my daughters didn't seem to mind. The swim did refresh us, so we could return to the apartment to sweep and mop. I slept that night with a fan and woke up with a swollen throat and the beginnings of a rash. Maybe Heather's Valencia gremlin somehow got me too. After I got home, I found out

I had scarlet fever. I wonder if that is what Heather had four months earlier.

29 July 2002   Granada to Madrid

Because I woke up sick, I slept until 10:00 AM. We got the car at 11:30, and what was supposed to be a station wagon, looked very small to me. I was worried, but Em, super packer, made everything fit. We left for Madrid at 1:45 and arrived at the airport at 6:00. We put all the big bags in three lockers that were in the hottest pit in Spain, and the damn lockers wouldn't work. A busy, irritating, hyper active, female attendant had to get the keys out for us. After turning the $130 car in at Hertz, we took a taxi to our hostel. The taxi driver stopped in the wrong place, and we had to hike four extra blocks with our overnight bags, which doesn't sound like much, but it was so hot and I wasn't well. That didn't slow us down. The Museo Nicional de Arte Reina Sofia was going to be closed tomorrow, so we went from 8:00-9:00 PM. We got to see some Miró, Dalí, and Picassos so it was worth it.

At 10:00 PM, we met Josie and Salva, her rugby player boyfriend, at a great big circular plaza where the streets head off like rays of the sun, Puerta dil Sol. We went with them for beer and tapas. Salva snuck and paid the bill—cute boy. Josie was the strong, athletic friend that missed meeting Heather in the Cinque Terra. She told a scary story about a mountain climb in a snowstorm that she experienced during her trek when she was to have met Heather. It sounded even more dangerous than running in front of the men who were running with the bulls.

We didn't get to bed until after midnight.

Subject: Yay!!!! we see you mañana!!!
Date: Tue, 30 July 2002 08:04

hey, dadder. i am at the internet with josie in madrid. mom and em are at the corte ingles looking for something to send to Carolina and her fam as a thank you. let's see, we got to madrid airport yesterday after talking to you, got rid of the car, got to our hostel, and then did a quick tour of the Reina

The Devil's Fingernail

Sofia museum before it closed at 9 pm, cuz it is closed all day on tuesdays. That is where picasso's famous black and white anti—war (the Spanish civil war when Franco had hitler bomb this tiny town in basque country called Gernika) or "Guernica" painting is. anyway that and some good Miró stuff, this Catalan artist guy that em likes. then we met josie and her Salva rugby guy friend who i know from granada. he lives in madrid for the summer. she is staying with him here for a while. so we 5 went to tapas. salva was sneaky and paid—very nice. this morning we met josie at the Prado—good museum, and then walked through the huge park, El Buen Retire, to here. mom and em just showed up. they didn't buy nuthingga.

    Dave the neighbor sounds cool. so, you and me hang out and have dad and daughter talk time, eh? that will be good. i am excited for our business class seat flights and then way excited to be home!! i love this place though, and know i will be back. mom and em love you too, and here is the flight shiznit: (we just checked it again to make sure) we arrive in SLC at 5:48 pm on delta flight 179, like we said. yep. k. we love you more than all the good art we walked by today. heather, and emmer, and mummer, and josie too

30 July 2002   Prado
    Had juice in the room. The girls had cheese and crackers. We stopped for coffee, and met Josie at noon at the Prado. Saw drawings by European Masters: Goya including his reclining nude and the same women dressed. The Garden of Delights with Heaven, Earth, and Hell by Bosch, The Maids of Honor or the Family of Philip IV: "Les Meniñas" by Diego Velázquez De Silva (1599-1660).
    At about 3:00 we walked to a big park by fountains and ate tortilla sandwiches by a beautiful lake with pillars around one end. We shopped with Josie and bought T-shirts for ourselves, lace couch pillow covers for Carolina's family, and a book and poster for Che. Heather had to have a Spanish style coffeepot to bring back, and we bought a CD, (probably for sale illegally) off a blanket in the metro in front of police. Back at the Hostel we cleaned

up leftovers and had cereal, milk, cheese toast, and sausage. Again our beds welcomed us after midnight.

31 July 2002   Madrid to NYC to SLC

We had purchased miles from a friend who got us Business Class tickets, so we had no line at the airport, and they took Heather's two huge bags—no problems. I did still have my sore throat and the rash was spreading, but I was so thankful that it waited until the end of the trip.

Our departure from Spain was 11:30 AM and we arrived 7:00 pm Spanish time or 1:00 PM NYC time. Customs took about half an hour. We couldn't wait to get to SLC, especially Heather who hadn't seen her dad since Christmas.

As I read through the previous journal, it struck me that I told a lot about what we did and saw, but not much about emotions and feelings; so I must share that the best part for me was being with my two wonderful, interesting, adventurous daughters. All of us were on and emotional "high" for the whole trip—we had so much fun and so much time to chat and share our feelings. The countless things to learn, see, and experience intrigued us and gave us more to talk about. I am and will be forever thankful that we three had that time together.

Heather had a few short emotional out-bursts, but Em and I were used to that and thought little of it. I, being an optimist, thought her boughts with depression were behind her. I was wrong.

Back in the USA

August, 2002

It took no time at all before Heather met Aaron, a new boyfriend, who was a student at the University of Utah.

After our wonderful adventure, both Heather and Emily helped me work in my classroom to get ready for the new school year. Denny and I had to send off both daughters for the first time. That was hard—so hard. Emily started college at Colorado State and Heather returned to Arizona State. She had to say goodby to both Aaron and to us, and head to her cute apartment near campus that she shared with April Bogórquez. Well traveled, open minded, interested in many cultures—April was a perfect roommate for Heather.

Heather's Journal   September 2, 2002

I am in Arid-zone—Arizona. I've had a week of classes at ASU, my senior year, which might be a year and a half, because I found out my scholarship, an eight-semester thing, was deferred for the first semester of Granada, because that was study abroad and not exchange (like the second semester), so I will have my scholarship until December of 2003.

We, the Lutheran Campus Ministry peeps, are in two vans driving toward Phoenix from San Diego. It was a good Labor Day weekend.

Salt Lake was awesome. Teresa, Hortin, my dad, and I met Aaron. Saw Greg thrice—He has a girlfriend of five months named Kim. Aaron is from Boulder, Colorado. Em is at Colorado State University in Fort Collins. I have not spoken with her since August 21—two Wednesdays ago when I left and drove 12 hours alone with all my shiznit, a bike on a bike rack on back, and 70 ounces of coffee, and an annual National Parks (for all over) Pass that I bought at the entrance to Zion National Park, when I drove through it in part of the drive. I drove in my car!!—Ford Contour, goldish, 1996. Yay! Me—21. Dad bought car and wax which was waiting for me when we las chicas returned de España. I will have a working phone line . . . . Then I can call Embily G.

This is the first year I did our Christmas letter instead of Heather. It tells about our trip to Spain—Ole'

Christmas Greetings, 2002
    Our girls are busy studying for finals, so this year we aren't sending our traditional poem and art. Having both of our girls gone is the biggest change for us in 2002. We've decided dealing with this change is easier when one considers some of the alternatives.
    Heather is back from her year of study and travel in Spain. She is still a Chemistry and Spanish major and a senior at Arizona State. She is now deciding if she should work after graduation or try to get right into a Graduate Program in Pharmacy.
    Emily, a freshman at Colorado State, is working hard with a Civil Engineering Major. She has gotten involved with the Christian Campus Crusade. Both girls are enjoying college life and will be home for Christmas.
    I am still teaching fifth grade and appreciate my job more than ever. Being an "empty nester" is a bit of an adjustment, and working with students helps keep me from getting too lonely.
    The highlight of my year was a three-week trip in Spain and Portugal with both girls. We were privileged to enjoy flamenco, Arab baths, and best of all—authentic Spanish hospitality. We met two of Heather's roommates' families at their summer beach homes on the Mediterranean and the Atlantic coasts. With all our shopping, cathedral and museum hopping, I often thought Denny made a good choice letting it be a girls' trip. We spent five hours at the Guggenheim Museum in Bilbao; Em drawing in her art sketchbook and Heather studying the translations on the art information. Heather was a wonderful tour guide, calling ahead on her cell phone for accommodations as we drove around the Iberian Peninsula. Emily was a trooper at helping Heather pack her

Granada household into two huge suitcases for our trip home.

While we were traveling, Denny put new siding on the front of our house and improved some of our landscaping. He is always fixing and improving things. He continues to work hard at his leasing and billing business. One of Denny's greatest loves is hiking in the beautiful Utah mountains, hunting for elk. Our family enjoys the lean meat, and he again provided us with some.

We all enjoy skiing together and will be up in "the best snow on earth" on Christmas Day. Please know that you, our friends, are welcome to come and enjoy the snow or any season with us.

Although change is a part of all our lives, we wish you this constant in your life: God's grace, joy, and peace for Christmas and the New Year.

    Love,
    The Grosses:
    Denny, Alyce, Heather, and Emily

Subject: Re: School
Date: Wed, 05 Feb 2003 22:58

  sorry i don't email enough. how you parentals doing? i talked to em for a while yesterday. i like my sister.

  yes, my house is very cleaned up from our BIG party, even the bathroom is sparkly and disinfected. so, i have been busy with school stuff, mostly for my Spanish Latin Am Civ class. Monday I had my physics lab, in which i'm in a group with Jewel.

  Tuesday, deaf Dave and I talked to the teacher for a while after class with questions about our presentation for next Tuesday. I told Dave that I want him to value the notes that I take for him, cuz I put a lot of time into it, and he just throws them randomly in his folder—ugh.

  I signed up to be in the rowing club. I think it will be cool, but... the practice is from 5-7 AM!! 2-4 days a week. i will probably be in a group that goes twice a week. we will see how this works. it starts next week. i studied biochem for a while today cuz i have a test in there next Wednesday.

  cool you guys will ski with aaron. he will fly here three

days after that. oh yeah, last night we, april and I; went to a small party with a bunch of foreigners to eat some num barbecued food complete with chicken made with saffron from Iran, by the Iranian—but has been living in Berlin for 7 years—Mehran, friend of Daniel's. I talked to this Arturo from Mexico City for a while, and helped him with some English pronunciations.

    Tomorrow I go to a meet-foreign-MBA-students-who-need-mentors-in-English thinger through the Honors college. i have signed up to do two bilingual service things—one friday morning—a radiothon to take pledges for a children's hospital with cancer research, and Saturday to help at a health fair. K, i love you guys more than all the translations of all documents, books, etc. that have ever been done! Heather

Subject: the Heath on the weekend
Mon, 17 Feb 2003 16:50 From: "Heather Gross"
Hi, Guys!

    Aaron here was good times. He got here Wed night. Thursday was exhausting and schoolnessy. I had class for three hours in the morning and three at night. aaron stayed home and read his <u>History of Economic Thought</u> and watched tv. Then that night we went to a karaoke bar with April, Luis of the Dom. Republic, Juan of Colombia, and Gil (a guy) of Angola. Other FES's (foreign exchange students) were there plus tons of the ASU types. Anyway, was fun.

    Friday, Aaron came with me in the morning. He got McDonald's while I went to Weight Watchers to learn that I had lost 1 pound. yay. Then we bought groceries for his making num sun-dried alfredo with mushrooms, broccoli, onion pasta and good salad, for our V.day dinner. We walked down Mill where he bought us Coldstone. Then to the Tempe Town Lake to sit under the Railrodad bridge. It was cool to look up through train tracks and see the moon and a plane fly by. good valentinesness!

    Saturday morning we went with April and four Germans (Daniel who knows Aaron from Mexico and others) to downtown Phoenix for a peace rally. Was cool, but I felt pretty useless parading around with a bunch of people who also see war as not the option, campaigning to police on horses and very few other listeners. Apparently 2/3 of Phoenix supports

The Devil's Fingernail

going to war now. Anyway, we in our two cars went to an African American festival thinger. This was all on April's initiative. The germans discovered Indian Fry Bread with sugar. i had a snow cone and aaron a burrito, not as good as his mexican one. we watched a Kapoiera group perform, the Brazilian African slave originated martial art/dance thing. Then April had to go to her parents' house to set up for a cousin's 15th b.day, a quincenera—very important for Mexican girls. so we (aaron and i) and four germans in my backseat drove back to Tempe.

    Then aaron and i went running around the lake. that was cool cuz there was a rowing regatta H.S. race going on. my coach had said that he wanted us to go check it out, so i got to see some rowing competition while we ran. i took aaron to where our beach to enter the lake is and to the boathouse too. these are on the far side from my house, the north side of the mill ave bridge, under the freeway. running was good with having good dinners every night. that night's was the best.

    Sunday morning i studied Italian. then he and i hiked Camelback Mountain. This is north in Paradise Valley, where the Robertsons (Cindy, Frank, Megan, Kyle) live. that is a way-steep but short hike. april said it would take an hour to an hour and a half, but aaron and i decided to speed climb up the hill and made it in 40 min. then we went fast down. i was jumpy and had a rhythm to land on my right ankle more often, cuz my left was hurting a little. aaron called me a gazelle.

    that evening we walked down mill once more; this time to the end to Monti's La Casa Vieja restaurant, to which i had a gift certificate from deaf Dave in my Spanish class. i didn't like my fish and chips and aaron's burger wasn't his fav, but we still had fun. i gave my leftover fish and chips to some homeless (yet have enough money to pierce their faces) kids on mill, who asked for them.

aaron's flight was at 7:10 this morning. i then did my physics lab report, and here i am. mom just called, but we were interrupted by some girl whose phone line is crossing with mine, hmmm... i will try to call you, mom. k. i love you guys more than all the leftovers ever taken from restaurants!
Heather

From: Heather Gross

Alyce Gross

Sent: Tuesday, March 11, 2003 1:58 PM
Subject: stuff ness
    besides school classes, i am working on getting something good together for the grant due friday. my director will email his recommendation, that is my modus operandi for now. i wanted to show you this email that barbara, who i work for at Building Great Communities sent me. she called me this morning and told me about it as well.

From: Sarah Auffret
Sent: Monday, March 10, 2003 4:23 PM
To: Barbara Shaw
Subject: Salt Lake City student
    Hi, Barbara, Virgil tells me you have a student intern, Heather Gross, who might make a good profile for the Salt Lake newspaper. I'd be glad to try to write about her—what sort of inner-city project is she involved in? Are there any awards, scholarships, etc. that I might be able to mention? I would appreciate some background on her and how to best contact her for phone interview/photo. Thanks.
Sarah Auffret

Assistant Director
Arizona State University Media Relations
    Hi! Heather is a National Merit Scholar, and a Sterling Scholar in foreign language from Utah. She is a senior at ASU in the Honors College with a double major in Spanish and Chemistry. She is currently involved in improving health in the East Van Buren Corridor (central inner city) in Phoenix. I have asked her to bring in a list of her awards and scholarships tomorrow when we meet and I'll forward it to you.
She is expecting your call. Let me know how else I can help.
Best, Barb

Nothing was ever published in Salt Lake newspapers that I was aware of, but it felt like an honor that Heather was considered. In contrast Heather wrote about herself that same month.

Heather's Journal:
March 6, 2003

The Devil's Fingernail

There is something very wrong with me. I just made myself throw up. I think it was the eighth time in 2003. According to the APA (American Psychology Association) a bulimic throws up three times a week for four weeks straight. Anyway, I'm not that regular. I'm not a smoker, or alcoholic. I am usually very healthy except when I abuse my body with food. . . . My parents are paying for Weight Watchers and I'm not following the program. I eat a lot when I'm stressed or upset, or it's almost like I want to depress myself, by eating random sh_ _. . . . I've definitely started to conquer my problem; I mean I have lost weight. A pressure is that I have to weigh in tomorrow, so why not fix what I did. The main cause of my binge and purge today is my worry over my Honors Thesis for which I wanted to apply for a research grant to go to Argentina this summer. My director (professor) is leaving to Buenos Aires tomorrow for ten days. The application is due one week from tomorrow. I may still have a chance if the Latin American Studies Department will allow him to email the recommendation, once I've written a proposal. I'm just stressed. . . . I have been ok lately and I need to step back and realize this. I am doing the ASU Rowing Club twice a week from 5-7 AM. I did well on my rowing time trial last Tuesday. . . . The rest of school is fine. I'm still with Aaron. He comes in a week for Spring Break. . . .

March 8, 2003—8:05 AM
   So now I say that eating too much, so much that I'd puke is just a lack of control issue—something that does not need to be a part of who I am. . . . Yesterday was wonderfully fulfilling. I enjoyed my job—being at ASU's Building Great Communities. I was proud to have been successful with Weight Watchers.

March 8, 2003—11:19 P M
   Today again—I feel like a drug addict, but my drug is f_ _ _ ing myself over by not doing my stuff—like studying, so getting depressed, so eating, so puking. . . . I love that tomorrow is a new day. I do not want to be bulimic, to hurt

my throat and teeth and self-image even more. . . . I talked to my parents on the phone yesterday. What a complete change of my mood they would have found if they had talked to me today. Well, tomorrow. Hope. Change. Do things. I know what causes this. I have to take control—a vow! Yes. No more puking. No more binging.

March 25, 2003
It seems I only write in here when I'm having some depressed eating disorder issue. Yep. I think that the March 8 entry was the last time I puked, and I didn't do that today, just over ate—too many Weight f-bomb Watcher points. OK, here's the situation. Spring break ended yesterday morning when Aaron left to drive back to UT after we drove back from California. So here I am with school and job—Building Great Communities at the ASU office—me in charge of health initiative—focus on central Phoenix poor Hispanic neighborhoods—the East van Buren Corridor. That's my job. School shmool.

I loved Disneyland and adjoining theme park—California Adventure, and Santa Barbara with Aaron. He was wonderful and patient and fun to travel with.

Starting now and into tomorrow I eat better, meaning less, and with more vegetables etc. I hate Weight Watchers and probably have gained 5 pounds since last weigh-in. . . . I do know I can run and eat well and get back toward my goal weight and finally reach and maintain it so that I don't have to keep paying Weight f-bomb Watchers.

Tonight I talked long on the phone with my sister and with Megan and yesterday with parents about being sad and crying when Aaron left. I don't know what I'm doing this summer, or what pharm schools prerequisites to do. These things are on my mind.

Subject: Re: Sad Computer
Date: Sun, 30 Mar 2003 13:06 From: "Heather Gross"
to my mom.
    hi wasssup. I'm sorry that you were disappointed at the lack of emails from you daughters, so me be writing. Well, I

think you know my goings on since friday. yep. i had been running, weight watchers, work meeting at macayo's, and then found your nummy package, into which i have made a significant nummy dent since it arrived.

[I have no idea what I sent her, but because of her struggle with weight, it sounds like I wasn't any help.]

friday night was fun with megan at dinner at a good cafe in mesa. we then went to this irish pub on mill. there are so many bars i have yet to experience. . . and i'm glad i still have time before i leave tempe. even though i haven't fallen in love with az, i know i will miss it.

first cool thing about this bar—Rula Bula, is that a nice forty something, but not annoying hitting on us, man bought our drinks. I had a Guinness beer. I learned to like these at the Irish bar we often went to in Granada. so, they had an irish music band and these girls dancing, kind of like Riverdance. the coolest thing was that the best girl, who they announced will be dancing in an international Irish Dance competition, was in my o chem two years ago and my p chem lab next semester. i had talked to her a lot about her dancing and stuff, so it was really cool to see her perform. she was excellent.

then i dragged megan, brenda, and this friend of megan's who i met that night, Christina, to the bar just down the street called Club LEVEL. this is where my rowing club peeps were, but that place was 18 and over and stinky high school bumpin and grindin music and dancing, so i said hi to my rowers, and then we moved on.

we four girls went to the Owl's Nest, the bar above Hooters on Mill, where the crowd is more our age (not older like at first bar, nor younger like at second) and there is a dance floor and good times. Megan and i were lucky to ask the right guy what we should drink, cuz he decided to just put it on his tab for us. wassup?—no paying that night. we danced and left before one.

so i got up, showered and was at school 9:30 am to drive painters to our site in Phoenix to paint three cute little old falling apart but ok houses. the old lady, who lives in one and rents the other two, appreciated it. twas cool. the photo student who works for Building Great Communities (will refer to it as BGC), David, took tons of pictures of me for that article in salt lake newspaper. twas weird. i had to keep painting where he told me to put my brush and move so he could get my ASU shirt as well, blah blah. we did the houses white with green trim. they looked fresh and new when we were done.

Saturday afternoon, i picked up my Chinese MBA student, mentee, and drove to my apt. we then walked to mill ave and walked up and down among the booths. i introduced her to kettle korn. she was funny asking about all the art and learning new terms.

(I think I'll send this to the em and dad too) sorry—I've reverted to my novel length spain email days. anyway, do you guys remember Brad? [I changed his name.] he was the boy i talked to over the summer after freshman year about meeting at the grand canyon etc, and then the thing just ended when i got back to asu. i saw him a while ago on campus. so he called, and wanted to hang out, but i think he just wanted to show me his new GT something leather interior (i don't care) car. he and his greasy hair friend came over, but they wanted to go to dinner and i had eaten—twas 9 pm. so i said we'd hang out some other time. i went to bed early.

this was cuz this morning i had to be at the Boat House at 5 am to meet my rowers to drive to Mesa and volunteer (get paid but funds go to our team) at an Iron Kids Triathlon. twas cool to see these kids. i helped with the run, directing 11-14 year olds and marking off their race numbers. after, we helped clean up and got to eat. they had tons of extra yogurts that they encouraged us to take. i got like 15. he he.

so now it is now. and it is a beautiful day outside. sun calls, homework too. i love you all, yep. Heather

Mom again: On April 17-20, 2003, I flew to Arizona to be with Heather over my spring break. I was concerned about her, because she didn't seem to be her happy self. I wish I had kept a journal, but I do remember sitting out on a bench, reading in the sun, on that beautiful campus, while Heather was in class. I also remember helping her make curtains for her bedroom in her cute apartment she shared with April. She was suffering with insomnia, so a darker room was our solution. We enjoyed shopping for art, and buying two Picasso prints, because they reminded us of our wonderful time together in Spain. They were for Heather's apartment, but I now have those prints hanging behind me in my computer room. Right above one with dancing figures, is a picture of Heather dancing at Jewel's wedding. The other Picasso print shows loving hands grasping cheerful flowers. Above it is a picture of Heather with her arm around Xinling's precious great grandmother. It will be explained later.

Heather was really upset at one point—much more upset then the incident called for. Her car wouldn't start. I called AAA who came right away, charged her battery, and told us we needed a new one. The water in batteries (even sealed ones) dries up in Arizona's heat. We made it to a garage just in time to purchase a new battery and get it installed. After that, Denny and I bought AAA cards for both our daughters. If only curtains and AAA cards could fix all problems.

Heather's Journal   April 27, 2003

I am in the Navajo Nation, the Indian Reservation that covers part of Utah, Arizona, and New Mexico, but we are near the town, Ganado, AZ. I came with some of my work people and a group of student volunteers, and I am freezing right now. It is 6 AM Arizona time, 7 AM Navajo time. (They do Daylight Savings.) I need sweat pants on. I am facing the sunrise. It is windy. I'm in shorts and sweatshirt. Yesterday at this time I went running with Jeremy, a kid who is on the ASU freshman track team, distance runner, and who is in the Honors College, likes Jesus, and wears an abstinence ring. There are other nice males on the trip, but not attractive to me. OK, originally I opened this book to reflect. I am in nature (quasi). Well, the stars are more and closer, and the people, although there are great incidences of domestic violence, alcoholism, and suicide, the people are closer to their souls—maybe—their inner selves. So I need to reflect on being in this other nation within my nation at war with Iraq since Wednesday March 19, the first day Aaron and I spent at Disneyland. . . .

It is open and sage brushy and beautiful here. So April wanted me to do this—bring a journal—write in the journal. That word comes from Latin for daily—I don't do that—write daily, but I like my sporadic updates. So, because April's birthday was yesterday and her birthday party at our house was Friday night; I was sad because I would miss the party. She said I should write. . . . I love her. She is beautiful and so helpful to sometimes defenseless, full of tears, me.

[Heather is getting depressed again and she is trying to figure out why.]

Now the chronological update: Three weekends ago, April 4th, I went with the Rowing Club to San Diego. Fun. The men's 8 did well. The next weekend, for Aaron's birthday on April 13, I flew to SLC, because he bought me a ticket 3 hours before the flight left. I have a scab/scar on my right elbow from mountain biking with him up behind the U. Palm Sunday was his birthday. We met mom at church and went home to a good lunch—flank steak (I still remember-num.), baked beans, potato salad, complete with German chocolate cake for Aaron. I put 22 candles on it. I flew back to Phoenix Monday morning. Then last weekend my parents were in Tempe. That was good. Parents and I went to Chandler Mall, pedal boated on Tempe Town Lake, and they saw the boat house where all the Rowing Club stuff is. We went to church on Easter, and then they flew home at 1:00 PM. I went to April's parents for an Easter meal. We all cracked dyed eggs with innards blown out, filled with confetti, on each other's heads—silly fun. This is a Mexican tradition.

So now it is now, and we came up here to work on a domestic violence shelter for these people, but all I did yesterday was sort clothing donations—I mean service wise, but that's OK.

So hey, I won a grant from the Latin American studies Department—only $700, to go to Argentina this summer for my theses—more on that later.

Now I go inside to group and breakfast. Good day, sun. ☺

Emily's spring break was later, May 23-27, 2003. She too,

spent it with Heather. They had a sisters' time together in Arizona, where Emily got to meet some of Heather's many college friends.

Heather stayed and worked in Tempe that summer as a hostess at Nick and Tony's Restaurant, and on July 16th she wrote in her journal, that she was almost a graduate of Weight Watchers. She must have had a better attitude about it because she left the f-bomb out of the description.

August 3-14, 2003, Aaron and Heather went to Argentina. Heather's motivation was to do research for a thesis which was a graduation requirement from Honors College. There is a substantial Italian settlement in Argentina and Heather's college minor was Italian. Somehow that, along with Heather's compassionate spirit, led to the topic she chose: "Italian Voices in La Boca of Buenos Aires." Heather arranged for and did interviews with Italian women who lost their sons and/or husbands, because they had been forced into military service in a bloody civil war. My husband and I remember her showing us a picture of her sitting around a table with several Italian women dressed in black.

To say Aaron was an avid skier is an understatement. While Heather interviewed, Aaron was somewhere in the Andes making "sick" turns (his terminology).

Heather's Journal
September 5, 2003, 2:56 AM
I am sleep deprived and at the moment I seem to be suffering from insomnia. Rowing starts Monday. Today my sister Emby G. turns 20! I have lots going on. Jobs: Fitness Fun instructor for 3-5 year olds at the Tempe Jewish Community Center and Mad Science Instructor for K-6th grades—I think. [The Mad Science didn't work out, because the pay wasn't enough to cover driving all over Phoenix to different schools.] *And I'm still Building Great Communities and not Nick and Tony's—nope, all good.* [She listed all her science pharmacy prerequisite classes including] *Inorganic Chemistry (Not in Spanish.* ☺

Remember the shitty experience in España.) and Honors Thesis.

About Aaron: . . . Travels with him are awesome. He is a tolerant of my freak-outs.

November 11, 2003
Hello, I feel sad. I just want to be done with school. . . . I am often depressed due to my thesis not being done. . . and the whole body image. . . . I dwell on things and plan on being sad and that's not good. . . . I have no motivation to care about all this. I need help to cheer up, to figure stuff out, to be happy again, to like being alive.

November 25, 2003
I am ugly, because my hair is dyed the color of poo. I've used up all my tears. There are none left. I went to the counseling services today. I don't know if they will help.
My thesis was done—defended on November 18 and turned in to the Honors College on November 20. My life is fine. I should be happy and excited to be going home for Thanksgiving. I am not. I mean I do want to go home. I am just not happy. I <u>hate</u> my hair. I don't have the energy to write any more negatives. It's 12:27 AM. Goodnight.

December 14, 2003
Sometimes I feel good, and I think, I should write in my journal so that there are some good things in it, but then I do not and then I do self-destructive things.
Dear God, help me to reclaim my life, my time management, decision-making, my sanity. Help me to not shovel shitty food into my body, throw it up, and then shovel again. . . . I cry so much and I have no problems. I create them for myself. It's like I'm trying to make this final exams end of college, graduation, moving away, saying goodbye thing harder than it already is. I have a headache as I often do after crying so hard and consuming so many random calories and hating myself over an over again. It is pathetic.

I went to that councilor again last Tuesday. I was honkey f_ _ _ ing dorey because I had gone running 10 miles the day before and had no huge deadlines to deal with. So he thinks I am just fine now. I am not. I miss loving being me. I just do not anymore. I don't want to take antidepressants. I just need to go to sleep and have a new day tomorrow. I want Aaron to call me back. I am so self absorbed and selfish and ick. The counselor said I do too much negative self-talk. Perhaps, eh? (sarcasm)

[Yes, Christmas letters never do tell the whole story, but the truth is we didn't know the whole story.]

December 2003   Denny wrote:

Season's Greetings from the Gross Clan,
    We seem to be healthy and happy. Our Heather will be graduating from Arizona State University as you receive this letter. She will finish with a major in Chemistry, a major in Spanish, and a minor in Italian. She will be moving temporarily back home into her old room. Changes are a comin'. We think that she might even get a real job someday.
    Our Emily is in her second year at Colorado State University. She started in Civil Engineering but expects to make a change to graphic design. She is a fairly gifted artist and has always done well in math, so the two strengths should be useful in graphic design. Emily has also been dating a guy named Greg Gross. Yes, you read that correctly. They have been an item for over a year and we like him very much. No, we aren't looking for a long-range nuptial, but we have enjoyed his company when he has visited. Can you say, Emily Gross Gross?
    Alyce has a nice 5th grade class this year. She comes home with great stories about her kids' behavior and always seems to sincerely like her students. She has mentioned retirement but that won't be a serious consideration for at least another 4-5 years. She remains active in a couple church groups and stays fit with regular exercising at home. She skies better

than any other women on the slopes who are beyond their 39th birthday.

Denny is closing his medical billing company because it just isn't growing. He'll make a career change and move into the Commercial Property & Casualty insurance industry. He has an offer from one company and expects to receive another shortly. His background seems to be suited for this industry. Changes are definitely a comin'.

After several years of mediocre snow for the ski season in Utah, this year is off to a great start. The resorts were all open for Thanksgiving and the snow is better than it has been in the last 5 years. This is a good thing for the 2nd driest state in the country. The ski lodge on Coventry Lane is always open for visitors.

We hope that your holidays are happy and blessed !!!

The Grosses (Denny, Alyce, Heather, Emily)

A sad event that Denny chose not to include in our Christmas letter was that on August 1, 2003, Grandma Gross, Denny's mother, died of Alzheimer's. Aunt Karen being in the same city did all she could for her mother. Karen should have been given sainthood for all the effort and time she took in making sure her mother had proper care. She too should write a book.

After College

Heather's Journal   February 26, 2003

So I can't sleep. It's 2:50 AM. I begin my job at Snowbird in two hours and 10 minutes. Anyway, I have been much happier since I've moved home—tons actually. One of my problems in Arizona—sporadic bulimia has completely exited my life. In my half-asleep feverish dream mind I've been in for the past few hours I thought of a paganish explanation for my "curse." When I lived in Granada, I inherited the keys of Marian [I changed her name], one of my compis' previous compis, the one who had lived in what became my room the year before I was there. Well, she was bulimic, desperately according Caro's stories. She had had a Corona Beer metal key chain on her keys. I inherited that as well, as she had left it behind. It was on my keys in Arizona, but one day in one of my mad rushes to the Language and Literature building on my bike (in order to turn in a worked-over till perfect paper) it broke off of my keys. I can think of it as the monkey paw in that story—it was an object that brought with it the bad luck of its previous owner. I threw it away in the moving out process in December in Arizona. I've not thrown-up since. This is all just a story; I mean it did happen like that, but I know that I am just plain happier, not depressed, not stressed out by school
('cause no school for now ☺ --weird I'm enjoying no school.) and eating more healthily with my parents and skiing tons with Aaron and his family. Then to Vail in January to see Em (and her Greg as well). Then just returned from Jackson Hole and Grand Targhee with Aaron. . . . K. I will try to shut my eyes the 2nd morning of Lent, for I must get up in 30 min. Goodnight.

February 28, 2004

I am writing by candle light so as to get my eyes ready for sleep. I would love some of that now, for it seems that I am incapable of switching off my brain. Dude, so I thought I would make a list of people in AZ whom I would *like to contact or see while I'm there in March to see Carolina.* [She then made a list of about 26 people and some other random things including this quote]: *Michelangelo "The greater danger is not that your hopes are too high and you fail to reach them; it's that they're to low, and you do."* ☺

[Insomnia continued to be a problem, but at least she was happy for a while; and I don't think she was ever bulimic again.]

After Heather graduated from ASU she came back to Salt Lake City. She lived with us for well over a year, but she was gone a lot; sometimes working double shifts saving for travel. She worked as a server at Snowbird Ski Resort. Her main motivation was to get a ski pass. During that work experience she practiced her Spanish and befriended the Mexican cooks. Through her sincere interest in people, she learned about their children and grandchildren back in Mexico. It sometimes paid off with free hamburgers cooked by her amigos, on the Tram Deck at Snowbird.

That spring, as planned back in Spain, Heather's beloved roommate, Caro or Carolina, came to the United States for a long visit. Carolina's brother and sister-in-law lived in Philadelphia, but that wasn't her only motivation for travel. The young man that Heather had introduced her to, Evan, lived in Phoenix. As it turned out, the relationship with Evan and Caro didn't last.

Heather got some time off in March and drove to Arizona to visit ASU friends, but mainly to get Carolina and bring her to Salt Lake City for a visit. I was happy to extend hospitality to Carolina, as her wonderful family had to us during our travels in Spain. I remember having a group of Heather's friends over for paella, which Carolina, Heather, and I prepared.

In April, Heather flew to Philadelphia to spend some time with Carolina and her sister-in-law, Lola. They took a train and visited Aunt Karen, Uncles Vic and Rick, and Cousin Anthony, in Pittsburgh. Uncle Vic was delighted to get to know Heather as a young adult and meet her friends. He recalled an unusual, enjoyable trip to a bead store with just Heather; where she was buying and showing him a variety of beads, which she would use to make earrings for her friends. She made several pairs of earrings for me as well, always being careful to use real silver as I am allergic to most metals. Those earrings are now some of my most cherished possessions.

Aunt Karen told us of a wonderful, many coursed, homemade, family meal with the Sarcones; Karen's daughter-in-law's Italian family; where Heather delighted and impressed everyone by chattering away in Italian to the Sicilian born parents and translating in Spanish for Caro and Lola. Sandra, Karen's daughter-in-law, said "I think her Italian is better than my English." Heather came back to Salt Lake City and back to work. Carolina eventually went back to Spain.

From Heather's Journal   June 28, 2004
I am still 22 years old, as it's 6:54 AM, and I do not consider my official birthday switching over time to be until 11:42 AM. I work at Snowbird today: 8:00 AM at the Forklift Restaurant, and 3:00 PM in Banquets at the Cliff Lodge. I have been working a lot lately, about 70 hours a week. Anyway I wanted to write something while I was still 22. Hi. This is Heather Aron Gross reporting. Man. I have many spiritual and life planning things to think about and give attention to and pray about. I guess that I've not had time for them lately. I hope this birthday goes OK. I miss resting my feet and head for a while. Aaron and travel are still the plan for now, and I'm not sure how I feel about that, but I will write as a more mature 23 year old soon. Love you, bye, wave. ☺

[She worked from 7 AM until 1 AM the next morning—18 hours straight on her 23rd birthday.]

August 5-8, 2004, we had a delightful Gross family gathering, in South Florida, to celebrate the wedding of our nephew, Stephan Gross, to Melissa. We stayed in a beach hotel, in an airy tower suite with tile floors and three levels, which Aunt

Karen arranged. The wedding was lovely and a great reason to get to spend time with Uncle Rick, Aunt Karen, and Florida cousins. Of course the bride and groom were quite busy, but it was a delight to see them as well. Emily hated the humidity, but I told her it felt like the moist Florida air was caressing my dry Utah skin.

A Heather memory I have from that trip: She and I were swimming together in the ocean. We weren't just splashing around like most people; we were really swimming for exercise, so we were headed out to sea. I could see a color change in the water ahead and decided that was a drop off and that it was time to turn back. I told Heather this, but she chose to keep swimming. Knowing my daughter, I started swimming back for shore hoping she would follow. If I had kept swimming with her, she would have attempted to make it to Key West. (That's an exaggeration, but you get the idea.) To my relief, she did turn and follow me, just as I first heard the frantic blowing of a whistle. I then could make out a lifeguard wildly gesturing, and a group of people staring out at us. As we got closer to shore I told Heather we should stop and play around in the water for a while, to let the growing crowd dissipate and let the excited lifeguard calm down. It worked. By the time we nonchalantly walked out of the water, the small crowd had lost interest and just the lifeguard approached. He authoritatively explained that there was a dangerous current out there, and we weren't to swim out that far again. We thanked him and let him know we appreciated his concern.

The day after we returned from Florida, August 9, 2004, Heather and Aaron flew to New Zealand. Aaron, who graduated from the University of Utah in May, and Heather had been saving and planning for a worldwide, post-graduation trip for about a year. Katie Gracia joined them for the European leg of the journey.

The Devil's Fingernail

Two Months of Travel: Down Under and Europe

"Heather Gross" <imahag@hotmail.com>
Sent: Thursday, August 12, 2004 10:51 PM
Subject: Me in Wanaka
Hi guys!
  I am again doing this like a journal thing kind of, but maybe less detailed cuz internetting is spensive here. So how you doing? I would love to read emails from you! so... write to me, k? Today is my Friday the 13th, oooh, but your Thursday the 12th, so HAPPY ANNIVERSARY, parents!! 26 years. hoochy capoochies. What's up with you, Em? Lots o working with mom/The Store/eh? I'm sure you've still found time to be socializing.
  So this is my third day in New Zealand, land of sheepies and rain and mountains and vineyards and beer and kiwis and snow and skiers.
  K. I arrived in Queenstown Wednesday August 11, after having left on August 9, so that day just disappeared for me, no August 10, 2004 in the existence of Heather Aron Gross. Aaron and I walked around the Queenstown Gardens and saw the whole town, it seemed, in a couple hours. Dude, it is very small and on a beautiful lake. And all the businesses there make money on adventure tourism—bungee jumping, jet boating, bogeying off a paragliding chute, bogeying off a huge mountain cliff, going around in a boat, plane, jet-ski, bike, etc. interesting... so then I napped. Next we went out and saw some bar life—tons o tourists, mainly british/australian/canadian/us/japanese my age-ish people. our hostel was called Southern Laughter, very cute with Gary **Larson** cartoons all big in color and framed all over the place—in the rooms, bathrooms, kitchen.
  yesterday we awoke to chillly rain, not good for skiing. mountain was closed, so we hiked to the top of a lookout at the town and lake point, for which one could pay $17 NZ dollars (about $12 USD—the exchange rate is about .65) to ride a gondola to the top and down. Instead, we hiked it and then got on the gondola to ride down without having to pay, cuz they don't check for tickets (as our hostel helpful lady had informed

Alyce Gross

us), wassup. so that was cool, but very wet. then to our hot tub at the hostel, yay. then i slept a lot. i have yet to fully get over the jet lag. i want to go to bed early, like 7pm (which is Utah's 1:00 am) and tis easy to **get** up early, but i will stay up later and hopefully get in the zone—the new Zealand time zone-zone soon.

Ok, so today we had planned to go to milford sound, this beautiful naturey mountainy water place to see seals and cruise around, but the road was closed! we found this out yesterday and canceled our other night in the queenstown hostel and moved to here—wanaka. now we are in the Altamont Lodge for one night and then move to the cheaper YHA hostel for two more nights. Wanaka is less touristy and more of a **ski** town. it is also on a lake and feels like a toned-down smaller version of queenstown. our bus ride here this morning was beautiful because the rain had stopped and we got to see the countryside—some nice pastoral scenes that mom would have loved. aaron and i went running around the lake, and now we are in town. our lodge is about a 15 minute walk to town. We came here cuz it is the base for Treble Cone, the largest best **ski** resort according to Polar Bear-jaron. [meaning **Aaron**] haha. So we will see. ski the next two days is the plan, then back to queenstown. hopefully milford sound one day, and then on the 18th fly to auckland, and then Sydney, australia!

i have been wearing my running shoes and the shorter dark jeans every day, but will use the other jeans when i know i don't have to worry about wet ground. thank you for the marvelous sew jobs!!

em, dude, my bags and their organization is working out great, much thanks to you, man. yep. and dad, aaron says that you did an awesome job sewing his **ski** pants! they have held up perfectly so far. thanks!

so write back and tell me how you guys be! and i will try to write every three days or so. probably won't call, if that's cool.

I miss you and love you more than all the cute sheepsies tromping and chomping around the steep hills and vineyards here! Heather the traveling floating feather
Ah! I will email Gunklevic [G speak for Uncle Vic] 'bout his bday! yes, hello from bajerin.
Love, me

The Devil's Fingernail

From: "Heather Gross"
Sent: **Tuesday**, August 17, 2004 1:24 AM
Subject**:** HAPPY BIRTHDAY TO THE MOMMA BAJOMMA!!

    Wassup! Sorry this email is to all, but it's mostly to mom on her bday! So, happy Bday, mom! How you doing? I hope that you have a marvelous day!

    I loved your long email the other day, mom. And thanks for writing too, dad, and tell Em to write!!

    So I am in Queenstown for my last night in New Zealand. I have to say I am ready to move on. We were in Wanaka three nights—Fri, Sat, and Sunday. We skied Saturday, but dudes, the skiing wasn't so great. I mean, the snow was ok, when I could see it. We couldn't see anything, which was disappointing because there is a marvelous view of Lake Wanaka, but not for me. the resort closed early as well. It just seems that we've gotten bad luck in the weather/planning what to do department. So, that day was bad, and then Sunday both ski resorts accessed from Wanaka were closed because the roads/avalanche blasting/get skiers to the mountainness are just not as efficient nor important here as in Utah... So Sunday we bummed around town. monday we awoke to beautiful clear skies, but had already booked our shuttle back to queenstown, so no skiing in clearness, and back to town of touristyness and a blizzard! was freezing and snowy. i decided snow in august is not good when I've just come from sun and getting tan and summer. well, i am actually in a good mood now, although it might not seem like it.

    Today aaron and i hiked to the top of that gondola place again, we rode a luge track on little sled things with wheels a couple times. twas fun. The track is concrete, not ice, but wider than an alpine slide. then we snuck on the gondola to ride down again. After that we went running through Queenstown Gardens. Tonight we might meet up with Nick, a New Zealander kid with whom i worked at Snowbird.

    We've been emailing Katie, so that is cool. She is very excited to take a six week hiatus from working. I emailed Uncle Vic and Aunt Karen too.

    That isn't surprising that you are your principal's best kept secret, mom. of course you are. :) also that em was a great helper at school. dad, nice you're doing more house fix-er up-ers. what else? seeing the Olympics from the kiwi perspective is interesting. we have lounge/tv thingers in the hostels. we cook too, to save money, cuz they have fridges and kitchens for hostel stayers to use. been doing some PB&J's, mom, like you suggested, but good that i didn't bring it into the country because they had food-sniffing dogs who would have found it when i came through customs. they take any food/animal/plant products and quarantine them. i lived on the wild side and didn't declare the apple jelly i was sneaking in for aaron. managed to pull that off.

    so tomorrow morning we fly to christchurch, then auckland, to Sydney, where we arrive at 5pm, and then will be only 16 hours ahead of you guys, so 8 hours behind but the next day.

    i'm excited for a little warmer climate and big city. i have been wearing my SLC 2002 hat, from the raisin bran box, all the time, (thanks, dad) and ski coats and many layers. sometimes tights under my jeans. what a change from Florida!!

ok. love and miss you guys more than all the spectators of the Olympics! heath bajeath

From: "Heather Gross"
Sent: Sunday, August 22, 2004 4:01 AM
Subject: From Stralia
Hi guys!

    I'm finally writing from here, my fifth night in Sydney. Sydney is beauutiful. Aaron and I have enjoyed the non-rain warmness of it. We have done tons of walking all over the place and touring. There are supposed to be 4 million people in the city, but it seems like a lot more, tis huge! The harbour and so many inny and outy—nesses of the land/water make for tons of cool views.

    Our hostel—The Jolly Swagman Backpackers has been interesting. We moved rooms, because we seemed to be right above the lounge TV downstairs that needed to be blaring at all hours of the night for the 24/7 partying going on; so that is good.

    the first day was the most walky. We went running through the Royal Botanic Gardens and around the Opera House. We walked across the Harbour Bridge and took a ferry back. We have lots of photos of the Opera House and the

The Devil's Fingernail

sunset by Bajaron. We've seen all the downtown sections and neighborhoods. We did a sky tour thinger on top of the Sydney tower, a thing on Australia's history that wasn't too informative, but we did get awesome views of the whole city from the top of the tower. We did a tour of the opera house Friday, and then experienced the show yesterday. That was cool, but I think I would be ok not being a regular opera-goer in my lifetime. Il trovatore is a big dude whose mom is a gypsy lady and whose love is loved by some other dude, and that's the story. I mean, it gets frustrating listening to someone sing, 'Oh my love' 17 times, he he. Aaron and I had fun though. I think we were the youngest people there for sure.

    We've been around Darling Harbour and Circular Quay and today took a ferry to Manly Beach. The weather is almost beachy, but we just strolled and ate thai food and of course ice cream. Tomorrow our safari thing starts. yay! we are cited, they take us to surf spots in national parks, we camp and surf and camp and surf. should be cool. that is until friday. I'm not sure if I'll be able to internet till then.

    So how are you guys? how are you in your new place, em? dad wrote that mom and em had a lot of rain driving and in ft collins. rain can suck. i'm glad there is less of it here.

    I love you guys more than all the voice undulations ever made by operatic vocal chords! Heath ba jeath
EM: WRITE TO ME, please ☺

From: "Heather Gross"
Sent: Friday, August 27, 2004 11:50 PM
Subject: yay most fun in Australia yet!

    Ok guys, I don't have much time to write so I will try to do more splaining again soon. I am in Byron Bay with Aaron and ten other sufari people. Dudes, the trip was so fun, and I am sooooo glad that we did it. ok.

    So we left Sydney Monday morning in a rickety van thing that runs on diesel, pulling a trailer with all of our backpacks, off to a place in one of the millions of national parks along the coast, about 7 hours north of Sydney. the campground was called Point Plomer. Ah! the group: Steve an Aussie from Cairns—50ish something. then 2 more Aussies—26 yr old Angie, and 33 yr old Susie, 2 Germans—28yr old Bjorn and 22 yr old Aleeda. Next,

Alyce Gross

Frenchies—20 yr old cute John, and 33 yr old Xavier. then Scottish—22 yr old Ross, 18 yr old Canadian Eli, and 25 yr old Irish Raelene. I love this group and twill be sad to leave them.

Ah, the instructors who were permanently high the entire trip are Kanga and Roo. (I changed their names.) They are funny and cute and i reckon (aussie talk) that it was safer to have them high the whole time. They are great surfers and excellent cooks. so point plomer where we had awesome waves and camped right on the surf spot and where kangaroos were going through the campground. aaron loves roos. he called the big guys Mr. Hopsies. It was easy to put up tents and so fun. then we drove up Wednesday to a new camp spot that i need the name of. surf conditions were not as good.

yesterday, friday, we surfed on the beach near our place. i swam with bjorn and John and dolphins!! right next to our boards, i guess ten feet away, and a family of them—two adults and a baby and then another group of about 20. i stayed out there all morning without reapplying [sunscreen], ooops. so now i am covered up. ah the surfing—I was an amazing first timer, mostly when kanga held on to my safety strap and pushed me and told me when to paddle right before the wave, the ocean will do whatever it wants with you. Man, those waves are scary and fun and frustrating and salty. ok. i have to go. the group is meeting at the beach to do a hike and then we have a dinner tonight where we get to see the documentary video that Roo made of our trip!

aaron and i are off to brisbane tomorrow, and then cairns by plane on monday to scuba dive. i can't believe this is winter, it is warm and wonderful, opposite of new Zealand, i could stay longer :). i miss you guys. i loved reading all of your newses. cool about all your classes and your place sounds just right, em! graphic design is perfect for you! you will have fun with your kids in 2 days, mom, and hi dad! write to me too. Cool about your 85 golf score about a week ago, dad.
i love you guys more than all the waves that have ever sucked or pushed or swallowed or slammed or been kind to the surfers of the world! Heathie surfpants gross

Sent: Monday, August 30, 2004 6:29 AM
Subject: in Cairns
HI Fambily!

The Devil's Fingernail

    Aaron and I arrived here an hour and a half ago, at 8:30 pm Monday, your 4:30 am. We hiked to a lighthouse with some thundery weather. Twas just Aaron, Eli, Eleeda, and I to the top. Canadian Eli and German Eleeda had a romance beginning so that was cute and cramped Aaron's style of joking with Eli all the time. Anyway, we met up with the frenchmen and aussie Suzi at the top. That night dinner, complimentary beer, and trip video watching were great. We said bye to Kanga and Roo and then were off to Cheeky Monkey's, a bar full of all the backpackers in Australia I reckon. There were metal tables textured like a floor, made to be danced on. I did lots of that with about twenty other people on my one table, wassup. Raelene taught me Ireland's national anthem in Irish (like Scotland's Gaelic, but they call their language Ireland, Erin means "my Ireland") Very fun. out till 3 am.

    then Sunday our group slowly left. :(our bus was at 4:30 pm to Brisbane. We were there last night and today, less than 24 hours. That is where Kate Heins lived.

    Today we took a boat cruise to the largest oldest Koala Sanctuary in the world. Cool to see the hugemongous homes along the river and get some history of the city. Then we got there to see cute fuzzy koala bums in many trees. They are almost always sleeping. They wake up munch on eucalyptus leaves, and this is so exhausting that they go back to sleep for another four hours. They sleep about 18 hours a day!   We fed kangaroos who were a lot tamer then the ones on the surfari. Then we got a picture with me holding a "walla bear" in "walla bear-jaron" language. Back on the boat to the city and then we had a 6 pm flight from Brisbane to Cairns, and now here i am.

    Aaron and i just walked down to the city centre. our hostel is cheap and quiet cuz it's not in the main street party area, so that is good because tomorrow at 7 am the Divers' Den dudes pick us up. Then off to dive the Great Barrier Reef! We sleep on the boat Tuesday and Wednesday nights and dive Thursday as well.

    Cool that it's nice weather in SLC. It is humid and 70ish feeling here. I can tell the days get hot. Man, if this is Cairns's winter, their summer must be icky hot.

    Oh mom, have you been saving these emails? Would you? I meant to be sending them to me too to save, but have forgotten some. So could you print them?

(I'm so thankful to God that I did.)
ok. I love hearing from you guys. Em, all your school stuff sounds fun and interesting, and I bet your bday will be goood times! I need your new Ft. Collins address, so write it to me! Love you guys more than all the hours ever slept by koala bears!
Heather ba jeather

Sent: Thursday, September 02, 2004 3:36 AM
Subject: Off the Boat
Wassup Family?
Twill be good to see you! and twill be Em's bday!! Dude. 21. Thanks for the address/phone/email, em. So we are back on land and have sea legs. That boat was pretty rocky at times. It's nice to not have to grab on to things to keep my balance while I walk. We did a total of ten dives—three the first day, four the second, and three today, Thursday. It was amazing, but I think so much diving is not my thing. we could have done four dives the first day, and five the second. It just got to be too much. We went out there on Reef Quest, a boat for day trippers, people who go out to snorkel or just do a couple of dives. We did two dives on that boat and then transferred to Ocean Quest, the boat that just stays out on the reef and survives because Reef Quest takes its garbage away and brings it fresh supplies every day. We were supposed to do a dive right after we'd gotten aboard the dive boat, but we napped instead. Then we did a night dive that was just kind of boring compared to what we did in Mexico.
So we did see some cool things—turtles, moray eel, white tip shark, tons of cute parrotfish that are awesome. You would like them, Em. the males are pink, blue, green, purple, yellow, with puffy blue lips and funny roily eyes. Lots of reef life— clown fish like Nemo, little shrimpies whose eyes glow at night, a halibut that blends in with the sand completely till his strange eyes on top of his flat body move around, so that was cool. We got some good pictures.
I made friends with funny strange 24 yr old Japanese Shuzo. Half the people on board were Japanese—interesting. many of the divers were doing training of some sort, not just doing a dive trip, so it was a lot less groupie camaraderieish than the surfing was. Shuzo took pictures of everything, i mean everything, all the time he'd kind of be sneaking up on aaron

and me with his little camera, ha ha. so we did three dives this morning that were pretty cool. the dive site was prettier than previous ones; then we got back on the day boat to take some very choppy waves home. we found out that now, because it was full moon time, was not the best; because the tides are bigger, this means more sediment in the water and reduced visibility. so, hmm.. now we get to sleep in a building that doesn't sway :)

    Ok. Aaron is hungry, so I have to go. Cool that your student teacher is good, mom. Write when you can, em, and of course I will call for your BDAY! Dad, what's up wichu?? Write if you can, please. Ok, guys, we fly back to Sydney tomorrow, Friday night, then from Sydney to Auckland to LA to SLC on Sunday, phew, then more on monday. ok I love you guys more than all the photos Shuzo can ever take! Heathie

September 5, 2004: Heather and Aaron arrive from Australia.
September 6, 2004: Heather, Katie Gracia, and Aaron flew to Chicago and then to Paris.

    If I remember correctly, Aaron decided that if they got right back on a flight they would only have to adjust once to the time change and jet lag. My job wasn't to give advice, just to pick them up and take them to the airport—which I did. In the short time that they had at home, we did go to REI, a sports store, and buy special backpacking towels and washcloths that are made of material that dries very fast. Aaron told me they had to throw away their towels from the previous trip.

From: "Heather Gross"
Sent: Tuesday, September 07, 2004 10:20 AM
Subject: here!
    hi guys, just to say hi we're at the hostel safe and happy. thanks, love heath

From: "Dennis Gross"
To: "Heather Gross"
Subject: RE: here!
Date: Tue, 7 Sep 2004 15:05
    Glad you made it. I just put $1,000 in your account. You should have access to it tomorrow. Love the

Alyce Gross

dadder!!!!!!!!!!!!!!!!!!

    grazie, papa. yay for paris and Katie! more fun with girl talk. aaron is being mr. photographer. John, who we met in stralia at safari, drove us around last night. paris is beauuutiful at all times of day! yep. luv the bajeeath

Heather paid for her own trip, but as you can see, we gave her some extra security along the way. When she dipped into it, she paid us back.

Saturday, September 11, 2004 2:46 AM
Subject: newses from Paris, finally
Hi guys!
    So John, who is 20, drove us around tuesday night. we got to see the eiffel tower lit up and most of thee other main seeey things—the louvre, arc de triomphe, champs elysees. just cool to be in a car, but crazy driving. good that the frenchman was behind the wheel.
    Wednesday was climb and use elevator to go up all levels of la tour eiffel. good views and good times with a billion other non parisians. then to the arc de triomphe and champs elyseess by day. the weather is good, a little on the warm side. i am happy with all that i packed and have gotten use of almost all the warm weather stuff.
    so that night was drinking on the grass with the sparkling e tower above. next day was slow and hung over :) hung out at our favorite place the e tower. we were joking about how that is all we will see of paris. but nope! thursday night antoine met us at the hostel, yay! another french tour guide. he came to paris from normandy just to hang with us, so that was very nice. that night we went to a delicious dinner, where i had beef and aborigine—eggplant. num. red wine choice by antoine too. a little higher quality than the 1 and 2 euro stuff katie and i had been finding in the supermarche.
    so yesterday aaron and i ran about 7 miles around paris, cuz i still have some australia time jet lag. twas marvelous with antoine making sure we saw lots more: moulin

The Devil's Fingernail

rouge first (i didn't get to see a flasher, mom)

[Mom's input: I had told Heather about a time when I was in Paris and my friends and I laughed at a flasher outside of the Moulin Rouge.]

then up the hill, where on the way, we saw the cafe where amelie worked in that movie. have you guys seen that? so up to sacre cour, the cool eastern influence style white cathedral at the top of mont martre. down to notre dame, and lunch at nummy greek—cheap.

aaron and antoine got along very well. aaron asking many questions about french football, rugby, lance Armstrong, etc. katie thought antoine was hot so that was good too. from there we saw the awesome many people lounging park—Luxembourg. next all the celebrity hotel places in paris, where madonna, princess di, and laura bush stay. jjaques shirac's house, the us embassy. finally on the metro to a dinner at lovely chez papa. more soon. i am having a great time and miss you guys. Love, the feath

From: "Heather Gross"
Sent: Tuesday, September 14, 2004 11:49 AM
Subject: RE: Disturbed

I wanted to say thank you, Dad, for the money in my account.
So, thanks! I think I will not have to dip too deeply into that, but it's good to have it.

It can be tough traveling with a friend and a boyfriend. We had a great time with Antoine because there was never a third wheel person. Well, the next day Katie woke up very sick and stayed at the hostel in bed. A French Canadian hostel boy got her sick. I bought her medicine from the pharmacy. Then Aaron and I went to the Louvre to see La Joconde, the Mona Lisa. Like you said mom, it's small. It was in a protective glass case cover thing. What was strange is that they allow tourists to take pictures all over inside the museum. I've never been to a museum that did that. I took a picture of all the people staring at the Mona Lisa and taking pictures of it. The next day, Katie felt a little better and we three went to Versailles, a huge Chateu castle thing outside of Paris. We decided to just pay to hang out in the amazing surrounding gardens behind it. There were fountains and grass and boats—little ones, and perfectly pruned trees. We had crepes and enjoyed calming classical music they play throughout the place on Sundays. Speakers are hidden in trees and bushes.

So, we took the Chunnel yesterday to London and then another train to Salisbury. This is the town where we girls went to get to Stonehenge.

The Three Ducks Hostel in Paris was loud and a constant party. That was annoying at times. Our hostel here is cute, cozy, and quiet. The town is too. Last night we went to the movie theatre and saw Farenheit 9/11—interesting to see it with a bunch of Brits surrounding us. Anyway, today we took a bus to a different stone circle place—Avebury and that was cool.

The stuff about traveling with Katie and Aaron will be ok, I think. We go to London tomorrow or Thursday, we're not sure. I will write more. Don't worry about me. I love you guys more than all stones ever dragged some place!! Love, Heathie

From: "Heather Gross"
Sent: Thursday, September 16, 2004 5:28 PM
Subject: RE: egos
Hi guys,

Mom, thanks for the nice email and good advice. We are in London. I'm glad that I've done the tourist stuff here, because now I can be chill with lots of shopping (although I have yet to find things I want to spend money on) and hanging out and not being a gung-ho tourist. We had a great getting along day today with Jenny taking us to the shopping street, and Katie in her element, and Aaron being very tolerant; so that was good. Also, there are two cool Aussies in our room, a guy and a girl. It's always good to be around other people, not just the three of us. I wrote a big email to Em about all the stuff I called parents about. For now Aaron and I are getting along though, so that is good for while we are traveling.

Your student teacher sounds way capable, mom. Nice that she checked the DOL tests! That <u>Love Actually</u> movie is way cute, and makes you like English people, huh?

Tomorrow is Katie's Bday, so if you guys want to send her a happy 24th in London. I bet she'd like it. So far I have a cute card and a funny book on dumb things that Bush has said for her. I will get something else. Plus we are taking her out to dinner and drinking and clubbing, and should be a perfect birthday I hope.

Aaron is so excited about the football (soccer) game we will see on Sunday. There is a huge ferris wheel [named the eye of London] that was built for the year 2000, so wasn't here when we girls did London. We might do that to see the city. I'm in the lobby of my hostel and I can smell weed, and it's not even Amsterdam.

K guys, I love you more than all the shoes ever sold in all the shoe stores in the world (there are tons on Oxford Street in London)!!!! Heathie

From: "Heather Gross"
Sent: Wednesday, September 22, 2004 5:05 AM
Subject: Hellooo from land of windmills and liberalness
Hi, Fambily,

It's interesting writing to you guys and having you be all over, each in a different state. So now I am six hours away from dad's time zone, and eight from mom and em. Ah! we are in Amsterdam. I think I haven't written for four days, or maybe five. I talked to parents Saturday night and em Sunday night.

Your last email wasn't boring, mom. I like hearing your "what's goings ons." You have lots of things you're doing outside of working it seems. I don't want to give up the two spaces between sentences, either. Cool you had fun with your Lois Circle ladies.

Dad, I wish I could argue with that dude about being gay being a choice or not. I would like to hear what his Biblical opinion thingers are. I am sure I have met people who had no choice, like my freezer guy at NWB Robb with two b's. Good that you get to learn lots of insurance particulars.

I need to run more times, but that often doesn't work in the traveling schedule. I have managed to do it once in each country so far.

Amsterdam is where we are. We are having fun and making it through. I think Katie will stay the whole time. The UK was spensivisssimo, especially cuz we took Katie out to sushi and drinking and the ferris wheel, but that was good. Aaron and I spent money on that, and Katie spent money shopping, so we all donated a chunk of our funds to the Queen Mother I guess. Or she died, right—so the queen. Anyway, now yay for the Euro!

Alyce Gross

Saturday was the Camden Markets. Sunday we went to the War Memorial Museum, where Katie and I saw the crimes against Humanity and Holocaust stuff, mostly stuff I had read about or heard before, but I learned about Cambodia. I was unaware of the hugeness of the ethnic cleansing that went on there, man. It seems like I just float around in first world countries and rarely meet someone who has to deal with war and disease and crazy governments, but I guess the crazy government thing is everywhere. We had a guy from Uganda in our hostel room in London. Besides snoring like he had the percussion section from the Philharmonic in his sinuses, he was interesting to talk to. He loved Americans and was in London to do a masters degree in administration of some sort, with a scholarship he had received from the U of Westminster. He had met Bill Clinton when Clinton and his family were in Uganda sometime ago. Anyway, we are lucky.

So Sunday, after sobering info at the museum, we were off to the not sober footy game. The CFC, the Chelsea Football Club, did not kill the Tottenham Hotspurs as we had hoped— no goal :(still interesting. We sat Katie, Aaron, me. I had a young Asian couple, to my right, Katie had some authentic soccer hooligans to her left. The older dude had a shaved head with a huge spider web tattoo and a bajillion other tattoos to go with it. He liked to yell things like "dirty f _ _ _ ing cock bastard." I think the Boca Juniors fans were more dedicated. Their songs were constant. Chelsea fans just yelled and sang sometimes.

Monday we flew with the wonderfully cheap Easy Jet to Amsterdam, where it has been cold, windy, and often rainy since we arrived. That's ok. Yesterday we did a mike's bike tour of the city where we rode to a windmill and a clog and cheese factory—nummy cheese. I didn't buy any clogs to match those red guys we have at the front door, mom; but we did get some cheese to eat.

We hung out with people we met on our tour, American girls and Aussie girl, and went to a comedy show, Boom Chicago—hilarious improv, like Whose Line is it Anyway?

Today is Wednesday, our first stop was here—the Easy Everything Internet, owned by the same guy who started Easy Jet. Anyway, those are my newses. Sorry this is never ending.... Ah, we go to Germany and stay with Anna and

Peter tomorrow! We arrive in Stuttgart and sleep near Munich at Peter's parents, I think. I will let you know, and then to Munchen Oktoberfest, yay! Ah did I tell you the funniest thing? Dasch had been trying to get a hotel in Munich forever, but in Paris. anyway now he has a place in Munich, so it's all good. I will be back in your Bavaria, parents.

Ok. Write, Emmy. I miss all you guys. Love you more than all the weed ever sold from a coffee shop! Heather

From: "Heather Gross"
Sent: Friday, September 24, 2004 12:07 PM
Subject: munchen

Yay! we are here with peter and anna, the nicest germans in the world. we stayed with them at peter's parents' house last night in pfalheim, a tiny 1200 person town between stuttgart and munich. his mom did our laundry and fed us a ton, even eggs in cups!!! yay ok i will write more soon. love, heath

Mom's input: When we took our girls to Europe, mainly Germany and England, we all enjoyed the soft boiled eggs that were often served in cute egg cups. In fact I bought three in London to remember our trip there.

From: "Heather Gross"
Sent: Wednesday, September 29, 2004 12:49 PM
Subject: in Zermatt
Hi guys

i again have little time on spensive internet but just want to let you know where i am. i hope to do a good long splainy email soon, Oktoberfest was wonderful. katie and i got bavarian girl costumes from a second hand store and wore them the last day we were there—monday. Tuesday we were on a train all day to here, beauuutiful. hiked today, ski on the glacier tomorrow, we saw dasch monday there, k. i will try to call. i love you so much, heathie

From: "Heather Gross"
Sent: Friday, October 1, 2004 12:25 PM
Subject: in Geneva

Hi guys!
    I am doing well and now here with Katie and Aaron. Katie is leaving from here on Sunday to Paris. :(Aaron and I go to Rome tomorrow. I guess this splitting up thing is ok, and will be for the best, as Dad wrote. I figured out that we went to Luzerne with the family when we were here.
    So, I need to write about so many things. As I said, Oktoberfest was so fun. It made it extra cool because we had German buddies to show us around. Geneva is beautiful, and feels like Paris. Back in warm weather, we are.
    It is hard changing my expectations in my head now that Katie won't be with us in Italy or Spain. She just really misses her family and wants some time to see them before the wedding she's in and then working again. Dad, I bet you are NUMB from that insurance class. Cool that you're flying home today. Write something, Em and Mom! I love emails from you guys! Miss you more than all the travel itineraries ever created or changed or planned!! Heather

From: "Heather Gross"
Subject: in Roma!!
Sent: Monday, October 04, 2004 2:56
Hello fambily, ok. the part below i wrote yesterday.
    i just wrote a long message to katie who is doing fine on her own in paris, her last night on this continent; and I'm pasting most of it into this email.
    On the train, we had a nice Swiss couple next to us on the way to Milan. The dude spoke German, French, Italian, Spanish, and English, of course. She worked in art, and he in psychology. Anyway from Milano to Rome, I was next to this so cute ballerina finance worker lady, who I got to speak to in Italian. She was going to Rome to meet this dude whom she had met on a train in Sicily. He's a doctor from Sicily and is 47. She's 35, and they were going to have dinner. They had only seen each other that once, but had been talking on the phone every night since they met. She was all nervous and excited. Then Aaron was talking to an Asian American doctor and her student from Cornell, who were interesting. Anyway, twas fun to speaka da talian.
    so i think all the tourists at oktoberfest, paris, etc. x 20 came to Rome. Dude, there are soooo many everywhere,

every monument thingy is pack-ola-ed, ha ha. tis ok. we saw the colosseum and roman forum and some famous plazas and fountains today. i am handling the "I've seen this before feelings," so that is good. tomorrow the Vatican, and then i think to napoli, yay! something new. then up to milan and then, yes, to Spain.

  now today, the 4th of October, we actually aren't going south to naples; because that would just be too south, so tomorrow we go to a small town in toscana!! tuscany, a place called Certaldo (Chair-tall-dough). we did Vatican city today, la capella sistina hasn't changed since i was here 2.6 years ago. :).

  ok. i love you guys more than all the tourists ever herded through the musei vaticani! write me some newses!
Heath

From: "Emily Gross"
Subject: what up
Date: Tue, 05 Oct 2004 10:45
Hola fam,

  I am sitting in my GD (graphic design) class, starting project number two. I am happy today, because we got our first projects back. I actually did not get mine back, because it is on display. I got one of the three A+ in class. It is cool. Also, we have to do thumbnail sketches for every project, and my teacher loved mine. That also makes me happy, because I don't have to redo mine.

  This weekend was fun. My NY buddy, Joe, was in town. He was in the dorms with us, and has come for these last two homecoming weekends. Thursday I did my cru thing, [a Christian group on campus] and then it was off to hang out with all of the boys that lived in Greg's hall in Allison. It was cool, because they all were at Greg's 24-7 this weekend, plus a few of us staple girls. We had parties on Friday and Saturday night, and watched a movie Sunday. Joe left on Monday afternoon, after we all met in the student center. It sucks that it has to take Joe to get everyone together. The weekend largely revolved around football. The boys have a video football game that they are playing whenever they are not watching a real game. Saturday, we had a pre-tailgate at Greg's (he missed this to work), then off to tailgate, then to watch a horrible loss to

BYU. While doing mass art sketches and thumbnails, I watched the Steelers victory as well as the Broncos.

I was glad to be gone all weekend, because both of my roommates' moms came to town. It made me sad to be home, because they never came home. I can't wait for you guys to come to CO.
Tonight I have a Snow Riders meeting at Woodies pizza, because one of our sponsors wanted to feed us. From there I am going with all of them to Ryan's (officer dude), because he is having a party till he turns 21 at midnight, when they all go to the bars. I don't think that I will join in that part of the festivities.
[Mom's input: Ryan the Snow Riders (officer dude) will become a much more important character in Emily's life!]

Thanks for the emails from the mom and the heath. It is way cool to hear all of the travels. I want to travel. Heath, I bet it will be good that Katie is gone. No more tension. Bajaron is used to not being home, just like you. I don't think Katie was ready for a month away.

Anyway, I love you all very much, Emmy

From: "Heather Gross"
Sent: Wednesday, October 06, 2004 7:51 AM
Subject: Under the Tuscan Bugs

Ha ha! They weren't that bad, Aaron and I just have many bites that must have taken place at night, but not too itchy. Hi. We're in Milan for 3 hours till we fly to Valencia tonight. We stayed at a 17th century converted convent—very cool, and now are headed for my European home base. yay. Twould be cool to come back and do two weeks in Tuscany, but we did get to see the castle district-Certaldo Alto, and then hang out with all the peeps staying at our place and cook (Aaron did a tasty pesto mozzarella invention) and drink good wine.

Em—You can see that you were meant to be in the art world—because of how well you're doing in all your classes.

aaron is getting way into the football of the rest of the world. american football is a good excuse for partying, yep.

mom, I'm cited to eat your cooking and talk to you and dad and relax for a second in utah, and go to CO for Halloween. Em-dude, i am going to be the bavarian beer girl, do you have parties planned? i hope so!!!

so ciao d'ttalia y pronto ci scrivo da Spagna! amore de la Heather :)

From: Alyce Gross
To: Emily Gross and Heather Gross
Subject: wow
Date: Thu, 7 Oct 2004 17:36
Hi daughters,

Em, it is exciting that you're doing so well. It must be such an honor to have your work displayed. I'm glad your friend Jo came for a visit. I remember you telling about how sad it was when he moved. Snow Riders seems to have opened a whole new area of fun.

[That was an understatement. It's where she met her future husband.]

Heath, any emails form Katie? Did she get safely to her Mom's? I would love to go with you to do two weeks in Tuscany. I bet Em would too. I'm sooo excited for all of us to be together in CO.

Em, did you have heavy winds? I saw news of a tornado in Denver area.

Love you both with whole heart, Mom

From: "Heather Gross"
Sent: Saturday, October 09, 2004 8:07 AM
Subject: in Granada
Hey guys!

Aaron and I got here Thursday night after all day on the bus from Valencia. We reached our hostel there at 1:00 in the morning, and were relieved to be in Mercedes's house after switching sleeping places 4 nights in a row. She lives in a different piso, not too far from where we lived before. So, we are still unsure if we will make it to mallorca to see caro. Aaron has seen all the cool street areas of Granada and has yet to see la Alhambra.

Em, you are awesome, like mom wrote. I am proud of you and tell people all the time what a great artist you are and how you like graphic design. I am very cited to see you in a few weeks!

Granada was hot when we arrived, and today is a little

chilly. We might fly home early if STA lets us. I would not mind for sure. Aaron wants to be in Salt Lake for the ski resort hiring fairs that are all on the weekend of the 16th and 17th. It's nice to be here and relax. Aaron and Mercedes are trying to communicate in Spanish and English and get along very well. We will meet up with Christian soon too.

K, guys. I'm 'cited to go home to carpet and hot water heaters always on and such. home is good. Aaron is learning that 3 months of traveling really makes him appreciate home. We are getting along well, and that is good. Ah! Katie made it home safely, and has yet to fly to her mom's. She is happy and glad she went home when she did.

Write, dad and em. Twas nice to talk to you, dad, on the phone Wednesday, k

love you more than all the bombonas (gas tank thingers) ever changed in peoples' homes! Heather

From: "Heather Gross"
Sent: Sunday, October 10, 2004 10:48 AM
Subject: coming home
Hello,

Mom, Mercedes is nice to house us. We are clean and not there too much. I'll tell her that you think she's wonderful. Her roommates are away for the weekend till Tuesday because that is the Dia del Pilar (Spain's patron saint- Pilar), so that worked out well. We did change the flight. We both fly out on the 14th from Paris. I called Caro, and it's ok that we're not going to Mallorca. We saw each other a few months ago. She said "no pasa nada" and that it's ok. So, Aaron and I take a bus to Madrid Tuesday morning. There we will see Pilar on her saint's day, (you just tell people "Happy your saint's day") and stay with her one night. The next day we fly to Paris. I'll give Pilar a big hug from you and ask about her people.

So, here is our info. We get into Salt Lake at 5:19 pm on Thursday.

Cool about the 5K, mom. Maybe I can go elk scouting with you dad. Ah, we saw Christian last night. He was telling us about how the Americans are just worse and worse each semester/year. He liked my small ASU group a lot. Now he works for ISA, a study abroad office that works with universities all over the US, mostly a lot of California schools.

He likes that too. He and his wife are cute and want to have kids soon.
    We did the Alhambra today. Aaron liked it, but man, there were a ton of tourists there; more it seemed than in the summer. I am excited to stop being a part of the crowd.
Thanks for writing so much mom.
Love you guys more than all the construction building chunks being moved around in Granada! Heather

It's so appropriate that the two months trip ended in Spain, and that Heather got to spend time with Christian and two of her three beloved roommates from 2001-2002. Her heart would have broken if she knew that was her last chance to see Carolina and she missed it. Thankfully none of us knew yet.

Back Home

October 14, 2004, Heather and Aaron arrived SLC at 7:37 AM. I was there to happily welcome them home. Heather started working at Tandem Labs on October 25th. It is where she had worked before, but the lab had an owner and name change.

Heather and Aaron had been together for almost two and a half years. They shared some wonderful experiences and had the love of travel and the love of skiing in common, but not much else. They broke up December 13th, just three days after the following Christmas letter was written. It was hard on both of them.

Greetings from the Grosses,   December 10, 2004
We want to extend warm wishes to friends and family from snow covered Utah.

Heather, 23, after graduating summa cum laude from ASU, in Chemistry, Spanish, and Italian; lived at home. She worked double shifts as a server, at Snowbird Ski Resort. That allowed her to ski for free, while saving all her earnings, with a worldwide trip as her goal. When Denny and I took our daughters to Germany in 1998, to show them where we first met, we had no idea what travel seeds we were sewing. After a family trip to south Florida, for our nephew's wedding in August, Heather skied in New Zealand, surfed in Australia, and scuba dived in the Great Barrier Reef. She toured Europe including Oktoberfest in Germany. She is now a scientist at Tandem Labs, a pharmaceutical contracts facility. Graduate school is in her future plans.

Emily, 21, is a junior at CSU. She changed her major from engineering to graphic design and couldn't be happier. We wish Emily were here to add her artistic flair to this letter, but with 18 units she is working hard toward finals. She serves in a leadership role with Christian Campus Crusade and is publicity chairman for the Snow Riders. Through the ski club office she earns great deals on ski trips and equipment. It is clear she isn't studying all the time. Those two diverse groups give her an interesting variety of friends. Both our girls have nice boyfriends, but we're happy there are no wedding plans yet.

Last year Denny was closing his office and shutting down two businesses. When most people his age are planning retirement; he is successfully launching a career change in Insurance sales. In Leasing he had to continually work at getting new customers, whereas in insurance he is building a solid cliental. He has amazing energy and isn't afraid to start something new. Fishing and hunting are still his passion. In fact he just got a deer. The Gross family seldom eats beef. We love lean game meat cooked any number of ways.

I guess I'm a good balance for him, because I keep doing the same thing—teaching fifth grade. I continue to enjoy my students and am never bored. I hope the students aren't either. Since the second day of school, I've had a student teacher. It's been fun teaching with a helpful partner the age of my daughters. Church activities, book club, and skiing still keep me happy and busy.

We hope you, our friends and relatives, are having happy holidays, and are looking forward to a prosperous 2005. God bless us every one.

Love, The Grosses
Denny, Alyce, Heather, Emily

Heather's Journal   April 12, 2005
Dear God, Let me hear this advice, these words of a poem, hung on the wall of an orphanage in Calcutta, founded by Mother Theresa.

> *People are often unreasonable, illogical and self-centered;*
> *Forgive them anyway.*
>
> *If you are kind*
> *People may accuse you of selfish, ulterior motives;*

Be kind anyway.

If you are successful, you will win some false friends and some true enemies;
Succeed anyway.

What you spend years building, someone could destroy overnight;
Build anyway.

If you find serenity and happiness, they may be jealous;
Be happy anyway.

The good you do today, people will often forget tomorrow;
Do good anyway.

Give the world the best you have, and it may never be enough;
Give the world the best you've got anyway.

You see, in the final analysis, it is between you and God;
It is never between you and them anyway

I fractured the left distal clavicle (end shoulder portion of the collar bone) 4.5 weeks ago—Friday, March 11th. I was skiing too fast on Silver Fox—a run just off the ridge under the tram, upper cirque, a double black—blah blah. Anyway, I've been sad some, and dumb with guys. . . . So I need to figure out how to be healthy Heather. . . .

    She tried so hard, but as the next journal entry indicates, she couldn't control the depression.
    She also dislocated her shoulder in that fall. Because she was in a sling, she had to move out of the lab and work in Quality Control for a while, at Tandem Labs. That experience, although

she wasn't happy about it, helped broaden her understanding for the lab work to which she later returned.

Heather's Journal
June 3, 2005
    In my black hole—I put up a thick blanket over my window, and my room stays fairly dark now and has been for about a week. I am depressed—very. Maybe the most I've ever been in this life. I go late to work all the time. . . . I'm still in bed. I hate work. I hate being awake. I went to a counselor two Tuesdays ago. . . . I am so sick of feeling like this. I sleep late to avoid being awake, and then it's worse because I have to stay late once I finally get to work. I do not see the point of any of this. We have a 20° C (-70° F) walk-in freezer at work. I think about going in there and staying. . . . I don't think I'm seriously or truly suicidal; I mean I don't want to cut myself or go through with any of that. I just do not want to be awake or to go to work or to be productive. I am lazy and depressed. The counselor man said I need to do creative things. He asked if I was suicidal. I said, "No." I wish I could stay in my house all day. I hate getting ready and figuring out clothes to wear over my boring chubbiness and driving and going into that metal sterile white coat environment. . . . I will get up now and drink coffee and then on with the day. My parents put up with the slug in their house. I know life will change. I need to be—have to be the changer. OK. Dear God.

July 28, 2005
    2:20 AM, depression, I am so over it, but not. Anyway I realized that my 24th birthday didn't even have a place in my last entry, so yes, now I've been 24 for 1 month. I'm on Wellbutrin XL/SR—antidepressant. I went to Dr. Susan Edwards (my mom's doctor), and that was the result. . . . I've had some OK ☺ times, but mostly not for a while. I went to Moab with Michelle Jensen to see Dasch last weekend—pretty fun—we rafted on the Colorado River. I should get some sleep. I have a job I have to keep so that I

can have insurance so I can take depression and acne drugs.

Heather was deeply depressed when she was away from home, away from the people who loved her the most, but she was in a "black hole" even when she was under our roof.

Something that cheered her and that she needed, was to move to her own place. After having a plan to live with friends, that didn't work out; Heather finally found an affordable, ideal location. On Sept 3, 2005, she moved to a darling red brick house, in Sugarhouse, Utah, with two roommates that she really didn't know. One roommate ended up moving out, so Heather was fortunate to share a nice sized house with just one other girl, Jana Hooper. Jana's mother owned the nicely kept house. I'm thankful that she and Jana became good supportive friends, because that is where Heather lived the last three years of her life.

Another something that cheered her that fall was dating a cute hockey playing, red-head from work, Scott Merkle (Smerkle). He shared Thanksgiving dinner and many other memorable dinners with us and had the nerve to steal our Heather away for our first Christmas without her. Our tradition of skiing on Christmas day wasn't the same without Heather. She and Scott were skiing, but in Lake Tahoe, not with us at Deer Valley. We did do a late Christmas with both girls.

December 2005
Greetings,
We enjoyed a traditional Thanksgiving with both daughters at home. It's never boring when they're here. They chose smart, fun, kind young men to bring home. We felt blessed with old friends, new friends, and family at our table. Emily brought a dog and two cute boys from her Snow Riders Club in Ft. Collins, Colorado. She is quite smitten with one boy and the dog. Heather also brought a new beau for us to meet and interrogate.

Emily is a senior at Colorado State in graphic design. Heather has moved to a very nice rented house, shared with roommates. She continues to work as a scientist at Tandem Labs in Salt Lake City. We enjoy seeing her almost every Sunday for dinner.

Denny is gratified that his career change, from his own leasing company to selling insurance, was the correct move. His efforts and successes have earned us a cruise to the Florida Keys and Cozumel in January, and another one to different Caribbean islands, in March. He considers cruises "happy prisons" but is willing to go for me.

I am beginning to think about retirement from teaching, but am not there quite yet. We're both looking forward to ski season.

We feel thankful for health, family, and friends like you. Warmest wishes for a blessed Christmas and a fruitful 2006.

God Bless Us Every One,

Denny and Alyce Gross

      Heather hated missing the 2002 Winter Olympics in Utah, (She was in Spain at the time.) and she loved using her language skills. With those two motivators, on February 15-28th, Heather attended the 2006 Winter Olympics in Torino, Italy. With Scott's blessing, she traveled there alone, but she stayed with a friend of a friend from work. She met up with her former Girl Scout leader, Marsha Gale and husband, Jim Gale. The first time we saw Marsha and Jim after Heather's death, Jim made me feel so good with these simple words, "Heather was one of my all-time favorites."

      In Italy, Heather also met her friend, Megan Ream, who was her roommate at ASU their sophomore year. Megan flew from Denver to get to Heather's funeral.

Alyce Gross

Facebook:
Marsha Gale
Thinking of you now that the Olympics have started....remembering our fun times with you in Torino, miss you!
February 13, 2010 at 7:55am

Megan Ream
I'm watching the opening ceremonies of the vancouver olympics n thinking of you. I will always remember juice box wine and bobsleds in torino.
February 12, 2010 at 11:20pm

From: "Heather Gross"
Sent: Tuesday, February 21, 2006 4:06 PM
Subject: see me on the Today Show!

    I am forwarding what Megan sent to me and to her fam about how to find the video clip of us on TV! Tis tough to see much of us, but yes—I'm in that tan cafe-con-leche-colored cap that was once yours, Em. Megan is to the left of me in a dark blue hat. I hope you see us!
    So I just got back to Torino, Carla and Elio's, from Bologna. I brought them some presents from there. I ski tomorrow and now need to research my skiing options.
    I had fun with Megan in Bologna. We climbed 490 steps in a tower to see the city. I was ahead of Megan as we were making the descent, and kept getting farther away, so her talking just got louder and louder until she was yelling down the tower to make sure that I could hear her. :) Good old Megan, ha ha. I did have fun with her. One of her many apt. mates (there are 8 in one apt!), a big black girl from LA named Nayasha, and I bonded over discussing a typical Megan monologue/conversation. Twas hilarious.
    Ah! Scott got to see me on the Today Show, and emailed that it was funny, that he saw me for about 20 seconds, and that I looked really good. It's good to have someone to miss and who misses me. I like my old man boy.
    k. Write me some newses. Tell me if you find the clip. Uncle Allan wrote. I love you guys more than all the molecules o' gas that have ever been burned to keep the fiamma (flame) olimpica going!

-the feath

From: ALYCE GROSS
To: "Heather Gross"
Subject: thanks
Date: Thu, 23 Feb 2006 17:35
    Hi Heath, Thanks for all the news. It was fun to get to talk to you last night. I'm glad you were with the Gales and still get to see the Giant Slalom event. Hope you feel like you've had an "Olympic" experience. How do you get to your flight to Germany? I'm sure you have it under control. We're excited to have a long visit when you get back and before we leave again.
    Love you more than all the times those curling brooms go back and forth, Mom
PS: I forwarded your last email to Al and Bev, and Aunt Karen.

From: "Heather Gross"
Sent: Sunday, February 26, 2006 9:48 AM
Subject: Deutschland
    Yay for Deutschland! I've been having good times with Daniel and his buddies. Although he and I hadn't seen each other since 2003, it was easy to get along right from the start. We've partied a bit and went to the Karneval (goodbye to meat—no eating meat during lent) parade today with music and candy being thrown. Braunschweig is the only place in northern Germany that Karneval is celebrated. Last night we were invited to his friends' apt. They tried to speak English with me, some very well, and were very welcoming. We hung out there to drink and eat berliners before going to a bar-DAX-named after the German stock exchange, because the beer prices are always changing according to demand—A very funny crowd and music that would never be in a club in the US—the soundtrack to Dirty Dancing etc. Anyway, this is a nice, non-touristy, relaxing end to my trip. I will eat some schnitzel for you, Dad. How you guys doing? Thanks for writing, parents. Is there new snow in SLC? It has snowed here a little. Wasssup, Em? How's school, work, your boy? k. I love you guys more than all the crazy fans who will see the World Cup games in Germany this summer!! Heath the Gross

Heather got home safely, back to her boyfriend, Scott, and to her work at Tandem Labs.

I debated and agonized with myself and with God, about including or not including her next journal entry. I finally decided that, although in life Heather chose to not have me share this, I believe in death she would want more of her whole story shared. I believe she would approve of the most honest depiction of who she was.

On October 30, 2006, she was diagnosed as having bipolar disorder. Heather came to us right away to tell her dad and mom all about it. My immediate response was, "Well, of course you have bipolar disorder. **How could we not have known?**" In retrospect, it explained so much, and it all made sense. Her mood swings and emotional turmoil started in middle school, but her father and I thought it was teenage girl hormone stuff. Actually, that probably was wrapped-up with the triggers at the onset of the disorder.

Heather seemed relieved to tell us, and to know we were completely accepting of it. We felt relieved with the diagnosis, and we were especially glad that she would be getting medication and counseling to help her deal with depression and impulsive manic behavior (remember the running of the bulls). At first Heather shared the diagnosis with close friends; but later she let us know she did not want us to share it, nor was she going to any more. She came to realize she didn't want to be defined by a disorder. Denny and I understood and respected her wishes those last few years of her life. But I had to reevaluate what I share and what Heather would want me to share. I think she would want me to show support to people with bipolar disorder.

The more I learn about it, the more compassion I have for those dealing with it. I pray that my words don't push stereotypes. I hope this book promotes more understanding from all the readers, and that it gives people with brain disorders motivation to get professional help, to take medication as prescribed, and to become knowledgeable about the disorder and share the knowledge with their families; so those who love them can help and support them.

Heather was still Heather, and her "Heatherisms" were not caused by her disorder. Her goodness, her values, her love of people, her brilliance was not a result of being bipolar. They were a part of who she was. She had great challenges because of her disorder, but they didn't keep her from achieving goals or from reaching out to people with her God-given capacity for non-judgmental love and acceptance of others. (She didn't reach out her first year of college, but I believe she learned from that experience.) Bipolar disorder can be managed as illustrated in the countless people in all walks of life who live/lived with this condition.

Now that the medical profession knows more about bipolar disorder, many famous deceased people have been studied and analyzed though their journals or through what others have written about them. From a web page, <u>Famous People with Bipolar Disorder Past and Present</u>: I learned that there have been so many famous people thought to have bipolar disorder that it is considered by some to be a mark of genius. That may or may not be true, but it is easy to see why the connection was made. I'll name a few from the hundreds that I read about: Abraham Lincoln, Winston Churchill, Ludwig van Beethoven, Wolfgang Amadeus Mozart, Sir Isaac Newton, William Faulkner, Mark Twain, Florence Nightingale, Margaret Trudeau, Vincent Van Gough, Buzz Aldrin, Patricia Cornwell, and of course, "the candle in the wind," Marilyn Monroe.

Bipolar people push boundaries and do not accept the status quo. I'm not saying all bipolar people will be famous, but there are some people who may never have made the contributions they did had they not been bipolar. I see it like this: There are plenty of infamous people who have bipolar disorder as well. There are all types of individuals with the disorder—good and not so good, smart and not so smart, talented and not so talented. Like anyone with a challenge, they can let it destroy them. (Some truly are not able to control it.) On the other hand, some may be pushed to meet the challenge and become stronger, more creative, passionate, and compassionate—closer to reaching their full potential—because of it.

At one point I remember saying to Heather, "Being bipolar is a part of who you are. Embrace it." That was easy for me to say. I didn't have to live with it, and I didn't know enough about it. I now would rephrase that and say "You are not bipolar; you are wonderful Heather who has a disorder. You have survived great challenges, and I'm proud of you."

I should have started researching and learning how to better support to my daughter as soon as I learned of her diagnosis, but even after some research I don't pretend to understand the difficulties that come with being bipolar. I do know, when hearing her diagnosis, it didn't make me love her less. It made me want to surround her with love and be with her through it. If I felt that way, how much more must God feel that way with his "children" who need him.

I believe Heather overcame many of her challenges because of her God-given goodness. She told me that her psychiatrist asked her if she ever wanted to take her own life, and she answered that she would never do that to her family. She kept working/running/praying her way out of depression, but as many of her journal entries indicated, not without anguish.

Heather's Journal   Written on March 31, 2007
I was diagnosed as having bipolar (manic depressive) disorder on 30 October, 2006. I have been taking lithium carbonate $Li_3 Co_4$, 45 mg tablets twice a day since then. I saw Dr. Linda Green [I changed her name.] twice alone and then once with Scott. Dr. Susan Edwards first diagnosed it. This is my regular general doctor who had prescribed Wellbutrin for depression in the summer of 2005. She sent me to a psychiatrist, Dr. Green. Anyway now is now.

[Heather told her father and me how much she respected her psychiatrists. I believe the key was that she felt Dr. Green truly cared about her.]

The Devil's Fingernail

On that October night, Heather was suffering from insomnia and acting goofy. Her concerned roommate, Jana, took her to Dr. Edwards; who gave Heather a sedative and referred her to Dr. Green. Thank you, Jana and Doctors.

Back in time: When Heather was a high school senior, she was required to keep a sketch book for her AP (advanced placement) English class. In recently reading some of her entries, I now see them as very big clues. Dr. Green probably would have considered them a clear red flag for bipolar disorder.

Heather's Sketch Book:
9/14/98   The Divided Self   Pride vs. Freedom
There are two people I can lump myself into. There is the psycho, school-driven, stress-filled being, and there is the liberal, imaginative, dancing weirdo. The achieve everything me often encompasses the free spirit me. Its drive is recognition, and it will stop at nothing until it has beaten all of the competitors. I find myself in a pit of stress, of thoughts, that as they materialize only send me down a hopeless path of perfection. I always think too much. I think to a dangerous level of analytical examination. In this world, I must do all to an extreme. I must get the best grade, be the smartest and be productive with every moment of my life. It is in this self that I run only to be fast or to go far. It is in this self that I do everything for the praise I will receive from others.

[Bipolar people are often not good students, but Heather's drive would not allow that. Her use of the word "dangerous" describing her level of analytical examination is an indication she knew something was wrong, even though she didn't know what at the time. Also doing everything to extreme was a clear indicator of bipolar behavior.]

I hate myself for being how I always am. The rules for excellence are deeply rooted in my soul. From my accomplishments, comes my pride. This pride is not stable; it must be built up again and again with each hurdle cleared.

I am scared that I am this self too often, almost all the time. I'm addicted to proving my worth. This dependency is not healthy. This is my dark side. I understand my dark side for I live it every day. It is who I am. It shows through, but never takes over, for there is always the other me. . .

The other me loves life unconditionally. I can think too much and not care if I'm buried under seventeen layers of contemplation. I can run half a marathon and not wonder if my miles are faster than the other guy's. I can play games with numbers off license plates and compare the initials of Jason Hughes to those of John Hancock without wondering if these amusements in my mind indicate intelligence. I am free to perform back flip front flip twists on the trampoline and to dance in my living room without caring about how weird I must look. I can be the most radical feminist alive while actively promoting the salvation of all bugs from the soles of evil-hearted shoes. I can express myself with rainbows, for the English language is a hindrance, and I am free.

[She had colored dark purple/blue clouds on one page, and a rainbow with orange, yellow, and green dancing, flipping figures on the other.]

Sketch Book   10/1/98   My Rivets Glue

My life is held together by everything it involves. Each part is a gear in my machine, and without one component, I would fall apart. I truly would, for I almost have. I'm a minor manic depressive, so I need my family, friends, school work, running, and religion to keep me balanced. [She clearly knew something was wrong.]

I believe I must first discuss the importance of my family and friends, for the people in my life are what keeps me from going insane. I genuinely love my family. I say, "Bye, love you," to dad, mom and sister every day because I really mean it. My dad is hilarious and impresses my friends with his weirdness. He cares about my future and helping me to investigate possible careers. My mom is wonderfully supportive. She listens to me and understands my feelings when no one else can. My younger sister Emily is my best friend. We have a healthy relationship, one rare among siblings. We still fight, but we have our own method for making peace. When one of us feels sorry, we just say, "Chee." And the other says it back. It's our secret way of forgiving and also saying that we love each other. I consider Katie, Jeff, and Trevan to be my best friends. They truly understand me. This is a good thing, since I often get wrapped up in achieving everything possible and forget that I'm just a kid in high school. I love hanging out with these three because we're very close and can have conversations on a deep level.

The things I do in school are the main source of my pride. I love to learn and to do a lot of it at once. I have a desire to excel in every subject. Accomplishing this is what makes me who I am. I also love to run on the cross country and track teams. I want to be something other than an academic freak. Running is my vent for stress and my outlet for energy. The people on the cross country team are a great influence on me. They keep me real.

Finally, my Lutheran religion defines me and holds my life together. I live in an area dominated by the LDS church. This only causes me to be stronger in my own faith, and in my ability to stand up for something I hold as sacred. I am an individual with views on political and societal issues often very different from the mainstream opinions. I love being able to fight for my convictions and back them up honorably.

I hope that these things will continue to hold me together, for without them I will become unglued. I can be proud to be made up of the people in my life, my achievements, and my faith. They are all integral parts of my framework and balance the person known as Heather Aron Gross.

Sketch Book   5/10/99
Insomnia = Dead lethargy filling my body while endless energy dances in my brain.
    [Heather often had trouble sleeping, another indicator of bipolar disorder.]

    Back to 2006: Scott and Heather were still together even after the disorder was revealed. We drove over the river and through the woods with Heather and Scott to Logan, Utah for a Thanksgiving with three other families. Scott and Heather were never engaged, but I vividly remember wedding talk in the car. It was our first Thanksgiving without Emily, because she spent it with her boyfriend's family in Colorado.

    Scott's Parents visited from New Hampshire and came to our home for Christmas Eve dinner. Ryan and Em were home too, so that year Ryan was included in our traditional Christmas skiing. We chose Solitude Ski Resort so Em and Ryan could snowboard. Scott was spending the day with his parents.

    On Dec 26, Heather thoughtfully had pleasant classical music on in her car as she drove Scott's Mom, Nancy, and me to Temple Square to see the lights. I remember thinking how considerate that was. She often had loud thumping music on when I got into her car. We stopped after, at Scott's apartment where he and his dad were enjoying a drink together. It was a fun night for me, and I thought I was getting to know Heather's nice new eastern in-laws to be.

December 2006
Holiday Greetings,

We really don't need to write this year, because we have almost no new news. Our girls have the same boyfriends, but no engagements yet. Our jobs are the same, with no retirement yet. We're in the same house that we've been in for twenty-eight years of marriage, with no upsizing yet. There is no need to downsize. Our health is good, and we have no man-made body parts yet.

Heather is at the same job as a research scientist and planning on graduate school in linguistics. In May, Emily graduated from Colorado State University with a major in graphic design. Go Rams! She is a resident of Colorado and going back to school to get a teaching certificate. That is great news to me (Alyce), because I now have a perfect place to unload my favorite teaching materials when I retire.

Although we have very little new news, we feel renewed and thankful as we remember our blessings: a committed, strong marriage; happy, independent daughters; fulfilling, worthwhile jobs; a friendly church family; and you, our friends and relatives.

We do need to write after all, because we value staying in touch with you.
We wish you renewal as you remember your own blessings this Holy Season.

Denny and Alyce Gross

Changes

Heather's Journal   March 31, 2007 (Continued)
I was accepted to the University of Utah, MA Linguistics program for this fall and await news regarding a Teacher's Assistantship and stipend. Scott graduated with an MBA in December, 2006. We still both work at Tandem Labs. I got a raise and am the official trainer of the lab as an associate research scientist. I will improve my approach to taking care of myself.

I worry about Scott and me. He needs to get a new job, and then we we'll see. I am missing something. I feel stuck. . . . I have to take care of me and make sure I know how to keep me happy and love myself—before I can fix Scott and my relationship. . . . We depress each other. I do love him.

April 18, 2007
Scott and I are on the breaking up path. Yep. We will be kind to each other and do it slowly, and it's sad. I feel good about it though. . . . I need to re-establish Heather.

When they did officially split on April 21, Heather came home for dinner and slept over. It felt good that she would turn to her dad and to me for comfort. We were sad with her, because we loved Scott too. In May she was a bridesmaid in Aundrea Klemz's wedding, and Scott was considerate enough to still be her date at the reception. As freshmen in college, Aundrea and Heather weren't much support to each other, but there is much to be said for the fact that they remained friends in spite of difficult times. Aundrea, when asking Heather to be a bridesmaid said, "I will always have you in my life."

Into the future: Scott and Lexy came together to see us after Heather died. They were a little hesitant about letting us know they were together. I'm sure their new relationship was Lexy's secret in the Facebook comment just after Heather's death. Denny and I value our continued friendship with them. We meet for dinner once in a while. Denny even helped Scott do some home improvements on a house Scott bought. We were thrilled to be invited to their wedding on September 17, 2011.

    Back to 2007: It was going to be another year with only one daughter home for Christmas. Emily and Ryan were in Fort Collins with his family, so on Christmas Eve we cooked turkey dinner for our good friends, Jan Heins and her daughter, Kate. On Christmas morning, after opening gifts with Heather, we went to the University dorms and picked up Koshin, a classmate of Heather's, who was here from Japan; and we met Jan and Kate in Park City for our traditional Christmas Day skiing. Koshin and Kate were on snowboards. All of us enjoyed a white Christmas on the slopes. Jan and Kate had family to get home to for dinner, but Heather, Koshin, Denny and I had Mexican dinner in Park City. I told Koshin about a Christmas years ago when I was teaching school in the Philippines and went skiing in Japan over Christmas break. Those two made dinner so interesting, entertaining, and fun. Of course we had no idea that this would be the last Christmas with our Heather.

December, 2007
Greetings,

Again we are sending our news with the motivation of not losing touch with important people like you. Denny and I are appreciating our empty nesting together even though we're at different career stages. Our theme this year is beginnings and endings.

Denny is still beginning. In January he will have been in the insurance business for just four years. He didn't want me to write this, but I've never been obedient. Last night at the Buckner Company annual dinner party, we were surprised that he was chosen from one hundred twenty five people as "Associate of the Year." It was awarded not only for his excellent production, but because he works to make the office environment a better place for everyone. Denny has always been happiest when he's busy. If he sees something that needs to be done, he does it; like moving furniture for secretaries, or organizing luncheons to show appreciation to support staff. Now all he needs this year to feel really successful is to get an elk, on his upcoming hunt.

After thirty-three years of teaching I'm enjoying a year of lasts, with a very good group of twenty-eight fifth graders. The finality comes with a little sadness, but more importantly a feeling of accomplishment and a sigh of relief. As I finish units, I go through folders, recycle papers, and save the gems for my daughter Emily. She will begin student teaching in fifth grade this January. If all goes as planned, she'll begin teaching in the fall. Emily fell in love with Colorado and will make her home there.

Like her Dad, Heather enjoys change. She went from scientist to linguistics student. She is studying Chinese and has timed a study abroad in China to end just as the 2008 Olympics begin. Of course, she plans to attend.

We pray this holy season is a time of remembering that Christ's birth brings new beginnings for all of us. We wish you blessings and joy for 2008.
Love, Denny and Alyce Gross

March 20-24, 2008   Easter in Fort Collins
We took a family Easter trip to Em and Ryan's—Heather in our back seat. She said her friends couldn't believe she actually liked traveling with her parents. Good Friday, the 21st, we were in Poudre Canyon where the girls started running back toward Fort Collins, to train together for a marathon. Denny and I hiked for a while and then picked them up while driving back to Emily's home. Emily played the adult that Easter, and prepared a lovely meal for fifteen people including the soon to be in-laws and their extended family, friends including Todd who was interested in Heather, and us. Ryan appreciated Heather's contribution to the preparations. While Emily and I were in the kitchen, Heather was cleaning the bathroom. She never did really learn to cook. It was an exciting transition day for me; having my younger daughter show she was grown-up enough to prepare a holiday meal.

May 4, 2008   Marathon and Diamond Ring
Heather drove back to Fort Collins by herself to run with her sister in the Colorado Marathon, which begin up in Poudre Canyon and ended in Old Town, Fort Collins. Emily said at some point, she and her blisters felt like giving up, but Heather kept her going and even did cart wheels across the finish line. Emily has a screen saver on her computer of Heather and Ryan goofing off on their back patio after the race. Ryan and Emily's good friend Todd was again Heather's companion for the festivities that weekend. During that trip, Ryan had taken Heather out to his secret hiding place in the garage to show her the engagement ring he bought for Emily. He swore Heather to secrecy. Heather came with Koshin to visit us shortly after her return. Denny and I both laugh at this memory. She had a sly smile with her shoulders slightly scrunched up and said in a small high-pitched voice, "I might know something." Denny and I immediately knew Ryan would soon be proposing.

Koshin shook his head and said, "You weren't supposed

to tell!"
  Ryan impressed us by calling and asking Denny's permission to marry our Emily. Sweet boy!

May 11, 2008
  There was yet another short trip. The following weekend Heather drove with linguistics friends to Goblin Valley and Dead Horse Point, in Southern Utah for a camping trip. Two photographs from those destinations ended up on the cover of her funeral program, and one on the cover of this book.

From: Emily
To my Family and Friends,
  May, 2008 is the best month ever. To start, I just finished school to become a teacher, and happened to already have a job in a great school district in Colorado. My school is small and I will only have about 15 students, so I will really be able to get to know them. Next, Heather and I ran a marathon which is one of those life goals that I have had. Now I am in Mexico with my wonderful boyfriend, Ryan, for a week-long vacation that was much needed. About an hour ago, Ryan took me for a walk on the beach, and asked me to marry him!!!!!!!!!!! I said yes!!!! I wanted to send the word to my family and friends around the world to let them hear the news. I will keep you informed.
Love, Emily

June 5-9, 2008
  Emily flew home, without Ryan, with many tasks in mind. The most important, although none of us knew it, was to see her sister for the last time. (It breaks my heart to write these words.) She worked a few half days at school with me, letting me know which of my many teaching treasures she wanted. The emotional decision to retire was made so much more satisfying, knowing my Emily would use my tried and true materials. We loaded much in my car to be temporarily stored in our garage until Em and Ryan came back with his pick-up the following month. Emily and I split our two days with school work and

The Devil's Fingernail

shopping for a wedding dress. The second day, when Heather didn't have to work, she joined us for the exciting dress search. We three had so much fun. Emily pinned down the style of dress she loved and was later able to find one that fit perfectly, on Crag's List—for free! (She has already paid it forward to another bride—for free.) That's my girl. Our family of four went out to a happy celebratory dinner at Macaroni Grill, again not knowing it would be the last with all four of us. Denny and I always had so much fun with our two entertaining daughters.

That evening, Emily got to meet many of Heather's girlfriends, while experiencing some of Salt Lake City's night life, which I've heard was always more exciting when Heather was a part of it. This was also the weekend that Emily tackled the monumental task of helping Heather organize her clothes (which were already in rainbow order), important papers, and other items. Just the shoes alone would have been noteworthy.

Heather had saved all of her trophies and awards from spelling bees to soccer plagues. Emily and Heather set them all out on the counter, and Heather stood by them while Emily took several pictures on Heather's camera. We have copies of those and her many other pictures on our computer and flash drives. Emily then made Heather throw the cumbersome trophies and plaques away. Heather needed her sister's determination and encouragement to be able to discard those hard-earned treasures. I don't know how Emily fit it all in; but she also went to church with us and helped her dad build our back fence that Sunday. I'm not lying. Efficiency is Emily's other name. June 18, 2008

Last Big Trip

I picked Heather up at her home in Sugarhouse, Utah, at 6:00 AM to take her to the airport for her trip to China and Japan. Her Utah roommate, Jana, kindly allowed Heather to park her car in their single car garage while Heather was gone.

Heather was a good money manager. She paid for her own travel, which was extensive. She often managed to stay with friends, or friends of friends, to help save money and to better experience the countries she was in.

China

From: Heather Gross <gross.h@gmail.com>
Sent: Saturday, June 21, 2008 4:31 PM
To: adgrossl@msn.com, emmylizg@hotmail.com
Subject: Hi from Chiiiiiiiiina!
    I am here safe! Both suit-cases arrived. The professor and his wife who i stayed with were so cute and nice and welcoming. He was Min from Tandem Labs chemistry professor. Then yesterday in Beijing, I got to hang out with a boy who will study at the U next year. He had churlish hair, and I told him that girls in the US will think he's cute. He graduated in English from Xinling's University, the same one where Min from Tandem went and where the professor worked before he retired. Anyway, that boy took me all around—to the summer palace where we went on a pedal boat with a roof and climbed many stairs up to a temple and walked a lot, then to a hill overlooking the forbidden city and then to Tiananmen Square! we had dinner with his friends who are all graduating, some who will go to school in the US too.
    this morning i had to get up at 4:30 to go on the bus to the airport to fly to Xiamen, where I'm staying now at Xinling's cousin's, on an island where there are no cars! i got to swim in the ocean today and then i took a 5 hour nap because i still have jet lag. tomorrow xinling and i take a 6 hour train to her hometown where i will stay for 5 days, then i fly to beijing from here on my bday. i will tell people it's my bday, em.
    tis so hot and humid here, but very pretty! thank you for taking me to the airport, mama. i love you guys! good luck with your parties, em. how are you dad? what else? i should go so i can shower in the crazy student dirty bathroom where you put a bucket under the spout that is off the wall right above the toilet—he he. tis ok. makes me appreciate how spoiled we are in the US! and then to bed. love you guys more than all the Chinese black hairs i have see here! Heather

From : Heather Gross
Sent: Monday, June 23, 2008 3:49 PM
Subject: update
    tonight i met xinling's 96 or 98 yr old great grandma

with tiny feet (she had them bound when she was a girl!) it's now 11:40 pm. this morning xinling, her dad, and i went to a provincial park where we hiked up between two very close rocks and could look up and see a tiny sliver of sky 100 feet above us. twas cool. we could look across the river and see a temple in the trees, then we had an awesome lunch with a pot for frying everything—duck, beef, pork, rice squares, etc. in the center of the table, twas delicious but sometimes tough since it was hot and humid, and we had hot tea and hot food. i think i will not be dry or cold until i get to beijing again.

  i want to talk to you guys! i got the linguist list stuff you emailed, dad. thanks! if you want to look on google earth or something, im in Fujian province in the south. Xiamen is the city i flew into, then a slow six hour train took us east to Yong'an, where all of xinling's fam is. k. i should sleep, email soon, love you more than the inflamed skin cells of the four mosquito bites on my right elbow.:) heath

From: Heather Gross
Sent: Tuesday, June 24, 2008 3:49 PM
To: "DENNIS ALYCE GROSS"
Subject: Re: Too much fun

  Hi fam! More good times have been had. Today i got to talk online to koshin with a webcam. twas cool. i went running in the park in the city, ten minutes from xinling's parents's apt. i got more stares than ever in my life i think—on the way there walking the crowded streets, crossing the road right behind ladies who were crossing so that a motor scooter wouldn't hit me. xinling's parents said it might be the first time a foreigner ever went running in that park.

  sorry your fishing resort place was too resorty, dad. so you are going to wash my car!? inside? that would be cool! do you have jana's phone number? nice you like retired life and get to hang and chill with friends, mom! how is the wedding planning, em? you can see that Beijing tour guide kid on facebook. Kelin Li should he be my next asian bf? just kidding.

  xinling's dad is a policeman, remember? he protects the "oods". that's how xinling was pronouncing "woods". he took the morning off to hike with us. her mom is an elementary teacher of Chinese. she still has some meetings to go to, but school is out.

The Devil's Fingernail

tonight we went to a delicious dinner with a cute young lady and her husband, both in the police with xinling's dad. they wanted to meet the laowai, the foreigner. i had to eat pig's blood mixed with starch, the color of liver, but tasted like slimy tofu. also, a very tasty stew and pig lung. every time you drink you have to toast somebody. beer is poured in tiny glasses, a little bigger than shot glasses and a toast is made for each drink. i made some to the whole table, but they made tons to me. was so nice. they kept commenting on my hair color and skin color and asking why my eyelashes were black and ha ha ha—good times. we then went shopping. clothes have a lot more flair here. usually it's good. i think you would like it, em. some shirts are crazy but most are just more interesting than ones in the US. i saw xinling's cousin's wedding photos—very cute, but kind of like a fancy prom in a wedding dress and then in a purple dress. those were just the wedding photos though, and apparently are not the same things they wear on the wedding day...

ah, to answer your question, mom, twas not the professor nor the boy who picked me up at the airport, but rather a girl friend of xinling's and that girl's boyfriend, who was awesome and grabbed my big suitcase for the bus and taxi. also no one would let me pay for stuff, even friends of friends who will never see me again! they called the professor so we could find his apt the first nights.

time for sleep, midnight here means your 10am! i love you guys more than all the interesting animal parts ever eaten by people around the world! love the feath

From: Heather Gross
Sent: Thursday, June 26, 2008 3:47 PM
Subject: Yong'an...XinIing's city
Hi jiating, family!

Thank you for the updates! Em, you are doing so much adulty house and yard stuff, eh? It sounds like the backyard will be perfect. I don't get home til August 21 (unless I change my flight), but school starts Aug 24th for me, so we will have to figure out some time for me to visit! Koshin is checking with JAL to see what options I have, but he says he will not pass his test, and that I should just come when we had planned.

Hmm. I am sleepy since today we got up at 6:30 to go to the farmer's (daily) market—live ducks and chickens, also just killed ones, pigs, everything, and tons of veggies. Xinling's mom bought 4 kinds of melons and a little meat. Yesterday Xinling and I went to the spa. They have a big swimming pool and then a separate one with all sorts of water sprays that act like massages or skin pounders or something. We had to wear swim caps the whole time. The swimsuits look like the ones ladies wore in the US in the 1930s but with colorful patterns. Most kids and adults don't know how to swim. I tried to teach Xinling breaststroke, backstroke, and freestyle. She got pretty good at breaststroke.

We have had many discussions about how Chinese are raised to just study, study, study so that they can take their entrance exam for college and go to a good university. Xinling got the highest score in her city (of 600,000 people) in 2003! The test includes Chinese, math, history, politics, and geography. She says she has forgotten a lot of it, and that raising kids like that might not be the best thing. She wants to raise her kids in the US so that they can do sports, be more well-rounded, and maybe date or do something more socially normal, at least according to me. She still hasn't dated anybody, and her parents bug her about it all the time.

Today I ran in the park around the lake and across it on a crazy bridge. Xinling and I just went to see her mom's family again. That great grandma is sooo cute. I have been working on Linguist List while Xinling works on an English to Chinese translation project.

Em, you are so going to be very ready for your wedding, eh? Like 200 days before it happens! Cool that you booked the Rio. Mom, I don't have the address at Nankai University yet. I will get it probably Saturday (my bday) and email it then. That day I get to hang out in the Beijing Airport for a while. Maybe I will figure out how to call you. I do like the amount of stuff I brought. Having two suitcases is a little tricky, but not bad.

Xinling and I sleep on her parents' bed because the only A/C is in here. Supposedly her mom always sleeps on the floor to avoid her husband's snoring, as she does while I'm here. Xinling's dad sleeps in Xinling's old bed. Right now, Xinling's mom is lying on the floor playing video games on her phone. She is a busy body! It's cute. There are two internet connection cords and only one long enough to be in the A/C room, so Xinling and I switch it back and forth between our laptops if we both want to be in that room.

Ah! the clothes dry on a rod outside the window. That is until the winds and pre-typhoon rains come (they just started!) and then we bring them in and hang them high from the ceiling with one of those long poles with a U hook that they use in clothing stores. Tis like Spain but smaller living space and a tinch less first world. We will see how the international dorm is, eh? Man, parents' house is huge and larger houses are unfathomable to these people, at least to have in China.

I will send a link to pics. This is stuff that Em could see on Facebook already. Anyway, I love you lots! (I think I don't want to keep thinking of big numbers of things every email.) yep. Heather

Heather stayed with her sweet friend, Xinling, at her parents' home before she began the language school in Nankai University, Tianjin. I found it interesting that Xinling's father belongs to the Communists Party and her mother doesn't. His job is something like a forest ranger, and her mother is a first grade school teacher. They live in Yong'an city in Fu jian province, where there are no tourists, so a blond jogging girl (Heather) was a first for the town's people. Xinling's parents, showing their hospitality, gave Heather and Xinling their air-conditioned bedroom. Also Heather had the privilege of meeting Xinling's great grandmother and eating a lot of her delicious cooking. She loved Heather because Heather would eat everything. I cherish a picture I have of Heather with her arm around this tiny sweet grandma who actually had bound feet.

Forward in time:
Facebook:
Xinling Chen   changchangchang, here I come.
Last year around this time, I was about to pick you up at Xiamen Airport. I remember waiting for you anxiously at the pick-up section. 20 minutes after your plane landed, you still did not appear. Finally, there came the cheerful girl with a

ponytail, looking all around for me, without any luggage. I ran toward you. You hugged me. We were so happy!!!
June 25, 2009 at 12:56 am

Xinling Chen
    Heather, my great-grandma passed away two days ago... I knew it just now. My family was trying to hide the news from me. I wish I could have been with her at her last moment.
    She was healthy when you two met. Then she fell and broke her leg half a year ago and she was sick in bed since. Now she is relieved, no more pains.
    I feel weird, because these two days I have been watching a Chinese soap opera. There was a scene that the actress's grandpa passed away. Was that a hint that my great-grandma was gone too? I kinda thought of it at that time, but I did not call home to check. I thought that was silly. Now I wish I did.
    Now will you two meet again? My beloved two ladies! I love and miss you two a ton!!!
April 18, 2009 at 12:04am

    June 28, 2008, was Heather's 27th birthday. She was in Beijing Airport—on her way to Nankai University, where she would study until August 10th.

From: Heather Gross
Sent: Sun 6/29/08 1:33 PM
here in tianjin safe
    safe and thank you for the happy bday! i have little time with the internet til i get it in my room. my room is awesome. i have a nice roommate. we made shelves, and i got to use glue and a screwdriver and duct tape already. :) love the feath

From : Heather Gross
Sent: Monday, June 30, 2008 8:58 AM
Subject: monday, first day o classes, etc.
Hi Family!!
    koshin sent me a funny email warning me about the tap water in china, as if i didn't know not to drink it after

being here 10 days, twas cute. anyway i have a boiler in my room and can make coffee with instant Nescafe for tasty kafei.

My roommate is cool. She studied for a semester in Iowa and then an intensive semester in Beijing. She's from Salt Lake. Her name is Amelia. Now she's here in the third year program with 6 other dudes. There are 3 girls in my class and 10 guys. Then only two guys in the first year class. We have two nice girl teachers, 24 and 26 yrs old. The other two girls are Louie, who I went running with this morning for 67 minutes (because we got lost for a while and couldn't get back to our dorm) and Katie [a new friend]. They are cute and nice and live next door to me and Amelia.

Hmmm.. ah, my bday. That night I went to a bar and some people bought me some drinks, but we were all tired because we had to go to Tianjin at 9:30 at night, after a bit of a messy meeting at the airport. This program is not as organized as the spain program, but it's better now after meeting our teachers. Anyway, Sunday was good. Amelia and I went to Carrefour, Jia Le Fu, to buy stuff for our rooms. We bought wooden shelves that we put together with wooden pegs, glue, and screws to put in our closets. They were 60 yuan, less than 10 bucks—way cool. we bought hangers and lots of bottled water, yep.

it will take 3 or 4 days for me to get internet in my room, then i could talk to you guys using Skype perhaps. we will see if this is an option. i don't think i will get a cell phone, but i might anyway. i love my room. tis very nice, especially for china. we have a/c and nice bathrooms with regular toilets and a bath/shower. there is a washer but no dryer. i expected that.

you guys are busy with church stuff, eh? how you em? survive the weekend? thank you for so many nice HAPPY BIRTHDAYs! yep. i love you family, i will speak Chinese well in 6 weeks, i think.
love, Guo He'an

From: Heather Gross
Sent: Sunday, July 6, 2008 6:58 AM
Subject: Sunday chillin

Alyce Gross

Hi family!!!!!!!!
   I'm alive and happy and busy and I think I might be too old to learn another language that does not have a phonetic alfabeto. Tis so tricky and time intensive to learn characters.
   Class is fun. I am about average. There are people who know a lot, and some very lost, and i'm in the middle. Let's see, I still don't have the internet in my room, and the computers at school are verrrry slow; so I'm now at a cafe/bar that has wireless. I hiked here with my laptop, yay!
   Check out tennis timmy's blog. He's a kid in my program and in my class. You can see pictures of Jesse and Soren, two dudes with whom Amelia and I hang out a bunch. There's a pic of me on the back of Jake's bike. I got to ride on the back of bikes for a few days til i bought a very newish bike from a Colombiana, a girl from Bogota, before they left Tianjin. i paid 150 kuai, about $21 for it with the lock; and then went to the crazy bike fixer man with gold teeth, to get the basket for another 10 kuai. my bike has a bell, back rack thinger, and basket, so i can bring a bunch of stuff home from Carrefour. there are various groups of students at our university, french Canadians, kids from michigan state, etc. i got to play soccer two days with random combos of Chinese and foreign kids, with 2 or 3 other girls, and tons of guys, very fun but crappy to fall cuz it's fake grass with ouchy little black turf thingers.
   friday our whole group went out for the 4th. we went dancing at a big place with foreigners and Chinese, twas soo fun. yesterday we explored Tianjin at some mall place and had lunch which you can see on timmy's blog. http://timmychina.blogspot.com/
   k... write about your stuff, mom, dad, em. yep. let me know how you are! time to do linguist list stuff and study.
   love you more than all the bicycle bell dinging that goes on here, heath

From: Heather Gross
Sent: Tuesday, July 8, 2008 1:57 PM
Subject: tuesday
   I'm at a bar on the internet because each time my roommate and i go to ask about the internet connection in our

The Devil's Fingernail

room, we get the "come back tomorrow at such and such time" answer. not cool. anyway, I need to bike home in the light warm rain and sleep, but just wanted to say hi.

i went running this morning and then had class, then i did laundry and, man, be thankful for a dryer; i have clothes hanging all over my room. hmmm.. i hope they dry. i then met a high school girl who is my language partner. her mom is a professor at my university. they lived in japan 5 years when the girl was little so she speaks Chinese and Japanese fluently, and english well—cool. she can help me learn some stuff before i go to japan, ah! koshin says he changed my flight to the 18th, so i'd fly home that day. i will confirm and tell you for sure.

the girl and her mom took me to dinner. they're nice. twas fun. I'm excited to see if you guys have done anything more to the house before i get home. when does school start for you, em? todd facebooked me that he has to work when he wanted to go to china, so i doubt he will come, which is totally cool with me because i have class til the 8th, and leave the IIth, with just a few days to try to go to some Olympics stuff with people in my program, yep. K, you can see some more on timmy's blog love you guys! the feath

hi bye
Heather Gross Sent: Thu 7/10/08 10:56 PM
i will be on a group trip til Sunday, i will write then!
love the feath

Heather passed on to us what Emily wrote to her:

On Wed, Jul 9, 2008 at 4:42 AM, Emily Gross wrote:
Hi Sister,
Yesterday was funny, because Brady called me to see if Ryan would be available to help him change his brakes, but Ry and I had to meet a pastor. I had Brady go buy the parts, and Todd and he came over so I could change the brakes. They kept making jokes about how they had to have me work on the car. Thanks to the dadder for giving me some training.

I just finished mowing, and I have to work tonight, so I am going to shower. I love you more than all of the blades of grass that I had to chop down.

Alyce Gross

From: Heather Gross
Sent: Sunday, July 13, 2008 3:53 PM
Subject: Confucius' stomping grounds and Tai Shan
Hi family!

    I had an awesome weekend on my group excursion, six hours south by bus to Tai'an in Shandong Province. We saw a bajilion Confucius thingers—his tomb in a forest, and temples and temples and temples... they kind of all start to look the same after a while. today we hiked 1600 steps up Tai Shan—shan means 'mountain.' the east holy mountain of china—beauutiful views with touristy crap being sold on the sides of the stairs the entire way up. it took us a little over 2 hours to do what our professor was saying would be 4. i hiked with spence and jake, two funny dudes.

    we went out dancing both nights in that town to a place with a bouncing dance floor. there is a dude in our group who is huge and 6'6". all the girls got on his shoulders at some point dancing, and all the Chinese just watched us dance. they don't know how to dance with their arms up. Chinese dudes bought me beer. they put ice in it for me.

    my shirt was drenched in sweat hiking while little Chinese old people are wearing street clothes and carrying their sun umbrellas and not sweating at all. Humidity!

    amelia and i managed to break the curtains off of the wall in our room. i tried to reinstall the hooks but we need a real screwdriver. i really just wanted to fix it, but we decided we should tell our professor guy. amelia thinks it's so funny that i'm like the stubborn guy who won't ask for directions, and our guy friends are telling us to just tell professor Wu. ha ha.

    i read Chinese dialogues with Linton, this tall blonde gay guy in our group who went on a mission to taiwan 6 years ago. i will take Chinese phonetics and Chinese syntax next year. that will be a way to have linguistic classes and still be in Chinese without necessarily taking the 3rd yr of the language class.

    em, it's awesome that you fix cars, i'm glad ryan is cool with the Lutheran thing and the pastor guy. parents, what did you do this weekend?

    ah! we got home from the sweaty adventure today at 8 pm and then went to the campus market to this Muslim place that most people in our group love, for lunch and dinner. then i went on a bike ride with the three ex-military dudes in our

The Devil's Fingernail

group to the local park near a man-made lake. twas like in xinling's town—the place where couples and some kids go after dinner to either dance or walk or listen to guys playing cool crazy instruments. the dancing is old school classical, cute for couples. it is sad that cities in the US don't have that type of thing, because people live so far from each other but could go out at night to mingle.

  i got internet in my room! i forgot to tell you! also, i left one suitcase with xinling! this worked out really well. i still have an extra backpack for extra stuff and managed from fujian (xinling's province) to beijing with everything in the bigger red one. xinling will use my other suitcase to bring stuff back to Utah and then buy a new suitcase in the US. she had wanted to do that anyway because her old suitcase had broken.

  so yes, i did change my flights to be earlier. i will be here for 4 days of the Olympics and then go to japan for a full week when i know koshin will be available. a lot of people in my program leave on the llth, so it is good to be leaving.

  tell me your newses! sleep time for me. love you guys more than all the empty water bottles collected by crazy teethed old people in china who hang out and make noises at tourists! Heath

Heather Gross
Wed 7/16/08 12:49 PM
Hey fam!
  I had fun dancing with Soren our first weekend and with Jake, the kid giving me the bike ride, last weekend, but no romances. Koshin and I write often to each other.

  I did my laundry a second time, much more successfully. The first time I washed too much for the washer to spin properly so it took toooo long to dry. Now all the stuff I put in the washer this morning is dry!! yay! today, we had a quiz in class, my best one yet I think. Then we all biked with our teachers to a restaurant for a big tasty lunch. Katie and I like sitting next to each other to eat, cuz we both love food and love trying weird things, fun. Then out for ice with milk, fruit spread, and beans—a weird but good dessert. Next I watched a DVD I bought (they are pirated and cost $0.86) called 'Beijing Bicycle' with Jake. It was in Chinese with engrish subtitles. Then to market with amelia and louie. Hmmmmm... Study time. Love you guys!

Heather Gross
Sent: Sun 7/20/08 3:21 PM
To: DENNIS ALYCE GROSS

hi. all is well! sleepy after being in beijing all day. we just got back at 10:30 pm, after the 1.5 hour train to Tianjin and taxi to our school.

Jimmy's blog left me out of the hike photos because those five boys climbed the mountain at night in the dark to see the sunrise, while the rest of us did it during the next day. that was interesting because our tour guide guy did not want them to hike on their own. in his bad english he said "i forbid you to go" !! ha ha. anyway, that was last weekend. this weekend our group activity was: yesterday—a bus in Tianjin to a rich family's courtyard, Shi, and then to Ancient Culture Street—a bargaining shopping place. that's what i did in Beijing too. i got you some stuff, but i want to ask you guys what you'd like me to buy. maybe i will figure out a cheapish way to call you some time. we saw Mao Zedong's body (or a plastic creepy weird pretend version of it, in a glass coffin). people worship him and bring flowers—so interesting.

now must hunt mosquitos and kill them and leave blood spots on the walls, so they don't eat me and amelia tonight, and then shower and sleep. nice, amelia just killed one. Ha ha. k. love, the feath

p.s. I'm ready to not see little kids squatting and peeing right on train platforms for all to see.

Great Wall etc
Heather Gross Sent: Sun 7/27/08 2:03 PM
To: DENNIS ALYCE GROSS
Hi Fambily,

The internet in my dorm, stopped working on Thursday. Tis fixed now though. So Hi!!!

Last week I had two quizzes and a big test on Friday—lots of studying. I did well on all I think.

My 16 yr old language girl came on Friday, and we (the 3 girls and I) took her shopping with us to a market—bartering good times. Yolanda is her English name. She is so cute and nice. She then went to dinner with us. I paid for her. She said she had a very happy day. She likes hanging out with Americans. It's cute.

Mom, do you want a big wall hanging Chinese style painting or fans or jade stuff or what? Em, tis tough for me to think of something you'd like. If you could call me here before August llth—call my room. that would be cool. I can give you the number. Twould be good to talk to you guys. I can ask my friends what cards their families have used to call them.

We went to the Great Wall yesterday. Awesome. Twas the tianjin section of the wall, two hours from the city. We rode in little open shuttle things up to it. Parts had huge stairs and towers I climbed up, tiny stairs too. I got to ride on a horse down from it. I talked to the lady guiding my horse the whole time. She said I looked a lot younger than 27 and asked why I wasn't married, ha ha. I told her about Em. On the bus I sat next to military guy Spencer who is hilarious.

Yesterday night we went to KTV—this huge casinoish place with many rooms for karaoke. A bunch of us in our group and two of our teachers all had one big room to share. Gay, tall Linton was the best singer. I danced to one song, and then they had me dance to all the lively songs after that—way fun. Today I slept a lot and went with Linton, Brandon, Brandon's tall Chinese language partner, and the girls to a hot pot dinner—so spicy and tasty. Then we walked around a street market where people sell everything, fun. We biked there and back. Tis so cool to have a bike and get around fast here.

K. have fun on your trips mom! How are you all? Keep letting me know. Love you! Heath

Heather Gross Tue 8/05/08 5:54 PM
hi family!!!!!!!!
    i am doing well... there are Italians here (have i told you about them?) one of them slipped a love letter under my door yesterday.. his name is yuri—speaks French and english well, and Spanish—almost as well as i do, and Chinese and of course Italian—fun to talk to him!! i confuse him cuz i keep switching languages..

this is the last week of our program. it's weird how quickly it has gone by. i will write more about activities soon. ah! i have tickets to an Olympic soccer game thursday—japan

vs US. yay! then our final test is friday and then beijing stuff this weekend and fly to japan monday. koshin is so excited for me to come, he has planned a lot for us to do.
    just wanted to let you know that I'm doing well. thanks for the big update emails, everybody! I'm glad you're busy and having fun. love you more than all the combinations of four or five or eight languages a person could learn! Heath

On Wed, Aug 6, 2008 at 5:25 AM, ALYCE GROSS
Hi Daughters,
    Heather, it is good to hear all your news. How old is the Italian note writer? I can understand how he could get confused talking to you in four languages, I get confused in just English. You haven't sent a phone number. Friday morning I go to book club cabin in Idaho. I'll be home Monday and celebrate our 30th wedding anniversary (a day early), because I drive to be with you, Em, on Tuesday.
Love you both with whole heart, Mom

Your Wednesday morning, my evening...call me. From: Heather G
Sent: Wed 8/06/08 2:16 PM
Hi parents and Em!
    I am sending my phone number:
the 011 is to make an international call, then 86 is china's country code, and 22 is Tianjin's code, the [next 8 digits] is my room number.
I'm sending this to dad's work email because i know he will get it soon and then maybe he could ask mom to call me soon! like your Wednesday 8:15 am, which is my 10:15 pm. would that work?
the Italian is 23. he is cool. i hung out with my language partner for the last time, she is soo cute, she told me I'm her first american friend and that she will miss me. ah i got a cheap good haircut today—just a trim. study and plan Olympic adventures time. call if you can or let me know when you could call!
love the Feath
[I did call and we had such a good visit.]

Heather Gross

The Devil's Fingernail

Sent: Sun 8/10/08 11:30 AM
Hi family!
It's my last full day in China. I have packed almost everything except a few drying clothes and bathroom stuff. I'm glad i just have my big backpack and one bigger suitcase. Tomorrow morning Yolanda is coming to say goodbye and then I take a 3 hour bus straight to the Beijing airport. that is better than using a taxi to the train station, to a taxi, to a subway, to the airport.
Yesterday we 4 girls took the fast (half an hour vs. the 1.5 hours it used to be) train to Beijing. It goes 190mph. We had fun, but I was a little sad because we could not get tickets for anything. This Olympics is weird, and that's what a lot of people we talked to thought. We met a guy from San Diego who had been to 6 Olympics. he could not believe that there weren't scalpers or available tickets anywhere outside or around Olympic park, where we were. it was like a big compound with many layers of fences, and only people with passes or tickets could get anywhere near the venues. that's not how the Tianjin soccer stadium was, so I'm glad we at least got to go those games. anyway, we still had fun going around Beijing with all the olympicsy atmosphere stuff. i think i would have had to buy tickets online sometime in the spring to get anything. we did try hard, and asked many people. an info number said there were no more tickets, and a website selling tickets also had none available. it was just hard to believe after it was so easy to get tickets in torino.
it is raining hard here now. we will see how the weather is in japan. koshin will be a great host, i think.
I'm attaching my corrected itinerary. i arrive monday the 18th at 7pm. how are you guys? when is mom going to Colorado? I'm excited to see you guys!! what else? i got cool stuff for you. yay! i hope you like it. it was fun to find.
i love you guys more than all the tickets ever sold or not sold!
Heath

Heather Gross
Sent: Wed 8/13/08 4:45 AM
Koshin and I are having lots of fun! I like Japan. It is more expensive than China—like US prices, but less stinky, with cleaner air, with cleaner nicer bathrooms, and less crazy

fashions. We went to the Osaka temple and to taaaasty meals. Koshin's buddy, Tetsya, who speaks almost no Engrish came along. Twas good times. Today we go to Kyoto. K. love you guys! How are you? Feath
Heather Gross
Sent: Sun 8/17/08 4:22 PM
HAPPPPPPPY BIRTHDAY! I LOVE YOU, MOM. SEE YOU SO SOON! HEATH

Facebook:
Nathaniel Smith
Here's how my summer played out: I went to China; I met a fearless traveler named Heather; thus, my summer was great!
They say that no one is ever really gone as long we keep the memory of her alive. Heather, rare human gem that she is, will surely live forever. Hasta que nos reunamos de nuevo, amiga.

Louie Andolsek
heather, one to never judge and loved by so many. you really lived your life in the moment. thanks for running with me in china :) you won't be forgotten, beautiful!!
your family and dear friends are in my prayers.
December 15, 2008 at 9:19am

Giorgia Ascenzi
Heather, I'm thinking about the time we spent together in China....you were so crazy! I loved you.....I'll remember you forever.... December 15, 2008 at 11:48am

Giada Geraci
Damn girl, you can't leave like this! It was yesterday we were in China switching shirts gettin ready for the ladies-night! So crazy dude! You'll be always in my memories.
December 15, 2008 at 12:05pm

Xinling Chen January 17, 2011 at 10:44pm
Re: Engaged
hi Alyce! How nice to hear from you! Sorry that it took me so long to respond. His name is Daniel. I knew him through his

The Devil's Fingernail

mom who also teaches Chinese in Canyons School District. He is an American-born Chinese. He served in the Air Force for four years and just came out in 2010. We have only known each other for about half a year, but we love each other so much that we decide to get married! The reception will be in May, and I will send out an invitation to you.
How have you been? I heard that you went to Europe last December. How was your trip?
Say hi to Dennis

Xinling Chen January 26, 2011 at 9:06pm
Re: Thrilled
Glad that you saw the memorial and also had one built at Snowbird. Heather is missed by so many people that met her. I am sure Heather would be happy. She was so worried about me not having a boyfriend and she would be so excited to know I am getting married!

The day before Mother's Day, 2011, Xinling and Daniel came by to give us an invitation to their reception. It made me so happy to see her. It really helped me get through my third Mother's Day without Heather.

While Heather was still in China, I took a trip to Fort Collins on August 12-16, 2008, where Emily and I had special mom/daughter times doing wedding planning and working to set up her classroom for her first year of teaching. I came home with the excitement of Heather's arrival on my mind.

Denny and I picked her up at the airport, on August 18, 2008, at 7:11 PM, and went to a China/Japan trip-information-filled Mexican dinner at the Red Iguana. Denny and I were so happy to have her home, but Heather had an air of sadness, because she had said good-by to Koshin, her Japanese boyfriend.

Todd Kreykes, the young man who two months later drove through a blizzard with our son-in-law to get to Heather's funeral, made a quick weekend trip to see Heather just after she got back from China. Heather almost always had boyfriends. I think she loved/cared about them all. That is why they were drawn to her. Many came to her funeral.

I don't know the date, but shortly after Heather returned from China and Japan, I can visualize myself on a sunny day, looking down at the sidewalk, and walking while praying (which I often did). One of my repeated prayers was that Heather would find the right partner and have a happy marriage. On that occasion, during that part of my prayer, I had a strong premonition/thought/feeling that she would never get married, and it seemed more disturbing information was to be revealed. Rather then "listening" I kept talking in my mind and moved forward with my walking and petitions asking that even if she never married, she would find a fulfilling profession. I now wonder if the Holy Spirit was trying to prepare me.

Heather kept moving too. On October 13-15, 2008, she took a last camping trip with linguistics friends during their fall break. As indicated in Facebook and other comments, those students have many fond memories of that trip and other times spent with Heather.

Early in November I especially remember how thrilled Heather was when President Obama was elected. Her hope was for peace. Following is the last time she wrote in her journal:

Heather's Journal
4 November 2008. . . Today is Election Day. Hopefully Barack Obama and Joe Biden will give the world a better next 4 years.

After her return from China, during those last four months of our Heather's life, Denny and I had some memorable times with her as well. She came to our house for dinner on several occasions; sometimes by herself and sometimes I fixed dinner for her friends, including Graham Twaddell, Jewel's husband who was in town on business; and Katie and Paul Dyson, who had come back from Australia to live and work in Steamboat, Colorado for about a year. Heather drove the mountain roads to visit them. She and Katie were so close and shared more than I know. Heather brought Xinling to an Oktoberfest meal at out church. She was good about sharing experiences with her many friends.

She was with us for Thanksgiving dinner, which we rotate hosting with three other families. It was at the Hackworth's that year. Heather was the last to arrive, because she had been skiing that morning. The day after Thanksgiving she went with Denny and me to view the Body Worlds exhibit. We had to stand in long lines. Normally she would have been chattering and entertaining us, but that day she was rather quiet and pensive. I wonder if she too had premonitions.

Fwd: LINGUIST List Daily Summary for Tue Dec 02 2008
Heather Gross

Hi Family,
How you doing? I have lots of school stuff to get done over the next two weeks, especially the next week. I have to ignore boys and the mountains. It's tricky.
Anyway, this email goes out to all people subscribed to LINGUIST List. Scroll down. The last one is my posting. You can click on the link and see the list of books that I generated and cleaned up to be posted.
Cool, eh? Love, the Feath

I didn't include her work here, but wanted to show that she was proud of it and wanted us to see it.

The following Christmas letter, which she proofread for me, was written and mailed just days before Heather died.

2008 Holiday Greetings,
We always look forward to hearing from friends and family. The holidays wouldn't be complete without your cards and letters, so don't forget us.
Here we are at Zion National Park, in November. My retirement allowed us to travel in the fall when it is cool and not

crowded. The weather was sunny and beautiful, but Let it snow! *Some of my motivation to retire was to ski on weekdays. I'm still sweeping dry leaves off of our driveway, but the snow is beginning to accumulate in the mountains. Retirement has come with a peaceful more relaxed feeling. While teaching, I always felt a sense of urgency; my work was never done. Now when it isn't done—who cares? I do miss the students, so I've volunteered with Utah Food Bank in their Kids Café program. It provides nutritious meals to children in low-income areas after school.*

As always, Denny is productive around the house, at work, and at church. He is now serving as church council president. Through work, he earned a wonderful trip to Hawaii, but his highlight this year was a trip back in time to his fortieth high school reunion in Pittsburgh. We thoroughly enjoyed time with family and old friends.

Heather is continuing work on a Masters in Linguistics and studying Mandarin Chinese language. Emily and Ryan are getting married in July! Yea! We love Ryan and are thrilled to finally have a son. Emily is now a third/fourth grade combination elementary teacher in Colorado.

We are thankful for our family, friends, and especially for the promise God gives us with the birth of his Son.
Love, Denny and Alyce Gross

The Devil's Fingernail

About three months later I sent this letter to people who didn't hear about Heather's death. (I put a copy of her obituary with it.)

March 23, 2009
       This is the hardest letter I have ever written. That is why it has taken me so long. Judging from your Christmas card, you didn't hear our tragic news.
       Heather came to our house on December 7th to help me put our picture on our Christmas letter. She was patient with me and with my computer impatience. She took time to download the program needed to make the process work. We spent a pleasant time together eating and visiting. She always loved to talk and share about her studies, her plans, and her

many friends. Denny and I were going to a Christmas concert that evening, so we hugged her and said we loved her, like we always did, and said good bye. That was the last time we saw her alive.

Denny and I are doing the best we can. Our church family has been a big support. We're working through our grief by reading many excellent books that people have given us, and we're doing Bible study. Spending time with friends (especially Heather's friends who like to talk about her) is comforting to us. We have a deepened appreciation for each other.

Emily, our 25-year-old, calls us almost daily on her way home from her teaching job. Her wedding, this summer, is something we all look forward to with a bitter/sweet feeling. Heather was to be her Maid of Honor.

Love, Denny and Alyce Gross

The Devil's Fingernail

Death
Never forget me, because if I thought you would, I'd never leave.
(A. A. Milne)

Journal Entry   March 25, 2009   Mom's Thoughts
on Heather's Death

    She lived an extraordinary life, and she died an extraordinary death. Why did that avalanche break at the exact moment Heather was in its path? On that huge mountain, it was only Heather who was snatched away. Where was her guardian angel? Was Heather in anguish or at peace with the angels? Did God do it? Was God protecting Heather, like I prayed every morning of her life? Maybe He was protecting her from future depression or from some other tragedy that would have been even more difficult. Will I ever know? Was it a random act of nature? Heather loved the Earth and its wonders. She especially loved the mountains and the snow. What a cruel trick to allow the very things she loved to violently kill her. Or was it a purposeful, sensational death fitting for one who lived a purposeful, sensational life?

Following are some of the Facebook responses right after her death:
Timmy Allin
TELL ME IT ISN'T TRUE... :(((((((((((((((((((((((((((
December 14, 2008 at 9:00pm

Kristen Schaub Lindahl
Heart broken.
December 14, 2008 at 9:43pm

Ben
Narrrrrrrr peng you. thanks for always keeping things fun and fresh. The way you lived doing what you loved and loving those around you will stick with me and many. Enjoy riding

the heavenly endless powder for me and know I'll be up there sometime to join you. Love you girl
December 14, 2008 at 9:47pm

Tara Paras
You are such a beautiful girl and I loved to see you skiing! It is a very sad day and you will be missed very much!
December 14, 2008 at 9:48pm

Heidi Bogus
Heather
I'll never forget Spanish class, running long distance with you or all of your cleverness. You were electric.
December 14, 2008 at 10:10pm

Monica Allen
You were an inspiration to me. You lived an incredible life, and I'll always remember you.
December 14, 2008 at 10:14pm

Ylenia Spagnoli
 i don't know how to say. . . i can't believe it. . . heather i'll never forget you. . . you were too young and too lifefull. . . bye i hope now you're in a better world.
December 14, 2008 at 10:21pm

Zebulon Pischnotte
Heather, why you? I will miss you SO much.
December 14, 2008 at 10:27pm

Jackie Van Buren
This is unreal. I love you, you have affected my life more than you could ever know. You're a beautiful beautiful person. No one who knows you could ever forget you.
December 14, 2008 at 10:45pm

Christine Kling
No spirit as yours has ever been or will be again..the shine of your light and your incredible life is in the hearts of many and will be held lovingly always. We will miss you. I will miss you dear one. Go well into the light. Much love.

The Devil's Fingernail

Your family will be in our thoughts and prayers. Sincerest heartfelt sympathy. We share your sadness and tears.
Christine
December 14, 2008 at 10:55pm

Megan Beckstead
Heather, My kids and I love you. We read the book you gave the kids tonight; for you. My kids love that book; I think it is their favorite. We miss your smiling face already. God Bless your family.
December 14, 2008 at 11:01pm

Bree DeGraw
I will never forget all of those memories in Girl Scouts, camp, sleep-overs, your laugh, your spirit....I will miss you! With all of my love!
December 14, 2008 at 11:06pm

Linton Dean
Heather, you are so awesome and always will be! ...all our fun conversations in China and running into you at school. You always make me smile! You will always be in my heart!
My thoughts and prayers go out to your family!
December 14, 2008 at 11:26pm

Jake Van Alstyne
I met you only a few very short months ago, but I got to know you well enough in that time to feel absolutely sick at having lost you. We didn't share as many memories as a fair world would have allowed us, but I'll never forget the times we did have. I know I miss you.
You never failed at making me laugh and you lived ...your life with passion. Your candle shone brighter than most. Indeed, it feels like looking back, it shone the brightest.
Our relationship meant more to me than I think you knew, and that is my biggest regret in this moment. There is a table in a bar on second south where I know I'll never be able to sit again. But I'll look in its direction and smile sadly, remembering how excited you were to show off your earrings to me.
You were amazing, brilliant, talented, brave, adventurous and

full of all the good things about life. You died doing what you loved. I'm certain that's how you would have wanted it.
December 14, 2008 at 11:33pm

Meghan Boldon Hunt
Heather, nobody can make me laugh like you could. I've always looked up to you and I will never forget you.
December 14, 2008 at 11:45pm

Ryan Adler
H...you were one of a kind. You certainly left your imprint on each of us. Whether skiing, dancing (both at the same time), running, or just hanging out...you knew how to make people smile. You will be missed :-(We all love you.
December 15, 2008 at 12:04am

Jonathan
I miss you babe. You truly were a person who truly radiated joy. My thoughts and prayers are with you and your family.
December 15, 2008 at 12:30am

Grace Yin
Heather, I'll always miss you. And I believe you are smiling in another world. Be good, my friend...
December 15, 2008 at 6:51am

Cortney Anderson
We, the Snowbird Family, will miss you so much, along with the rest of the world. Mom and Dad Gross, close family, friends and all who knew her, please be strong, you know she is, for ever...
December 15, 2008 at 6:58am

Tristan Gale Geisler
you were a great friend to me. I will always treasure the memories we made together. i miss you!
December 15, 2008 at 7:38am

Annika Anderson
You will be missed. I have fond memories of Zion days. You and your family will be in my heart!

The Devil's Fingernail

December 15, 2008 at 8:06am

Yuri Esposito
There are so many words that I would have told you, there are so many days that I wished to stay with you, there is so much love that I would have given you, I always wished that everything in your life would be great, and now I smile because I know that you're lookin' at me and we still stand together. I'll miss you Heather. With love. Your Mr. Pants
December 15, 2008 at 12:27pm

Barbara Spencer Thornton
Oh, what a horrible tragedy! Heather—you were a shining light to everyone who knew you! The world will be dimmer now that you are gone.
December 15, 2008 at 12:07pm

Todd Kreykes
HG, God bless you for everything that made you who you are. This is not how I had envisioned my next trip out to see you. I will miss you
December 16, 2008 at 1:45am

Todd drove ten hours through a snowstorm with Ryan, our future son-in-law, to get to Heather's memorial service. They had to wait several hours, in Rawlins, Wyoming while the cell of a blizzard caused the closure of I-80. As I explained in Book I, Ryan initially flew to Salt Lake City with our daughter Emily, on December 14, the day of Heather's death. After a few days he flew back to Fort Collins, Colorado, to work part of the week. Then he drove back with Todd, on Friday night, to come to the funeral. I'm so thankful to Todd that Ryan didn't have to make that harrowing trip alone.

Sadie Dickman
It's become a tradition to have a dance in your honor at our parties.
We totally just cut loose and try to do as you did.
So, really, you're still in our lives every day.

Alyce Gross

I think all the time about the way you lived—all about freedom and love and passion—and I wanna be just like you when I grow up.
I don't think I'm the only one.
February 5, 2009 at 11:42am

News Articles and Reports

Mike DeBernardo, a camera man for a local TV station, Fox News, who was one of the four young men who had been skiing with Heather on the day she died, and who patiently waited with us at The University of Utah Hospital, warned us about reporters. That helped prepare us. One called that very night, and several called or came starting the next morning and continued throughout the next few days. All were very polite and respectful.

For several days running, Heather's death was reported in the local newspapers and television stations. It was also mentioned more than once on the Today Show and Good Morning America. We have friends who were teachers for international schools in South Korea, and they even heard it there. Following are copies of a few of the many reports:

ABC 4 News (KTVX.) granted me permission to use this direct quote:

The awesome power of an avalanche took its toll in the Wasatch back-country Sunday, a woman died after being swallowed up in a slide at Snowbird Ski Resort.

The Salt Lake County sheriff's office has released the name of the woman who died as a result of that avalanche. She is 27-year-old Heather Gross of Salt Lake City. Rescuers say it took nearly an hour to locate Gross in that debris field.

Response to the avalanche was immediate. "She was skiing with a friend who witnessed the avalanche," said Salt Lake County Deputy Levi Hughes. It happened in an in-bound area of the resort called "High Baldy" on Snowbird's eastern edge, an area that requires hiking to reach. "This is a very unusual event to have an avalanche in bounds in a ski resort, incredibly unusual," said Salt Lake County Sheriff Jim Winder.

Snowbird officials say the area had been cleared to enter at 9:30 this morning after avalanche control was completed. It was the first time the area had opened this season. At 12:24pm the avalanche was triggered. "That person was recovered at 1:18

pm in critical condition," said Snow Bird's Dave Fields.

Seven avalanche dogs and dozens of search and rescue people from the Salt Lake County Sheriffs' Office, Snowbird safety personnel and Wasatch Back Country Rescue were on scene. It's not known if Gross was wearing a beacon. It has been confirmed she was found by a probe. It has also been confirmed she was the only victim but the search continued even after she was located. "Standard protocol is you continue looking and probing and trying everything you can to verify the debris field is clear," said Fields. Just after 5 pm the search was called off.

Heather Gross was airlifted to the hospital in critical condition. She died just after 5 pm. She was well known at Snowbird. "This individual has been a long time skier at Snowbird and it's affected the snow safety personnel—very deeply," Sheriff Jim Winder said. The last time a fatality happened in an in-bound area of Snowbird was more than 30 years ago.

Mom's Input:

Heather was not in back-country and she wasn't wearing a beacon, which almost no one wears while skiing inside the resort boundaries. I don't believe the reported time of death is accurate. I believe she died while under the snow for 54 minutes.

Avalanches are very rare inside the boundaries of ski resorts. Heather's death was the first in-bound avalanche death at Snowbird since 1977. In The Salt Lake Tribune, on December 15, 2008, Bruce Tremper, director of the Utah Avalanche Center, is quoted as saying, "People come from all over the country to study how [Snowbird and Alta] do avalanche control . . . because they're considered to be the best." Statistically, he said, a person is "100 times more likely to be killed by lightning in Utah than by an in-bounds avalanche at a ski area."

Accident Report
Date: 2008-12-14
    Submitted by: Jim Collinson, Snowbird Snow Safety Dept. Place: Mt. Baldy, Snowbird Ski Resort State: UT
Fatalities: 1 Summary: One skier caught, carried, buried, died later in the hospital.
Location: Mt. Baldy separates the ski areas of Snowbird/Alta,

The Devil's Fingernail

rising to 11,068'. The avalanche occurred on the northwest exposure at an elevation of 10,470'.

History: This was the first day which the Mt. Baldy side of Snowbird was opened this season. Previous control work on the slope included: a 105 mm rifle bullet on November 20, 2 lb. HE on December 9, and two separate shots of 2 lb. HE on December 14; one shot in the starting zone of the subsequent avalanche, the other shot on the lower flank of the subsequent avalanche, all with no results. All five of the Baldy routes were run on December 14th; these routes cover West Baldy, Northwest Baldy, and the western exposure of the Peruvian Ridge. 55 starting zones were tested with explosives or skis with no significant results. Access to Mt. Baldy was opened at 09:28. Prior to the avalanche, which occurred at 12:24, an estimated 300 people crossed the starting zone and or skied the slope that failed. A public cell phone call was placed to Ski Patrol dispatch while the slide was in motion.

Accident and Rescue Summary: At 12:24 a male snowboarder was on the high traverse of Northwest Mt. Baldy and initiated the avalanche; the crown face bisected the high traverse. The event occurred as he was crossing the slope but did not involve him. According to witness reports from near the starting zone, as the slide was in motion they spotted a person in the middle of the track who was hiking up the slope to retrieve a ski. Warnings were yelled, but when visibility returned, the slope was empty, the alarm was sounded to the ski patrol, and many public skiers and snowboarders in the area began a search for missing people. A hasty search team was immediately dispatched with dogs, beacons, and Recco. Probe teams were assembled and dispatched along with extra probes for the public on scene already searching. Due to approximately 150 people on site, their scattered equipment, and the resulting contamination of the deposition, the dogs had interest in numerous locations but were unable to locate the victim. The victim, a 27-year-old female, was the same person who had been seen hiking in the track. She was not equipped with a beacon or Recco and was located with a probe line at 58 minutes, 3' deep.

Avalanche Data: This slope has a northwest aspect, elevation of 10,470', and a slope angle of 36 degrees. The initial release was 1' deep, 35' wide, and 20' from crown face to stauchwall. As this pocket traveled down slope, it released the skier's left flank and reached a maximum width of 120'. The average depth of the crown face was 1', with pockets of up to 3'. As the avalanche descended, it gouged into old faceted snow and entrained much of the snow in the track. The avalanche ran 1,000' vertically, classified as HS-AR-R3-D2-O. The deposition had tongues that were up to 10' deep, averaged 5'.

Weather and Snowpack History: After receiving a record amount of precipitation in the form of both rain and snow in early November, the Wasatch Mountains were under high pressure until the end of November building a very faceted snowpack. On November 28 a significant rime/rain event occurred to the highest peaks. Early December returned to high pressure and cold temperatures further deteriorating the snowpack above and below the rime event. December 8th broke the high pressure spell with a storm which deposited 1' of 6% snow. The night of December 12th had strong southwest winds; a finger/pencil slab was deposited. December 13th was the second storm of the month with 17" of 6% snow.

Danger Rating: The UAC [Utah Avalanche Center which does backcountry danger rating] rated the hazard at the upper end of moderate for this day. [Again, Heather was not in backcountry.] There had been no avalanches reported in the Cottonwood Canyons previously.

Mom's Input:

After the warm weather and no snow the end of February and beginning of March, I skied at Alta on Thursday, March 5, 2009—just under three months after Heather's death. It was the day after there had finally been a big snow storm with 12 inches of new snow. I knew ice, from that warm weather, under new powder would be a cause for increased avalanche danger, but felt confident Alta would not open unsafe runs. (I believe Heather felt that same confidence at Snowbird, on December, 14, 2008.) On the morning of March 5, as I stood in line for the ski lift, I saw on the Collins electronic sign, over and over, that the gates to

The Devil's Fingernail

Snowbird and the High Baldy Chutes were closed. Right then, while looking at that sign, I knew in my heart that the closure was partly due to Heather's death, and that her death may have saved and may continue to save lives. I also know that right after Heather's death, as reported to us by Snowbird Ski Patrollers, the avalanche blasting was thorough. I think those precautions, and probably others that I'm not aware of, were and will continue to be taken, in part, because of Heather's life being lost in an in-bounds avalanche. There were other avalanche deaths that winter, but not inside the boundaries of ski areas. Heather's death may have saved many other lives.

I would rather that my spark should burn out in a brilliant blaze than it should be stifled by dry rot. I would rather be a superb meteor, every atom of me in magnificent glow, than a sleepy and permanent planet. Jack London

Goblin Valley

Great Wall of China

Alyce Gross

Obituary

How it was inspired:
I lift my eyes to the [mountains]—from where will my help come? My help comes from the LORD, *who made heaven and earth* (Psalm 121:1&2).

The Psalm uses hills but I changed it to mountains, because I can step out on my deck or look from my kitchen window and see the powerful grey granite of the Western Rockies, snow covered into August and highlighted by the sun.

The heavens are telling the glory of God (Psalm 19:1a).

This spoke to me, because the morning after Heather's death I stepped out on my deck and saw a most stunning sunrise. It shot up vividly with an intense splash of color—peachy, pinky, orange—and then it was gone. It was over the area of the mountains in which Heather died. It was a perfect tribute to my beautiful daughter's short life, and it, with the power of the Holy Spirit, along with some of the Facebook comments, motivated me on what to write for my Heather's obituary.

The Devil's Fingernail

Heather Aron Gross
6/28/81—12/14/08

      Heather was never meant to die of old age; instead she died causing international news. The inbounds avalanche at Snowbird, on December, 14th, ended her life at age 27. She was an avid Snowbird skier and would never want her death to stifle anyone's love for skiing or for the resort.

      Our daughter did a life's worth of living in her 27 years. Her candle burned brightly but not long enough. She needs the many people whom she has touched, to keep it burning. Her prayer for you would be to remember her goodness and zest for life and continue to share and spread it.

      Heather had a passion for adventure and learning. Travel was a part of who she was. She open-mindedly accepted and befriended people from all over the world. She combined travel and learning with studies in Spain, China, Argentina, and more.

      She will be deeply missed by her parents, Dennis and Alyce Gross of Salt Lake City, and her sister, Emily

Gross, of Ft. Collins Colorado. Heather left a void that will be partially filled by hilarious memories.

Anyone caring to memorialize Heather should make a donation to the Utah Food Bank in her name.

As an infant she was baptized, on August 23, 1981 into the Body of Christ and anointed with the Holy Spirit, at Zion Lutheran Church, 1070 S. Foothill Drive, where the Celebration of her Life will be held on Saturday, December 20th at 3:00 PM. Guests will be greeted as early as 2:00 PM.

More than two years after Heather's death, I found this in her sketchbook, written while she was a senior in high school. Maybe the candle analogy was a good one, because she wrote:

Goo   11/18/98

It seems to me, dear Cornelius, that the meaning of life can be explained by this candle. We all begin with so much wax under us. Once ignited, we can choose to flicker, grow weak, and give up, or take hold, grow strong, and burn all that life gives us. These drips are what we leave behind, legacies of melted goo.

My prayer is that Heather leaves behind lives made better because she has touched them with her God-given light.

Celebration of Life

Sunday's child full of grace...

    Heather was born on a Sunday and died on a Sunday. We scheduled the memorial service at our church to be held on the following Saturday so that working people and students would be able to attend. I hadn't really thought how many people may show, but they came from far and wide. They came and kept coming. Many of Heather's young friends, some who probably couldn't afford it, flew to Utah from other states. People flew into our winter snow from Arizona, California, Montana, Colorado, Washington, Pennsylvania, Michigan and more. One friend came across the Pacific from Japan. Pastor Neale E. Nelson who had served Zion Lutheran Church as Pastor from 1957-1970 and returned as a member in retirement, said to his daughter, I have never seen the Church this full in the thirteen years I served or since. He was correct. Zion Lutheran Church, where Heather was baptized, attended Sunday school regularly, and was confirmed, has never been as full as it was on December 20, 2008. It was filled not only with people, but with Spirit. Every pew was full. The balcony and both choir lofts were full. Chairs were set up in the narthex and people stood behind the chairs and up and down the side aisles.

    The atmosphere was not that of a funeral dirge, but quite the opposite. It was electric with what I'll call God's Holy Spirit and with the love, devotion, and compassion from Heather's numerous and varied friends. There were also many people there who didn't know Heather, but came to show support to Denny, Emily, and me. Ethel Olsen, a church and book club friend of mine said, "Our church has never had so many culturally diverse people in attendance." I think there were people there from every continent except Antarctica. This, of course, was partially due to the fact that Heather was studying linguistics with a diverse group of students. Also the scientists she had worked with included many foreign nationals. There were college professors, high school teachers, and school friends from elementary through the graduate level. There were linguistic students and scientists of many nationalities, as well as skiers and ski patrollers. Heather's friendships were deep and wide.

The music was of highest quality with our professional musicians: David Chamberlin, Organist, and Susan Swidnicki, Oboist. The Processional Hymn was an old traditional one that my brother reminded me was sung at our Mother's funeral: "My Hope Is Built on Nothing Less." But from there, we went with more up-beat music that better reflected Heather's personality: "I Danced in the Morning," "On Eagle's Wings," "Earth and All Stars!" and ending with "Shine, Jesus, Shine." They were sung with such emotion and passion, they truly were a reflection of the kind of life Heather lived. No one was bored. My husband, Dennis Gross, was able to share "remembrances" about Heather with a comedian's storytelling and timing ability. I don't know how he did it, except that, as always, the angels were with him. He had everyone laughing and crying. Denny took ideas sent by two close friends, Katie Gracia Dyson and Jewel Kling Twaddell to incorporate into his message. Next, Heather's scientist friend, Brittney Weber, read an emotional tribute to Heather that she had written shortly after Heather's death. Brittney moved on to graduate school to study writing. A copy of her piece is included directly below, followed by Katie's and Jewel's input. Our Pastor, Steve Klemz, who knew Heather since she was about ten years old, did an excellent job of relaying her exuberance for life and the likelihood that she is now skiing the eternal fresh. From her Facebook page he got Heather's word for what heaven may be like—"FRESHNESS!"

Scripture readings included:
You have turned my mourning into dancing;
You have taken off my sackcloth and clothed me with joy,
so that my soul may praise you and not be silent.
*O L*ORD *my God, I will give thanks to you forever* (Psalm 30; 11-12).

Pastor Steve said that only Heather could explode onto the dance floor, as he remembered her at his daughter's wedding.

Let us then pursue what makes for peace and building up of one another (Romans 14:19).

Denny talked about her love and concern for her many friends. She spent her life "building up" others.

I came that they may have life, and have it abundantly (John 10:10b).

If anyone ever lived life abundantly, it was our Heather. She did "take hold, grow strong, and burn all that life gave her."

Her memorial service lasted over an hour, and then all were invited to a meal downstairs in the church where people were fed by our welcoming congregation. We had childhood albums spread out on tables and Heather's high school dance pictures were filling a wall. Some of her high school friends were taking pictures of the pictures. My daughter Emily and her boyfriend Ryan did a power point loop of choice pictures from Heather's childhood and from her many activities and travels. All was topped off with a champagne toast. It really felt like a celebration of a life—a celebration fitting my beautiful firstborn child. I hope her spirit knows and sees how many lives she touched. Brittney was one of them and wrote this and read it at the service:

> I miss my mercury. My Hg. Girl, if you could only see how you've threaded all of our lives together. So many souls warmed by your mischievous grin and laughter that moved rooms. You are what happens when love meets blonde and spirit and the richness of life. You proudly displayed all the treasures you collected around the world, treasures that reminded you of people you'd loved and your adventures. Your natural gifts for language and culture moved every person, but none more than your own Gspeak. Yar. Danceables. Countryness. I'm trying to catch you in memories and photographs and stories but it's me that's caught, Heather. Caught in your whirlwind of love and light and happiness that swept us all up and moved us into better places in our lives. I am so lucky to have loved you for the scrap

of time I had, because you had so much to do and so many people to change. I feel like I'm pouring you out of me along with all of the grief and the ache because I cannot bear it. I don't know in which pocket of the universe your light is scattered now but I know it's dancing. My heart is breaking, Heather, but you're dancing.
I love you. Bdub (Brittney Web)

    I believe Brittney has written more about Heather, and I'm sure someday I'll get to read it. She
lovingly gave us a copy of the above piece framed and surrounded with a collage of wonderful pictures of Heather and friends. It hangs in our computer room along with other treasured art and photos.

Katie Gracia   Thu 12/18/08 9:08 PM

    We were alphabetically fated to know one another...it's as if the powers that be knew that one day we would be best friends. 16 years of memories...laughing till we cried, crying till we laughed, summers spent sleeping on the trampoline, sneaking out of your parents yard to go play video games at matt's house until 5 in the morning—we were such rebels :) i bought you a battery powered curling iron to cut down on the time it took you to get ready in the morning...I thought if you could curl your hair in the two miles it took to get to school all of our problems would be solved, matching hair ties to t-shirts and writing down every outfit your wore so you never doubled up in the same two weeks, jars of clay "flood" and the most beautiful interpretive dance i have ever witnessed—100 times over again in your living room in 9th grade, you found beauty in all things ugly, you opened my world to travel and are a part of what i am today, we shopped for dirndls in Munich for hours...finding the perfect ones and danced on tables and ate pretzels the size of our heads. i am who i am because of you...it's as if over 16 years our molecules had intertwined and got all mixed up together and we became part of one another, i speak heather fluently and can translate to anyone the what's, why's and how's of what you were trying to say. just like the last 100 times we spoke   "i love you miss heather g" "i love you miss katie g"

The Devil's Fingernail

Our Heather, by Jewel
Sent: Wed 12/17/08 11:40 PM Dear Alyce, Denny and Em
    I have so many memories of Heather—it was hard to sort through and pick my favorites (I have included full stories, but I think you were looking for shorter snippets...please feel free to pull out whatever works). Your daughter made such an impact on my life and who I have become. I am having a very difficult time imagining my future without her, as both my husband and I knew she would be an important part of our lives forever. I know she still will be. It's just so hard to say goodbye. Here are some memories/stories, etc. I hope they help. I really enjoyed putting in words some of my favorite Heather moments and characteristics. You raised a truly unique individual that touched this world like no other. Thank you.
    During our study abroad year, Heather and I took a lot of trips together. One of the trips was to Germany to visit a foreign exchange student my family had had when I was growing up, Alexandra. Alex's parents came to visit during our trip because I had not met them and they were excited to meet part of Alex's American family. Her parents did not speak any English, nothing, no single word, besides maybe hello. They spoke German and Polish. We spoke neither of those languages and needed Alex to translate for us. However, Alex did not come with us when her parents drove us the 2 hour journey to the airport. As you can imagine it was difficult to communicate. This did not stop Heather! She continued to tell Alex's mom story after story, sometimes in English, sometimes in Spanish. I think she even threw in some Italian as an attempt to find some way to communicate with Alex's parents. It was clear they could not understand her, but the passion and enthusiasm Heather had during her story telling made for a memorable experience that has transcended the 2 hour car journey.
    During another one of our trips we had probably one of my favorite study abroad stories ever. We were in Venice, Italy during carnival.
    [I included the Venice memory in the Junior Year in Spain Chapter. Denny did tell about it at her Celebration of life.]

Heather is probably one of the most athletic & fit people I know. When she was in AZ & Granada and far from skiing, she ran, rowed, played soccer, hiked and anything else she could do to move! I think that's why it was always so charming that she liked candy soooo much. Honestly, I think she had a sweety or sucker in her pocket at all times. This became most obvious to me in Spain where there were sweety shops at each corner (and full of very yummy candies). It was a common detour to stop in the candy shop and get some snacks. I can close my eyes now and picture her reaching in her sweater pocket, pulling out a hard candy, un-wrapping it and tossing it in her mouth.

It's either completely understandable or so confusing that although Heather was studying linguistics, she totally made up her own language. The most recent addition to this quirky syntax was the word "yar." To be honest, I don't even know what it means but I assumed it was yes or some other happy exclamation. Her language was how our college group of best friends became the Itro's. There were four of us, Heather or Hitro, Jewel or Jitro, Tracy or Titro and Lauren or Litro (with an honorary fifth, Andy, but his name didn't work as well). The idea was Heather's and came from the word Nitro, a sporting equipment name. It instantly became how we referred to each other, all four of us intelligent honors ladies throwing around our cute, quirky names as though we belonged in a secret club. Titro even made us necklaces to wear when we all went our separate ways during Junior year of college.

Heather had this great ability to look at the world and create unique geometric and other descriptive comparisons. For example, if we walked into a room of four people she would point out that two had blonde hair and two had brown while all were wearing something yellow and had a book whose name started with P. I began to crave these comparisons and so enjoyed seeing the world through Heather's eyes. She brought people together with her comparisons because she was always able to find some characteristic or trait that people shared, before they could even start to find their differences. I loved when I became part of the observations as I felt I was being inducted into a club or special gang. It's a beautiful way to honor peoples uniqueness

while illustrating how interconnected we are in the world. Sometimes I do this now and each time I think of Heather.
Much love,
Jewel

Sent: Thu 12/18/08 8:46 PM
Lauren, Tracy, Josie, April, and Dominica will all be coming as well to the funeral (some college and some Spain friends). There are so many others that would be there too, if they could.

I found one more thing today. It's my journal entry from 12/19/2000 when we all lived in the same dorm together (second year of college):

Heather is fantastic. I look at her and I see this incredible energetic light, totally on fire, lighting everything she touches. She shines. She inspires to shine also. This girl is so smart. She's adorable and cute and sweet and wonderful. She inspires me to love living every day and helps make me a better person. Being with her is so uplifting.

Heather and I were meant to meet. Just as our friendship helped pull her from a low, it inspired me daily to push my boundaries and embrace life in a way I didn't know how before Heather.

Others Wrote About Heather

Facebook
Mike Peterson
G, I love you and miss you so much. I know you are now watching over all of your family and friends who you loved so genuinely. You taught me many things. Foremost how to love and live life with every last bit of energy you have. You touched the hearts of so many, effortlessly but profoundly. You should know that I would not be the person I am today without having had the great blessing of your friendship. I hope you are enjoying skiing the Eternal Freshness.
PS You always asked/promised to be at my wedding. You will be the first person I talk to if and when that ever happens.
Dec 15, 2008 at 12:44 pm

Missing you like crazy G! All I can do is celebrate many of the happiest moments of my life that were spent with you. You made me feel incredibly happy and completely at peace every time we were together.
December 27, 2009 at 7:32 pm

From: Scott Reuschel
Sent: Tuesday, December 16, 2008 2:21 PM
Subject: Rememberences from Tandem
Denny, Alyce and Emily,
    I don't have the words to express how sorry I am for your loss, but I just wanted to let you know that there are a lot of people here at Tandem who are still remembering and "celebrating" the life and times spent with Heather.
    Rest assured, there has been many a story told in the last 2 days that has had us in tears, both from laughing and from crying. Needless to say, she was "one of a kind" who will never be forgotten. Scott Reuschel
01 February 2009
Dear Denny, Alyce and Emily,
    Your daughter/sister, Heather, has been in my mind very much lately. I have known and worked with Heather at Tandem over 7 yrs.
    I think it was in the summer of 2001 that I first worked

with her (and also Rob Shell) in the Sample Management department. I remember being so impressed with her liberal-minded attitude and acceptance of people, especially for one so young. She was funny, sensitive, light-hearted and smiled a lot: I remember Rob affectionately referring to her as "Heather-Poo".

    She had been amused at my former job experience as a chorus dancer (many years ago) in shows in Las Vegas: she would, from time to time, ask me questions about what it was like and even though I may have exaggerated my stories at times, she was always delighted, appreciating my dramatic embellishments. And I loved how she appreciated my earrings!!! I received more compliments about my earrings from Heather than anyone I have known!

    Over the years I saw her learn, grow-up and mature. The first couple of years there I used to think: how could someone so young have so much confidence! Oh, that I had had that confidence when I was her age! When she started traveling, I admired her courage to be able to go to foreign countries, like Spain and later China on her own, learning new languages and making new friends.

    I remember when she fractured her clavicle in a skiing accident, I believe, a few years ago, and she couldn't work as a scientist in the lab. So she came up into the QC (Quality Control) department where I trained her.

    Granted, this work was not exactly her cup of tea! She didn't appear to enjoy flagging the errors of her fellow scientists in the lab during our document review! However, I think she acquired a new awareness and appreciation of the importance of our work at Tandem, as it was later reflected in her own documentation in the lab notebooks and run folders.

    During this time, I remember when she would have some concerns about her observations in the lab (and I cannot even remember what they were now) and she would sometimes use the expression, "Am I being ridiculous?!" It is an expression I shall always associate with Heather; I found it so endearing because it was not self-deprecating yet had innocence to it.

    There is no question that Heather had a free spirit, but I also think she was an "old soul" as well. I remember talking to her about a book I had read, <u>Between a Rock and a Hard Place</u>, by Aron Ralston, a nonfiction story of a young man's survival from an accident in which he ended up amputating his hand. After recounting the story to her, I was astounded at her wise assessment of his character, which, as it turned out, was eventually reflected by the young man, himself, at the end of his story! I have fond memories of her becoming so involved in things at work, like running in the Corporate Races several years ago as a representative of Tandem, and supporting and participating in the many charitable events that took place over the years. I saw her mature as she became a trainer in the lab and helped other people. And I have memories of watching her speaking Chinese during lunch breaks to the Chinese members of our lab and embracing the culture of others, such as Yasir, who is from the mid-east.

[The remainder of this letter is about acceptance of death and is in Part One in the Doubt, Questioning and Cancer chapter.]
Strength, love, peace, and healing,
Bonnie Fletcher

The Devil's Fingernail

The following poem was written in the spring of 2009 by Anne
Haroldsen, a high school friend of Heather's. In November, 2010 she
contacted me through Facebook.

Anne Haroldsen   November 25, 2010 at 9:01am
Re: poem about Heather
Hi Alyce,
That is neat that you are writing a book about Heather. I hope
I get to read it! You can of course do whatever you want with
the poem. I would be honored if you included it in your book!
Have a good Thanksgiving,
Anne

For Heather

Maybe it was written in the snow,
In the way the water that winter froze, crystallized,
Fell to the earth in millions of tiny white flakes,
Delicate as lace, and weightless,
A sky of misaligned stars

Maybe it was written in the water
In the droplets that hung from the needles of pine trees,
In the melting slabs of ice under the drifts of powder
I sometimes think the mountains understood, and grieved,
The pillars and crests of granite silent under the wisps of cloud
You can sense it in the stillness of the ice on the frozen streams,
The silent trees
A quiet grief holds them still

By the end of that deadly winter, I had lost count
Of the lives lost, the bodies recovered,
The number of avalanches that fell down the mountains
Like a scythe

I still think of the last moments,
When you must have fought,
Unable to breathe,

Alyce Gross

Under all of that snow

All of us who love you are still,
In our minds, frantically digging,
Tearing snow away from the earth
The ice cutting the raw skin of our hands
Which are numbed from disbelief, and panic
We will never let those moments go
We will never give up our frantic search through the snow and ice
As though, if we replay it over,
We could be there, in the last moments, when you were alone
As if the impossible hope will win out,
And we will find you there, a few minutes sooner,
Brush the snow from your blue lips,
And carry you to warmth

Heather, it is spring, and you should be here,
Surrounded by your friends
Who believe that somewhere, you are dancing,
Interpreting the faint music of the stars,
That you are filled with laughter,
That you are, as always, unafraid of anything,
That your heart is free
Outside the window, a bird is singing
I want to end this elegy with its singing,
With the clear, sweet notes of its simple joy
We carry within us the imprint of your voice,
The last of your laugh we are still able to hear
Its faint echoes call to us, as though from very far away
We think of you,
And are glad that you were, for your brief moments, here

By Ann Haroldsen

Memorials

Well before a Snowbird Memorial was complete, some of Heather's Linguistics friends lovingly created a web page Memorial as well as a physical Memorial, at the Linguistics Department at The University of Utah:

Facebook:
August 12, 2009 at 2:04pm
Brian Cragun Hi G,
Long time, no chat.
Along with reminding you how much I miss you, I have an exciting piece of news.
We've been working really hard at it, and finally have our Heather Aron Gross Memorial Project web page online. You, and anyone else that would like to see it, can do so by going to:
http://www.hum.utah.edu/linguistics/?&pageId=4023

This page has a passage that all of our friends are working to translate into as many languages as we can, and some pictures of places you once were.

Heather Aron Gross Memorial Project
On the actual web site, this message can be translated by clicking on all these various languages:

English   Español (Spanish)   Deutsch (German)   ქართული (Georgian)
Gwich'in   বাংলা (Bangali)
Français (French)   Magyar (Hungarian)   Nederlands (Dutch)
   Svenska(Swedish)   Eifel Platt (Platt German)
日本語 (Japanese)   Русский (Russian)   简体中文 (Simplified Chinese)
繁體中文 (Traditional Chinese)

Recently we lost a friend, mentor, and valuable member of our community. Heather Aron Gross, a graduate student nearing completion of her MA degree, passed away as the result of injuries that she sustained when caught in an avalanche while skiing at Snowbird.

Heather's positive energy, enthusiasm, and a strong spirit of unity enriched the lives of many in the time we had together. Her bright smile and friendly words inspired and will continue to inspire many of us for the years to come.
Our deepest condolences go out to Heather's family and friends.
May her spirit always dance on.

We're holding a vote to decide which of the beautiful pictures will be displayed in the Department for a long time to come; so that you can leave as much of a mark on the place we spent the most time together, as you did on all of us.
我好想念你,老郭. Brian

Brian Cragun   March 11, 2010   我親愛的...
You should be happy to know that there is now a memorial for you in the Department. We finally got all of the pictures together, and got a beautiful plaque. I just got the pictures Sadie sent me. They made me cry tears of joy. I hope you like it.
Loving and missing you daily

    Brian, and other students from the Linguistics Department, put in much time and effort to complete both the virtual and physical memorials for Heather, at an intensely busy point in their lives. They were taking finals, graduating, and moving. Brian moved to Taipei, Taiwan to teach English and study at the National Taiwan University, yet he stayed on this project to see it finished. I'm forever grateful to Brian and all the others who contributed to this heartfelt project.

The Devil's Fingernail

The snowbird ski patrol also put effort into remembering Heather.

Thank You Note	December 21, 2009
Dear Snowbird Ski Patrol,
	Thank you for coming to Porcupine with the plaque to honor our daughter's memory. Your show of support on December 14, 2009 was a reflection of that same dedication you exhibited exactly a year earlier. We know the whole ski patrol and many others did their best to try and save Heather's life. She shared and we share your love and respect for nature. We also share the knowledge that although we humans would like to control nature, we never will. That is a part of its awesome wonder and power.
	We don't get to know why Heather died that day, but we do know she would not want to blame anyone, or have her death stifle anyone's love for skiing or for Snowbird Resort.
	We do hope that what was learned from her death may have already and may continue to save lives.

With gratitude, respect, and love,
Alyce and Dennis Gross

Facebook:
Brady Newton
Heather, we will all miss your infectious smile and quiet demeanor on the tram and while skiing with you. I will never forget while we sat on the tram deck Friday evening watching the sun set on High Baldy and you called our attention to how beautiful the last sunlight of the day hitting Fields of Glory was: Oranges and yellows and long shadows. Maybe you knew somehow that that's where your last run would be. A fitting run to go out on: Fields of Glory... My thoughts and prayers go out to your family.
December 15, 2008 at 3:07pm

Letter	February 6, 2010
[Judy is one of four childhood friends who did Emily and Ryan's rehearsal dinner.]
Hi Judy,

Barb and Linda did make it here, and a few weeks later Denny's sister, Karen, came too. She just left a few days ago. It was fun for me to show them around Salt Lake, and take them up beautiful canyons to the ski areas. They didn't ski, but were interested in the sites. Of course, we had lots of time for visiting and eating which are some my favorite things to do.

Barb is starting to cook up ideas for getting together in the spring and summer. Maybe August, so Margaret can join us.

I have had no physical problems or side effects from my lymphoma or from the radiation, which was way back in September. I really hardly ever think about having cancer.

We're going to Ft. Collins for a long weekend around Feb. 20th. It's always good to see Emily and Ryan. We were there twice in December, to help us get through some of the hardest times.

On December 14th, the anniversary of Heather's death, we drove home from Ft. Collins to a big gathering of Heather's friends that took up the whole upstairs of a local pub. There were childhood friends, linguistic students, scientists, and ski patrollers with a plaque they are going to put on Mt. Baldy (where she died). While with Barb and Linda, on a tram ride at Snowbird, I decided that Mt. Baldy is Heather's tombstone. Only my Heather would have a tombstone 11,000 ft. high. The ski patrol asked me ahead of time what I wanted on the plaque. As is typical, it has her name, birth and death dates, but the rest, like Heather, is not typical:

Heather Aron Gross
June 28, 1981 to December 14, 2008
She lived life abundantly
and died in the Fields of Glory

"Fields of Glory" was the name of the ski run where the avalanche killed her. The plaque will be attached to a rock near where her body came to rest.

I'm still grieving and probably always will, but it is getting a little less painful, especially with good friends like you and others who grieve a little with me. Thank you for your many cards.

Love, Alyce

Yes, in my mind, Heather's tombstone is the 11,000 feet high Mt. Baldy, and yes, the Ski Patrol did honor our Heather with a small plaque on lower Baldy, inscribed with what I consider Heather's epitaph. At first the patrollers thought they would put the plaque at the top of Mt. Baldy, but only extreme skiers would ever see it there. It would not be a safe place to hike, so they decided to place it close to where her body came to rest. During the summer and fall hikers can now get to it on Peruvian Gulch Trail.

There ended-up being two plaques at Snowbird. The first was hung on a wall under Heather's picture along with pictures of many deceased ski patrollers. This wall of honor and remembrance is in "The Peak House" near the top of the Snowbird tram. It is where ski patrollers prepare rounds for blasting to cause avalanches before the lifts open, where they do dispatching for mountain rescues, and where they come to warm up or to just hang out.

Being shown that first plaque on the first year anniversary of Heather's death, and having the ski patrollers present it in the company of so many of her friends, was another overwhelming tribute to our daughter. Also, around the year anniversary of Heather's death, her Facebook friends still remembered her. These are just some of the postings that gave me so much comfort:

Tristan Gale Geisler
So tomorrow is my wedding anniversary. I was married at the top of the tram at Snowbird. The next week you died there. I have such mixed feelings about the place now. Whenever I get to ski there I think of you and how much I miss you.
I am in Italy tonight. Thanksgiving was lame. I had fish... not T-day food!
November 27, 2009 at 9:30am

Alyce Gross

Our family had a few Thanksgiving dinners and an Easter dinner with Tristan's family because of our Girl Scout connection. Tristan was a gold medal winner in Skeleton in the 2002 Utah Winter Olympics. Heather was in Spain at the time, but was so excited for Tristan and hated missing the festivities at home.

Alexandra Scott
ggggggggggggggggggggggggggggggggggggggg
December 9, 2009 at 10:05pm

Sadie Dickman
So, snow down here so far has been sad and windy this year. I'm sure it'll pick up soon. Had dreams last night about you and my grandma. How are you guys doin up there?
You know how Brian's been working on the memorial thing for the department? Well, now Dominique has got some pics of your favorite places framed and ready to hang in the Ling Dept, plus one of you on top of that rock in Goblin. You probably think that's ridiculous, but in a good way. Maybe it'll become a tradition, like in locker rooms, for people to touch your face every time they have a big syntax test in Aniko's class. Hahaha. Seems oddly appropriate. And creepy. Both. Have this image lately of you sort of bouncing across my lawn in your green Halloween dress with leaves pinned all over you. love it
miss yooooouuu!!!!
December 8, 2009 at 12:06am

Brian Cragun
I can't believe how long it's been. It doesn't seem possible that this much time's already passed. Like Sadie said, we've somehow coordinated everything and the pictures of you should get put up soon. I'm loving life in Taiwan, but constantly think of you; miss you G.
December 13, 2009 at 8:05pm

Jewel Kling
I'm gonna dance tomorrow to celebrate you Miss HG. I still miss you dearly.

The Devil's Fingernail

December 13, 2009 at 8:49pm

Jake Marshall
Going to the bird today. It's been a year. Missing you still all the time.
December 14, 2009 at 8:21am

Ryan Adler
Miss you H. Can't help but think you had something to do with the 40+ inches that fell in the cottonwoods this weekend. Don't worry, I got my fair share of the fresh down here, as I am sure you got yours up there.
December 14, 2009 at 8:34am

Jana Hooper [Heather's housemate]
Kensington still doesn't feel like home.... you are missed.
December 14, 2009 at 9:21am

Andrea Klemz Bagioli
I can't believe it has been a year, I'm really still having a hard time believing it at all... I miss you. Love you Heathie :)
December 14, 2009 at 10:13am

Tracy Doyle
Love you, Heather. Totally gonna get my groove on tonight.
December 14, 2009 at 11:21am

Greg Jensen
Miss you, Heather!! Thanks for the 40 incher over the weekend!!
December 14, 2009 at 12:12pm

Todd Kreykes
"If I must die I will inspire while I live alongside the dreamers." Heard that and thought of you. Thanks for sending down the snow. Miss you.
December 14, 2009 at 3:29pm

Bree DeGraw

The poem in yoga class tonight was filled with your energy.
May I be generous and helpful. May I be pure and virtuous.
May I be patient and able to bear and forbear the wrongs of
others. May I be strenuous, energetic and persevering. May I
practice meditation and attain concentration and oneness to
serve all beings. May... I gain wisdom and be able to give the
benefit of my wisdom to others. Oh and this song, is you.
December 14, 2009 at 8:31pm

Tristan Gale Geisler
I am in Germany and it's a frozen wonderland outside. Snow
is growing sideways on trees and buildings. Beautiful but very,
very cold. I have been thinking of you for the past few days. I
miss you much HG.
December 15, 2009 at 9:31am

Jamie Christensen Johnston
Miss you Heather. We all went to the dinner for you last night
and my boys got a little upset. I just told them that you are
skiing the fresh with their brother and then they were ok. Still
expect to see you whenever we walk past Kensington!
December 15, 2009 at 9:53pm

Katie Calvert
我很像你朋友！
December 17, 2009 at 12:01am

Xinling Chen
It has been a tough year, but you have always made me
laugh and let me feel encouraged whenever I think of you!
Happy New Year!
December 31, 2009 at 9:31pm

One of the memorials can be found with a keyboard and a mouse, the other isn't so easy.

Giant Tombstone

Journal Entry   Monday, September 13, 2010
A year and nine months after Heather's death

      After receiving a message from our new friend, Steve Miller, (the patroller who found Heather's body) informing me that the plaque had been placed at memorial site, I drove to Snowbird for a strenuous and emotional hike. I usually hike with a new group of friends on Tuesdays and Thursdays, but this time I wanted to be alone. In the cold shadow of Mt. Baldy, I ascended toward its base. The steep switch backs started from the tram deck, at about 8,000 feet to Peruvian Gulch at about 10,000 feet. As I came closer to my destination I felt a tightening in my chest and I begin to cry. I was so impressed by the natural beauty of the huge rock the patroller chose. It is a greenish slab with streaks of oxidized orange coloring, and it has a large textured, yet almost smooth area perfect for placement of a flat object. The nine-foot angular chunk of limestone is settled in a rock slide and from those rocks the patroller chose and artfully placed two perfect flat topped rocks as "benches" perpendicular to each other. One is facing and one is next to the larger rock that has Heather's epitaph affixed to it. Coming from the right side of the relatively tiny rectangular plaque, there is an almost invisible tear of epoxy. Trying out both of the lovely benches, I spent about an hour there in quiet contemplation. I wasn't alone. As the shadows moved, a fat furry marmot came out to sun himself and join me in looking north across an impressive expanse to yet another artfully sculpted ridge of the western Rockies. Heather would have approved of both the cute companion and perfect setting. She used to call the Wasatch "her mountains." The last prayer I remember her saying, was on Thanksgiving, a little more than two weeks before she died. We were at the home of friends. Heather was the last to arrive, because she had been skiing at Snowbird that morning. Our hostess, Tracy Hackworth, had a tree branch on which we were to hang decorative leaves. On the leaves we each were to write what we were most thankful for. Of course, almost everyone wrote "family and friends," but not our Heather. Her prayer of thanks was for "the proximity of the mountains." So it is fitting that her tombstone is of those mountains and her ashes are spread on them, in The Fields of Glory, her place of death.

A week after I first visited the memorial Denny and I arranged another Porcupine gathering with some Snowbird Ski Patrollers. I asked who had been working on Heather's Memorial and exclaimed how beautiful it was. I found out it was Dennis Durrant. He explained that he had positioned smaller rocks so the heavy stone "benches" could come to rest on them. By using gravity he slid the heavy "benches" into perfect placement. A heart shaped stone backs one bench. Dennis said he hoped to replace the small plaque with something bigger and with more information on it. Steve Miller suggested that we include a picture. I started working on what to put on a larger plaque, incorporating some of what I wrote in Heather's Obituary. I even used a line from what Brian Cragun and others had written. The following is what I had forged and cast in bronze on an 18 x 24 inch plaque, with Heather's picture at the top.

On August 26, 2011, just two days after I first submitted this book to a publisher, the new larger plaque was put in place. The small one is back under Heather's picture at the peak hut.

The Devil's Fingernail

Steve Miller, Dennis Durrant, Alyce and Dennis Gross

Memorial Plaque

**Heather Aron Gross
June 28, 1981 to December 14, 2008**

"Unable are the loved to die, for love is immortality." Emily Dickinson

Heather lived an extraordinary life, and she died an extraordinary death. Here on Mount Baldy, her giant tombstone, it was only Heather who was snatched away by an inbounds avalanche on 12/14/08.

She used to call the Wasatch "her mountains," so it is fitting that her ashes are spread on them, in The Fields of Glory, her place of death.

She was an avid Snowbird skier and would never want her death to stifle anyone's love for skiing or for the resort.

Heather lived most of her life in Salt Lake City. She worked as a scientist but changed paths to pursue the study of languages. Travel was a part of who she was. She combined travel with learning, and the love of languages through studies in Spain, Argentina, China, and more. She open-mindedly accepted and befriended people from all over the world.

In her 27 years she did a life's worth of living. Her positive energy and strong spirit of unity enriched the lives of many. Her candle burned brightly but not long enough. She needs the many people whom she has touched, to keep it burning. Her prayer for you would be to remember her goodness and zest for life and continue to share and spread it.

Heather left a void that will be partially filled by hilarious memories, and there is consolation with the belief that she now skis the eternal fresh.

The light shines in the darkness, and the darkness did not overcome it. John 1:5

Rather than hiking up to the memorial site, one can take either the Tram or Peruvian chair lift. Both of those lifts are running almost all year around and both leave you just west of Mt. Baldy; so in the summer and early fall (after the snow melts and before the new snow falls) one can ride up and hike down. It's about a forty minute walk from the tram or thirty minutes from the chair lift, to the rough summer road that cuts across the fall line beneath Mt. Baldy. Turn right or east on the road which is beneath the memorial.

Unfortunately, by the time there is enough snow to ski to the memorial, the plaque is covered. My husband and I went on the third anniversary of Heather's death, and a ski patroller with a shovel, efficiently dug it out for us. When my living daughter was able to visit after Christmas another patroller did the same. Snowbird's Ski Patrol has continued to treat us with respect, consideration, and kindness.

Alyce Gross

Heart shaped stone at her Snowbird memorial

Spreading of Ashes

Is that all there is? Scientific evidence teaches us that matter and energy are neither created nor destroyed. So where is Heather? Where is her energy? Where are the elements that made her physical body? Is all that was Heather now just four pounds of ash? It can't be. I have hope that her energy lives on with her spirit.

According to Wikipedia, *cremation is the process of reducing dead bodies to basic chemical compounds in the form of gases and bone fragments. This is accomplished through high temperatures and vaporization. Contrary to popular belief, the cremated remains are not ashes in the usual sense, but rather dried bone fragments that have been pulverized. Cremated remains are mostly dry calcium phosphates with some minor minerals, such as salts of sodium and potassium. Sulfur and most carbon, is driven off as oxidized gases during the cremation process, although a relatively small amount of carbon as carbonate may remain.*

Vapor or oxidized gases are matter. Matter has weight and takes up space. All of Heather's body still exists, but in a changed state/phase. It is mostly vapor which dissipated into the air on December 17, 2008, when she was cremated. Most of her physical body is now a part of the atmosphere. Denny, Emily, and I had to decide what to do with the remaining four pounds of compounds that I will still call "ashes."

We were sure she would want cremation. That decision was soon reinforced when Heather's scientist friend, Lisa Rohde, asked us about her burial. We told her Heather would be cremated, and Lisa said, "Oh good, that is what she wanted." I was relieved that Heather had discussed it with friends, because she hadn't discussed it with us. The spreading of her ashes around the world seemed most appropriate for our daughter who had such a passion for travel.

Shortly after Heather's death, Denny gave a few ounces of Heather's ashes to Koshin Fukuyoshi, a young man who had been in a linguistics program at the University of Utah with

Heather. With some help from fellow linguistics students, who collected and sent him money, Koshin flew to Utah all the way from Japan, for Heather's funeral. He reverently took the tiny package of ash home to Japan in late December, 2008.

Emily took a trace amount to put in a silver locket necklace, lovingly given to her by her long time childhood friend, Sydney Holbrook. She almost never takes the necklace off. We purchased two small urns to hold some of Heather's ashes, one for Emily and Ryan, and one for Denny and me.

When scooping a small amount of ashes from the larger container, I go out to my garden where I have a stepping stone that Heather made for me several years ago. On it she wrote "Dad the hunter and Mom the gatherer." If a little ash spills in the process; it is there in the garden or on the stepping stone, my treasured Mothers' Day gift.

In March, 2009, Emily was originally coming to Utah to join her sister and friends for the Urban Iditarod. It was to involve teams with decorated shopping carts being pulled and pushed, by costumed "huskies" and "mushers," from bar to bar. Denny and I were to be included as part of the cheering section. (This is a whole other story, but it helps tell a little about Heather's ability to gather friends for unusual experiences.) Instead she gathered her mom, dad, sister, and the ski patroller, who found her lifeless body.

Journal Entry   March 7, 2009   Three months after Heather's Death

We met Steve Miller at Snowbird Ski Resort's Tram Deck so he could kindly escort us; with about half (the rest to be spread elsewhere) of Heather's ashes tucked safely in Denny's inside coat pocket, next to his heart. We took the tram to the top of Hidden Peak. From there we skied down a short distance and shot up toward Mt. Baldy, until we came to a stop and had to remove our skies. I had Heather's newly purchased fat powder skies, which she never got to use. We carried our skies and Emily her snowboard, for a ten minute climb to the High Baldy

The Devil's Fingernail

Traverse. Our heavy stiff ski boots just fit in the foot holds, fashioned by the Patrollers, for those who are willing to work to get to the steepest and deepest powder. This is still in the resort boundaries, but not accessible to the casual skier. It is for expert skiers only. Steve roped it off behind us so we could be alone. With our skis and Emily's board back on, we were led by Steve around Mt. Baldy, on a narrow traverse with a very steep drop off to the left. We were following Heather's last living trek, to the top of Fields of Glory, which is close to 11,000 feet high.

When we reached the area where Steve said the avalanche began, I stood with the edges of Heather's skies holding me in place at the top of the shoot, and read the words to one of the songs sung at her funeral: *On Eagles Wings* (some of which is from Psalm 91 and Isaiah 40:31), while Denny cried and dug in the snow to bury some of Heather's ashes. Emmy sat quietly weeping, with her head bent over her snowboard. After reading in the strongest voice I could muster, I wanted to throw some ashes in the air. I threw some saying, "We'll never forget you, Heather. We love you." We were in a light cloud which kindly enveloped us in privacy. We would look like mere specks from the tram deck, but privacy was a comfort. I kept looking to the sky, hoping to see a rainbow; but in those weather conditions, there wasn't one. Our cloud dropped a little snow, yet it was a warm sunny day. I could barely side slip my way down the steep killing slope, while I thought of my Heather being slammed with the hard, fast crush of snow. I saw the rugged, steep shoots, one just west of "The Eye of the Needle" where her body was dragged and propelled over a distance of 300 yards (three football fields). I tossed more ashes at about the point where she was swept up and again at the bottom of Peruvian Gulch, where her battered body came to rest. There I read Psalm 139:1-18. For the word "me" in the Psalm, I substituted Heather's name. I foolishly kept looking for a rainbow, but the sun came out and other skiers were now in the lower area. We said good-bye to our patient guide, Steve, who would meet us later.

We three skid the rest of the way down to the tram line. Was it fate or coincidence that we ran into Sam, Alex, and Mike? All who had skied with Heather the day of her death, and all who sat for hours with us in the University Hospital Emergency waiting room. We skied with them a few runs, but felt emotionally drained, which made us physically exhausted; so we stopped and sat in the sun, on the tram deck, and had beer and pizza. Of course there was a toast to Heather. Steve came and gave us a bag of gifts (Snowbird T-shirts and caps).

That evening we invited The Tandem Lab (where Heather used to work) kids: Lexy, Scott, Lisa, Brittany, and Emily M. to dinner so they could see our daughter, Emily. They're the ones who would have been in the Urban Iditarod. It seemed a fitting day and evening to remember our Heather. The kids (actually young adults) all went to a local bar to continue commemorating and celebrating Heather.

How differently Emily's trip turned out from what she and Heather had planned.

In June, 2009, Emily and Ryan, on their pre-wedding honeymoon to Ireland, took a small amount of Heather's ashes in a powder compact. Emily told me a plastic bag would look suspicious. While in Northern Ireland, they met with Heather's friends, Jewel Kling and her husband Graham Twaddell (a native of Ireland). At an interesting geological formation, Giant's Causeway, in Northern Ireland, Emily and Jewel walked down to the sea and spread some of Heather's ashes.

Facebook:
Jewel Kling
I'm so glad you were with us at the Giant's Causeway. I had an amazing time with your sister and Ryan. Love you HG
June 11, 2009 at 6:38pm

Letter to Australia   December, 2009
Hi Katie,

The Devil's Fingernail

It was so good to hear from you. Denny and I both get comfort by staying close to Heather's friends, especially you and Paul. It sounds like you have been having some wonderful experiences, but I know you. You need a job where you feel fulfilled. I'm sure, with your talent and experience, you'll find one.

In some ways I wish I would not have retired, just for the sake of staying busy. Yet, I think it is better for me to face my grieving head on, plus I think I would have been a very distracted school teacher. My retirement has allowed us the freedom to travel when we want. In November, we took a beautiful trip to Northern Italy. We were on an educational tour with 14 people. It was an interesting group which made the many delicious 5-course meals more enjoyable. We were drawn to the Cinque Terre because Heather was there in 2002. We spread a small amount of her ashes on the beach and water at Monterosso. She had written an email from there, exclaiming of its beauty. I was hoping it would be a "feel good" experience, but it was very sad for both of us. I think we're still looking for Heather. It is so hard to not find her when we get to a destination, or when we arrive back home. Facing the rest of my life, without her to brighten it, is overwhelming; so I just face one day at a time.

We returned home with the task of preparing for three families plus Em and Ryan who joined us for Thanksgiving. Last year we were with the same three families plus Heather. We've found it best to surround ourselves with people during these "firsts" without her. Ryan has been very supportive of Emily, and she is doing well. She calls me almost every day while driving home from school. I'm so thankful for those two.

Denny and I are driving to Fort Collins the weekend before Dec. 14th. We'll drive home on the 14th, and hopefully see some of Heather's friends that evening. We'll go back to Fort Collins again for Christmas.

My cancer seems like nothing compared to losing Heather—especially because I have never felt sick, not even during or after radiation. I'm scheduled for a CT scan on Dec. 9th, and I'll have check-ups about every 4 months for a while. Because we caught it in stage 1, the radiation may have cured it.

Alyce Gross

I wish you and Paul the very best. Did you celebrate Thanksgiving, and what are your Christmas plans?
Hugs and love, Alyce

Into the future:

Katie came home in October, 2010 for her mother's wedding. Even with a very busy and tight schedule she managed to come see us. I fixed her lunch and Denny came home so he could visit too. We enjoyed hearing about her happy marriage to Paul and their life in Australia. I stay in touch with Katie through email:

6/5/11
From: Katie Dyson
Hi Alyce and Denny, What a crazy last few weeks it's been! Up until the 17th of May my pregnancy was going really well—happy and healthy and growing a nice little bump. I went in for my regular midwife appt and they found that I had pre eclampsia (a condition where my bp is high and unstable and it causes a whole bunch of problems for bub and me and the only cure is delivery of the baby). I was 29 weeks+4 days at that stage so it was too early. . . . I stayed in the hospital for 11 days and then went home for a week. In one of the follow-up appts they did a trace of her heart rate and checked my bp which led to a cesarean on Friday night. I was almost 32 weeks. She is tiny and in the NICU but doing really well and breathing on her own.

Paul and I are so happy and in love with our little girl. We have a very long road ahead of us, she will be in hospital for 5 or 6 weeks. We have named her Grace *Heather* Dyson. I can't wait to tell her all about Heather and how special she is. I know Heather is helping us right now and watching over Grace. She was just under 3 pounds and 16 inches long.
The Dysons

From new life back to ashes:

The spreading of ashes seemed fitting until our trip to Italy. Then my mind started stirring up questions. Shouldn't she

The Devil's Fingernail

be all in one place? What does the Bible say? In the Bible, weren't bones raised up? What am I doing leaving these ashes in this cold, damp country far from home? I was in torment in my mind. Shortly after the trip, I called Pastor Steve, to ask if he had an opinion or Biblical knowledge on the subject. He said he thought spreading her ashes was a prefect tribute to our Heather. It helped to hear his encouragement, but what had helped most, was my simple prayer the night before we left Italy. I wrote about it in Book One explaining how it calmed my torment.

Denny and I generally are not worriers. But as explained earlier, around July 4, 2002, we were worried to distraction. Emily and I had a three week trip to Spain already planned starting July 11th. When we didn't hear from Heather for four days, I begin to picture the planned vacation becoming a hunt for my missing child.

Heather had been traveling and backpacking on her own, but was to meet Josie in northern Italy. I felt very confident that she would be with the perfect traveling companion. Heather had told us about Josie, a tall strong athletic girl. Having been mugged in Granada; she fought off her attacker, and as she ran away he shouted "Bravo!" to her. Josie got away unharmed.

Something happened to prevent Josie and Heather's planned meeting. Her cell phone didn't work in Italy. We usually communicated by email, but unknown to Denny and me the computer cafes in Chinque Terre were few and very expensive. She finally called saying Christian had tracked her down, and was sorry she worried us. She said how beautiful the Chinque Terre was.

In my retirement, I registered with Exploritas, an educational tour group (that used to be called Elder Hostel and now is called Road Scholar). I was looking for a trip to celebrate radiation being completed and hoping for a distraction from our grief. Exploritas sent information on many travel opportunities; and of course, I was drawn to The Chinque Terre. I have always loved to travel but not with tour groups, yet I knew that Denny and I, in our sad state of mind, needed to be around other people;

so we decided a small group was the way to go. On our November flight across the Atlantic, we carried a small amount of Heather's ashes in a powder compact. I was very cognizant of my precious cargo tucked in my carry-on.

Journal Entry   Sunday, November 15, 2009
Northwestern Italy:
Mountain villages on the Mediterranean Coast

    On a "free day," from our tour group, Denny and I took a bus from Lerici to La Spezia. I had the compact of Heather's ashes in my purse. From there we took a train to Monterosso, the largest and furthest west of the five Cinque Terra villages. We purchased tickets that included walking trails and getting on and off the train at the five villages. Because it was Sunday and off season, few people were about. Denny and I walked to a "new" part of town and up a steep road. Because I pictured Heather entering this town from above; I was looking for upper hiking trails, but didn't find any. We were also putting off the decision on how and where to disperse the ashes. Back down by the beach we sat on a bench by the Ligurian Sea, which is part of the Mediterranean. I read from a copy of "On Eagles' Wings" and Psalm 139. We went down to the deserted beach, and Denny dug a hole in the sand by a concrete barrier and buried a small amount of ashes. I spread the rest in the sea while saying, "He will raise you up on Eagles' wings. We love you, Heather; and God help us." We took the train to Vernazza where we shared warm minestrone soup and perfectly cooked veal. It was a wonderful meal, but a very hard day for both of us. After our lunch we again caught the train, continuing east to Corniglia Station, and climbed a steep road to a very small picturesque town tucked in the mountains above the sea. Three old stout Italian women were visiting on a bus stop bench. It made me lonely to see them. I wished I could share my sad story and feel their compassion. I moved to take their picture, but they motioned me away. Denny and I descended three hundred and eighty-one steps leading

The Devil's Fingernail

back to a trail. We walked at sunset, along a fenced plunging cliff bordering the sea, to Monarola. I kept wondering if our Heather walked the same trail and saw a similar beautiful sunset over the water seven years earlier. Just missing the train, we had to wait fifty minuets for the next one to La Spezia. We thought we might also miss the dinner, in a private home, planned for the tour group. As it got darker and colder we waited and talked about Heather, and about how thankful we were to have each other, but we were a forlorn duo sitting there in the cold. The train finally took us back to bustling La Spezia. Our short bus stop wait, among friendly Italians, and the warm cozy ride back to Lerici, made us start to feel better. But nothing could top the companionable, dinner that was being prepared for us that evening.

We got to our hotel at 6:42 PM, to find a note by the elevator stating that dinner was postponed to 7:15—perfect timing. The chef's house on the mountain side was in a neighborhood above Lerici. Our hotel dinners were almost always seafood, but that night, as we entered the welcoming home, delicious smells were wafting out to greet us. The first thing we saw was an open hearth with a rotisserie skewering sausage, fowl, and other delicious meats. The wine was plentiful, and the appetizers numerous and excellent. The freshly made ravioli was displayed on a massave tray for us to see, before the chef plunged them into huge pots of boiling water. The abundance of meats and breads, and the excited talk of every ones' adventures of the day, made for the healing warmth Denny and I needed. For dessert there was canolli filled with ricotta cheese that tasted like sweet cream. Most of the group was too full to finish one, but I ate two.

After dinner we carefully walked down winding cobbled pathways, in the dark. Denny was well behind me offering both arms to steady ladies a bit older than he. Arm and arm with my new best friend, Jane, we forged ahead calling back when there was a step down. I was filled with much boldness, as well as much food, wine, lemon liqueur, and grappa. I had sampled everything. Heather would have approved.

My family edited the first line of our Christmas letter. I had written: In the worst year of my life, some of the best things happened.
Christmas, 2009

Greetings to Our Dear Friends and Family,
In a most difficult year, following Heather's death, some of the best things happened.
We gained a wonderful son, who is devoted to our Emily. Ryan and Emily White were married in July, with three days of festivities that brought family from both coasts and Canada. Lifelong friends prepared a delicious rehearsal dinner in Ryan and Emily's perfect back yard. Love, support, and a white horse and carriage created the atmosphere for a sacred and fun filled wedding. Ryan and Emily live in Fort Collins, Colorado, where he has a career as a construction superintendent, specializing in water treatment plants. Construction is in his blood, and he can fix and build anything. Emily is in her second year as a dedicated elementary school teacher. She managed to cram in completing a

master's degree, while planning her wedding and teaching. We're thankful for their solid marriage and jobs. So we can visit them often, Denny and I purchased a condominium in Fort Collins.

Heather's many and varied friends have shown that she will not be forgotten. Skiers: by sponsoring a Snow Ball fund raiser, in her honor, for an educational scholarship; scientist friends: by organizing a 5K race and bar-b-q on what would have been her 28th birthday; and linguistic students: by creating a memorial, written in many languages, with beautiful photos. We take comfort in knowing she died on a mountain she loved, in an area named The Fields of Glory. She lived life with abundance and passion, as though she knew there was no time to waste. We are proud that she was our daughter.

Denny and I just returned from an educational trip to Northern Italy. We met a very interesting and enjoyable group of people on our Exploritas tour. In part we went to spread some of Heather's ashes. We'll continue to plan for suitable destinations in the future.

Our commitment to each other, faith, and prayers from you have held us through the darkest time. In this Advent season, we look for the light in Christ's birth to guide us.

John 1:5 The light shines in the darkness, and the darkness did not overcome it.
Love, Denny and Alyce Gross

Alyce Gross

December 26, 2010

We hope you had a blessed and MERRY CHRISTMAS and look forward to a fruitful NEW YEAR!

Heather sent us on yet another quest: last year to Italy and this year to the Czech Republic.

With the second anniversary of her death, on December 14th, Denny and I decided to spend it with family. First we had three nights in Prague, on our own. It was a destination Heather had in mind. She considered teaching English there. Together we decided on the Charles Bridge at the Pieta (above), as a suitable place from which to spread some of her ashes. This has become our new bitter/sweet custom. We think Heather would be pleased that she is sending her parents all over the world in her honor and memory.

On the second phase of the trip we were with my two brothers and their wives, so the six of us were on a nine day river boat cruise: Holiday Markets of the Danube. We began in Germany and cruised east across Austria, stopping each day in a different city or small town, including Bratislava, Slovakia. We ended in beautiful Budapest, Hungary. Braving the cold while seeing interesting sites each day and having leisurely dinners with family each evening, was perfect.

Emily and Ryan came from their home in Fort Collins, Colorado, shortly after we got back. With them, on Christmas

day, we skied as is our old custom. Today Denny and Ryan are elk hunting in the snow, and Emily and mom are having a cozy relaxing time together.
Find me on Facebook for more trip pictures.
God bless us everyone!
Love, Denny and Alyce Gross

Alyce on Charles Bridge

On April 1, 2011, Denny and I flew to Phoenix Arizona to look at some investment property. We took our precious powder compact with us, as we had two other more important events to look forward to. That evening we met up with two of Heather's beloved Itros; Jewel Kling, Tracy Doyle, their partners, and the smallest yet largest and most endearing presence—wee Enler, Jewel and Graham's baby. It was fitting that we met at an Irish Pub in Old Town, Chandler, because Jewel's husband is Irish and he and Jewel were with Emily and Ryan when they spread some of Heather's ashes in Northern Ireland. It was a happy coincidence that the property we were thinking of buying is in the same town as Jewel and Graham's home, and an even happier coincidence was that we chose the same weekend to visit as

Alyce Gross

Tracy and Ryan. We hadn't seen Tracy since Heather's funeral and it was our first time to meet her beloved partner, Ryan. Our time together was emotionally charged with memories of Heather, and our thirst was quenched with good Irish beer. Graham was thoughtful and happy to share Heather memories. He reminded us that she used to say, "Her drinking team had a rowing problem."

The next morning, before meeting our realtor, Denny and I visited Tempe Town Lake. Heather would sometimes get up at 4:40 AM to practice with her ASU Rowing Team at 5:00 AM. We couldn't help but notice all the beautiful improvements and changes around the lake, and we thought how Heather would have loved to see it all. We chose a spot on the dock area, a little distance from where a rowing instructor was calling out advice to a rower in the water. On that hot morning, as is our new custom, I read from "On Eagle's Wings" and Psalm 139. Then Denny spread some of our Heather's ashes in the Tempe water. I wiped tears from my eyes, and accidently knocked my prescription sunglasses into the lake, through the gray cloud of Heathers ashes. Interestingly I've changed—losing the glasses would have upset me before Heather died. Instead I thought it fitting to leave something personal of mine with our daughter.

Denny and I then drove around ASU, as we reminisced about the times we went there to visit while Heather was in college. We were also able to find the apartment building that she lived in, with April Bojorquez, after they finished their year studying in Spain.

Heather also had made trips back to Arizona. She was a bridesmaid in Jewel and Graham's wedding and even designed and made the jewelry for all the bridesmaids. She did that for Andrea Klemz's wedding as well. We have a framed picture of Heather in a beautiful red dress, dancing with Jewel's brother, at that reception. Heather couldn't miss her beloved friend's weddings. She and Koshin flew to attend April's wedding in April, 2008. One of the pictures that Koshin took of Heather in rapt attention, watching April get married, is the very picture we used to help us remember and honor Heather during Emily's wedding. Heather and Koshin stayed at Jewel and Graham's new home, so we have fun-filled pictures of them enjoying the backyard swimming pool. Denny and I also got to see their house and pool.

After spending a long afternoon looking at condominiums; we were welcomed to Jewel and Graham's lovely home, with Tracy and Ryan still there, and where wee Enler is king. We were privileged to share and receive affirmation about spreading ashes at the rowing site. They all thought it was a wonderful way to show tribute to Heather. We will continue to look for suitable locations and events to honor and remember our daughter by spreading her ashes as we read these words:

On Eagle's Wings:
> *You who dwell in the shelter of the Lord, who abide in this shadow for life, say to the Lord: "My refuge, my rock in whom I trust!"*
> *And he will raise you up on eagle's wings, bear you on the breath of dawn, make you to shine like the sun, and hold you in the palm of his hand.*
> *The snare of the fowler will never capture you, and famine will bring you no fear; under God's wings your refuge, with faithfulness your shield.*
> *You need not fear the terror of the night, nor the arrow that flies by day; though thousands fall about you, near you it shall not come.*
> *For to the angels God's given a command to guard you in all of your ways;*
> *Upon their hands they will bear you up lest you dash your foot against a stone.*
> *And he will raise you up on eagle's wings, bear you on the breath of dawn, make you to shine like the sun, and hold you in the palm of his hand.*

Alyce Gross

Psalm 139:1-18 NRSV & 139:18b NIV: I substitute Heather's name for "me and I" as I read.

> *O LORD, you have searched Heather and known her.*
> *You know when she sat down and when she rose up; you discern her thoughts from far away.*
> *You search out her path and her lying down, and are acquainted with all her ways.*
> *Even before a word was on her tongue, O LORD, you knew it completely.*
> *You hem Heather in, behind and before, and lay your hand upon her.*
> *Such knowledge is too wonderful for me; it is so high that I cannot attain it.*
> *Where can Heather go from your spirit? Or where can she flee from your presence?*
> *If she ascends to heaven, you are there; if she makes her bed in Sheol, you are there.*
> *If she takes the wings of the morning and settles at the farthest limits of the sea,*
> *Even there your hand shall lead her, and your right hand shall hold her fast.*
> *If Heather says, "Surely the darkness shall cover me, and the light around me becomes night."*
> *Even the darkness is not dark to you; the night is as bright as the day, for darkness is as light to you.*
> *For it was you who formed Heather's inward parts; you knit her together in my womb.*
> *I praise you for Heather was fearfully and wonderfully made.*
> *Wonderful are your works; that Heather and I know very well.*
> *Heather's frame was not hidden from you, when she was being made in secret, intricately woven in the depths of the earth.*
> *Your eyes beheld her unformed substance.*

> *In your book were written all the days that were formed for her, when none of them as yet existed.*
> *How weighty to me are your thoughts, O God!*
> *How vast is the sum of them!*
> *I try to count them—they are more than the sand;*
> *When Heather awakes, she is still with you.*

I know she was *fearfully and wonderfully made.* Whether her bipolar disorder was caused because *the devil's fingernail* touched Heather's DNA when she was *being knit together in my womb,* or because it was a part of God's plan *when she was being made in secret, intricately woven in the depths of the earth*—I do not know, but I do know that with times of greatest challenge there was a gift. It was learning to rely on God more and self less.

My greatest challenge was not cancer. It was losing Heather, and when I was fighting with demons and pushing God away, God didn't turn his back on me. *I could not flee from His presence,* and I don't think God turned his back on Heather—even in the avalanche. *Your right hand shall hold her fast.*

> *The Spirit of the Sovereign* L<small>ORD</small> *is on me . . . . He has sent me to bind up the brokenhearted. . . to comfort all who mourn and provide for those who grieve . . . to bestow on them a crown of beauty instead of ashes, the oil of gladness instead of mourning, and a garment of praise instead of a spirit of despair. They will be called oaks of righteousness, a planting of the* L<small>ORD</small> *for the display of his splendor (Isaiah 61: 1-3).*

If there were no earthly death, life would not be cherished. Life would not be complete.

> *The day which we fear as our last is but the birthday of eternity.* Seneca

Epilogue

Parts of Emails from friends who chose *Heather* as the middle name of their daughters:

12/20/11

Kennedy will be turning two in January, and she is the only one in the family with blonde hair. Eric and I consider that Heather's sense of humor! You may think I'm crazy to say this, but I think Heather goofs around with Kennedy sometimes. She will be alone in her room at night and suddenly begin laughing hysterically—Eric and I just say "she's laughing at Aunt Heather." I know Heather is our family's guardian angel, especially Kennedy's. She has touched our lives just as much in death as she did in life. I am sorry if these things were difficult to hear; but I have found my own way of adjusting for the last three years, and sensing her presence in my life just feels right.

We love you,
Teresa, Eric, Kennedy, and Brixton

6/23/11

Hi, things are going as well as they can with Grace. She is slowly growing—3.3 pounds now but still so small. . . . They have told us that we can most likely take her home in 3 and a half weeks. Then the real adventure begins! I had a dream about Heather last night and I haven't dreamt about her in a while. I was telling her all about Grace. With Heather's birthday in a few days, she has been on my mind a lot; and with everything happening with Grace I was so wishing she was here. . . . I hope you and Denny are well.

Lots of love,
Katie

3/02/12

I have been meaning to write you for some time but what prompted me this morning was a dream I had last night about Heather. It was the most real and vivid dream I have ever had. She was wearing the most beautiful emerald green

top and her hair was down and past her shoulders. Each dream I have about her she knows she is not alive. This one was the same. I had so many questions for her. I wanted to know if she was ok and how it felt when she passed. I was crying and telling her how much I missed her. She was so calm and kept saying that she was ok and that she was happy. I told her I wanted her to meet and see Grace. She said she has and she watches her and she thinks she is beautiful. As I write this I can't stop crying and missing her. But I feel like I got to see her last night and it makes me so happy when I get a chance to be with her in my dreams.
    Thinking of you and Denny.
    Lots of love,
    Katie

A part of my reply:
3/03/12 (three years and three months after Heather's death)
Oh Katie,
    I cried with you through your email. It's strange how joy and sorrow can be so mixed together at times. Some of the books I've read say sorrow expands your soul. I don't know.
    I've been praying for a dream like that, but I'm still waiting. I have had dreams with Heather in them where she was happy, but not with such clarity and not with such a sense of communication. Thank you for sharing your very personal, beautiful dream. For now I'll accept it as my message from Heather through you.

Printed by Libri Plureos GmbH in Hamburg, Germany